**Public Capital, Growth and Welfare |**

# PUBLIC CAPITAL,

PIERRE-RICHARD AGÉNOR

# GROWTH AND WELFARE

## ANALYTICAL FOUNDATIONS FOR PUBLIC POLICY

PRINCETON UNIVERSITY PRESS
PRINCETON AND OXFORD

Published by Princeton University Press, 41 William Street, Princeton, New Jersey 08540
In the United Kingdom: Princeton University Press, 6 Oxford Street, Woodstock,
Oxfordshire OX20 1TW

press.princeton.edu



Library of Congress Cataloging-in-Publication Data
Agénor, Pierre-Richard.
Public capital, growth and welfare : analytical foundations for
public policy / Pierre-Richard Agénor.
p. cm.
Includes bibliographical references and index.
ISBN 978-0-691-15580-7 (hardback : alk. paper) 1. Capital investments.
2. Economic development. 3. Public welfare. I. Title.
HG4028.C4A275 2012
332′.041–dc23
2012022671

British Library Cataloging-in-Publication Data is available

This book has been composed in Times New Roman and Myriad Pro

Printed on acid-free paper. ∞

Printed in the United States of America
Typeset by S R Nova Pvt Ltd, Bangalore, India

10 9 8 7 6 5 4 3 2 1

To my wife, Nicole,

and my daughters, Madina and Laurence,

for their love and support

# Contents

Introduction and Overview 1

**1 | Basic Channels** 11

1 Background 11
1.1 Productivity and Cost of Private Inputs 11
1.2 Complementarity Effect on Private Investment 14
1.3 Crowding-Out Effects 15
2 The Economy 16
2.1 Households 17
2.2 Firms 20
2.3 Government 23
2.4 Market-Clearing Conditions 25
3 Equilibrium and the Balanced Growth Path 26
3.1 The Case Where $\mu = 1$ 27
3.2 The Case Where $\mu < 1$ 28
4 Growth Effects of Public Policy 32
5 Optimal Fiscal Policy 34
6 Extensions 37
6.1 Indirect Taxation 37
6.2 Complementarity Effect 38
6.3 Public Capital and Household Utility 39
6.4 Partial Depreciation and Maintenance 40
6.4.1 Partial Depreciation 40
6.4.2 The Investment-Maintenance Trade-Off 41
Appendix: Optimal Policy under Welfare Maximization 45

**2 | Public Capital and Education** 49

1 Background 49
2 The Economy 51
2.1 Households 51
2.2 Production of Goods 52
2.3 Production of Human Capital 53
2.4 Government 54
2.5 Savings-Investment Balance 55
3 Equilibrium and the Balanced Growth Path 55
3.1 The Case Where $\mu = 1$ 57
3.2 The Case Where $\mu < 1$ 59

4 Sensitivity of Education Technology 62
5 Public Policy 63
5.1 Increase in Public Spending 63
5.2 Optimal Expenditure Allocation 64
6 Extensions 65
6.1 Endogenous Rearing Costs 65
6.2 Time Allocation and Infrastructure 66
6.3 Schooling Quality 67
Appendix: Stability Conditions and Steady-State Effects with $\mu < 1$ 69

**3 | Public Capital and Health** 72

1 Background 73
1.1 Health and Economic Growth 73
1.2 Infrastructure and Health 75
1.3 Health Persistence 78
2 A Two-Period Framework 79
2.1 Households 79
2.2 Production of Goods 81
2.3 Health Status and Productivity 81
2.4 Government 83
2.5 Savings-Investment Balance 83
3 Time Allocation and Growth Dynamics 84
4 Public Spending, Growth, and Human Welfare 88
5 Optimal Spending Allocation 89
6 A Three-Period Framework with Endogenous Fertility 91
7 Endogenous Life Expectancy 100
8 Interactions between Health and Education 104
8.1 Impact of Health on Education 104
8.2 Impact of Education on Health 106
8.3 Magnification Effect 107
Appendix: Stability Conditions with Health Persistence 110

**4 | Public Capital and Innovation** 111

1 Background 112
2 The Economy 113
2.1 Households 114
2.2 Production of the Final Good 114
2.3 Production of Intermediate Goods 116
2.4 Human Capital Accumulation 117
2.5 Research and Development Sector 117
2.6 Government 119
2.7 Savings-Investment Balance 119
2.8 Labor Market 119

3 Balanced Growth Path 120
4 Public Policy 121
4.1 Basic Intuition 121
4.2 Numerical Illustration 122
5 From Imitation to True Innovation 124
Appendix: Dynamic System and the Steady State 128

**5 | Public Capital and Women's Time Allocation** 132

1 Background 133
1.1 Women's Time Allocation Constraints 133
1.1.1 Transportation 134
1.1.2 Water and Sanitation 134
1.1.3 Electricity 135
1.2 Intergenerational Health Externalities 136
1.2.1 Mothers' Health Status and Child Development 136
1.2.2 Mothers' Educational Status and Child Development 137
1.3 Analytical Implications 139
2 The Economy 139
2.1 Family's Utility and Income 141
2.2 Home Production 143
2.3 Market Production 143
2.4 Human Capital Accumulation 144
2.5 Health Status and Productivity 145
2.6 Government 146
2.7 Savings-Investment Balance 147
3 Women's Time Allocation and Fertility 148
4 The Balanced Growth Path 150
5 Public Policy 154
6 Women's Labor Supply and Development 156
7 Extensions 158
7.1 Public Capital and Gender Gaps 158
7.2 Nonunitary Household Framework 158
Appendix: Solution, Stability Conditions, and Steady-State Effects 163

**6 | Public Capital and Poverty Traps** 174

1 Background 174
2 The Economy 177
2.1 Individuals 177
2.2 Firms 177
2.3 Government 178
2.4 Savings-Investment Balance 178
3 Balanced Growth Path 178
4 Network Externalities 179

5 The Big Push 182
6 Other Channels 184
6.1 Time Allocation 184
6.2 Health-Induced Poverty Traps 184
6.3 Technology Choice 186
7 Aid Volatility and Time to Build 188

**7 | Research Perspectives** 192

1 Heterogeneous Infrastructure Assets 192
2 Political Economy of Government Spending Allocation 193
3 Excludable Public Goods 195
4 Debt, Public Capital, and Fiscal Rules 196
5 Spatial Dimensions of Public Capital 203
6 Infrastructure and Trade 206
7 Public-Private Partnerships 207
8 Public Capital and Income Distribution 209
9 Negative Externalities 212
10 Testing for the Impact of Public Capital on Growth 215

**Lessons for Public Policy** 219
**References** 225
**Index** 247

# Public Capital, Growth and Welfare |

# Introduction and Overview

Over the past three decades, significant economic and social progress has been achieved in the developing world. Infant mortality rates have been halved, primary school enrollment rates have doubled, and in some countries life expectancy has increased by more than 20 years. During the 1990s alone, per capita income increased on average by 2.6 percent.

However, progress has been uneven. In some countries, the rapid spread of HIV/AIDS has literally erased many of the gains achieved in increasing life expectancy. And although the *proportion* of people in extreme poverty fell slightly as a whole over the past decade, the *absolute number* of poor people increased in almost all regions (except in East Asia), with large concentrations in South Asia (which contains the largest number of the world's poor) and in sub-Saharan Africa (which continues to have the largest proportion of its population living in poverty). Today, one in every four people, or 1.3 billion persons, lives in extreme poverty in the developing world. In the past 10 years alone, the number of poor people in sub-Saharan Africa increased by more than a third. Although access to clean water and sanitation is now recognized as a human right by the United Nations, almost 900 million people continue to lack access to safe drinking water and more than 2.6 billion do not have access to basic sanitation. Because of water- and sanitation-related diseases, each year about 1.5 million children under the age of five die and millions of school days are lost (see United Nations (2005)). Malaria, by itself, claims the lives of 1 million children under the age of five every year. Through various channels, the global financial crisis triggered by the collapse of the subprime mortgage market in the United States has set some countries back by more than a decade.

The persistence of poverty and lack of progress in human development has led policymakers to put renewed emphasis on policies aimed at promoting economic efficiency and improving the productivity of the poor, generating income-earning capabilities and creating opportunities for using them productively, through education and health (which affect productivity), increasing opportunities to invest in small- and medium-size enterprises (which depend in part on access to credit), and improving housing and basic infrastructure services.

Much of the current international debate on how these policies should be sequenced has centered on the need to promote a large, front-loaded, increase in public investment. Reports by the United Nations (2005), the Commission for Africa (2005), and the World Bank (2005*a*) and prominent advocates like Jeffrey Sachs (2005, 2008) have indeed recommended a "Big Push" in public infrastructure investment in poor countries, financed by generous debt relief and a substantial increase in aid, to spur growth, reduce poverty, and improve the quality of human life in low-income developing countries. In a report on sub-Saharan Africa, for instance, the World Bank (2005*a*) called for a doubling of spending on infrastructure in the region, from 4.7 percent of GDP in the years prior to the report to more than 9 percent over the subsequent decade.

A common argument for a large increase in public spending on infrastructure is that infrastructure services have a strong growth-promoting effect through their impact on the productivity of private inputs and the rate of return on capital—particularly when, to begin with, stocks of infrastructure assets are relatively low. In that regard, and with the exception of cellular telecommunications, low-income countries are at a particular disadvantage. In sub-Saharan Africa, for instance, only 16 percent of roads are paved, and less than one in five Africans has access to electricity. The average waiting time for a fixed telephone connection is three and a half years. Transport costs are the highest of any region, and high freight charges continue to represent a major constraint on the expansion of exports to industrial countries. Given the scale and lumpy nature of many infrastructure projects, and the fact that prospects for public-private partnerships in infrastructure investment for the region, and low-income countries in general, remain limited (if not nonexistent, in some cases), closing the infrastructure gap will indeed require a substantial increase in *public* investment.

At the same time, recent analytical and empirical research has highlighted the fact that, beyond its effects on the productivity of private inputs and the rate of return on private capital, public infrastructure may spur growth through a variety of other channels. For instance, it has been argued that good public infrastructure (such as a reliable power grid or well-maintained roads), by reducing the need for the private sector to spend on maintenance of its own stock of physical capital, may raise the rate of capital formation. A large body of evidence, based on microeconomic studies, suggests also that infrastructure may have a significant impact on health and education outcomes. Accounting for the externalities associated with infrastructure may thus be essential in designing and quantifying growth and human development strategies.

This book focuses precisely on these externalities and their implications for growth and human welfare—that is, the well-being of individuals, as opposed to social welfare or the well-being of the community as a whole—in low-income developing countries. Its purpose is threefold. First, it provides a systematic overview of the recent evidence on the different channels, beyond those deemed conventional, through which infrastructure may affect growth. Second, it takes a resolutely analytical approach by developing an integrated series of formal models for understanding how these channels operate. Possible extensions of these models are also indicated. Third, policy implications, with respect to formulating growth and human development strategies, are drawn.

Reflecting this multiplicity of purpose, chapters 1 to 6 all begin with a background section, which reviews the evidence on the issue at stake, and then present a rigorous analysis of a particular channel. Chapter 7 outlines a comprehensive research agenda, and the conclusion of the book draws together the main policy lessons of the analysis. Of course, given that throughout the book only small analytical models, rather than applied, country-specific models, are developed, only broad policy lessons can be drawn; nevertheless, there are good reasons to believe that these lessons provide a solid foundation for more operational analysis and country-specific policy advice.

By its very nature, the book can also be used as a single reference for a short, specialized course on economic growth or development economics, or as a supplement to more general advanced courses in those areas. It is largely self-contained and the step-by-step solution of all models (provided in either the text itself or chapter appendices) makes it relatively easy to follow. Students who have no prior exposure to this area will find the literature review on each topic covered in the book to be fairly comprehensive and will welcome the research perspectives provided in the last chapter. At the same time, this book is not a comprehensive textbook; as such, it assumes familiarity with basic concepts in microeconomics (such as utility and profit maximization) and macroeconomics (such as aggregate production functions), as well as core elements of modern growth theory. Although some key concepts are defined when appropriate, this is done in a rather succinct manner. Readers familiar with the basic chapters in Barro and Sala-i-Martin (2003) or Acemoglu (2008), for instance, would be well equipped to tackle the issues discussed here.

Throughout, the analysis is based on the Allais-Samuelson Overlapping Generations (OLG) model.[1] OLG models have proved to be a powerful analytical tool to address development issues in general; this book shows that they are particularly well suited to address the links among infrastructure, growth, and human welfare. Given its analytical focus, the book is most suited for professional economists and graduate students specializing in either macroeconomics or development economics, who also firmly believe (as I do, hence the subtitle) in the role of economic theory in providing analytical foundations for public policy.

Throughout the book, the terms "public infrastructure" and "public capital" are used interchangeably, in line with the literature in the field. Of course, public capital is a broader concept—it also includes school buildings, hospitals, public libraries, and all other physical assets owned by the state. However, there is no risk of confusion because references to these other components of public capital will be made only sparingly—if at all. Moreover, the focus

[1] See Allais (1947), Samuelson (1958), and the extension by Diamond (1965) to include physical capital. P. Weil (2008) offers a brief history of the OLG model and some of its recent applications, whereas De la Croix and Michel (2002) provide a comprehensive analytical treatment. The baseline OLG model is discussed in many textbooks on economic growth, including Acemoglu (2008).

will be on "core" public capital, which includes transport, water supply and sanitation, information and communications technology, and energy.

To facilitate the task of the reader, and references across chapters, common notations for both variables and parameters are used as much as possible throughout the book. The main symbols are summarized at the end of this introduction.

The book is organized as follows. Chapter 1 begins by focusing on "conventional" channels through which public capital is deemed to affect growth, namely, productivity, complementarity, and crowding-out effects. It presents a basic two-period OLG model, which is extended in subsequent chapters to address a host of other issues. At the core of this model is a production function in which, following the seminal contribution of Arrow and Kurz (1970), public capital is complementary to private capital. In addition, the production of new public capital depends not only on the flow of investment in infrastructure but also on the existing stock of public capital. The latter assumption is shown to be critical in generating dynamics in the public-private capital ratio.

Several extensions of the basic model are then considered, including indirect taxation, a complementarity effect operating through the efficiency of private investment, an effect of public capital on household utility, and maintenance expenditure. The allocation of government spending between maintenance and new investment in infrastructure, possible trade-offs that may arise between these two components of public outlays, and the possibility that public spending on maintenance may also affect directly the durability of private physical assets are discussed as well.

The chapter also provides a discussion of optimal fiscal policy, which is studied from the perspective of growth maximization by a benevolent government, rather than in terms of *social* welfare maximization. A key reason for doing so is the fact that the purpose of this book, in line with the practical concerns of policymakers today, is how public capital can promote growth; and sustained economic growth is critical to achieving progress in reducing poverty and improving standards of living across the board. There are other reasons as well, related in particular to the coexistence of several generations at any given moment in time and the difficulty of defining a social welfare function in such conditions. It should be pointed out, nevertheless, that the book does examine the implications of public capital for *human* welfare, in addition to growth, to the extent that it considers education and health outcomes.

Chapters 2 to 6 are devoted to the various externalities that public capital may generate. Chapter 2 focuses on the links among public capital, knowledge accumulation, and economic growth. It is common to argue that knowledge spillovers are a key determinant of economic growth (see for instance Jones and P. Romer (2010)). In this chapter, the view that is emphasized, in line with the empirical evidence, is that knowledge accumulation itself may depend critically on access to public capital. It also considers the possibility of a trade-off between public spending on education and investment in infrastructure. The point is that even though these expenditure components may be strongly complementary at the microeconomic or sectoral level, they may be substitutes at the macroeconomic level due to a financing constraint. The question that arises, then, is how to allocate optimally (limited) resources among alternative uses. It is addressed by assuming, as discussed earlier, that the government's goal is to maximize growth.

Chapter 3 examines interactions among public capital, health, and economic growth, using both two- and three-period OLG models. The first model dwells on the large body of evidence that suggests that access to infrastructure may be critical to improving health outcomes. The second accounts, in addition, for the fact that there is persistence in health outcomes between childhood and adulthood, the first two stages of life. This creates the possibility that public capital may affect health in ways that are different than commonly thought: if, for instance, greater access to infrastructure services allows parents to devote more time to child rearing, and if children's health depends positively on parental time, their productivity and earnings in adulthood will also be affected. In effect, what this analysis shows is that time allocated to child rearing, which is often considered as unproductive in growth models, may turn out to be a critical channel through which public capital affects growth. The chapter concludes by noting that interactions between health and education, which are well documented, may serve to magnify the effect of public capital on growth and human welfare.[2]

Chapter 4 focuses on the links among public capital, innovation and the diffusion of new products, and economic growth. Potential trade-offs associated with the provision of infrastructure and government support for innovation (as well as education, as in chapter 2) are discussed once again: if governments have access to limited resources to cover their expenditure, different types of government interventions entail dynamic trade-offs at the macroeconomic level—even though at the microeconomic or sectoral level these interventions are largely complementary. In addition, different types of government intervention may generate spillover effects on other sectors, which may have an indirect impact on innovation capacity. In particular, there is much evidence to suggest that access to telecommunications and highly skilled labor are important determinants of innovation capacity. Thus, if lack of infrastructure and low quality of tertiary education are key constraints on research and development activities, increasing spending on infrastructure or universities may ultimately prove to be more efficient to stimulate innovation than, say,

[2] A critical point that also emerges from the models presented in Chapters 2 and 3 (albeit unrelated to public capital *per se*) is that when thinking about human capital, and in contrast to commonly held views, it is essential to distinguish between health and knowledge; while the latter can be accumulated without bounds, the former cannot. This distinction has important analytical and policy implications.

subsidies for research activities in the private sector. Trade-offs involved in the allocation of public expenditure between infrastructure investment and support for R&D activities are illustrated through both an intuitive discussion and numerical experiments. The last part of the chapter discusses the role of public capital in the transition from *imitation* activities (copying or adapting foreign products or technologies to local markets) to *true innovation* (which involves the creation of new products, at the cutting edge of technology). It argues that this transition may necessitate not only a more qualified workforce in a range of areas but also a different *type* of public capital: whereas imitation may require only access to "basic" infrastructure (roads, basic telecommunications services, electricity, and so on), to switch to true innovation may require a more "advanced" type of physical assets, which exhibit a greater degree of complementary with skilled labor. Recent research provides robust evidence to suggest that access to broadband infrastructure, in particular, is critical for the rapid generation and distribution of decentralized information and ideas, which in turn are important steps to promote innovation. Without the provision of this type of capital there is a risk of being caught in an "imitation trap," a situation in which economic growth is positive—both in absolute and per capita terms—but moderate, lengthening therefore the process of convergence to high-income status.

Chapter 5 presents a gender-based model to analyze the links among public capital, gender, and economic growth, taking into account women's time allocation among market work, home production, child rearing, and theurt own health care. Women are assumed to bear the brunt of domestic tasks (processing food crops, providing water and firewood, caring for children, and so on), in line with the evidence for developing countries. As in chapter 3, health status in adulthood (which affects productivity and wages) is taken to depend on health status in childhood as well as time allocated to own health care. Thus, health persistence and time allocated by mothers to child rearing become again key factors in the growth process. The implications of the analysis for the debate on the relationship between women's labor supply and the level of development as well as various extensions (including intrahousehold bargaining) are also discussed. Although the analysis focuses on the impact of infrastructure on women's time allocation, the model can be used to study a variety of gender-based policies; the chapter may therefore prove to be of independent interest to those working on gender and growth issues.

Chapter 6 focuses on the network effects of public capital and considers how a Big Push in public investment may help a poor country escape from a poverty trap, that is, an equilibrium characterized by low or zero growth in income. Network effects typically imply nonlinearities or threshold effects, often resulting in the degree of efficiency of infrastructure being nonlinearly related to the existing stock of public capital itself. Specifically, the marginal benefits of public capital, in terms of its own efficiency, may be highly positive at first, once a core network is completed; but beyond that, these marginal benefits, while they remain positive, may increase at a decreasing rate. The analysis shows that, depending on how strong nonlinearities are, multiple equilibria may emerge. Provided that the quality of governance is adequate enough to ensure a sufficient degree of efficiency of public investment, a large increase in the share of spending on infrastructure may shift the economy from a low-growth equilibrium to a high-growth steady state. The chapter also studies how the choice of production technology is affected by access to public capital, in a setting where the critical value of that variable (that is, the point at which a switch in technology occurs) is endogenously determined through a rate-of-return arbitrage condition. Similar conclusions on the impact of public investment are obtained. The analysis provides therefore a conceptual underpinning to the Big Push idea, with the important proviso that for this policy to work, the quality of governance may need to be improved at the same time. The practical implications of these results for the ongoing debate on "scaling up" public investment in poor countries cannot be overemphasized.

Chapter 7 outlines a research agenda for improving further our understanding of how public capital, economic growth, and human welfare interact. It addresses issues such as heterogeneous infrastructure assets, the political economy of government spending allocation, excludable public goods, interactions between government debt and public capital accumulation in the presence of fiscal rules, spatial and regional dimensions of public capital, public-private partnerships, the impact of public capital on income distribution, negative externalities associated with infrastructure, and empirical tests of the impact of public capital on growth. The view that underlies this book is that the scale of infrastructure projects and the lack of access to private capital markets by the poorest countries hamper their ability to invest in this area. However, even though public investment will continue to be needed to address a range of needs (such as new road capacity in sparsely populated areas), the issue of private sector provision of infrastructure services will become increasingly important in the coming years. Some low-income countries have also started to leverage their natural resources. Understanding what the best long-term arrangements with the private sector are in a context where promoting growth is a key objective remains therefore an important area of investigation. The discussion points out as well that most existing studies, based on linear, single-equation regressions, seriously underestimate the true impact of public capital on output. To a significant extent, this is the consequence of the fact that many of these studies did not attempt to account for some of the externalities associated with infrastructure, as discussed in this book.

Even though the last chapter suggests that there is still a lot to understand in the relationship among public capital, economic growth, and welfare, my hope is that this book makes it clear that there has been much progress toward that endeavor—both conceptually and empirically. Its key message is that, beyond the conventional productivity and cost effects, as well as complementarity and crowding-out effects that economists tend to emphasize, there is a wide range of externalities associated with public capital—and these should be accounted for in analytical models and introduced in policy debates. It is not a gross exaggeration to argue that investing in infrastructure may be as much about promoting markets as it may be about achieving health and education targets, fostering a culture of innovation, and empowering women. What this means, paradoxically, is that in some circumstances the best way to improve, say, education or health outcomes could be to spend less on schooling and health facilities and instead spend more on infrastructure. This does not mean of course that intrinsic challenges in those sectors should be ignored; in the education sector, for instance, there are serious quality issues in low-income countries that need to be addressed. The point, however, is that lack of access to public capital may be an equally important, if not more important, constraint in some cases. This also has implications for the selection, monitoring, and evaluation of infrastructure projects; in addition to conventional methods for project assessment (often based solely on internal rates of return), it is essential to account for the benefits that these projects may provide in terms of human welfare. The fact that measuring these benefits can be difficult in practice should not be used as an excuse for ignoring them.

• • •

This book is the product of the research that I have conducted for the past few years at the University of Manchester and the Centre for Growth and Business Cycle Research on public capital, economic growth, poverty reduction, and welfare. The university has provided me with a superb environment and unique conditions for developing this agenda, and for that I am most grateful.

In conducting this work, I have benefited from collaborative projects and interactions with several colleagues and students at Manchester, including Keith Blackburn, Kyriakos Neanidis, and Devrim Yilmaz. Many of the practical insights upon which this book dwells emerged from the research agenda on growth and poverty reduction that I initiated during my time at the World Bank, and more recently through a collaborative project on women's time allocation and growth. Economists from the bank with whom this collaboration has been most fruitful include Otaviano Canuto, Karim El Aynaoui, Emmanuel Pinto Moreira, and Luiz Pereira da Silva. Last but not least, I am grateful to my daughter Madina, a doctoral student at the Harvard School for Public Health at the time of this writing, for getting me to think harder and more creatively about women's health and gender issues in general—issues, unfortunately, that remain foreign territory for too many macroeconomists. I am thankful to all for their contributions, although I retain sole responsibility for the opinions expressed herein.

In preparing this book, I have used material from several of my papers published in professional journals. I thank *Economica*, the *Journal of Development Economics*, the *Journal of Economic Dynamics and Control*, the *Journal of Macroeconomics*, *Oxford Economic Papers*, and the *Journal of Public Economic Theory* for permission to dwell on these contributions.

## Main Notations

**Variables**

| | |
|---|---|
| $a_t$, $A_t$ | Individual and average labor productivity |
| $B_t$ | Stock of public debt |
| $c^t_{t+j}$ | Consumption at period $t + j$ by individual born at $t$ |
| $e_t$, $E_t$ | Individual and average human capital |
| $e^P_t$ | Human capital-private capital ratio |
| $\varepsilon^h_t$ | Time allocated to activity $h$ |
| $G^h_t$ | Government spending on category $h$ |
| $h_t$ | Individual health status |
| $h^C_t$, $h^A_t$ | Individual health status in childhood and adulthood |
| $H^G_t$ | Government supply of health services |
| $i_t$ | Interest rate on public debt |
| $I_t$ | Private investment |
| $K^P_t$ | Private capital stock |
| $K^I_t$ | Public capital stock |
| $k^I_t$, $J$ | Public-private capital ratio |
| $N_t$, $n_t$ | Adult population, fertility rate |
| $p_t$ | Survival probability from adulthood to old age |
| $r_t$ | Rental rate of private capital |
| $s_t$ | Individual saving rate |
| $U_t$ | Individual or family utility |
| $w_t$ | Actual or effective wage in efficient units of labor |
| $Y_t$ | Output of final goods |

**Parameters**

| | |
|---|---|
| $\alpha$ | Elasticity of final output with respect to public capital |
| $\beta$ | Elasticity of final output with respect to (effective) labor |
| $\delta^P$, $\delta^I$ | Depreciation rates, private and public capital |
| $\zeta$, $\phi$ | Congestion parameters, final output |
| $\eta_N$, $\eta_H$ | Preference parameters, household utility |
| $\theta$, $\theta^R$ | Shares of after-tax income allocated to child rearing |
| $\Xi$, $\Xi_1$, ...$\Xi_n$ | Scale parameters or composite terms |
| $\kappa$ | Degree of persistence in health |
| $\varkappa$ | Elasticity of supply of health services with respect to public capital |
| $\mu$ | Elasticity of new public capital with respect to public investment |
| $\rho$ | Individual discount rate |
| $\sigma$ | Individual savings rate |
| $\tau$ | Tax rate on adult income |
| $\upsilon_h$ | Share in tax revenues of public spending on category $h$ |
| $\chi$ | Sensitivity of labor productivity to health status |
| $\varphi$ | Efficiency of infrastructure investment |

# 1 | Basic Channels

Macroeconomists typically emphasize three basic channels through which public capital may affect growth: a direct *productivity and cost effect* on private production inputs, a *complementarity effect* on private investment, and a *crowding-out effect* on private spending through the financial system.

This chapter begins by reviewing the evidence on all three effects. It then presents a basic OLG framework, with full capital depreciation, that accounts for the productivity effect. The equilibrium and the balanced growth path (along which key macroeconomic variables grow at a constant rate) are then derived, and the growth effects of public investment are examined, under alternative assumptions about the importance of the existing public physical assets for the production of new capital. The cost effect of public capital is also discussed, with respect to labor inputs. Optimal fiscal policy is analyzed next. The chapter concludes by discussing various extensions, including indirect taxation, the complementarity effect of public capital on private investment, public capital in the utility function, partial depreciation, and maintenance expenditure.

## 1 | Background

### 1.1 | Productivity and Cost of Private Inputs

The direct productivity and cost effects of infrastructure is the argument that is most commonly referenced to account for a growth effect of public capital. If, as is normally the case, production factors are gross complements, a higher stock of public capital would tend to raise the productivity of other inputs, such as labor and the stock of private capital, thereby reducing unit production costs. Given decreasing returns, the magnitude of this effect would depend, of course, on the initial stock of public capital. In mature economies, marginal productivity effects are likely to be limited; but in low-income countries, where stocks of infrastructure assets are relatively low to begin with, they could be substantial.[1]

[1] Many economic historians believe that today's rich countries owe much of their development to massive (public and private) investments in infrastructure. The development of the western part of the United States, for instance, was driven mainly by a massive expansion of railways, supported by land grants and subsidized credit. Between 1865 and 1873 alone, 28,000 miles of track were laid. However, there is also evidence that the frantic pace of railway expansion pushed up construction costs significantly. The role of railways—which were invented in the 17th

Sub-Saharan Africa is a case in point.[2] In most countries of the region, particularly the lower-income ones, infrastructure remains a major constraint on economic activity, depressing firm productivity perhaps by as much 40 percent (Escribano et al. (2008)). For one set of countries power is the most constraining factor by far; a majority of firms cites it as a major business obstacle.[3] Africa's power infrastructure delivers only a fraction of the services found elsewhere in the developing world (Eberhard et al. (2008)). The 48 countries of sub-Saharan Africa (with a combined population of about 800 million) generate roughly the same amount of power as Spain (with a population of about 45 million). For a second set, inefficient functioning of ports is equally significant. Deficiencies in transport and in information and communication technologies (ICTs) are less prevalent but substantial in some cases.

Africa's road density is sparse when viewed against the size of the continent and the distribution of its population. In rural areas over 20 percent of the population lives in dispersed settlements, where typical population densities are less than 15 people per square kilometer. Only one-third of the population living in rural areas are within two kilometers of an all season road, compared with two-thirds in other developing regions. In cities, population density is relatively low by global standards and does not benefit from large economies of agglomeration in the provision of infrastructure services. As a result, the costs of providing a basic infrastructure package can easily be twice as much as in other, more densely populated cities in the developing world (Foster and Briceño-Garmendia (2010)). Lack of railways in the region is a key constraint to trade expansion, especially for agriculture and extractive industries.

Estimates by the African Development Bank suggest that in sub-Saharan Africa transport and energy costs, at 16 and 35 percent of total costs, respectively, represent by far the largest share of firms' indirect costs. A large fraction of these costs is the result of the poor quality of basic infrastructure. For instance, because of inadequate transport facilities and unreliable supply of electricity, firms often incur additional expenses in the form of more expensive transportation means and onerous energy backup systems. Poor quality of electricity provision has a particularly large impact on the poorest countries (Escribano et al. (2010)). In many countries of the region, lack of irrigation also represents a major constraint on agricultural productivity (see Food and Agriculture Organization (2008)). With the availability of fresh water

century to haul coal in mines, and from mines to canals or rivers—in the context of the Industrial Revolution is discussed by Allen (2009).

[2] There is also evidence for other regions. Romero and Kuroda (2005), for instance, found that public infrastructure lowered production costs and improved the productivity performance of agriculture in the Philippines over the years 1974-2000. Evidence for industrial countries is provided in Romp and de Haan (2005).

[3] Africa's firms report losing an average of 5 percent of their annual sales because of frequent power outages—a figure that rises to 20 percent for informal firms unable to afford backup generators. Overall, the economic costs of power outages can easily reach 1 or 2 percent of GDP.

becoming increasingly vulnerable to climate change, in coming years the continent may face severe losses in annual grain production, as well as drastic reductions in energy capacity production.

The productivity and cost effects of public infrastructure may be magnified in the presence of externalities associated with the use of some production factors, such as, for instance, *learning-by-doing effects* resulting from a high degree of complementarity between physical capital and skilled labor.[4] In addition, independent of its direct effect on the marginal product of factor inputs in the production process (as discussed earlier), public infrastructure may also have an indirect, additional impact on labor productivity. The idea, as suggested for instance by P. Ferreira (1999), is that with better access to roads and other means of public transportation (such as railways), workers can get to their job more easily, therefore spending less time commuting from home or moving across different work locations. This would tend to reduce traffic-related stress, which can be detrimental to concentration on the job. With greater access to electricity and telecommunications, workers can perform a number of tasks more rapidly (such as checking price quotations), as well as additional tasks away from the office (such as checking electronic messages from home). In poor countries, improved access to mobile phones has led to the development of new data services, such as mobile-phone-based agricultural advice, health care, and money transfer, which may all provide significant benefits in terms of productivity. By providing easier access to information, broadband networks may have a large impact on productivity as well. In turn, higher productivity would tend to enhance growth. Czernich et al. (2011), for instance, in a study of OECD countries during the period 1996–2007, found that a 10-percentage-point increase in broadband penetration (measured as the number of broadband subscribers per 100 inhabitants) raises annual per capita growth by 0.9 to 1.5 percentage points.

Another indirect effect of public capital could be through *inventories* that firms hold. In a study covering 36 major Chinese cities, Li (2010) found that infrastructure investment since the mid-1980s led to a dramatic reduction in inventories, from an inventory/sales ratio of 0.8 to approximately 0.15. Road investments alone reduced raw materials inventories by 25 percent during the period 1998–2007. In fact, one dollar of road spending caused 1 to 2 cents of inventory decline, which is similar in magnitude to the estimates for the United States prior to the 1980s (Henckel and McKibbin (2010)). In a study of India's Golden Quadrilateral (GQ) Program—a major highway project aimed at improving the quality and width of existing highways connecting the four largest cities of the country—Datta (2011) found that firms in cities affected by the GQ highway project reduced their average stock of input inventories by between 6 and 12 days worth of production. Thus, transport infrastructure investment may contribute to economic efficiency not only by

[4] In general, externalities exist if economic or other interactions create social gains or costs beyond those taken into account by those involved in the interaction.

reducing transport costs but also by reducing the need to maintain high (and expensive) inventories.

Of course, the positive effect of public capital on the marginal productivity of private inputs may hold not only for infrastructure but also for other components of public capital—such as in education and health, which may both affect the productivity of labor. Moreover, other components of public spending, related for instance to the enforcement of property rights and maintenance of public order, could also increase productivity, reduce costs, and exert a positive effect on private investment and growth, despite the fact that they may not be considered as being directly "productive." Improved public safety for instance could reduce the need for firms to spend resources to protect employees and physical assets by hiring guards, building fences, reinforcing doors, and buying security systems. But, as noted earlier, infrastructure capital may have a particularly large effect in countries where initial stocks are low and basic infrastructure services (such as electricity and clean water) are lacking, as is the case in many low-income countries.

## 1.2| Complementarity Effect on Private Investment

Another channel through which public capital can exert a positive effect on growth is through its effect on private capital formation. As noted earlier, public infrastructure increases the marginal productivity of private inputs. In so doing, it raises the perceived rate of return on, and may increase the demand for, physical capital by the private sector. For instance, the rate of return to building a factory is likely to be higher if the country has already invested in power generation, transportation, and telecommunications.

The complementarity effect has been well documented in the empirical literature on private capital formation in developing countries (see Agénor (2004, chap. 2)). Albala-Bertrand and Mamatzakis (2004) for instance found that in Chile, public infrastructure capital had a significant positive effect on private investment. In Vietnam, the decision to improve National Highway No. 5 and rehabilitate the port of Haiphong in the early 1990s led to a massive increase in investment (much of it foreign) in major industrial zones, spurring growth and employment in the northern part of the country in general (see Mitsui (2004)). The provision of infrastructure services (particularly in the area of telecommunications) has also been shown to be a key determinant of foreign direct investment in a number of other countries (see Vijayakumar and Rao (2009)).

Conversely, the study of Uganda by Reinikka and Svensson (2002) illustrates well how inadequate public infrastructure may adversely affect private investment. A survey of 243 manufacturing firms conducted in 1998 in that country showed that the lack of adequate electricity sources was ranked as the most important constraint to investment. Firms did not receive electricity from the public grid for 89 operating days on average, which led to 77 percent of large firms (in addition to 44 percent of medium and 16 percent of small firms) purchasing generators, representing 25 percent of their total investment in equipment and machinery in 1997. The same survey showed that for a firm without a privately owned generator, a 1 percent increase in the number of days without power resulted in a 0.45 percent reduction in investment. Thus, lack of access to, and poor reliability of, public infrastructure may affect both the *level* and the *composition* of private investment, in the latter case by biasing private capital formation toward the accumulation of assets that may alleviate the constraints that firms face in their day-to-day activities.

In the short run, public capital may also affect private capital formation indirectly, through changes in output and relative prices. As noted earlier, improved access to infrastructure may raise the marginal productivity of all factor inputs (capital and labor), thereby lowering marginal production costs and increasing the level of private production. In turn, this scale effect on output may lead, through a standard accelerator effect (or increased expected demand), to higher private investment—thereby raising production capacity over time and making the short-run growth effect more persistent.

Another indirect channel is through the effect of public infrastructure on the price of domestic consumption goods relative to the price of imported goods, that is, the (consumption-based) real exchange rate. An increase, for instance, in public investment in infrastructure would raise aggregate demand and put pressure on domestic prices. If the nominal exchange rate does not depreciate fully to offset the increase in domestic prices, the domestic-currency price of imported consumption goods will fall in relative terms (that is, the real exchange rate will appreciate), thereby stimulating demand for these goods. The net effect on domestic output may be positive or negative, depending on the intratemporal elasticity of substitution between domestic and imported goods. If this elasticity is low (as one would expect in the short run), the net effect may well be positive. Again, through the accelerator effect, private investment may increase, and this may translate into a more permanent growth effect.

At the same time, to the extent that the increase in government spending on infrastructure raises the relative price of *domestic* capital goods, and the switch in private consumption demand toward imports translates into a nominal appreciation, the domestic-currency price of *imported* capital goods may fall in relative terms, resulting in a drop in the user cost of capital. If a large fraction of the capital goods used by the private sector is imported (as is often the case for machinery and equipment in developing countries) this may lead to an increase in private investment. The relative price effect is not necessarily only short term in nature; as suggested by the evidence reported in Sala-i-Martin et al. (2004), it may translate into a more persistent growth effect.

## 1.3| Crowding-Out Effects

In the short term, an increase in the stock of public capital in infrastructure may have an adverse effect on activity, to the extent that it displaces (or crowds out) private investment. This short-run effect may translate into a longer-lasting adverse effect on growth if the drop in private capital formation persists over time.

Crowding-Out effects may take various forms. For instance, if the public sector finances the expansion of public capital through an increase in distortionary taxes, the reduction in the expected net rate of return to private capital may lower the propensity to invest. A similar, and possibly more detrimental, effect on private capital formation may occur if the increase in public infrastructure outlays is paid for by borrowing on domestic financial markets, as a result of either higher domestic interest rates (in countries where market forces are relatively free to operate in the financial system) or a greater incidence of rationing of credit to the private sector. Moreover, if an investment-induced expansion in public borrowing raises concerns about the sustainability of public debt over time and strengthens expectations of a future increase in inflation or explicit taxation, the risk premium embedded in interest rates may increase. By raising the cost of borrowing and negatively affecting expected after-tax rates of return on private capital, an increase in the perceived risk of default on government debt may have a compounding, depressing effect on private capital accumulation.

In principle, crowding-out effects associated with public infrastructure should be short term in nature; to the extent that an increase in the public capital stock raises output growth in the medium and longer term, future government borrowing needs may actually fall as a result of higher tax revenues. In that sense, deficits today may pay for themselves tomorrow, a common logic when discussing tax cuts and increases in productive expenditure in a growth context (see for instance Agénor and Yilmaz (2011)). However, as noted earlier, these effects may also persist beyond the short term, and turn into longer-run (adverse) effects on growth. For instance, if higher (anticipated) tax rates create permanent incentives for tax evasion, lower resources may reduce durably the government's capacity to invest in infrastructure and other areas in the future, or its ability to ensure adequate maintenance of the public capital stock. If so, then, despite the productivity and complementarity effects mentioned earlier, the net effect of an increase in public spending on infrastructure may well be to hamper, rather than foster, economic growth. Moreover, as discussed in more detail in chapter 7, the crowding-out effect associated with excessive public debt can be a source of instability and prevent the economy from reaching an equilibrium with constant growth.

## 2| The Economy

To illustrate the link between public capital and productivity highlighted in the foregoing discussion, and its implications for growth, a simple overlapping-generations (OLG) model is presented. A fairly detailed description of the model is given in this chapter because the same fundamental apparatus (with various extensions and modifications) will be used in subsequent chapters.

The point of departure is an economy populated by three types of agents: individuals (or households), firms, and an infinitely lived government.[5] Time is discrete and indexed by $t = 0, 1, 2, \ldots$ Firms produce one homogeneous good, which can be either consumed in the period it is produced or stored to yield capital at the beginning of the following period. Its price is constant and normalized to unity. Although the horizon of the model is infinite, households live for two periods only, young (period 1) and old (period 2). Thus, in any one period of time there is an overlapping generation of young and old. Households are also endowed with one unit of labor services when they are young and zero units when they are old. Consequently, they can work only when they are young; the only source of income is wages in the first period, which serves to finance consumption in both periods. Savings can be held only in the form of physical capital. Agents have no other endowments, except for an initial stock of physical capital, $K_0^P$, which is the endowment of an initial old generation. The government invests in infrastructure and spends on unproductive (or, more accurately perhaps, not directly productive) services. It taxes the wage income of the young only, not the interest income of the old. It cannot borrow and therefore must run a balanced budget in each period.

All markets clear, and there are no explicit monetary transfers across generations, neither from parents to children nor from children (while working) to parents. Transfers and bequests are of course important in practice in many developing countries—particularly transfers from the young to the old, in line with the *old age security hypothesis* discussed for instance in Ehrlich and Lui (1991), Raut (1990), and Morand (1999). Indeed, in the absence of well-functioning capital markets, and no public pension system, parents may need to rely on their children for old age income support. As a result, they may view the allocation of resources to their children's education or health as an investment decision, rather than the result of pure altruistic concerns. However, these issues are somewhat tangential to those that are the focus of this book, and for simplicity are left out. In addition, to the extent that parents allocate time to tutoring their children (as in chapter 2) or caring about their health (as in chapters 3 and 5), and that such activities affect children's behavior in adulthood, and to the extent that there is knowledge and health persistence (as in chapters 2 to 5), the analysis does not completely abstract from intergenerational links.

## 2.1| Households

Households have perfect foresight and are identical within and across generations. At each period $t$, $N_t$ individuals are born; they become old in $t+1$. The total population alive at $t$ is thus $N_{t-1} + N_t$. Let $N_{t+1}/N_t = n$, where $n \geq 1$;

[5] Until chapter 5, where a gender-based OLG model is used, the terms "individuals," "agents," and "households" are used interchangeably.

this implies that the population as a whole also grows at the constant rate $n$, because $(N_t + N_{t+1})/(N_{t-1} + N_t) = (N_{t-1}n + N_t n)/(N_{t-1} + N_t) = n$. Total labor supply (given that only the young work) at $t$ is given by $N_t$.

Let $c^t_{t+j}$ denote consumption at period $t + j$ of an individual born at the beginning of period $t$, with $j = 0, 1$. The discounted utility of that individual is given by

$$U_t = \ln c^t_t + \frac{\ln c^t_{t+1}}{1+\rho}, \tag{1}$$

where $\rho > 0$ is the rate of time preference, or equivalently the subjective discount rate, and $1/(1+\rho)$ the discount factor. The utility function in (1) is assumed to be additively separable, which implies that consumption is a normal good in each period—that is, demand for it is positively related to income, as shown later. For tractability, throughout the book the utility function in each period is assumed to be logarithmic.[6]

Because labor is inelastically supplied by young households, it does not appear explicitly in the intertemporal utility function. In fact, throughout this book the analysis will abstract from labor-leisure choices.[7] Time allocation between *productive* uses will be endogenously determined in chapters 3 and 5.

Because taxes are levied only on the young, the period-specific budget constraints are given by

$$c^t_t + s_t = (1-\tau)w_t, \tag{2}$$

$$c^t_{t+1} = (1 + r_{t+1})s_t, \tag{3}$$

where $w_t$ is the wage rate, $\tau \in (0, 1)$ a constant tax rate, and $r_{t+1}$ the rate of return on holding assets between periods $t$ and $t + 1$.[8] Because in this model savings (the acquisition of assets) take only the form of capital accumulation, the rate of return on assets is by definition equal to the rate of return on private capital. Conditions (2) and (3) hold because there are no bequests or debts to future generations. Young agents are thus all born without assets.

Substituting for $s_t$ from (3) in (2) yields the lifetime or intertemporal budget constraint,

$$c^t_t + \frac{c^t_{t+1}}{1 + r_{t+1}} = (1-\tau)w_t. \tag{4}$$

[6] This functional form implies that $\lim_{c^t_{t+h}\to 0}(d \ln c^t_{t+j}/dc^t_{t+j}) = \infty$, which avoids the possibility of corner solutions.

[7] As argued by García-Peñalosa and Turnovsky (2005, p. 1052), doing so may not be a bad approximation when it comes to poor countries, given the low overall levels of consumption to begin with in these countries.

[8] If interest income were taxed, then equation (3) would be $c^t_{t+1} = [1 + (1-\tau)r_{t+1}]s_t$. The government budget constraint, given in equation (19), would need to be adjusted accordingly.

Each individual maximizes (1) with respect to $c_t^t$ and $c_{t+1}^t$, subject to the intertemporal budget constraint, that is,

$$\{c_t^t, c_{t+1}^t\} = \arg\max \left\{ \ln c_t^t + \frac{\ln c_{t+1}^t}{1+\rho} \right\},$$

subject to (4) with $w_t$, $r_{t+1}$, and $\tau$ given, and $c_t^t, c_{t+1}^t > 0$.

Let $\lambda_t$ denote the Lagrange multiplier associated with (4); first-order conditions are given by

$$1/c_t^t = \lambda_t, \tag{5}$$

$$1/(1+\rho)c_{t+1}^t = \lambda_t/(1+r_{t+1}), \tag{6}$$

which can be combined to give

$$\frac{c_{t+1}^t}{c_t^t} = \frac{1+r_{t+1}}{1+\rho}. \tag{7}$$

Equation (7) is the *Euler equation*. It essentially indicates that, at the optimum, a household cannot gain from shifting consumption between periods. A 1-unit reduction in consumption in period $t$ lowers utility by $1/c_t^t$. The unit saved in period $t$ can be converted (by investing it) into $1+r_{t+1}$ units of consumption in period $t+1$, raising utility by $(1+r_{t+1})/c_{t+1}^t$; this is discounted "back" to period $t$ by $1+\rho$.

Substituting (7) in constraint (4) yields

$$c_t^t = \left(\frac{1+\rho}{2+\rho}\right)(1-\tau)w_t, \tag{8}$$

so that[9]

$$s_t = (1-\tau)w_t - c_t^t = \sigma(1-\tau)w_t, \tag{9}$$

where $\sigma = 1/(2+\rho)$ is the marginal propensity to save out of after-tax income.

This result shows that, in the simple case of a log-linear utility function, the savings rate depends only on the wage rate, not the rate of return of capital, because income and substitution effects cancel each other out.[10] The low interest elasticity of savings in low-income countries is actually well

[9] Solution (9) could be obtained more directly by substituting (2) and (3) in (1) and solving $\max \ln[(1-\tau)w_t - s_t] + (1+\rho)^{-1}\ln[(1+r_{t+1})s_t]$ with respect to $s_t$, with $\tau$, $w_t$, and $r_{t+1}$ given; the first-order condition is $-[(1-\tau)w_t - s_t]^{-1} + (1+\rho)^{-1}s_t^{-1} = 0$.

[10] With a Cobb-Douglas utility function, of the form $(c_t^t)^{\omega}(c_{t+1}^t)^{1-\omega}$, where $\omega \in (0, 1)$ and $\rho = 0$, the Euler equation would take the form $\omega c_{t+1}^t/(1-\omega)c_t^t = 1+r_{t+1}$, then $c_t^t = (1-\tau)\omega w_t$, and the savings rate would be $s_t = (1-\tau)(1-\omega)w_t$, which is also independent of $r_{t+1}$. As illustrated by Lin (1998), however, if it had been assumed that second-period noninterest income is nonzero, the use of a log-linear utility function would not result in savings being perfectly inelastic with respect to the interest rate.

documented, as discussed in Agénor (2004, chap. 2) and Agénor and Montiel (2008, chap. 3).

Let $C_t$ denote total household consumption at time $t$; it is given by the sum of consumption of the young and the old generations alive in period $t$:

$$C_t = c_t^t N_t + c_t^{t-1} N_{t-1}. \tag{10}$$

Until chapter 3 (where fertility decisions are explicitly analyzed), the following assumption is imposed for simplicity:

**Assumption 1.1.** *Population is constant* ($n = 1$)

The zero-growth assumption implies therefore that $N_t = \bar{N}$, $\forall t$. Using (2) and (3), total private consumption can also be written as

$$C_t = \{[(1-\tau)w_t - s_t] + (1+r_t)s_{t-1}\}\bar{N}. \tag{11}$$

## 2.2| Firms

There is a continuum of identical firms, indexed by $i \in (0, 1)$. They produce a single nonstorable good, which is used either for consumption or investment in physical capital. Production requires the use of private inputs, labor and private capital (which firms rent from the currently old agents), and public capital in infrastructure. There is also a negative externality associated with the *aggregate* stock of private capital. Firms do not invest in publicly provided services because they cannot internalize their benefits.

Assuming a Cobb-Douglas technology, the production function of individual firm $i$ takes the form[11]

$$Y_t^i = \left[\frac{K_t^I}{(K_t^P)^{\zeta}}\right]^{\alpha} (N_t^i)^{\beta} (K_t^{P,i})^{1-\beta}, \tag{12}$$

where $K_t^{P,i}$ denotes the firm-specific stock of capital, $K_t^P = \int_0^1 K_t^{P,i}$ the aggregate private capital stock, $K_t^I$ the stock of public capital (core infrastructure), $\alpha, \zeta > 0$, and $\beta \in (0, 1)$. Throughout this book, the rate of utilization of each production factor is taken as constant over time and normalized to one. So the quantity $K_t^j$ for instance, with $j = P, I$, represents at the same time the capital input $j$, a flow, and the available stock of capital $j$. Similarly, the quantity $N_t^i$ represents both the labor input, a flow, and the number of adults employed by firm $i$, a stock.

[11] The Cobb-Douglas specification is used systematically in this book because of its simplicity and tractability. Duffy and Papageorgiou (2000) found that the elasticity of substitution between physical capital and human capital exceeds unity for rich countries, but that it is less than unity for developing countries. Baier and Glomm (2001) consider the case of a constant elasticity of substitution (CES) function in a related context, but they must resort to numerical analysis to analyze the properties of their model.

Equation (12) implies that production exhibits constant returns to scale in firm-specific labor and capital. In equilibrium, firms make zero profits. In what follows the restriction $\alpha < 1$ will also be imposed, to ensure (as shown later) a positive effect of the savings rate on the steady-state growth rate.

Public capital in infrastructure is exogenous to the private production process and affects each single firm's output in the same way. However, its productivity effects are diminished by excessive use: thus, although not excludable, public infrastructure is partially rival because it is subject to *absolute congestion*, in the sense that it is directly proportional to the size of the aggregate private capital stock.[12] For instance, the greater the number of trucks operated by the private sector, the greater the likelihood of traffic jams and lost time for workers driving to their work location. The greater the use of electricity-powered machine equipment by private firms, the higher the pressure on power grids, and the greater the likelihood of power failures. The higher the number of phones operated concomitantly by the private sector, the greater the risk of calls being dropped. These are particularly important considerations for low-income countries, where public assets in transportation, energy, and telecommunications are, to begin with, limited. The strength of the congestion effect is measured by the coefficient $\zeta$, whereas the magnitude of the productivity effect is measured by $\alpha$.[13]

Markets for both private capital and labor are competitive. Each firm's objective is to maximize profits, $\Pi_t^i$, with respect to labor services and private capital, taking as given $K_t^I$ and $K_t^P$:

$$\max_{N_t^i, K_t^{P,i}} \Pi_t^i = Y_t^i - (r_t + \delta^P)K_t^{P,i} - w_t N_t^i, \tag{13}$$

where $r_t$ is the rental rate of private capital and $\delta^P \in (0, 1)$ the rate of depreciation of private capital. The term $r_t + \delta^P$ measures therefore the user cost of capital.

The solution of each firm's (static) profit maximization problem yields

$$w_t = \beta Y_t^i / N_t^i, \quad r_t = (1 - \beta) Y_t^i / K_t^{P,i} - \delta^P,$$

which implies that private inputs are paid at their marginal product.

Given that all firms are identical, in a symmetric equilibrium $K_t^{P,i} = K_t^P$, $\forall i$. In addition, the labor market equilibrium condition requires $\int_0^1 N_t^i di = \bar{N}$.

[12] In the present context, a public good is excludable if a firm can prevent other firms from using it concomitantly, and it is rival if the use of it by one firm reduces availability of the good for use by other firms. Excludable public goods are by definition goods for which it is possible to charge a price or fee for their use, an issue discussed in chapter 7. Until then, the provision of all public services is assumed to remain free of charge.

[13] As in Glomm and Ravikumar (1994), congestion could be measured both in terms of the private capital stock and labor supply—or alternatively, in terms of aggregate output. See Barro and Sala-i-Martin (1992) and Eicher and Turnovsky (2000) for a discussion of various concepts of congestion in endogenous growth models.

Thus, the first-order conditions become

$$w_t = \beta Y_t / \bar{N}, \tag{14}$$

$$r_t = (1-\beta) Y_t / K_t^P - \delta^P. \tag{15}$$

Because the number of firms is normalized to unity, aggregate output is thus, using (12),

$$Y_t = \int_0^1 Y_t^i di = \Xi \left( \frac{K_t^I}{K_t^P} \right)^{\alpha} (K_t^P)^{1-\beta+\alpha-\zeta\alpha}, \quad \Xi = \bar{N}^{\beta} \tag{16}$$

Because the public-private capital ratio $K_t^I / K_t^P$ is constant in the steady state and population is constant, endogenous growth requires $Y_t$ to be linear in $K_t^P$; that is, aggregate output must exhibit constant returns to private capital in order to generate growth in the long run.[14] This requires therefore imposing the following condition on the parameters of the production function:

**Assumption 1.2.** $\beta - \alpha(1-\zeta) = 0$.

In quantitative terms, this assumption can be interpreted as follows. In practice, the marginal product of capital is of the order of 0.35-0.4, implying that $\beta$ is of the order of 0.6-0.65. Because assumption 1.2 implies that $\zeta = 1-(\beta/\alpha)$, for the congestion effect to be strictly positive ($\zeta > 0$) it must be that $\alpha > \beta$. Recent estimates suggest instead values of $\alpha$ in the vicinity of 0.15 (see Bom and Ligthart (2010) and Agénor (2011*a*)). However, as discussed in more detail in chapter 7, there are strong indications that many existing studies (based on linear, single-equation regressions) seriously underestimate both the direct and indirect (that is, the general equilibrium) effects of infrastructure on output. Inadequate adjustment for the efficiency of investment flows may also lead to overestimating capital stocks, and thus to underestimation of its marginal benefits.

At a more conceptual level, the existence of network effects (which are explored in chapter 6) may provide a conceptual rationale for imposing $\alpha > \beta$—at least over a certain range of values of the public-private capital ratio. Alternatively, the restriction $\alpha > \beta$ can be entirely sidestepped by assuming the existence of a second positive externality, associated this time with the aggregate stock of *private* capital, in the tradition of P. Romer (1986).[15]

[14] The production function takes then the form of a standard $AK$ function. See, for instance, Barro and Sala-i-Martin (2003), Agénor (2004), and Acemoglu (2008) for a discussion of $AK$ models.

[15] This externality is similar in spirit to the *learning by doing* effect first introduced by Arrow (1962), and according to which knowledge (as embodied in the economy's stock of private capital) plays a critical role in raising labor productivity.

The individual production function (12) would then take the form

$$Y_t^i = \left[\frac{K_t^I}{(K_t^P)^\zeta}\right]^\alpha (K_t^P)^\eta (N_t^i)^\beta (K_t^{P,i})^{1-\beta},$$

where $\eta > 0$ measures the strength of the private capital stock externality. Instead of (16), aggregate output would therefore be given by

$$Y_t = \Xi (k_t^I)^\alpha (K_t^P)^{1-\beta+\alpha-\zeta\alpha+\eta},$$

implying that the restriction for ensuring steady-state growth would now be $\beta - \alpha(1-\zeta) - \eta = 0$, or equivalently $\zeta = 1 - (\beta - \eta)/\alpha$. Thus, with $\alpha = 0.15$ (as in some recent estimates) and $\beta = 0.65$, any value of $\eta > 0.5$ would be sufficient to ensure that $\zeta > 0$. For higher values of $\alpha$, as discussed in chapter 7, the threshold value of $\eta$ (a parameter for which there is limited consensus) would be correspondingly lower. For $\alpha = 0.25$ for instance, the relevant value for $\eta$ drops to 0.4.

Maintaining therefore assumption 1.2 for simplicity, aggregate output becomes

$$Y_t = \Xi \left(\frac{K_t^I}{K_t^P}\right)^\alpha K_t^P. \tag{17}$$

Private capital accumulation is driven by

$$K_{t+1}^P = I_t + (1 - \delta^P) K_t^P, \tag{18}$$

where $I_t$ is private investment.

### 2.3| Government

As noted earlier, in any given period the government taxes only the young, at the constant rate $\tau$.[16] The tax rate is announced at the beginning of time and the government commits fully and credibly to it. There is therefore no *time inconsistency problem*, that is, the possibility that the government may renege on fiscal policy announcements, after expectations are formed and private decisions have been taken.[17]

The government spends a total of $G_t^I$ on infrastructure investment and $G_t^U$ on other (unproductive) items. Because it cannot issue bonds, it must run a

[16] Given the focus of this book on the expenditure side of the budget, taxation is assumed to be at a uniform rate. Studies that examine the optimal tax composition (between labor and capital) include Baier and Glomm (2001). See also Glomm and Ravikumar (1999) for a growth model with public capital and time-varying tax rates.

[17] In general, time inconsistency refers to a situation where a private agent or a social planner must make a choice about an action or decision in some future plan, and where what is optimal initially is no longer so at a later date. This change in what is optimal occurs despite the fact that nothing new is learned and the environment remains the same, except for the fact that decisions of the past are locked in place.

balanced budget; thus[18]

$$G_t = G_t^I + G_t^U = \bar{N}\tau w_t. \tag{19}$$

Shares of spending are both assumed to be constant fractions of government revenues:

$$G_t^h = \upsilon_h \bar{N}\tau w_t, \quad h = I, U \tag{20}$$

where $\upsilon_h \in (0, 1)$. Combining (19) and (20) therefore yields

$$\upsilon_I + \upsilon_U = 1. \tag{21}$$

In conventional macroeconomic models, the production of new public capital is related directly to investment spending only, using the so-called *perpetual inventory method*. Suppose instead that producing new capital requires also the use of existing infrastructure assets. For instance, to build or expand a power plant may require public land on which to build, the use of roads to carry construction materials, and electricity to operate machine tools and construction equipment. The law of motion of public capital can therefore be written as

$$K_{t+1}^I = (\varphi G_t^I)^\mu (K_t^I)^{1-\mu} + (1 - \delta^I)K_t^I, \tag{22}$$

where $\delta^I \in (0, 1)$ is a depreciation rate and $\mu \in (0, 1)$ a technology parameter. The conventional case, in which only current investment matters to build new capital, corresponds therefore to $\mu = 1$. As it turns out, the value of $\mu$ plays an important role in understanding the properties of the model; in what follows the cases $\mu = 1$ and $\mu < 1$ will be considered separately. Note also that public capital, in this specification, is not subject to congestion associated with private use, as in (12). At this stage, doing so would only complicate the analysis.

Another parameter that appears in (22) is $\varphi \in (0, 1)$, which measures the extent to which investment flows translate into actual accumulation of public capital.[19] The case $\varphi < 1$ reflects the view that investment spending on infrastructure is subject to inefficiencies, which tend to limit their positive impact on the public capital stock. Arestoff and Hurlin (2005) and Hurlin (2006), for instance, estimate the value of $\varphi$ to vary between 0.4 and 0.6. Using a larger sample of 71 developing countries, Dabla-Norris et al. (2011) estimate a median value of $\varphi$ (renormalized in a 0-1 range) to be 0.4. As it

[18] By adding debt to the model, it could be assumed that the government is allowed to borrow to finance government capital formation, but not consumption; see Agénor and Yilmaz (2011, 2012) and references therein. More general models of growth with public capital and debt accumulation include Corsetti and Roubini (1996), P. Ferreira (1999), and Greiner and Semmler (1999), whereas Hung (2005) considers the case of seigniorage. The issue of public debt is discussed in chapter 7, together with alternative fiscal rules.

[19] This specification, which was first proposed by Pritchett (2000) in a discussion of growth accounting, was used in a macro/development setting by this writer in a paper first circulated in 2006 and published a few years later (see Agénor (2010)).

turns out, this parameter (which can broadly be thought of as an indicator of the quality of public sector management, or governance, or as a measure of absorptive capacity) plays an important role in the dynamic response to shifts in investment spending, including the role of public policies in escaping from a low-growth trap (see chapter 6). Chapter 7 will discuss various ways through which $\varphi$ can be endogenized, by linking it to the degree of corruption or political incentives.[20]

For the moment, the following assumption is imposed:

**Assumption 1.3.** *Both private and public capital depreciate fully after production.*

Thus, $\delta^P = \delta^I = 1$, so that $K^P_{t+1} = I_t$ and $K^I_{t+1} = (\varphi G^I_t)^\mu (K^I_t)^{1-\mu}$. Assuming full depreciation of capital within periods is reasonable in the present setting, given that a "period" corresponds to one-half of the representative individual's life cycle.[21] For simplicity, it is also assumed that capital is irreversible, that is, once invested, it cannot be consumed.

## 2.4| Market-Clearing Conditions

With wages free to adjust, the labor market is always in equilibrium. Given the long-term nature of the analysis and the evidence on the degree of wage flexibility in low-income countries (see Agénor (2006) for instance), this assumption is quite reasonable.

Because goods cannot be transferred across periods, the equilibrium condition for the goods market is

$$Y_t = C_t + I_t + G_t,$$

that is, given (19) and assumption 1.3,

$$Y_t = C_t + K^P_{t+1} + G^U_t + G^I_t. \tag{23}$$

This condition indicates that output must be divided between private consumption and public unproductive consumption in period $t$, and public and private investment available for production in $t+1$.

The asset market clearing (or capital market equilibrium) condition requires equality between private investment and aggregate savings by young individuals:

$$I_t = K^P_{t+1} = \bar{N} s_t, \tag{24}$$

[20] Note that, as in Rioja (2003*a*), the effectiveness of the stock of public capital could be measured as $\varphi K^I_{t+1}$, but this specification is less appealing conceptually.

[21] With full depreciation, it must be assumed that public capital and goods are combined during period $t$, or an instant before the end of period $t$, to produce the capital to be used at the beginning of $t+1$.

Because of *Walras's Law*—according to which, if there are $m$ markets in the economy, and $m-1$ markets are in equilibrium, then the $m$th market must also be in equilibrium—the equilibrium conditions (23) and (24) are not independent. To establish this result is simple enough. Using the period-specific budget constraints (2) and (3), aggregate consumption of the young can be written as $C_t^t = \bar{N}(1-\tau)w_t - \bar{N}s_t$, whereas consumption of the elderly, using also (24), is $C_t^{t-1} = (1+r_t)\bar{N}s_{t-1} = (1+r_t)K_t^P$. Economy-wide consumption is thus $C_t = C_t^t + C_t^{t-1} = \bar{N}(1-\tau)w_t - \bar{N}s_t + (1+r_t)K_t^P = \bar{N}w_t + (1+r_t)K_t^P - \bar{N}s_t - \bar{N}\tau w_t$. From equations (14) and (15), and $\delta^P = 1$, $\bar{N}w_t + (1+r_t)K_t^P = Y_t$.[22] Thus, the previous expression becomes $C_t = Y_t - \bar{N}s_t - \bar{N}\tau w_t$. Substituting this result in the economy-wide budget constraint (23) yields $Y_t = Y_t - \bar{N}s_t + (G_t - \bar{N}\tau w_t) + K_{t+1}^P$. Given the government budget constraint (19), this yields indeed $K_{t+1}^P = \bar{N}s_t$.

Throughout the book, only the savings-investment equilibrium condition will be used.

## 3| Equilibrium and the Balanced Growth Path

Determining a balanced growth path for this economy requires first defining a competitive (market) equilibrium.[23] In generic terms, and in an economy with no government, a *competitive market equilibrium* is a vector of prices and an allocation that are such that, given that agents maximize their objective function (profit, preferences) subject to their technological possibilities and resource constraints, these prices make all net trades compatible with one another by equating aggregate supply and demand. In the present setting, given the initial capital stocks $K_0^P$ and $K_0^I > 0$, a competitive equilibrium for this economy is a sequence of factor prices $\{w_t, r_{t+1}\}_{t=0}^{\infty}$, consumption and savings allocations $\{c_t^t, c_{t+1}^t, s_t\}_{t=0}^{\infty}$, physical capital stocks $\{K_{t+1}^P, K_{t+1}^I\}_{t=0}^{\infty}$, a constant tax rate $\tau$, and constant spending shares $\upsilon_I$ and $\upsilon_U$, such that individuals maximize utility, firms maximize profits, markets clear, and the government budget is balanced.[24]

A *balanced growth equilibrium* is then a competitive equilibrium in which $c_t^t$, $c_{t+1}^t$, $K_{t+1}^P$ and $K_{t+1}^I$ grow at the constant, endogenous rate $\gamma$, and the rate of return on private capital is constant.

[22] The last equality simply illustrates *Euler's theorem*, according to which the value of (aggregate) output is exhausted by wage payments to the young and capital income accruing to the old.

[23] In general, a competitive equilibrium is a vector of prices and an allocation such that given prices, agents maximize their objective function (profit, preferences) subject to their technological possibilities and resource constraints, and these prices make all net trades compatible with one another by equating aggregate supply and demand.

[24] With constant returns to scale in private inputs, firms also earn zero profits in a competitive equilibrium.

To study the dynamics of this economy, note first that using (9), and substituting for $w_t$ from (14), equation (24) yields

$$K_{t+1}^P = \bar{N}\sigma(1-\tau)w_t = \beta\sigma(1-\tau)Y_t. \tag{25}$$

To make further progress, it is convenient to consider the two cases of $\mu = 1$ and $\mu < 1$ separately.

### 3.1| The Case Where $\mu = 1$

With $\mu = 1$, from (22) with $\delta^I = 1$, together with (14), and (20),

$$K_{t+1}^I = \varphi G_t^I = \varphi\beta\upsilon_I\tau Y_t. \tag{26}$$

Combining (25) with (26) yields

$$k_{t+1}^I = \frac{K_{t+1}^I}{K_{t+1}^P} = \frac{\varphi\upsilon_I\tau}{\sigma(1-\tau)}. \tag{27}$$

Thus, both stocks of capital grow at the same rate and their ratio remains constant not only along the balanced growth path but at all times.

Equations (17) and (25) imply that aggregate output in $t+1$ is

$$Y_{t+1} = \Xi(k_{t+1}^I)^\alpha\beta\sigma(1-\tau)Y_t.$$

In turn, using (27), this implies that the growth rate of output is constant at all times and given by

$$1+\gamma = \frac{Y_{t+1}}{Y_t} = \Xi\left[\frac{\varphi\upsilon_I\tau}{\sigma(1-\tau)}]^\alpha\beta\right]\sigma(1-\tau)],$$

or equivalently

$$1+\gamma = \Xi(\varphi\upsilon_I\tau)^\alpha\beta[\sigma(1-\tau)]^{1-\alpha}. \tag{28}$$

From (17) and (27), this is also the growth rate of the two capital stocks.

Equation (28) implies that the steady-state growth rate depends on public policy, through $\tau$ and $\upsilon_I$, governance (as captured by the degree of efficiency of public investment, $\varphi$), as well as technology ($\alpha$ and $\beta$) and household preferences, as captured by the savings rate, $\sigma$. In particular, as long as $\alpha < 1$, there is a positive relationship between thriftiness and growth—even though more savings magnifies the congestion effect on infrastructure associated with private capital.

Note also that there is a *scale effect* on growth; through $\Xi$, the steady-state growth rate depends on the size of the population, $\bar{N}$. In the present setting, where population is constant, this is inconsequential. With endogenous fertility, however, this is more problematic; there is no robust evidence to suggest that countries with the highest rates of population increases are also countries with the highest rates of output growth. Chapter 3 discusses a simple alternative specification of congestion effects that "neutralizes" this scale effect when population changes endogenously.[25]

Equation (23) together with (14), (19), and (25) yield a linear relationship between aggregate consumption and output,

$$C_t = Y_t - G_t - K_{t+1}^P = [1 - \tau\beta - \beta\sigma(1-\tau)]Y_t,$$

which implies that total consumption also grows at the rate $\gamma$ in the steady state.

To derive the steady-state rental rate of private capital, note first that from (15) and (17), and given assumption 1.3,

$$r_{t+1} = \frac{(1-\beta)Y_{t+1}}{K_{t+1}^P} - 1 = (1-\beta)\Xi(k_{t+1}^I)^\alpha - 1,$$

which implies, using (27), that on the balanced-growth path the rental rate of capital is constant at

$$\tilde{r} = (1-\beta)\Xi\left[\frac{\varphi\upsilon_I\tau}{\sigma(1-\tau)}\right]^\alpha - 1. \tag{29}$$

However, because of the log-linear utility function (which implies that the savings rate is constant), and the fact that the old do not pay taxes, the interest rate does not have any direct effect on the growth rate.

To summarize then, with $\mu = 1$ the economy is always on the balanced growth path, characterized by a constant growth rate of output. The public-private capital ratio is constant at all times, which implies that the output-private capital ratio is also constant at all times. Thus, if a change in public policy affects the stationary values of both the growth rate $\gamma$ and the public-private capital ratio, the adjustment to the new equilibrium path takes place in just one period, without transition.

### 3.2| The Case Where $\mu < 1$

Suppose now that $\mu < 1$. Using (14) and (20), and setting $\delta^I = 1$, equation (22) can be written as

$$K_{t+1}^I = \varphi^\mu\left(\frac{G_t^I}{K_t^I}\right)^\mu K_t^I = (\varphi\upsilon_I\tau\beta)^\mu\left(\frac{Y_t}{K_t^P k_t^I}\right)^\mu K_t^I,$$

or, using (17),

$$\frac{K_{t+1}^I}{K_t^I} = (\Xi\varphi\upsilon_I\tau\beta)^\mu(k_t^I)^{-\mu(1-\alpha)}. \tag{30}$$

[25] This essentially involves using population as a congestion factor. In the present setting, if as in Glomm and Ravikumar (1994) congestion is defined as $(K^P)^\zeta\bar{N}^\phi$, with $\phi > 0$, the scale effect can be eliminated by imposing $\zeta + \phi = 1$, or equivalently $\phi = \beta/\alpha$. See chapter 3.

Similarly, using (17) equation (25) can be rewritten as

$$\frac{K^P_{t+1}}{K^P_t} = \beta\sigma(1-\tau)\Xi(k^I_t)^\alpha. \tag{31}$$

Combining (30) and (31) yields

$$k^I_{t+1} = \Phi(k^I_t) = \frac{(\varphi\upsilon_I\tau\beta)^\mu}{\Xi^{1-\mu}\beta\sigma(1-\tau)}(k^I_t)^{(1-\alpha)(1-\mu)}, \tag{32}$$

where $\Phi(k^I_t)$ is the transition curve.

This equation corresponds to (27) with $\mu = 1$. However, when $\mu < 1$ the public-private capital ratio is no longer constant and movements toward the steady state exhibit transitional dynamics. Because $(1-\alpha)(1-\mu) < 1$ and $\lim_{k^I_t \to \infty} \Phi'(k^I_t) = 0$, there is a nontrivial equilibrium, which is unique and globally stable (see Azariadis (1993) and Galor (2006)). Indeed, note first that $\Phi(k^I_t) > 0$ for $k^I_t > 0$. Second, it can be shown that $\lim_{k^I_t \to \infty} \Phi'(k^I_t) = 0$, that is, the slope of the relationship between $k^I_{t+1}$ and $k^I_t$ becomes less and less concave and eventually becomes a flat line. These two conditions imply therefore that, for some $k^I_t > 0$, $\Phi(k^I_t) < k^I_t$, that is, $\Phi(k^I_t)$ falls below the 45-degree line in Figure 1.1. Therefore, a steady-state equilibrium exists.[26]

The adjustment process is illustrated in Figure 1.1. The relationship (32) is shown as the concave curve $KK$. Coefficient $(1-\alpha)(1-\mu)$ measures the speed of convergence; the lower $\mu$ is (the more "essential" the existing stock of public capital is to produce new capital), the faster the adjustment to the long-run equilibrium. Starting from an initial value $k^I_0$, the economy moves over time from point $A$ to point $E$, where the public-private capital ratio is equal to its steady-state value, given by, setting $k^I_{t+1} = k^I_t$ in (32),

$$\tilde{k}^I = \left[\frac{(\varphi\upsilon_I\tau\beta)^\mu}{\Xi^{1-\mu}\beta\sigma(1-\tau)}\right]^{1/[1-(1-\alpha)(1-\mu)]}. \tag{33}$$

From (17) and (25),

$$Y_{t+1} = \Xi\left(\frac{K^I_{t+1}}{K^P_{t+1}}\right)^\alpha K^P_{t+1} = \Xi\beta(k^I_{t+1})^\alpha\sigma(1-\tau)Y_t,$$

which implies that the growth rate of output is

$$1+\gamma_{t+1} = \frac{Y_{t+1}}{Y_t} = \Xi(k^I_{t+1})^\alpha\beta\sigma(1-\tau). \tag{34}$$

[26] More generally, an exponential function of the form $\Phi(x_t) = x_t^\omega$ satisfies $\Phi' > 0$, $\Phi'' < 0$, $\lim_{x_t \to 0}\Phi'(x_t) = \infty$, and $\lim_{x_t \to \infty}\Phi'(x_t) = 0$ if $\omega \in (0, 1)$; and $\Phi' > 0$, $\Phi'' > 0$, $\lim_{x_t \to 0}\Phi'(x_t) = 0$, and $\lim_{x_t \to \infty}\Phi'(x_t) = \infty$ if $\omega > 1$, which are necessary and sufficient conditions for the existence of a unique nontrivial steady state. This steady state is stable if $\omega < 1$ and unstable if $\omega > 1$.

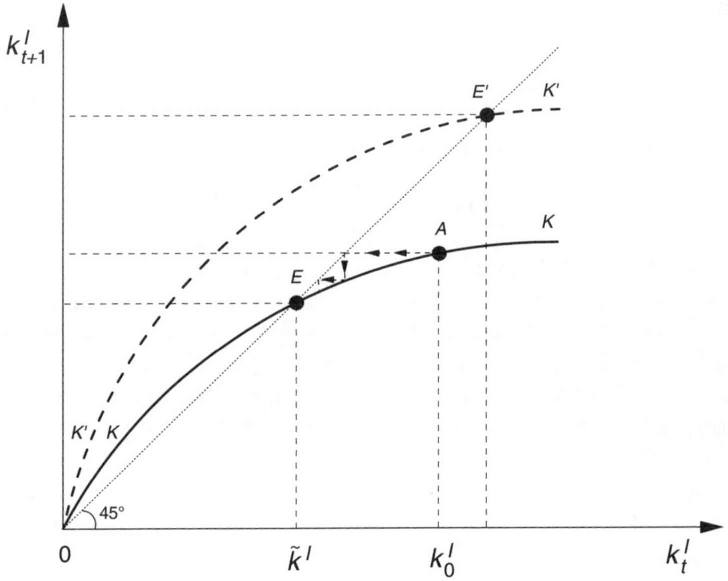


Figure 1.1. Dynamics of the Public-Private Capital Ratio ($\mu < 1$) and Increase in the Share of Public Investment.

Substituting (33) in this expression yields the steady-state growth rate of output:

$$1+\gamma = \Xi\left[\frac{(\varphi\upsilon_I\tau\beta)^{\mu}}{\Xi^{1-\mu}\beta\sigma(1-\tau)}\right]^{\alpha/[1-(1-\alpha)(1-\mu)]}\beta\sigma(1-\tau), \qquad (35)$$

which, as before, is also the growth rate of the two capital stocks.

The determination of the equilibrium public-private capital ratio is illustrated in Figure 1.2 as well, where the growth rates of the public and private capital stocks are represented. Curve $II$ represents the growth rate of the public capital stock; it is decreasing in the public-private capital ratio, as implied by (30), because of diminishing marginal returns in the (congested) public input. Curve $PP$ represents the growth rate of the private capital stock and is instead increasing (although at decreasing rates) in the public-private capital ratio, as implied by (31). This is because of the positive impact of infrastructure on the marginal productivity of private capital. Starting as in Figure 1.1 from an initial value $k^I_0 > \tilde{k}^I$, corresponding to points $A$ and $A'$, the two capital stocks approach their common equilibrium growth rate (corresponding to a constant public-private capital ratio) from opposite directions. The steady-state equilibrium obtains when the two curves intersect, at point $E$.

Finally, note that a simple way to account for the effect of infrastructure (or lack thereof) on production costs, as discussed in section 1.1, is to assume that they translate into higher labor costs, which can be written now as

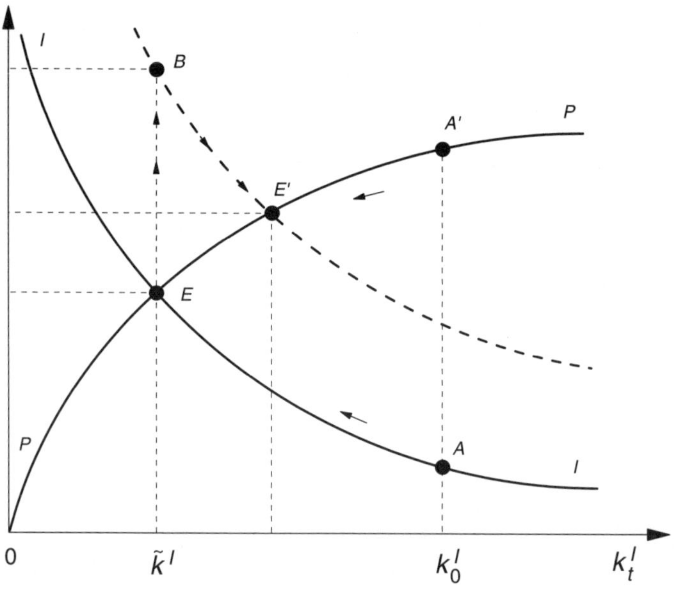


Figure 1.2. Determination of the Equilibrium Public-Private Captial Ratio ($\mu < 1$) and Increase in the Share of the Public Investment.

$(1+x_t)w_t N_t^i$, where $x_t = x(k_t^I)$, with $x' < 0$.[27] Thus, poor access to public capital, as captured by a low value of $k_t^I$, raises proportionally the cost of labor for all firms. Inserting this expression in (13) and solving the representative firm's optimization problem implies that the equilibrium wage is now, instead of (14), $w_t = \beta Y_t/\bar{N}(1+x_t)$. Substituting this result in (24) and solving the model as before, it can be shown that the public-private capital ratio (as defined in (27)) remains independent of $x_t$, but that the steady-state growth rate, with $\mu = 1$ for simplicity, is now

$$1+\gamma = \Xi \frac{(\varphi \upsilon_I \tau)^\alpha \beta[\sigma(1-\tau)]^{1-\alpha}}{1+x[\varphi \upsilon_I \tau/\sigma(1-\tau)]}.$$

This result implies that increased investment in infrastructure (a rise in $\upsilon_I$) not only raises productivity of private inputs but also lowers production costs, thereby raising the equilibrium wage. Through higher wages, it also promotes savings, private investment, and thus long-run growth. By contrast, the long-run relationship between the private savings rate and growth, which was shown earlier to be positive, is now ambiguous: congestion, by reducing the

[27] Transportation costs (which also vary inversely with access to infrastructure) are explicitly introduced in chapter 4, in a setting where production requires, in addition to labor and capital, intermediate inputs.

public-private capital ratio, exerts an additional negative effect on growth through an increase in production costs.

## 4| Growth Effects of Public Policy

To examine the growth effects of public capital, consider first the impact of a budget-neutral increase in the share of government spending on infrastructure $\upsilon_I$, that is, with $d\upsilon_I + d\upsilon_U = 0$. From (33) and (35), it can be verified that the log-derivatives of $\tilde{k}^I$ and $1+\gamma$ with respect to $\upsilon_I$ are

$$\frac{d\ln\tilde{k}^I}{d\upsilon_I} = \frac{\mu}{[1-(1-\alpha)(1-\mu)]\upsilon_I} > 0, \tag{36}$$

$$\frac{d\ln(1+\gamma)}{d\upsilon_I} = \alpha\left(\frac{d\ln\tilde{k}^I}{d\upsilon_I}\right) > 0. \tag{37}$$

Thus, both effects are positive, regardless of the value of $\mu$. It can also be shown from these expressions that $d^2\ln\tilde{k}^I/d\upsilon_I^2$, $d^2\ln(1+\gamma)/d\upsilon_I^2 < 0$. An increase in $\varphi$ has the same qualitative effects. These results can be summarized as follows:

**Result 1.1.** *A budget-neutral increase in the share of government investment in infrastructure, $\upsilon_I$, or an increase in the efficiency of public investment, $\varphi$, raises the steady-state value of the public-private capital ratio and increases the long-run growth rate. However, there are diminishing marginal returns in both cases.*

The transitional dynamics when $\mu < 1$ are illustrated in Figures 1.1 and 1.2, in both cases under the assumption that the economy is initially in a long-run equilibrium position, with the public-private capital stock equal to $\tilde{k}^I$. In Figure 1.1, curve $KK$ shifts upward to $K'K'$ (with no change at the origin) and the equilibrium shifts from point $E$ to point $E'$. As can be inferred from (30) and (31), in Figure 1.2 curve $II$ shifts upward, implying a jump in that rate from $E$ to $B$, whereas curve $PP$ does not change. During the transition, the public-private capital ratio increases continuously (albeit at decreasing rates), due to the fact that as this ratio rises, the productivity of private capital improves, whereas the productivity of public capital declines. The growth rate of the private capital stock increases from $E$ to $E'$, whereas the growth rate of the public capital stock decreases from $B$ to $E'$. Again, after the initial jump from $E$ to $B$ for the public capital stock, the two capital stocks approach their common steady-state growth rate from opposite directions. The new long-run equilibrium is at $E'$.

Consider now the growth effects of an increase in the tax rate, $\tau$. With $\mu = 1$, taking the log-derivative of equations (27) and (28) yields

$$\frac{d\ln\tilde{k}^I}{d\tau} = \frac{1}{\tau} + \frac{1}{1-\tau} > 0, \tag{38}$$

$$\frac{d\ln(1+\gamma)}{d\tau} = \alpha\frac{d\ln\tilde{k}^I}{d\tau} - \frac{1}{1-\tau}. \tag{39}$$

The first term in (39), which is positive, captures a *productivity* (or *crowding-in*) *effect* on growth, whereas the second, which is negative, captures a *crowding-out effect*. On the one hand, a rise in the tax rate increases the amount of resources that the government can invest in public capital, which raises the productivity of private inputs, *gross* income, the public-private capital ratio (as captured in (38)), and tends to promote growth. On the other, it tends to reduce *after-tax* income and savings, which dampens private investment.[28] Even though a lower stock of private capital mitigates congestion effects (thereby magnifying the productivity effect), it also tends to reduce growth directly. Note also that the higher $\alpha$ is, the larger the productivity effect, and that the higher the initial tax rate is, the larger the crowding-out effect.

Using (38), equation (39) can be rewritten as

$$\frac{d\ln(1+\gamma)}{d\tau} = \frac{\alpha[(1-\tau)+\tau]-\tau}{\tau(1-\tau)} = \frac{\alpha-\tau}{\tau(1-\tau)} \lesseqgtr 0. \tag{40}$$

Thus, the impact of a higher tax rate on the growth rate is ambiguous in general and depends on the initial value of the tax rate itself; if $\tau < \alpha$ ($\tau > \alpha$), the productivity (crowding-out) effect dominates, and the growth rate increases (falls).

With $\mu < 1$, the corresponding result is

$$\frac{d\ln(1+\gamma)}{d\tau} = \frac{\alpha}{1-(1-\alpha)(1-\mu)}\left(\frac{\mu}{\tau} + \frac{1}{1-\tau}\right) - \frac{1}{1-\tau},$$

or equivalently

$$\frac{d\ln(1+\gamma)}{d\tau} = \frac{\mu(\alpha-\tau)}{\tau[1-(1-\alpha)(1-\mu)](1-\tau)} \lesseqgtr 0, \tag{41}$$

which implies again that the sign of $d\ln(1+\gamma)/d\tau$ depends on whether initially $\tau \lesseqgtr \alpha$.

[28] Note that a reduction in private investment also increases the rate of return on private capital, because the stock of private capital is now relatively scarce compared with the stock of public capital. Equation (29) shows indeed that the equilibrium rate of return to capital goes up, that is, $d\tilde{r}/d\tau > 0$. However, given the assumption of a log-linear utility function, the change in savings depend only on after-tax income, not the interest rate.

These results can be summarized as follows:

**Result 1.2.** *An increase in the tax rate always increases the public-private capital ratio but has in general an ambiguous impact on steady-state growth, due to conflicting productivity and crowding-out effects. The net effect is negative (positive) if the initial tax rate exceeds (falls short of) the elasticity of output with respect to the public-private capital ratio.*

## 5| Optimal Fiscal Policy

In the present setting, optimal fiscal policy involves determining the tax rate and the share of government spending allocated to investment in infrastructure so as to maximize a benevolent government's objective.[29] There are two standard approaches to this issue: one is to assume that the government maximizes growth, the other that it maximizes social welfare, defined in terms of household utility.

Throughout this book, the focus is on growth maximization. There are three reasons for this choice. The first is practical; as discussed in the Introduction and Overview, the main concern of policymakers today in many poor countries is to accelerate growth to speed up poverty reduction and foster human development. Consequently, it is natural to focus on maximizing growth as the criterion for setting public policies. The second is that in OLG models, defining a welfare function is not as natural as it may seem, because of the heterogeneity of agents.[30] The traditional approach is to define social welfare as the discounted sum of lifetime welfare of the different cohorts. However, this is quite arbitrary. If a fraction of households is working and another fraction is retired, they are likely to have different utility functions; evaluating social welfare in such conditions is difficult. Welfare benefits may also be unevenly distributed across generations if, as in Heijdra and Meijdam (2002), capital ownership expands with age and wages rise only gradually. Ideally, a benevolent government could reallocate consumption to make sure that social

[29] In the literature, it is common to identify the share of taxes in output with the share of government spending in output. For reasons that will become apparent shortly, the choices of $\tau$ and $\upsilon_I$ are treated separately.

[30] In infinitely lived, representative agent models—in which agents can be interpreted as dynasties, where parents take the utility of their descendants fully into account by leaving bequests—this issue does not arise and it is generally straightforward to base welfare maximization on household utility. S. Turnovsky and his collaborators have made important contributions to the analysis of welfare effects of fiscal policy in these models, both analytically and numerically; see Turnovsky (1996, 1997, 2000), Turnovsky and Fisher (1995), Fisher and Turnovsky (1998), Chatterjee et al. (2003), Chatterjee and Turnovsky (2005), Ott and Turnovsky (2006), Monteiro and Turnovsky (2008), Turnovsky and Pintea (2006), and Turnovsky and Basher (2009). Other studies that analyze welfare-maximizing policies in continuous time models of growth with public inputs include Rioja (1999), Piras (2001, 2005), Glomm and Ravikumar (1999), Baier and Glomm (2001), Tsoukis and Miller (2003), Yakita (2004), and Agénor (2008*a*, 2008*b*).

welfare (utility shared by all households combined) is as high as possible. In practice, however, it is not possible to shift consumption from the retired to the working population, or vice versa.

The third reason is that imperfect knowledge about the preferences of the household makes it difficult to pursue a first-best strategy to maximize welfare. Because growth is a central determinant of welfare, and because changes in income are easier to measure than welfare, a policy of growth maximization is a sensible second-best strategy. Indeed, the numerical simulations conducted by Misch et al. (2008) for instance suggest that even when there is some degree of uncertainty as to how public capital affects the production function, growth maximization often yields growth outcomes (and, in many cases, welfare outcomes) that are very close to those obtained under welfare maximization.[31]

Consider then the determination of the growth-maximizing value of the tax rate. It is obtained by solving $d\ln(1+\gamma)/d\tau = 0$ for $\tau$. From (40) and (41), it is immediately obvious that this condition yields $\tau = \alpha$, regardless of the value of $\mu$. Thus, the following result holds:

**Result 1.3.** **(Barro rule)** *Maximizing the growth rate requires setting the tax rate equal to the marginal productivity of public capital in output:*

$$\tau^* = \alpha. \tag{42}$$

This rule, first identified in a seminal contribution by Barro (1990), is an important benchmark in growth policy analysis.[32] Intuitively, the optimal tax rate balances the conflicting effects of the tax rate on growth (the productivity and crowding-out effects identified earlier) by equalizing the marginal benefit and the marginal cost. If public capital exerts no positive effect on output, then the optimal tax rate is zero; the reason is that, from (28), with $\alpha = 0$ the growth rate is then $\Xi\beta\sigma(1-\tau)$, which is monotonically and negatively related to the tax rate.

The derivation of the optimal tax rate can also be illustrated graphically, by representing the relationship between $1+\gamma$ and $\tau$, as given in (28). This function, defined for $\tau \in (0, 1)$, has an inverted-U shape. It is also skewed to the right: increases in $\tau$ raise at first the growth very rapidly, until the maximum

[31] The appendix to this chapter shows that, if a benevolent government maximizes welfare for the current generation and all future generations, the growth- and welfare-maximizing tax rates coincide. However, they differ if the government maximizes only the utility of the current generation of adults.

[32] Barro uses a different analytical setting than the OLG framework developed here—an infinitely lived, representative agent framework. Qualitatively, however, the result is fundamentally the same. Futagami et al. (1993) proved that Barro's result extends to the case where infrastructure services are (produced by) a stock rather than a flow of expenditure, as in Barro's original specification.

point, corresponding to (42), is reached. Beyond that point, further increases in $\tau$ lower the growth rate, but at a more gradual pace.

Now, to determine the growth-maximizing share of spending, it suffices to observe that, from result 1.1, the steady-state growth rate is monotonically increasing in $\upsilon_I$, independently of the value of $\mu$. This is because, with the tax rate and tax revenues taken as given, there is no crowding-out effect associated with changes in the composition of spending. From (36) and (37), and regardless of the value of $\mu$, in order to have $d\ln(1+\gamma)/d\upsilon_I = 0$ it must be that $\upsilon_I$ tends to infinity, which is not feasible. Thus, the optimal policy is to set $\upsilon_I$ to the highest possible value:

**Result 1.4.** *With unproductive spending as the only alternative to investment in infrastructure, maximizing the growth rate requires spending all tax resources on infrastructure:*

$$\upsilon_I^* = 1. \tag{43}$$

From (14), (20), (42), and (43), this result implies that the share of infrastructure investment in output, $G_t^I/Y_t$, is also constant at $\alpha$. Thus, the size of the government, measured either by the tax rate or the share of spending in output, is the same (as in Barro's original contribution) and equal to the marginal productivity of public infrastructure in output.

However, suppose for a moment that the government provides simultaneously two categories of public capital, roads and power plants for instance, whose stocks are denoted $K_{1,t}^I$ and $K_{2,t}^I$, respectively. Suppose also that both are nonexcludable but partially rival, and affect private productivity in different ways. Assuming that the congestion factor is again the aggregate stock of capital, the aggregate production function (17) takes now the form

$$Y_t = \Xi \left( \frac{K_{1,t}^I}{K_t^P} \right)^{\alpha_1} \left( \frac{K_{2,t}^I}{K_t^P} \right)^{\alpha_2} K_t^P,$$

where $\alpha_1, \alpha_2 \in (0, 1)$.

Assuming that investment in both categories of public goods are fixed fractions of tax revenues, and that there is no unproductive spending ($\upsilon_U = 0$) for simplicity the government budget constraint (21) becomes

$$\upsilon_I^1 + \upsilon_I^2 = 1. \tag{44}$$

With $\mu = 1$, it is straightforward to establish that the steady-state growth rate is now given by, instead of (28),

$$1 + \gamma = \Xi(\varphi\tau)^{\alpha_1+\alpha_2}(\upsilon_I^1)^{\alpha_1}(\upsilon_I^2)^{\alpha_2}\beta[\sigma(1-\tau)]^{1-\alpha_1-\alpha_2}. \tag{45}$$

Using (44), the growth-maximizing solution for $\upsilon_I^1$ is determined by setting $d\ln(1+\gamma)/d\upsilon_I^1 = 0$. This condition yields

$$\frac{\alpha_1}{\upsilon_I^1} - \frac{\alpha_2}{1-\upsilon_I^1} = 0,$$

that is, $\upsilon_I^1 = \alpha_1/(\alpha_1+\alpha_2)$, with $\upsilon_I^2$ determined residually from (44). A similar result can be established with $\mu < 1$. Thus,

**Result 1.5.** *With two types of productive public capital, maximizing the growth rate requires setting each spending share equal to the elasticity of output with respect to each type of capital, divided by the sum of the elasticities of output with respect to the two types of capital:*

$$\upsilon_I^{h,*} = \frac{\alpha_h}{\alpha_1+\alpha_2}, \quad h = 1, 2 \tag{46}$$

This formula, which follows from the results in Agénor (2008*a*), can be viewed as a generalization of the Barro rule to the case of two productive public goods—with the important caveat that it relates to the optimal *composition* of public spending, independent of the tax rate. Intuitively, because both types of public capital are productive, and because the government budget constraint is binding, there is now a trade-off that must be internalized in the allocation of spending. Naturally enough, the optimal policy accounts for relative differences in productivity among the two types of capital.[33]

## 6| Extensions

The basic framework presented earlier can be extended in several directions. In what follows the following extensions are considered: indirect taxation, a complementarity effect of public capital on private investment, a direct effect of public capital on household utility, and endogenous depreciation and maintenance.

### 6.1| Indirect Taxation

In the foregoing discussion, it has been assumed that the government taxes only wages. This is consistent with the evidence for many low-income developing countries: personal income taxes are rarely comprehensive and often do not amount to much more than withholding taxes on labor income in the formal sector. Similarly, among corporate firms, taxes are collected mainly from those that are highly dependent on the formal financial sector. However, there is also evidence to suggest that poorer countries tend to rely relatively

[33] As also follows from the results in Agénor (2008*a*), and as can be verified directly from (45), the optimal tax rate is now $\tau = \alpha_1 + \alpha_2$. From (46), the share of spending on each category of public good in output is thus $\tau\upsilon_h = \alpha_h$, $h = 1, 2$.

more than richer ones on *indirect* taxes. As documented for instance by Gordon and Li (2009), consumption taxes account for more than half of total government revenues in poor countries, whereas personal income taxes represent about 30 percent and corporate income taxes 13 percent of total revenues—compared to 33 percent, 54 percent, and 10 percent, respectively, in richer countries.[34]

Adding consumption taxes on can be done in a relatively simple way, by multiplying $c_t^t$ and $c_{t+1}^t$ by $1+\tau^C$, where $\tau^C \in (0, 1)$ is the consumption tax rate, on the left-hand side of (2) and (3). However, it is easy to verify that this would not affect the Euler equation (7); much of the foregoing analysis would remain qualitatively similar. Because the focus of this book is on the expenditure side of the government budget, rather than a more detailed analysis of tax policy, the assumption of a single tax on wages will be maintained throughout this book.

### 6.2| Complementarity Effect

As discussed in the first section of this chapter, one of the conventional effects of public capital (potentially of great relevance for low-income countries) is the fact that poor access to infrastructure may act as a constraint on both domestic and foreign private investment.

To capture this effect in a simple way, equation (18), with $\delta^P = 1$, could be modified as follows:

$$K_{t+1}^P = \Gamma(k_t^I)I_t,$$

where $\Gamma \in (0, 1)$, $\Gamma' > 0$, and possibly $\Gamma'' > 0$ as well, if stocks of infrastructure assets are very low to begin with. Thus, a higher public-private capital ratio raises the efficiency of private investment and translates into a higher private capital stock. With $\mu = 1$, the key modification is to equation (27), which now becomes

$$k_{t+1}^I = \Phi(k_t^I) = \frac{\varphi \upsilon_I \tau}{\sigma(1-\tau)}\Gamma^{-1}(k_t^I).$$

This result implies that the model may now display transitional dynamics, even with $\mu = 1$. Stability requires $|\Phi'| < 1$; in addition, because $\Phi' < 0$, the adjustment process displays oscillatory behavior.[35] However, the key point is that although a budget-neutral increase in infrastructure investment raises on impact the public-private capital ratio (as before), this in turn stimulates

[34] As discussed by Agénor and Neanidis (2009), the existence of high collection costs on personal and capital income may explain why the tax structure in many developing countries is dominated by indirect taxes. In a broad sense, these costs include not only those associated with collecting revenues, enforcing payments, and implementing audits, but also the budgetary costs incurred in preparing and promulgating tax laws.

[35] With $\mu < 1$, $\Phi'$ may be either positive or negative, given that there are now two opposite effects of $k_t^I$ on $k_{t+1}^I$.

private investment and raises the private capital stock, thereby mitigating the initial positive effect. Thus with (absolute) congestion effects as modeled here, a strong complementarity effect does not necessarily translate into higher growth in the steady state.

### 6.3| Public Capital and Household Utility

In the basic model of this chapter, public capital was assumed to affect directly only production, not household utility. Suppose now that current-period consumption is also a function of access to (congested) public services.[36] For instance, improved access to roads, if they are not too jammed by trucks transporting raw materials or delivering goods, allows households to travel to parks and scenic areas and may raise the utility gain from consuming market goods. In that sense, as noted early on by Arrow and Kurz (1970, p. xiii), public capital can contribute to consumer satisfaction.

To capture this effect in a simple manner, the household utility function (1) can be replaced by

$$U_t = (k_t^I)^\kappa \ln c_t^t + \frac{\ln c_{t+1}^t}{1+\rho},$$

where $\kappa > 0$. Utility is thus *nonseparable* in current consumption and public capital services.[37]

Suppose that households take the public-private capital ratio as given when optimizing. The first-order conditions are now

$$(k_t^I)^\kappa / c_t^t = \lambda_t,$$

$$1/(1+\rho)c_{t+1}^t = \lambda_t/(1+r_{t+1}),$$

which can be combined to give the modified Euler equation,

$$\frac{c_{t+1}^t}{c_t^t} = \frac{1+r_{t+1}}{(1+\rho)(k_t^I)^\kappa}.$$

Substituting this result in the intertemporal budget constraint (4) yields

$$c_t^t = \left[\frac{(1+\rho)(k_t^I)^\kappa}{1+(1+\rho)(k_t^I)^\kappa}\right](1-\tau)w_t,$$

so that

$$s_t = \sigma(k_t^I)(1-\tau)w_t, \quad \sigma(k_t^I) = \frac{1}{1+(1+\rho)(k_t^I)^\kappa}. \tag{47}$$

[36] Models of growth with public services in the utility function include Baier and Glomm (2001), Balducci (2006), Chen (2006), and Agénor (2008*a*, 2008*b*), among others.

[37] If the utility of consumption in adulthood is separable, for instance because the first term takes the form $\ln[(k_t^I)^\kappa c_t^t]$, the optimality conditions derived earlier would not be affected.

The savings rate depends now negatively on the public-private capital ratio ($d\sigma/dk_t^I < 0$). Intuitively, improved access to infrastructure today makes consuming now more attractive, thereby reducing the incentive to save. Public policy toward capital accumulation affects therefore household decisions.

Moreover, with $\sigma$ being now a function of $k_t^I$, the model exhibits transitional dynamics even in the case where $\mu = 1$. Indeed, combining (25), with $\sigma$ defined as in (47), and (26) yields

$$k_{t+1}^I = \Phi(k_t^I) = \frac{\varphi \upsilon_I \tau}{\sigma(k_t^I)(1-\tau)}, \tag{48}$$

which corresponds to (27) with $\kappa = 0$. the transition curve is increasing and concave, just as in Figure 1.1. The balanced-growth rate is now, instead of (28),

$$1 + \gamma = \Xi(\tilde{k}^I)^\alpha \beta[\sigma(\tilde{k}^I)(1-\tau)]. \tag{49}$$

The difference equation (48) is again (locally) stable around the steady state equilibrium point $\tilde{k}^I$ if $\Phi'(\tilde{k}^I) < 1$, a condition that depends on $\kappa$. The value of $\kappa$ affects also the adjustment process; an increase in $\kappa$ for instance shifts the transition curve upward (with no change at the origin), implying from (47) and (48) that the steady-state value of the public-private capital ratio is higher. The reason is that the savings rate (and thus the private capital stock) is lower, mitigating the strength of the congestion effect. However, the higher public-private capital ratio does not necessarily translate into a higher growth rate, as can be seen in (49), given the fall in the savings rate.

## 6.4| Partial Depreciation and Maintenance

### 6.4.1| *Partial Depreciation*

Consider first the case where assumption 1.3 no longer holds, that is, both private and public capital depreciate only partially after production. For expository purposes, it is sufficient to focus on the case where $\mu = 1$. With partial depreciation, the stock equations (25) and (26) become

$$K_{t+1}^P = \beta\sigma(1-\tau)Y_t + (1-\delta^P)K_t^P,$$

$$K_{t+1}^I = \varphi\beta\upsilon_I\tau Y_t + (1-\delta^I)K_t^I.$$

Substituting (17) for $Y_t$ in these expressions yields

$$k_{t+1}^I = \Phi(k_t^I) = \left[\frac{\varphi\beta\upsilon_I\tau\,\Xi(k_t^I)^{-(1-\alpha)} + 1 - \delta^I}{\beta\sigma(1-\tau)\Xi(k_t^I)^\alpha + 1 - \delta^P}\right] k_t^I, \tag{50}$$

which of course corresponds to (27) with $\delta^I = \delta^P = 1$ . In general, however, the public-private capital ratio is *not* constant over time, even with $\mu = 1$. The model therefore displays transitional dynamics. For the adjustment process to be (locally) stable, the condition $|\Phi'| < 1$ must be satisfied. Establishing whether this condition holds, however, is more involved.

It can also be verified that, for plausible empirical values, the transition curve in the case where $\mu < 1$ remains in fact concave; accounting for partial depreciation, therefore, does not change qualitatively the results obtained with full depreciation. However, the adjustment process to a change in, say, the share of investment spending is now more protracted.

### 6.4.2| *The Investment-Maintenance Trade-Off*

The foregoing analysis did not account for the need to maintain the stock of infrastructure assets. Yet, this is a very important practical issue in many low-income countries. Indeed, lack of public spending on core infrastructure maintenance (as opposed to "new" investment) has been a recurrent problem in many developing countries. According to the World Bank (1994, p. 1), in the early 1990s technical inefficiencies in roads, railways, power, and water in developing countries caused losses equivalent to a quarter of these countries' annual investment budget in infrastructure. In a more recent study, Foster and Briceño-Garmendia (2010) estimate that on average about 30 percent of the infrastructure assets of a typical African country are in need of rehabilitation. This share is even higher for rural infrastructure and for countries affected by violent conflict. This reflects a legacy of underfunding for infrastructure maintenance, and over time represents a major waste of resources because the cost of rehabilitating depreciated infrastructure assets can be several times higher than the cumulative cost of a well-designed preventive maintenance program. A clear example of this is the roads sector, where many countries fail to cover basic maintenance and rehabilitation needs, and thus face a rapid deterioration in the quality of their road network. Safeguarding maintenance expenditure is thus essential to avoid wasting resources on the repeated rehabilitation of existing assets.

The importance of maintenance for growth has been emphasized in a number of studies. In an early contribution, Hulten (1996) argued forcefully in favor of paying more attention to the *quality* of infrastructure capital in the growth process. In a subsequent study, Buys et al. (2006) estimated that upgrading the road transport network in sub-Saharan Africa could expand dramatically cross-border trade within the region, with major benefits for the rural poor and large urban centers. By implication, some reallocation of resources from investment to maintenance may be warranted.

To account for maintenance spending and its effect on depreciation in a simple manner, consider the case where $\mu = \delta^P = 1$, so that only public capital depreciates partially across periods. Suppose also that the rate of depreciation of public capital is endogenous and depends linearly on the ratio of maintenance spending, $G_t^M$, to the public capital stock:

$$\delta^I = 1 - \theta^G \left( \frac{G_t^M}{K_t^I} \right), \tag{51}$$

where $\theta^G \in (0, 1)$ is an efficiency parameter.[38] Thus, maintenance expenditure enhances the durability of public infrastructure capital. In addition, if the government spends nothing on maintenance ($G_t^M = 0$), public infrastructure would depreciate entirely within a period. This specification, which dwells on Agénor (2009*b*), differs from the formulation adopted for instance by Rioja (2003*b*, p. 2290), Kalaitzidakis and Kalyvitis (2004, p. 699), and Dioikitopoulos and Kalyvitis (2008, p. 3764), which assumes that the depreciation rate is a function of the ratio of maintenance expenditure over *output*, rather than public capital. The latter may be a more natural scaling variable, given that one would expect maintenance needs to depend on the prevailing stock of public infrastructure assets, independent—at least to some extent—of usage. Regardless of the flow of cars, for instance, roads are likely to deteriorate over time as a result of weather conditions. Similarly, power grids need to be inspected and upgraded on a regular basis (even when private usage is low) to prevent malfunction and losses.

For simplicity, suppose that all "unproductive" spending consists of maintenance spending, so that $G_t^M = G_t^U$. Using (14), (17), and (20) yields

$$\frac{G_t^M}{K_t^I} = \left( \frac{\beta \upsilon_U \tau Y_t}{K_t^P} \right) (k_t^I)^{-1} = \beta \upsilon_U \tau \, \Xi (k_t^I)^{-(1-\alpha)}.$$

Substituting this result in (51), and then (51) in (50) with $\delta^P = 1$, yields

$$k_{t+1}^I = J = \frac{\tau(\varphi \upsilon_I + \theta^G \upsilon_U)}{\sigma(1-\tau)},$$

which shows that the public-private capital ratio is again constant along the balanced growth path. Substituting the spending allocation constraint (21) yields

$$J = \frac{\tau[\theta^G + \upsilon_I(\varphi - \theta^G)]}{\sigma(1-\tau)}. \tag{52}$$

This equation illustrates in a simple way the trade-off between investment in "new" infrastructure (that is, an increase in the stock of public physical assets) and spending on maintaining the existing stock of assets: whether increasing the share of public spending on infrastructure or maintenance raises the public capital stock depends on the size of $\varphi - \theta^G$, the relative efficiency of the two categories of spending. If the benefit from maintenance, in terms

[38] The restriction on $\theta^G$ is sufficient to ensure that $\delta^I \in (0, 1)$, as long as $G_t^M / K_t^I < 1$. A convex specification would be much less tractable analytically. Note also that spending on maintenance could be subject to the same efficiency problems associated with investment spending.

of improved durability of the public capital stock is relatively high, compared to the degree of efficiency of public investment ($\theta^G > \varphi$), then reallocating spending toward infrastructure investment and away from maintenance may actually reduce growth. This result shows the importance of ensuring that sufficient resources are allocated to maintenance. From (28) for instance and (52), it can be verified that the growth-maximizing policy entails a corner solution, with $\upsilon_I = 1$ (or $\upsilon_U = 0$) for $\varphi > \theta^G$, and $\upsilon_I = 0$ (or $\upsilon_U = 1$) for $\varphi < \theta^G$. This is of course an extreme illustration of the trade-off between new investment and maintenance.[39]

Maintenance spending by the public sector may also affect the durability of the *private* capital stock (see Agénor (2009*b*)). Maintaining the quality of roads, for instance, enhances the durability of trucks and other means of transportation used by the private sector to move labor and goods. With a more reliable power grid, electrical equipment may last longer. For instance, the World Bank (1999, p. 44) estimated that in Vietnam reducing a road's roughness from 14 IRI (International Roughness Index, a standard international metric) to 6 IRI would save between 12 and 22 percent in vehicle operating costs. A reduction from 14 IRI to 3 IRI would save from 17 to 33 percent in those costs. In a study for Latin America and the Caribbean, Gyamfi and Ruan (1996, p. 5) estimated that each dollar not spent on road maintenance leads to a \$3.00 increase in vehicle operating costs as a result of poor road conditions. Conversely, by helping to reduce power losses, telephone faults, and so on, increased maintenance expenditure would improve the durability (as well as the quality) of public capital, thereby enhancing its productivity effects on private production and spurring growth.

This effect can be captured by assuming that $\delta^P$ is endogenous and linearly related to the ratio of government spending on maintenance to the private capital stock:

$$\delta^P = 1 - \theta^P \left( \frac{G_t^M}{K_t^P} \right), \tag{53}$$

where $\theta^P \in (0, 1)$ measures the marginal benefit of higher maintenance spending on the durability of private capital.[40] "Usage" of public infrastructure is therefore measured by the size of the private capital stock.

Suppose again that $G_t^M = G_t^U$. Using (14), (17), and (20) yields

$$\frac{G_t^M}{K_t^P} = \frac{\beta \upsilon_U \tau Y_t}{K_t^P} = \beta \upsilon_U \tau \Xi (k_t^I)^\alpha. \tag{54}$$

[39] See Agénor (2009) for the derivation of a more general solution.

[40] The restriction on the parameter $\theta^P$ is, again, sufficient to ensure that $\delta^P \in (0, 1)$, as long as $G_t^M / K_t^P < 1$.

Combining (53) and (54), and substituting the result in (50), with $\delta^I = 1$ for simplicity, yields

$$k^I_{t+1} = J = \frac{\varphi \upsilon_I \tau}{\sigma(1-\tau) + \theta^P \upsilon_U \tau},$$

that is, given the spending allocation constraint (21),

$$J = \frac{\varphi \upsilon_I \tau}{\sigma(1-\tau) + \theta^P (1-\upsilon_I)\tau}. \tag{55}$$

Now a budget-neutral increase in $\upsilon_I$ unambiguously increases the public-private capital ratio. The reason is that in addition to the direct, standard effect on the public capital stock, the concomitant reduction in spending on maintenance raises the rate of depreciation of the private capital stock, which in turn contributes to lowering the existing level of that stock. However, the growth-maximizing policy does not involve a corner solution here; with $\mu = 1$ for instance, substituting (55) in (28) and solving for $d\ln(1+\gamma)/d\upsilon_I = 0$ yields

$$\frac{1}{\upsilon_I} - \frac{\theta^P \tau}{\sigma(1-\tau) + \theta^P (1-\upsilon_I)\tau} = 0,$$

or equivalently,

$$\upsilon_I^* = \frac{\sigma(1-\tau) + \theta^P \tau}{2\theta^P \tau},$$

which shows that a higher marginal benefit of maintenance spending on the durability of private capital lowers the optimal share of spending allocated to new investment. This provides therefore an additional rationale for allocating sufficient funds to maintaining public infrastructure assets.

• • •

This chapter began with a review of the conventional channels through which public capital may affect growth, namely, productivity and cost, complementarity, and crowding-out effects. The evidence in favor of these effects is quite strong, particularly for countries where, to begin with, public capital is available in limited supply. It then presented a basic two-period OLG model, whose key feature is a production function in which public capital is complementary to individual private capital but subject to a negative externality associated with the aggregate stock of public capital. Thus, although nonexcludable, public capital is partially rival. In addition, the model also assumed that the production of new public capital depends both on the flow of investment in infrastructure and the existing stock of public capital. The latter assumption was shown to be critical in generating dynamics in the public-private capital ratio.

Next, the chapter studied the growth effects of a change in the share of spending allocated to public investment and the tax rate, and provided a discussion of the growth-maximizing fiscal policy. The rationale for focusing on growth maximization, rather than (social) welfare maximization was also discussed. It was shown that to maximize the growth rate requires setting the tax rate equal to the marginal productivity of public infrastructure capital in output, the so-called Barro rule. In addition, it was shown that with a single type of public capital, and with unproductive spending as the only alternative to investment, maximizing the growth rate leads to a rather obvious result—all tax revenues should be allocated to the accumulation of public capital. However, with two types of productive public capital, maximizing the growth rate requires setting each spending share equal to the elasticity of output with respect to each type of capital, divided by the sum of the elasticities of output with respect to the two types of capital. This formula, which of course generalizes to any number of public capital goods, provides a good practical benchmark for expenditure allocation.

Several extensions of the basic framework were then considered, including indirect taxation, a complementarity effect operating through the efficiency of private investment, an effect of public capital on household utility, physical asset depreciation, and maintenance expenditure. The allocation of government spending between maintenance and new investment in infrastructure and possible trade-offs that may arise between these two components of public outlays were discussed, and so was the possibility that public spending on maintenance may affect the durability of the private capital stock.

## APPENDIX: Optimal Policy under Welfare Maximization

To illustrate the implications of welfare maximization for optimal public policy in an OLG context, consider the determination of the tax rate, $\tau$. Suppose that a benevolent government aims to maximize (subject to appropriate constraints) a welfare function defined as the discounted sum of the utility of the representative individual of the present and all future generations (or cohorts), by choosing the tax rate:

$$\max_{\tau} W_t = \sum_{t=0}^{\infty} \omega^t U_t, \tag{A1}$$

where the constant discount factor $\omega \in (0, 1)$ reflects social time preferences and may differ from each individual's subjective discount factor, $1/(1+\rho)$. The assumption that $\omega$ is less than one implies of course declining weights on successive generations.

This maximization problem can be solved along the equilibrium growth path as follows. The utility function (1) can be written as

$$U_t = \ln c_t^t + \Lambda \ln c_{t+1}^t, \tag{A2}$$

where $\Lambda = 1/(1+\rho)$. From (8), $c_t^t$ can be written as

$$c_t^t = (1-\sigma)(1-\tau)w_t. \tag{A3}$$

Substituting this result in the Euler equation (7) yields

$$c_{t+1}^t = \Lambda(1+r_{t+1})(1-\sigma)(1-\tau)w_t. \tag{A4}$$

Substituting (A3) and (A4) in (A2) implies that the equilibrium level of lifetime utility is

$$U_t = \ln[(1-\sigma)(1-\tau)w_t] + \Lambda \ln \Lambda(1+r_{t+1})(1-\sigma)(1-\tau)w_t,$$

that is,

$$U_t = D_1 + (1+\Lambda)\ln(1-\tau) + \Lambda \ln(1+r_{t+1}) + (1+\Lambda)\ln w_t,$$

where

$$D_1 = (1+\Lambda)\ln(1-\sigma) + \Lambda \ln \Lambda.$$

Thus, welfare is increasing in the wage rate and the rental rate of capital, but decreasing in the tax rate.

Using (14) and (15), with $\delta^P = 1$, to substitute out for $r_{t+1}$ and $w_t$ yields

$$U_t = D_1 + (1+\Lambda)\ln(1-\tau) + \Lambda \ln(1-\beta)\left(\frac{Y_{t+1}}{K_{t+1}^P}\right) + (1+\Lambda)\ln \beta Y_t,$$

or equivalently

$$U_t = D_2 + (1+\Lambda)\ln(1-\tau) + \Lambda \ln\left(\frac{Y_{t+1}}{K_{t+1}^P}\right) + (1+\Lambda)\ln Y_t,$$

where

$$D_2 = D_1 + \Lambda \ln(1-\beta) + (1+\Lambda)\ln \beta.$$

In the steady state, and as implied by (17), $Y_{t+1}/K_{t+1}^P = Y_t/K_t^P = \Xi(\tilde{k}^I)^\alpha$. Thus, the above expression, evaluated along the balanced growth path, becomes

$$\tilde{U}_t = D_3 + (1+\Lambda)\ln(1-\tau) + \alpha\Lambda \ln \tilde{k}^I + (1+\Lambda)\ln \tilde{Y}_t, \tag{A5}$$

where

$$D_3 = D_2 + \Lambda \ln \Xi.$$

Along the steady-state equilibrium path, $\tilde{Y}_t = Y_0(1+\gamma)^t$, whereas from (27), with $\mu = 1$, $\tilde{k}^I = \varphi \upsilon_I \tau/\sigma(1-\tau)$. Substituting these results in (A5) yields

$$\tilde{U}_t = D_4 + (1+\Lambda)\ln(1-\tau) + \alpha\Lambda \ln\left(\frac{\tau}{1-\tau}\right) + (1+\Lambda)t\ln(1+\gamma),$$

where

$$D_4 = D_3 + \alpha\Lambda \ln(\varphi \upsilon_I/\sigma) + (1+\Lambda)\ln Y_0.$$

This expression implies that welfare is increasing in the growth rate $\gamma$, given in (28), and depends on time. It can be rearranged as

$$\tilde{U}_t = D_4 + [(1+\Lambda) - \alpha\Lambda]\ln(1-\tau) + \alpha\Lambda \ln\tau + (1+\Lambda)t\ln(1+\gamma).$$

Taking the derivative of this expression with respect to $\tau$ and setting it to zero yields

$$\frac{d\tilde{U}_t}{d\tau} = -\frac{1+\Lambda(1-\alpha)}{1-\tau} + \frac{\alpha\Lambda}{\tau} + t(1+\Lambda)\left[\frac{d\ln(1+\gamma)}{d\tau}\right] = 0,$$

where the last term represents the long-run growth effect.

From Equation (28), or (38)–(39),

$$\frac{d\ln(1+\gamma)}{d\tau} = \frac{\alpha}{\tau} - \frac{1-\alpha}{1-\tau}. \tag{A6}$$

Substituting this expression in the previous one yields

$$-\frac{1+\Lambda(1-\alpha)}{1-\tau} + \frac{\alpha\Lambda}{\tau} + t\left(1+\Lambda)(\frac{\alpha}{\tau} - \frac{1-\alpha}{1-\tau}\right) = 0. \tag{A7}$$

Consider first the case where $t \to \infty$. Expression (A7)b becomes

$$\frac{\alpha}{\tau} - \frac{1-\alpha}{1-\tau} = 0,$$

which is the same condition as the one required for maximizing growth (see (40)). Thus, to maximize the welfare of the current and all future generations, the welfare- and growth-maximizing solutions are the same and require setting the tax rate to $\alpha$.

Consider now the case where $t \to 0$. Expression (A7) yields

$$\frac{\alpha\Lambda}{\tau} = \frac{1+\Lambda(1-\alpha)}{1-\tau},$$

which can be rearranged to give

$$\tau^{**} = \alpha\left(\frac{\Lambda}{1+\Lambda}\right) < \alpha.$$

Thus, to maximize the welfare of the current generation of agents only, the optimal tax rate must be *lower* than the growth-maximizing tax rate, $\alpha$. Intuitively, the benefit of growth for social welfare is weaker in that case because although the welfare of present-day adults depends positively on their consumption in old age, the latter is discounted. The more the current generation discounts the future (that is, the higher $\rho$ is, or equivalently the lower $\Lambda$ is), the lower the utility benefit of old age consumption, and the lower should be the optimal tax rate: the benefit of reducing after-tax income and consumption today in order to invest and increase income tomorrow is weaker. If future consumption is entirely discounted, that is, $\rho \rightarrow \infty$, then $\Lambda \rightarrow 0$ and the optimal tax rate is zero. It can also be shown that the first-order condition for welfare maximization with respect to $\upsilon_I$ implies that the optimal policy, regardless of the value of $t$, is the same as under growth maximization. This condition, however, would not hold if alternative productive uses of government spending are taken into account, as discussed in subsequent chapters.

# 2 | Public Capital and Education

A large strand of the literature on economic growth focuses on human capital, which is often broadly defined as consisting of the abilities, skills, and knowledge of individual workers.[1] In that perspective, it has been emphasized that human capital, very much like conventional economic goods, requires a variety of inputs to be produced. However, the impact of public capital on human capital accumulation, and more generally education outcomes, has only recently begun to receive much attention.

This chapter begins with a review of the evidence on the link between public capital and education. It then extends the OLG model presented in the previous chapter to account for human capital accumulation and a role for public capital in that process. After characterizing the long-run properties of the model, it is used to perform several experiments—including increases in the elasticity of the education technology with respect to public capital and in the share of public investment in infrastructure (as in the previous chapter). Optimal expenditure allocation is now discussed in a setting where both infrastructure investment and education outlays are productive components of public spending. Several extensions are then considered, namely, an endogenous effect of infrastructure on child-rearing costs and parental time allocated to education, and the effect of schooling quality on the allocation of public expenditure between education and infrastructure.

## 1 | Background

A large body of evidence, based predominantly on microeconomic studies, has documented the existence of a significant link between infrastructure and educational attainment in developing countries. As documented in an early summary by Brenneman and Kerf (2002), and more recently by Agénor (2008*a*, 2011*a*), these studies have found a direct positive impact of various types of infrastructure services (namely, roads, electricity, water and sanitation, and telecommunications) on learning indicators.[2]

[1] See for instance Barro and Sala-i-Martin (2003), Agénor (2004), and Acemoglu (2008) for a review of the literature.

[2] Evidence is available also for industrial countries. Jones and Zimmer (2001) for instance found that "capital" (defined as the physical assets owned by public schools that are essential inputs in the production of education) had a positive impact on academic achievement in the United States.

Indeed, a better transportation system and a safer road network (particularly in rural areas) have been found to be instrumental in raising school attendance. In the Philippines, for instance, after rural roads were built, school enrollment went up by 10 percent and dropout rates fell by 55 percent. A similar project in Morocco raised girls' enrollment rates from 28 percent to 68 percent in less than 10 years (see Khandker et al. (1994) and Levy (2004)). The quality of education also improved, as greater accessibility made it easier to hire more experienced teachers and facilitated their ability to commute between rural and urban areas.

Similarly, researchers have found that greater access to safe water and sanitation in schools tends to raise attendance rates (particularly for girls) and the ability of children to learn. In Bangladesh, for instance, girls' attendance rates in schools went up by 15 percent following improved access to water and sanitation facilities. In Morocco, the sharp increase in girls' enrollment rates mentioned earlier was in part also due to improved access to water and sanitation in schools. This effect may operate in part by enhancing children's health; indeed, in many developing countries (particularly among the poorest) schools that lack access to clean water supply and sanitation services tend to have a higher incidence of illnesses among their students.[3]

A number of micro studies have also found that access to electricity helps to improve the learning process, by allowing children to spend more time studying and by providing more opportunities to use electronic equipment. Computers, for instance, may enhance the quality of learning by improving access to information. A study of the Philippines suggests that electricity increases study time by approximately an hour an evening (World Bank (2008*a*)). In purely quantitative terms, access to electricity can make a sizable difference in terms of its impact on schooling. In the late 1990s in Nicaragua, 72 percent of children living in a household with electricity were attending school, compared to only 50 percent for those living in a household without electricity (see Saghir (2005)). As also documented by the World Bank (2008*a*), the failure of teachers to take up positions in remote locations and frequent absenteeism from such postings are often indirectly related to poor access to infrastructure; studies suggest that the availability of electricity (just like adequate access to roads) does make rural positions more attractive to teachers.

This brief review of the evidence suggests that, overall, the benefits of public capital for education outcomes can be sizable. To capture these benefits and examine their implications for long-run growth and public policy, the core OLG model developed in chapter 1 is next extended to account for the accumulation of knowledge.

[3] As discussed in chapter 3, poor sanitary and hygienic conditions in schools may have longer-run effects on health as well.

## 2| The Economy

Consider again an economy populated by three types of agents: households, firms, and the government. There are now two production sectors in the economy, one producing a physical good (which can be consumed or invested as before), and the other, operated by the government, which produces knowledge or human capital. Individuals live now for three periods: childhood, adulthood, and old age. They accumulate knowledge in the first period, supply human-capital-enhanced labor in the second, and retire in the third. Education is public, mandatory, and free of charge. These assumptions are particularly relevant for low-income developing countries where the scarcity of human capital has led governments to pursue active policies to promote education, and private schooling opportunities remain limited.[4]

Individuals are identical within and across generations. They are endowed with one unit of time in childhood and adulthood, and zero units when they are old. All individuals have access to a common schooling technology, which converts time invested during childhood into human capital, permitting a higher flow of labor services per unit time in adulthood. In childhood all time is devoted to education.[5] In adulthood, a fixed fraction $\varepsilon \in (0, 1)$ of parental time is allocated to home tutoring, and the rest $1 - \varepsilon$ is devoted inelastically to market work. Human capital investment has an intergenerational external effect: it causes growth in the economy-wide stock of knowledge, which increases the effectiveness of time spent in school by later generations. The government invests in infrastructure and spends on education and unproductive services; as before, it taxes individuals only during adulthood.

Other assumptions are the same as before. There are no bequests or debts to future generations and the only source of income is wages in the second period of life. Consumption of children is part of their parents' consumption in adulthood. In order to consume in old age, agents must set aside some of the income earned during middle age. Savings can be held only in the form of physical capital. Agents have no other endowments, except for an initial old generation, which is endowed with an initial capital stock $K_0^P$. There is no population growth, and the number of adult workers is set at $\bar{N}$.[6]

### 2.1| Households

All households value consumption in adulthood and old age. The utility of an adult born in period $t$ takes the same form as before:

$$U_t = \ln c_{t+1}^t + \frac{\ln c_{t+2}^t}{1+\rho}, \tag{1}$$

[4] See Agénor (2012) and the references therein.

[5] Child labor is therefore excluded, despite its importance in some developing countries. Note that it could also be assumed that the level of effort (that is, the time allocated by children to studying, beyond time spent in school) is a choice variable.

[6] See Becker et al. (1990) for a seminal contribution to the analysis of human capital and fertility.

where $\rho > 0$. Note that in this setting, the discount rate could be related to education outcomes. Bauer and Chytilová (2007) for instance, in a study of Uganda, found a strong negative association between the level of education and individual discount rates; more educated individuals appear to be more patient, even after controlling for other characteristics (age, income group, gender, marital status, and clan linkage). For simplicity, however, the impact of education on individual patience is ignored.

Let $e_{t+1}$ denote individual human capital at $t+1$. Each agent born at $t$ supplies inelastically $e_{t+1}(1-\varepsilon)$ efficiency units of labor during adulthood, and receives gross labor income of $(1-\varepsilon)e_{t+1}w_{t+1}$, where $w_{t+1}$ is the *effective* wage rate (that is, the wage in terms of efficient units of labor). In addition, time spent in schooling while in childhood requires a loss of adult consumption equal to a fixed fraction $\theta \in (0, 1)$ of the adult's net wage. Thus, although schooling per se is free (in the sense that the government does not charge any fees to students), it is costly, because parents must also devote time to tutoring (which entails an opportunity cost) and provide clothes, books, and so on, to allow children to get an education. The total cost of taking care of children, accounting for its opportunity cost, is thus equal to $(\varepsilon+\theta)e_{t+1}w_{t+1}$.

Because there is no consumption in childhood, the period-specific budget constraints are

$$c^t_{t+1} + s_{t+1} = \Omega e_{t+1} w_{t+1}, \tag{2}$$

$$c^t_{t+2} = (1 + r_{t+2}) s_{t+1}, \tag{3}$$

where $\tau$ and $r_{t+1}$ are as defined in the previous chapter, and

$$\Omega = (1-\theta)(1-\tau)(1-\varepsilon) < 1.$$

Combining (2) and (3) yields the intertemporal budget constraint:

$$c^t_{t+1} + \frac{c^t_{t+2}}{1 + r_{t+2}} = \Omega e_{t+1} w_{t+1}. \tag{4}$$

## 2.2| Production of Goods

As in chapter 1, firms are identical and their number is normalized to unity. They produce a single nonstorable good, using now "effective" labor, $E_t N^i_t$, where $E_t$ is average human capital in the economy, private capital, $K^{P,i}_t$, and public infrastructure, $K^I_t$, which is again a common external input for firms. The production function of individual firm $i$ takes now the form

$$Y^i_t = \left[\frac{K^I_t}{(K^P_t)^\zeta}\right]^\alpha [(1-\varepsilon)E_t N^i_t]^\beta (K^{P,i}_t)^{1-\beta}, \tag{5}$$

where $K^P_t = \int_0^1 K^{P,i}_t$, $\alpha, \zeta > 0$, and $\beta \in (0, 1)$.

Again, each firm's objective is to maximize profits, $\Pi_t^i$, with respect to labor services and private capital, taking as given $K_t^I$, $K_t^P$, and $E_t$:

$$\max_{N_t^i, K_t^{P,i}} \Pi_t^i = Y_t^i - (r_t + \delta^P)K_t^{P,i} - w_t(1-\varepsilon)E_t N_t^i.$$

Given that all firms are identical, and that labor market equilibrium imposes $\int_0^1 N_t^i di = \bar{N}$, in a symmetric equilibrium the first-order conditions are

$$w_t = \beta Y_t/(1-\varepsilon)E_t\bar{N}, \quad r_t = (1-\beta)Y_t/K_t^P - \delta^P, \tag{6}$$

and aggregate output is

$$Y_t = \int_0^1 Y_t^i di = \Xi(k_t^I)^\alpha \left(\frac{E_t}{K_t^P}\right)^\beta K_t^P, \quad \Xi = [(1-\varepsilon)\bar{N}]^\beta, \tag{7}$$

where again assumption 1.2 in chapter 1, $\beta - \alpha(1-\zeta) = 0$, is imposed to ensure constant returns to private capital in the long run. Note also that, as in chapter 1, the assumption of constant population is not innocuous.

With full depreciation, private capital accumulation is driven by

$$K_{t+1}^P = I_t, \tag{8}$$

where again $I_t$ is private investment.

### 2.3| Production of Human Capital

Human capital depends on the time devoted by parents to tutoring their children, $\varepsilon$, government spending on education per child, $G_t^E/\bar{N}$, which includes the provision of books, pencils, school meals, and so on, the stock of public infrastructure, and the average level of human capital of parents, $E_t$:[7,8]

$$e_{t+1} = \varepsilon \left(\frac{G_t^E}{\bar{N}}\right)^{\nu_1} (K_t^I)^{\nu_2} E_t^{1-\nu_1-\nu_2} + (1-\delta^E)e_t, \tag{9}$$

where $\delta^E \in (0, 1)$ is a depreciation rate, and $\nu_1, \nu_2 > 0$. Thus, the parent generation's human capital affects children's human capital externally. Because individuals are identical within a generation, the human capital of parents is

[7] For tractability, constant returns to scale in $G_t^E/\bar{N}$, $K_t^I$ and $E_t$ are imposed on the education technology. The effect of parental time is also assumed linear, although this is inconsequential, given that $\varepsilon$ is constant over time.

[8] It could also be assumed that parental spending on education per child, $\theta(1-\tau)(1-\varepsilon)e_{t+1}w_{t+1}$, also affects the quality of schooling. For simplicity, this effect is abstracted from. Blankenau and Simpson (2004) consider endogenous private choices in education. Note also that, as in Galor and Weil (2000), it could be assumed that technological progress (as measured by the aggregate capital-labor ratio) erodes human capital. This mechanism, however, has limited relevance for most developing countries.

taken to be equal to the average human capital of the previous generation, $E_t$. Consistent with the evidence discussed in Agénor (2011*a*) and Agénor and Neanidis (2011), increasing returns in the education technology with respect to public capital are ruled out; thus, $\nu_2 < 1$. Decreasing marginal returns to government spending on education is also assumed, so $\nu_1 < 1$. To ensure that average human capital at $t$ has a positive impact on individual human capital at $t + 1$, the following condition is imposed:[9]

**Assumption 2.1.** $\nu_1 + \nu_2 < 1$.

The presence of $E_t$ on the right-hand side in equation (9) can be viewed as reflecting the individual's initial level of human capital at birth. Indeed, as pointed out by Azariadis and Drazen (1990, p. 510), it could be assumed that each agent born in period $t$ inherits (is born with) the average stock of knowledge available at that time, that is, $e_t = E_t$. Knowledge and technical skills are thus disembodied, that is, they do not die with the individual agents but rather are passed on in an automatic fashion to the newborns. There are consequently *intergenerational externalities* associated with human capital. At the same time, the newborns can add to the stock of knowledge inherited from the previous generation by benefiting from parental time, public capital, and government spending on education.

## 2.4| Government

In each period the government invests in infrastructure and spends on education and other (unproductive) items. Again, it runs a balanced budget, so that

$$G_t = \sum G_t^h = \tau E_t(1 - \varepsilon)w_t \bar{N}. \tag{10}$$

Spending shares are all assumed to be constant fractions of government revenues:

$$G_t^h = \upsilon_h \tau E_t(1 - \varepsilon)w_t \bar{N}, \quad h = I, E, U. \tag{11}$$

Combining (10) and (11) therefore yields

$$\sum \upsilon_h = 1. \tag{12}$$

With full depreciation, and new public capital requiring both a flow of goods and existing capital (as discussed in chapter 1), the stock of infrastructure assets evolves as

$$K_{t+1}^I = (\varphi G_t^I)^{\mu}(K_t^I)^{1-\mu}, \tag{13}$$

where again $\mu \in (0, 1)$.

[9] As discussed in the appendix to this chapter, this assumption is also needed for stability.

### 2.5| Savings-Investment Balance

The asset market-clearing condition requires, as before, equality between investment and savings:

$$I_t = \bar{N} s_t. \tag{14}$$

## 3| Equilibrium and the Balanced Growth Path

Given initial physical and human capital stocks, $K_0^P$, $K_0^I$, $E_0 > 0$, a *competitive equilibrium* for this economy is now a sequence of prices $\{w_t, r_{t+1}\}_{t=0}^{\infty}$, consumption and savings allocations $\{c_t^t, c_{t+1}^t, s_t\}_{t=0}^{\infty}$, physical capital stocks $\{K_{t+1}^P, K_{t+1}^I\}_{t=0}^{\infty}$, a human capital stock $\{E_{t+1}\}_{t=0}^{\infty}$, a constant tax rate $\tau$, and constant spending shares $\upsilon_I$, $\upsilon_E$ and $\upsilon_U$, such that individuals maximize utility, firms maximize profits, markets clear, and the government budget is balanced. In equilibrium, individual human capital must also be equal to the economy-wide average human capital, $e_t = E_t$. A *balanced growth equilibrium* is a competitive equilibrium in which $c_t^t$, $c_{t+1}^t$, $K_{t+1}^P$, $K_{t+1}^I$ and $E_{t+1}$ grow at the constant, endogenous rate $\gamma$, and the rate of return on private capital is constant. By implication, output also grows at the rate $\gamma$, and the effective wage is constant.

All individuals face the same interest rate and learning technology so that they will choose the same consumption and saving plans. Individuals take their human capital, wages, the interest rate, and the tax rate as given and maximize (1) subject to (4) with respect to $c_{t+1}^t$ and $c_{t+2}^t$. With $\lambda_t$ denoting the Lagrange multiplier associated with (4), this yields the first-order conditions:

$$1/c_{t+1}^t = \lambda_t, \tag{15}$$

$$1/(1+\rho)c_{t+2}^t = \lambda_t/(1+r_{t+2}). \tag{16}$$

Equations (15) and (16) yield again the Euler equation

$$\frac{c_{t+2}^t}{c_{t+1}^t} = \frac{1+r_{t+2}}{1+\rho}, \tag{17}$$

which equates the marginal rate of substitution between consumption in adulthood and consumption in old age (discounted to working age period) to their relative prices.

Substituting (17) in (4) yields

$$c_{t+1}^t = \left(\frac{1+\rho}{2+\rho}\right) \Omega e_{t+1} w_{t+1}. \tag{18}$$

From (2) and (18), individual savings are given by

$$s_{t+1} = \Omega \sigma e_{t+1} w_{t+1}, \tag{19}$$

where again $\sigma = 1/(2+\rho)$.

Deriving the dynamics of this economy proceeds as follows. First, note that substituting (6), (14), and (19) in (8) yields

$$K_{t+1}^P = (1-\theta)(1-\tau)\sigma\beta Y_t. \tag{20}$$

Substituting for $Y_t$ in this expression using (7) implies

$$\frac{K_{t+1}^P}{K_t^P} = \Xi_2 (k_t^I)^\alpha (e_t^P)^\beta, \tag{21}$$

where $\Xi_2 = (1-\theta)(1-\tau)\sigma\beta\Xi$, and $e_t^P = E_t/K_t^P$ is the human capital-private capital ratio.

Similarly, from (6), (11), and (13),

$$K_{t+1}^I = (\varphi\upsilon_I\tau\beta Y_t)^\mu (K_t^I)^{1-\mu} = (\varphi\upsilon_I\tau\beta)^\mu \left(\frac{Y_t}{K_t^P k_t^I}\right)^\mu K_t^I.$$

Using again (7) to eliminate $Y_t$ yields

$$\frac{K_{t+1}^I}{K_t^I} = \Xi_3 (k_t^I)^{-\mu(1-\alpha)} (e_t^P)^{\beta\mu}, \tag{22}$$

where $\Xi_3 = (\varphi\upsilon_I\tau\beta\Xi)^\mu$.

Combining (21) and (22) yields

$$k_{t+1}^I = \frac{\Xi_3 (k_t^I)^{-\mu(1-\alpha)} (e_t^P)^{\beta\mu} K_t^I}{\Xi_2 (k_t^I)^\alpha (e_t^P)^\beta K_t^P},$$

or equivalently,

$$k_{t+1}^I = \Phi^1(k_t^I, e_t^P) = \Xi_4 (k_t^I)^{(1-\alpha)(1-\mu)} (e_t^P)^{-\beta(1-\mu)}, \tag{23}$$

where $\Xi_4 = \Xi_3/\Xi_2$.

From (9), with $\delta^E = 1$ for simplicity,

$$E_{t+1} = \varepsilon \left(\frac{G_t^E}{E_t}\right)^{\nu_1} \left(\frac{K_t^I}{E_t}\right)^{\nu_2} E_t,$$

that is, using (6) and (11),

$$E_{t+1} = \varepsilon \left(\frac{\upsilon_E\tau\beta Y_t}{K_t^P}\right)^{\nu_1} (k_t^I)^{\nu_2} (e_t^P)^{-(\nu_1+\nu_2)} E_t.$$

Using (7) to substitute for $Y_t$ yields

$$\frac{E_{t+1}}{E_t} = \varepsilon(\upsilon_E\tau\beta\Xi)^{\nu_1} (k_t^I)^{\alpha\nu_1+\nu_2} (e_t^P)^{-\nu_1(1-\beta)-\nu_2}. \tag{24}$$

Combining (21) and (24) yields

$$e_{t+1}^P = \Phi^2(k_t^I, e_t^P) = \Xi_5 (k_t^I)^{-\alpha(1-\nu_1)+\nu_2} (e_t^P)^{-\nu_1(1-\beta)+(1-\nu_2)-\beta}, \tag{25}$$

where $\Xi_5 = \varepsilon(\upsilon_E\tau\beta\Xi)^{\nu_1}/\Xi_2$.

Note that, in general, both an increase in the public-private capital ratio and the current private physical capital-human capital ratio have an ambiguous effect on the future private-human capital ratio. On the one hand, an increase in either variable raises the future human capital stock; on the other, they increase output and thus savings and the future private capital stock. Which effect dominates cannot be ascertained a priori and depends on the values of the various parameters characterizing the production functions for goods and human capital.

As in the previous chapter, to examine the behavior of the economy, the cases $\mu = 1$ and $\mu < 1$ are studied separately.

### 3.1| The Case Where $\mu = 1$

Setting $\mu = 1$ in (23), the public-private capital ratio becomes constant over time at

$$J = \Xi_4|_{\mu=1} = \frac{\varphi \upsilon_I \tau}{(1-\theta)(1-\tau)\sigma}. \tag{26}$$

Substituting this result in (25) yields

$$e_{t+1}^P = \Xi_6 (e_t^P)^{(1-\beta)(1-\nu_1)-\nu_2}, \tag{27}$$

where $\Xi_6 = \Xi_5 J^{-\alpha(1-\nu_1)+\nu_2}$. Equation (27) is a first-order difference equation in $e_t^P$ implying that the model now displays transitional dynamics. Its steady-state solution is

$$\tilde{e}^P = \Xi_6^{1/[1+\nu_2-(1-\beta)(1-\nu_1)]}. \tag{28}$$

With $e^P$ constant in equilibrium, the rate of growth of private capital (and thus public capital, as implied by (25)) is the same as the rate of growth of human capital.

Equations (7) and (20) imply that aggregate output in $t+1$ is

$$Y_{t+1} = \Xi J^{\alpha} (e_{t+1}^P)^{\beta} (1-\theta)(1-\tau)\sigma\beta Y_t, \tag{29}$$

which implies that the steady-state growth rate of output is

$$1+\gamma = \Xi J^{\alpha} (\tilde{e}^P)^{\beta} (1-\theta)(1-\tau)\sigma\beta. \tag{30}$$

Stability of the adjustment process described by (27) requires

$$|(1-\beta)(1-\nu_1) - \nu_2| < 1,$$

or equivalently $(1-\beta)(1-\nu_1) < 1+\nu_2$. This condition always holds. Thus, whether one considers the "standard" model of human capital accumulation, in which public capital plays no role in the education technology (so that $\nu_2 = 0$), or the "augmented" model, with $\nu_2 > 0$, stability is guaranteed. In addition,

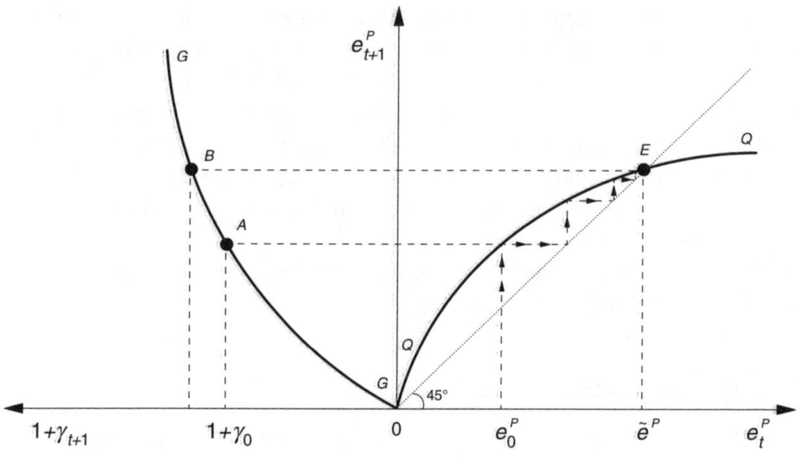


Figure 2.1. Dynamics of Growth and the Human–Private Capital Ratio ($\mu = 1$).

a higher value of $\nu_2$ speeds up convergence to the long-run equilibrium.[10] Intuitively, a higher $\nu_2$ implies that the effect of an increase in the public capital stock on human capital accumulation is magnified, thereby raising output by more. Because higher output translates into higher tax revenues, it further stimulates investment in infrastructure and public capital accumulation, thereby increasing the speed of convergence to the steady state.

The adjustment process corresponding to (27) is illustrated by the concave curve $QQ$ in the right-hand panel of Figure 2.1. The left-hand panel in the figure displays the concave curve $GG$, which corresponds to (29) and shows the relationship between the growth rate of output $1+\gamma_{t+1} = Y_{t+1}/Y_t$ and the human-private capital ratio, $e^P_{t+1}$. Starting from the initial value $e^P_0$, the economy converges gradually over time to $\tilde{e}^P$, with growth increasing from point $A$ to point $B$.

Inspection of (26), (28), and (30) yields the following result:

**Result 2.1.** *With $\mu = 1$, an increase in parental time allocated to children's education, $\varepsilon$, has a positive effect on the steady-state human-private capital ratio but an ambiguous effect on the economy's steady-state growth rate.*

As can be inferred from the definition of $\Xi_6$, an increase in $\varepsilon$ always leads to a higher human capital-private capital ratio.[11] On the one hand, it stimulates directly human capital accumulation; on the other, it lowers labor allocated to market work, which leads to lower output. In turn, lower output reduces

[10] Note that convergence may be oscillatory if $\nu_2$ is large enough to exceed $(1-\beta)(1-\nu_1)$. However, this is not of much interest in the present case.

[11] After appropriate substitutions, it can be shown that $\Xi_6$ depends on $\varepsilon(1-\varepsilon)^{-(1-\beta\nu_1)}$. With $\beta\nu_1 < 1$, it is clear that an increase in $\varepsilon$ raises $\Xi_6$ and thus, from (28), $\tilde{e}^P$.

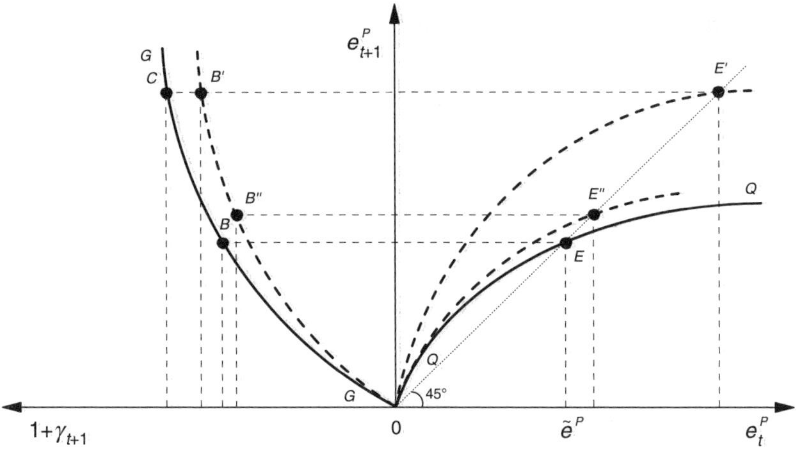


Figure 2.2. Increase in Parental Time Allocated to Tutoring.

private savings (which also tends to increase the human capital-private capital ratio) and to reduce government spending on education (which has the opposite effect). In the present setting, the latter effect is dominated by the direct effect and the savings effect, and a higher $\varepsilon$ unambiguously raises the human capital-private capital ratio.

This result is illustrated in the right-hand side panel of Figure 2.2. An increase in $\varepsilon$ shifts the transition curve $QQ$ upward (with no change at the origin) with the equilibrium moving to from point $E$ to either point $E'$ or $E''$. From (26), the public-private capital ratio is unaffected, because both public investment and private savings are linear in output with $\mu = 1$ (see (20) and (22)). However, curve $GG$ shifts inward, because the increase in $\varepsilon$ lowers the supply of raw labor and (all else equal) the growth rate.[12] The net effect on *effective* labor is thus ambiguous. If the shift in $QQ$ is large, with the equilibrium human capital-private capital ratio rising from $E$ to $E'$, the steady-state growth rate will also be higher, increasing from $B$ to $B'$. By contrast, if the shift in $QQ$ is muted, steady-state growth will fall from $B$ to $B''$. Thus, even if the net effect on the human capital-private capital ratio is unambiguously positive, the growth effect can be negative because labor supply falls.

### 3.2| The Case Where $\mu < 1$

With $\mu < 1$, the public-private capital ratio is no longer constant over time; equations (23) and (25) now form a simultaneous, nonlinear first-order difference-equation system in $e_t^P$ and $k_t^I$. Defining $\hat{e}_t^P = \ln e_t^P$ and $\hat{k}_t^I = \ln k_t^I$,

[12] From (29), given that $\Xi$ depends on $(1-\varepsilon)^\beta$, an increase in $\varepsilon$ lowers output unambiguously. The magnitude of this effect depends on $\beta$.

this system can be written in linear form as

$$\begin{bmatrix} \hat{e}^P_{t+1} \\ \hat{k}^I_{t+1} \end{bmatrix} = \begin{bmatrix} a_{11} & a_{12} \\ a_{21} & a_{22} \end{bmatrix} \begin{bmatrix} \hat{e}^P_t \\ \hat{k}^I_t \end{bmatrix}, \tag{31}$$

where

$$a_{11} = (1-\beta)(1-\nu_1) - \nu_2,$$

$$a_{12} = -\alpha(1-\nu_1) + \nu_2,$$

$$a_{21} = -\beta(1-\mu) < 0,$$

$$a_{22} = (1-\alpha)(1-\mu) > 0.$$

Setting $\Delta k^I_{t+1} = \Delta e^P_{t+1} = 0$ in (23) and (25) yields the steady-state solutions

$$\tilde{k}^I = \Xi_4^{1/\Pi}(\tilde{e}^P)^{-\beta(1-\mu)/\Pi}, \tag{32}$$

$$\tilde{k}^I = \Xi_5^{-1/a_{12}}(\tilde{e}^P)^{(1-a_{11})/a_{12}}, \tag{33}$$

where $\Pi = 1-(1-\alpha)(1-\mu) \in (0, 1)$.

These equations define the steady-state relationships between $e^P_t$ and $k^I_t$. Equation (32) defines a curve with a negative slope depicted as $KK$ in Figure 2.3. The slope of this curve is, in absolute terms, $\beta(1-\mu)/\Pi$, which is less than unity if, in particular, $\alpha+\beta<1$. Assuming that this condition holds implies that $KK$ is convex.

The slope of the curve defined by (33), denoted $SS$ in Figure 2.3, depends on $(1-a_{11})/a_{12}$, that is

$$\frac{1-a_{11}}{a_{12}} = \frac{1+\nu_2-(1-\beta)(1-\nu_1)}{\nu_2-\alpha(1-\nu_1)}.$$

The numerator is always positive, but the denominator is ambiguous in sign. In the "standard" case where public capital does not affect the education technology ($\nu_2 = 0$), $a_{12} < 0$; thus, the slope of $SS$ is unambiguously negative. In addition, $[(1-a_{11})/a_{12}] - 1 < 0$ if $\alpha+\beta<1$. Assuming that this condition holds implies that $SS$ is also convex. By continuity, if $\nu_2$ is sufficiently small (that is, $\nu_2 < \alpha(1-\nu_1)$, so that $a_{12} < 0$), these results continue to hold. For convenience, conditions for convexity of both $KK$ and $SS$ are imposed:

**Assumption 2.2.** $\alpha+\beta<1$, $a_{12} = \nu_2 - \alpha(1-\nu_1) < 0$.

As can be inferred from Figure 2.3, the system (23) and (25) has a unique equilibrium, which obtains at Point $E$. The appendix to this chapter shows that

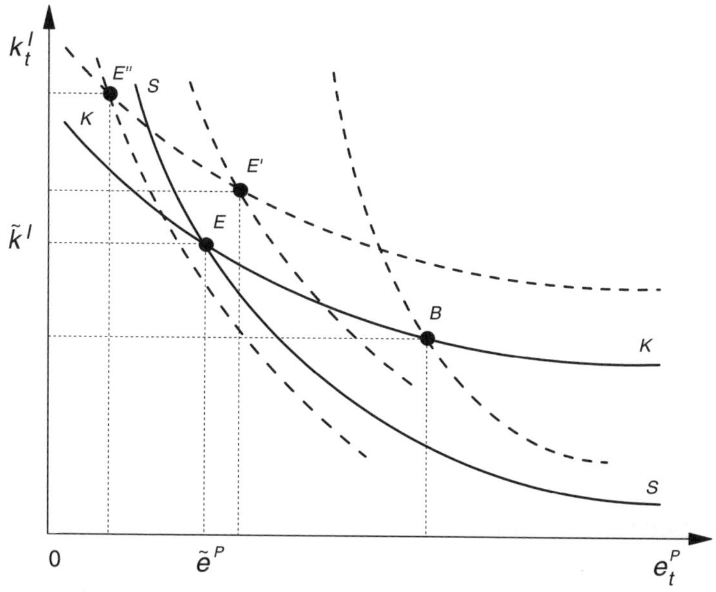


Figure 2.3. Steady-State Equilibrium with $\mu < 1$ and Increase in Parental Time Allocated to Tutoring.

stability of the equilibrium requires $KK$ to be steeper than $SS$, as shown in the figure.[13]

From (7) and (20),

$$Y_{t+1} = \Xi(k_{t+1}^I)^\alpha(e_{t+1}^P)^\beta(1-\theta)(1-\tau)\sigma\beta Y_t,$$

which implies that the steady-state growth rate of output is

$$1+\gamma = \Xi(\tilde{k}^I)^\alpha(\tilde{e}^P)^\beta(1-\theta)(1-\tau)\sigma\beta, \tag{34}$$

where $\tilde{e}^P$ and $\tilde{k}^I$ are the solutions of (32) and (33).

Consider again an increase in $\varepsilon$. The effects on the human capital-private capital ratio and the growth rate remain ambiguous. Graphically, as shown in Figure 2.3, curve $KK$ shifts upward; the lower output associated with the reduction in labor supply always has a stronger effect on private savings than public investment in equilibrium. Curve $SS$ also shifts upward as long as assumptions 2.2 hold.[14] With both curves shifting up, the steady-state effects

[13] Note that if $\nu_2$ is sufficiently large, $a_{12}$ could be positive, implying that $SS$ would have a positive slope. However, the equilibrium would remain unique.

[14] After substitutions, it can be shown that $\Xi_4$ in (23) depends on $(1-\varepsilon)^{-\beta(1-\mu)}$, which implies that an increase in $\varepsilon$ raises $\Xi_4$ and from (32), all else equal, $\tilde{k}^I$. Just like $\Xi_6$, $\Xi_5$ depends on $\varepsilon(1-\varepsilon)^{-(1-\beta\nu_1)}$; however, even though an increase in $\varepsilon$ raises $\Xi_5$ (given that $\beta\nu_1 < 1$) it does not necessarily increase $\tilde{k}^I$ in (33), because it depends on $\Xi_5^{-1/a_{12}}$. If $\nu_2$ is not too large, $a_{12} < 0$ and $\tilde{k}^I$ in that equation increases, all else equal.

are ambiguous. Intuitively, the reason for this ambiguity is that an increase in $\varepsilon$, by lowering labor supply and reducing output, lowers private savings and the private capital stock, which tends to reduce the human capital-private capital ratio. However, because at the same time the public-private capital ratio increases, the fall in the human capital-private capital ratio is mitigated. the net effect on that ratio is thus ambiguous. Two possible outcomes are illustrated in Figure 2.3: both steady-state values increase (shift from point $E$ to $E'$) and only the public-private capital ratio increases (shift from point $E$ to $E''$). Thus, in contrast to the case where $\mu = 1$ (in which the public-private capital ratio is constant and independent of $\varepsilon$), the trade-off in the allocation of parental time—even though both components (tutoring and market work) can be considered productive—is more acute and translates now into the possibility that an increase in the former may not raise the equilibrium human capital-private physical capital ratio.

## 4| Sensitivity of Education Technology

Suppose now that in the education technology defined in (9), the sensitivity with respect to public capital, $\nu_2$, increases. With $\mu = 1$, as shown in Figure 2.2, curve $QQ$ becomes steeper and shifts upward (again, with no change at the origin). Because $GG$ does not depend directly on $\nu_2$, it does not shift. As with the experiment involving $\varepsilon$, the equilibrium moves from $E$ to $E'$, and from $B$ to $C$, characterized by a higher human capital-private capital ratio and a higher growth rate in the steady state. The public-private capital ratio, by contrast, does not change. This can be summarized as follows:

**Result 2.2.** *With $\mu = 1$, an increase in the sensitivity of the human capital technology to public capital, $\nu_2$, raises the equilibrium human-private capital ratio and the economy's steady-state growth rate. It has no effect on the public-private capital ratio.*

With $\mu < 1$, and supposing that assumptions 2.2 continue to hold, curve $SS$ in Figure 2.3 shifts to the right and becomes steeper, whereas curve $KK$, which does not depend directly on $\nu_2$, remains the same. The equilibrium shifts from $E$ to $B$, characterized by not only a higher human capital-private capital ratio (as before) but also a lower public-private capital ratio. The reason is that now the higher human capital-private capital ratio raises the private capital stock by more than it raises the public capital stock, as a result of a stronger effect on private savings than public investment. The net effect on the steady-state growth rate is now ambiguous, unlike what occurs with $\mu = 1$. Nevertheless, the following result can be established:

**Result 2.3.** *With $\mu < 1$, an increase in the sensitivity of the human capital technology to public capital, $\nu_2$, raises the equilibrium human-private capital* *ratio, and possibly the economy's steady-state growth rate, if the productivity externality of public capital, α, is not too large.*

Thus, what matters for this experiment is how strong the externality of public capital is with respect to knowledge accumulation, relative to its conventional productivity effect.

## 5| Public Policy

### 5.1| Increase in Public Spending

To illustrate the impact of an increase in public spending, it is sufficient to focus on the case where $\mu = 1$.[15]

From (26), (28), and (30), a budget-neutral increase in the share of public investment on infrastructure ($d\upsilon_I + d\upsilon_U = 0$) yields, under assumptions 2.2,

$$\left.\frac{d\ln J}{d\upsilon_I}\right|_{d\upsilon_I + d\upsilon_U = 0} = \frac{1}{\upsilon_I} > 0,$$

$$\left.\frac{d\ln \tilde{e}^P}{d\upsilon_I}\right|_{d\upsilon_I + d\upsilon_U = 0} = \frac{\nu_2 - \alpha(1-\nu_1)}{\upsilon_I[1+\nu_2 - (1-\beta)(1-\nu_1)]} < 0,$$

$$\left.\frac{d\ln(1+\gamma)}{d\upsilon_I}\right|_{d\upsilon_I + d\upsilon_U = 0} = \alpha \left.\frac{d\ln J}{d\upsilon_I}\right|_{d\upsilon_I + d\upsilon_U = 0} + \beta \left.\frac{d\ln \tilde{e}^P}{d\upsilon_I}\right|_{d\upsilon_I + d\upsilon_U = 0} \lesseqgtr 0.$$

Thus, although the public-private capital ratio increases, the equilibrium human capital-private capital ratio falls (due essentially to the larger increase in the private capital stock), implying that the net effect on long-run growth is in general ambiguous.

Similarly, a budget-neutral increase in the share of public spending on education ($d\upsilon_E + d\upsilon_U = 0$) yields

$$\left.\frac{d\ln J}{d\upsilon_E}\right|_{d\upsilon_E + d\upsilon_U = 0} = 0,$$

$$\left.\frac{d\ln \tilde{e}^P}{d\upsilon_E}\right|_{d\upsilon_E + d\upsilon_U = 0} = \frac{\nu_1}{\upsilon_E[1+\nu_2 - (1-\beta)(1-\nu_1)]} > 0$$

$$\left.\frac{d\ln(1+\gamma)}{d\upsilon_E}\right|_{d\upsilon_E + d\upsilon_U = 0} = \beta \left.\frac{d\ln \tilde{e}^P}{d\upsilon_E}\right|_{d\upsilon_E + d\upsilon_U = 0} > 0,$$

[15] The appendix to this chapter considers the case where $\mu < 1$ and shows that even a budget-neutral increase in spending on education can have an ambiguous effect on the steady-state growth rate.

In this case, the increase in spending has no effect on the public-private capital ratio, and raises both the equilibrium human capital-private capital ratio and the steady-state growth rate. Figure 2.1 can be used to illustrate both of these experiments.

The important point, however, is that now there are two productive components of spending. Consider then the case where the increase in infrastructure is financed by a reduction in spending on education, so that $d\upsilon_I + d\upsilon_E = 0$. It is intuitively clear that the net effect on growth must be ambiguous: the positive benefit from improved access to infrastructure may be offset by a lower stock of human capital and a lower supply of effective labor. Indeed, from equations (26), ( 28), and (30) it can be established that

$$\left.\frac{d\ln(1+\gamma)}{d\upsilon_I}\right|_{d\upsilon_I+d\upsilon_E=0} = \frac{\alpha}{\upsilon_I} + \frac{\beta\{[\nu_2 - \alpha(1-\nu_1)]\upsilon_I^{-1} - \nu_1\upsilon_E^{-1}\}}{[1+\nu_2-(1-\beta)(1-\nu_1)]} \lesseqgtr 0. \quad (35)$$

By implication, there must also be an optimal allocation of government spending that balances these two effects.

### 5.2| Optimal Expenditure Allocation

To determine the optimal allocation of public expenditure between infrastructure investment and education, it is sufficient to consider again the case where $\mu = 1$.[16] Suppose that initially $\upsilon_U = 0$, so that from (12) $\upsilon_I + \upsilon_E = 1$. This condition now implies that any shift in one (productive) spending share, to be budget neutral, must be offset by an opposite change in the other (productive) share.

Using this condition, and using (35), the condition for determining the optimal share of spending on infrastructure is

$$\left\{\alpha + \frac{\beta[\nu_2 - \alpha(1-\nu_1)]}{1+\nu_2-(1-\beta)(1-\nu_1)}\right\}\upsilon_I^{-1} - \frac{\beta\nu_1(1-\upsilon_I)^{-1}}{1+\nu_2-(1-\beta)(1-\nu_1)} = 0. \quad (36)$$

Before the general solution to this condition is derived, consider first the case where $\nu_2 = 0$; the solution to (36) yields

$$\upsilon_I^* = \frac{\alpha}{\alpha+\beta} \in (0, 1), \quad (37)$$

which is the formula derived in Agénor (2008*a*, 2012). Thus, if the human capital technology does not depend on public capital, the optimal allocation of public expenditure depends solely on the parameters characterizing the goods production technology, $\alpha$ and $\beta$.[17]

[16] The case where $\mu < 1$ is a bit more tedious to analyze but leads to similar results—with the exception that the optimal share $\upsilon_I$ depends (as one would expect) positively on $\mu$.

[17] In related work, Monteiro and Turnovsky (2008) found that, if private physical capital enters also in the production of human capital, the optimal allocation of expenditure depends upon the parameters characterizing *both* the production and human capital technologies. However, this is

In the general case where $\nu_2 > 0$, the solution to (36) yields

$$\upsilon_I^* = \frac{\alpha\nu_1 + (\alpha+\beta)\nu_2}{(\alpha+\beta)(\nu_1+\nu_2)} \in (0, 1), \tag{38}$$

which is the formula derived in Agénor (2008*a*, 2011*a*). The key difference, however, is that in contrast to the case where $\nu_2 = 0$, the optimal share of spending on infrastructure investment depends now not only on the parameters characterizing the goods production technology, but also on those characterizing the human capital technology, $\nu_1$ and $\nu_2$. By implication, the following result can be established:

**Result 2.4.** *An increase in the elasticity $\nu_1$ ($\nu_2$) in the human capital technology lowers (increases) the growth-maximizing share of spending on infrastructure investment.*

And naturally enough, if government spending on education services has no effect on the production of human capital (so that $\nu_1 = 0$), then $\upsilon_I^* = 1$.

## 6| Extensions

The basic model developed in the previous sections can be extended in a variety of directions. This section focuses on an endogenous effect of infrastructure on child-rearing costs and parental time allocated to education, and the effect of schooling quality on the allocation of public spending between education and infrastructure.

### 6.1| Endogenous Rearing Costs

In the foregoing discussion, it was assumed that the fraction of income allocated to child rearing, $\theta$, is fixed. Suppose instead that $\theta$ depends negatively on the public capital ratio, so that $\theta = \theta(k_t^I)$, with now $\theta' < 0$. For instance, part of the cost of rearing a child may consist of transportation costs; with improved access to roads, these costs may fall—at least over a certain range.[18]

To illustrate the implications of an endogenous $\theta$, it is sufficient to consider the case where $\mu = 1$. First, given that the fraction of time parents allocate to home tutoring, $\varepsilon$, is fixed, labor supply is not affected. Second, equation (26) can now be written in the form

$$F(J, \upsilon_I) = [1-\theta(J)]J - \frac{\varphi\upsilon_I\tau}{(1-\tau)\sigma} = 0.$$

hard to rationalize if education is a public good, as assumed here. In the absence of that effect, their formula ((22*b*), p. 68), is essentially (37).

[18] A somewhat related idea, proposed by Cavalcanti and Tavares (2011), is that public *spending* may reduce the per child cost of raising children. However, given their focus on explaining the size of government, they do not pursue in any detail the implications of this assumption for long-term growth and (as discussed in the next chapter) time allocation decisions.

Intuitively, an increase in the share of investment in infrastructure has now two opposite effects on the public-private capital ratio. On the one hand, it raises that ratio directly, as before; on the other, however, it tends to lower it, because the share of spending on child rearing falls, thereby increasing savings and magnifying congestion effects. However, applying the implicit function theorem shows that $dJ/d\upsilon_I = -(\partial F/\partial \upsilon_I)/(\partial F/\partial J) > 0$. Thus, in the present case, the fall in rearing costs mitigates the direct effect but does not reverse it. From (30), the effect of an increase in infrastructure investment on growth not only remains positive, it is magnified by the higher savings associated with lower rearing costs. Chapter 3 will discuss an alternative channel through which endogenous rearing costs may affect growth (through time allocation decisions), this time with a possible adverse effect on growth.

### 6.2| Time Allocation and Infrastructure

In the foregoing discussion it was assumed that all adults allocate a fixed fraction of their time $\varepsilon$ to tutoring their children. In chapters 3 and 5, time allocation will be endogenized and subject to individual choice, first based solely on preferences and the opportunity cost of time, and second by explicitly analyzing the impact of infrastructure on time allocated to home production.

Even in the present setting where $\varepsilon$ is not chosen optimally, a preliminary analysis can be conducted. Suppose indeed that, even though $\varepsilon$ is exogenous from the perspective of each parent, it depends across all individuals on access to (congested) infrastructure services. Electricity for instance may allow parents to use television programs or the Internet for educational purposes. Thus, improved access to infrastructure may raise the *efficiency* of time allocated to tutoring. This relationship can be captured in a simple manner by multiplying $\varepsilon$ in the human capital technology (9) by a coefficient $\xi$, which is positively related to the public-private capital ratio; thus with $\delta^E = 1$ for simplicity,

$$e_{t+1} = \xi(k_t^I)\varepsilon \left(\frac{G_t^E}{\bar{N}}\right)^{\nu_1} (K_t^I)^{\nu_2} E_t^{1-\nu_1-\nu_2},$$

where $\xi' > 0$. The important point here is that the time allocation constraint does not change. To fix ideas, suppose that $\xi(k_t^I) = (k_t^I)^{\vartheta}$, where $\vartheta \in (0, 1)$.

To illustrate the implications of this link, it is again sufficient to consider the case where $\mu = 1$. Given the definition of $\Xi_6$, the dynamic equation (27) becomes

$$e_{t+1}^P = \frac{\varepsilon(\upsilon_E \tau \beta \Xi)^{\nu_1}}{\Xi_2} J^{-\alpha(1-\nu_1)+\nu_2+\vartheta} (e_t^P)^{(1-\beta)(1-\nu_1)-\nu_2},$$

which implies that the stability condition does not change. However, the parameter $\vartheta$ affects the steady-state value of the human capital-private capital ratio; the positive effect of an increase in the share of spending on infrastructure investment on the human capital-private capital ratio and the rate of growth in the steady state is magnified.[19] This provides an additional channel through which infrastructure affects growth. Chapter 5 will consider a more detailed treatment of this issue, by solving explicitly for the optimal allocation of time in a gender-based environment.

## 6.3| Schooling Quality

In the foregoing discussion the quality of education was not discussed. However, as documented by UNESCO (2008) and the United Nations (2010), although in recent years enrollment in primary schools has increased sharply in poor countries (from 58 percent in 2000 to 74 percent in 2007 in sub-Sahara Africa), there are indications that, in many cases, this improvement was accompanied by higher student-teacher ratios and quality deterioration. In 2006, the pupil-to-teacher ratio in primary education was 25 on average for the world and 14 for North America and Western Europe (down from 16 in 1999), but 40 for South and West Asia (up from 37 in 1999) and 45 for sub-Saharan Africa (up from 41 in 1999). This ratio was as high as 52 for Mali and Tanzania, 67 for Mozambique, and 69 for Rwanda. In secondary education, although the pupil-to-teacher ratio remained constant at 18 for the world as a whole between 1999 and 2006, and at 13 for developed countries, in sub-Saharan Africa it rose from 24 to 27 during the same period. As noted by Glewwe and Kremer (2006), shortages of teachers and school buildings in developing countries have resulted not only in very large class sizes but also in double shifts—which shorten the school day for individual pupils and therefore affect the quality of education.

To the extent that school quality lowers the return from investing in education, it may affect potential trade-offs associated with the allocation of public spending between education and infrastructure services. The fact that both components of spending are productive, and that the government faces a balanced budget constraint, makes this issue nontrivial from a growth perspective—particularly for low-income countries, where needs are great in both education and infrastructure. Agénor (2012) addresses these issues in a setting where the quality of education is inversely related to the degree of congestion in schools, which itself is measured in two ways: the proportions of teachers (determined endogenously through the government budget constraint) and students in the population, and the ratio of government spending on education to effective teaching capacity, which is defined as the number of teachers multiplied by the prevailing stock of human capital. A key result of

[19] Note that if it had been assumed that it is "raw" time allocated to child schooling, $\varepsilon$, that depends (negatively) on access to infrastructure services, the impact of an increase in $\upsilon_I$ on growth would be in general ambiguous: the reason is that although a reduction in $\varepsilon$ is beneficial for growth (because it raises the effective supply of labor in market production) it lowers the rate of accumulation of human capital.

the analysis is that the growth-maximizing share of government spending on education services, when the second measure of congestion is used, depends negatively on the degree of congestion in schools. Equivalently, the share of spending on infrastructure is higher. If indeed the externality of public capital on education outcomes is high, this result—which could in principle be derived in the model of this chapter after relevant extensions—means that to improve the quality of education it may be optimal to improve the environment in which schools operate.

However, it is important to note that this result does *not necessarily* imply that spending on education should be reduced; quality problems may be intrinsic to the education sector (being related, for instance, to low teacher pay) and this need to be addressed directly. Note also that in a number of developing countries, perceived deficiencies in the quality of public education has led to a rapid expansion of the *private* education sector—to the point where it may be of equal importance to (if not more important than) the public education sector. A useful extension of the analysis in this chapter would therefore be to consider how the presence of this sector affects optimal public policy, namely, the choice between direct spending on public schools (possibly in combination with spending on some types of infrastructure) and subsidies to private schools.

• • •

This chapter has focused on the links among public capital, knowledge accumulation, and growth. The first part provided a review of the evidence on the various ways through which public capital may affect educational outcomes. A number of microeconomic studies have indeed documented a positive impact of infrastructure services on educational attainment. A better transportation system and a safer road network (particularly in rural areas) help to raise school attendance. Electricity allows more time to study and more opportunities to use electronic equipment and other devices that may improve the learning process. Greater access to safe water and sanitation enhance the health of individuals, increasing their ability to learn. In quantitative terms, the difference that access to infrastructure makes can be sizable. In many countries, the percentage of children living in a household with electricity and attending school tends to be higher than the percentage for those living in a household without electricity.

An extension of the OLG model presented in the previous chapter was then presented. In line with the evidence, the key feature of the extended model is that the production of human capital (an activity in which only the public sector is engaged) requires not only public spending on education services but also access to infrastructure capital. After deriving the balanced growth path, several results were established. It was shown, in particular, that a higher impact of public capital on the rate of human capital accumulation increases the speed of convergence to the steady state. In addition, although an increase in parental time allocated to children's education has a positive effect on the human-private capital ratio in the long run, it has an ambiguous effect on the economy's steady-state growth rate because the net effect on the effective supply of labor is also ambiguous.

The possibility of a trade-off between public spending on education and investment in infrastructure (both of which representing productive categories of expenditure) was also considered. The key issue that the analysis brings to the fore is the fact that even though these expenditure components may be strongly complementary at the microeconomic or sectoral level, they may be substitutes at the macroeconomic level due to the government budget constraint. The question that arises, then, is how to allocate optimally (limited) resources among alternative uses. An explicit formula, which account for various elasticities in the production functions for goods and human capital and may again provide a useful practical benchmark, was derived and used to illustrate the trade-offs involved. Extensions linking public capital, rearing costs, parental time allocated to tutoring, and the quality of education were also considered. These provide alternative channels through which infrastructure may affect economic growth.

## APPENDIX: Stability Conditions and Steady-State Effects with $\mu < 1$

To examine the stability of the dynamic system described in (31), standard techniques can be used (see Azariadis (1993) and Galor (2006)). Let $\mathbf{A}$ denote the matrix of coefficients in (31) and let $\det \mathbf{A}$ denote its determinant and $\mathrm{tr}\mathbf{A}$ its trace. Let $\lambda_j$, $j = 1, 2$ denote the eigenvalues of $\mathbf{A}$; the characteristic polynomial is thus $p(\lambda) = \lambda^2 - \lambda \mathrm{tr}\mathbf{A} + \det \mathbf{A}$. Thus, $p(1) = 1 - \mathrm{tr}\mathbf{A} + \det \mathbf{A}$, whereas $p(-1) = 1 + \mathrm{tr}\mathbf{A} + \det \mathbf{A}$.

For convenience, $a_{ij}$ coefficients are reported here:

$$a_{11} = (1-\beta)(1-\nu_1) - \nu_2,$$

$$a_{12} = -\alpha(1-\nu_1) + \nu_2,$$

$$a_{21} = -\beta(1-\mu) < 0,$$

$$a_{22} = (1-\alpha)(1-\mu) > 0.$$

From assumptions 2.2, $a_{12} < 0$, that is, $\nu_2 < \alpha(1-\nu_1)$; and $\alpha + \beta < 1$, that is, $\alpha < 1 - \beta$. By implication, $\nu_2 < (1-\beta)(1-\nu_1)$. Thus, $a_{11} > 0$.

$$\mathrm{tr}\mathbf{A} = (1-\beta)(1-\nu_1) - \nu_2 + (1-\alpha)(1-\mu) > 0,$$

$$\det \mathbf{A} = (1-\mu)\{[(1-\beta)(1-\nu_1) - \nu_2](1-\alpha) + [\nu_2 - \alpha(1-\nu_1)]\beta\}.$$

To ensure that $\det \mathbf{A} > 0$ requires

$$[(1-\beta)(1-\nu_1)-\nu_2](1-\alpha) > [\alpha(1-\nu_1)-\nu_2]\beta.$$

By manipulating this expression, it can be shown that it boils down to $\nu_1 + \nu_2 < 1$, which corresponds to sssumption 2.1.

Given the signs of $\mathrm{tr}\mathbf{A} = \lambda_1 + \lambda_2$ and $\det \mathbf{A} = \lambda_1\lambda_2$, then $p(-1) > 0$. Now,

$$p(1) = 1 - [(1-\beta)(1-\nu_1)-\nu_2] - (1-\alpha)(1-\mu)$$

$$+(1-\mu)\{[(1-\beta)(1-\nu_1)-\nu_2](1-\alpha)+[\nu_2-\alpha(1-\nu_1)]\beta\}.$$

Even with $\nu_2 = 0$, this expression cannot be easily interpreted. To make progress, note that in terms of the $a_{ij}$ coefficients, $p(1)$ can be written as

$$p(1) = 1 - (a_{11} + a_{22}) + (a_{11}a_{22} - a_{12}a_{21}).$$

To ensure that $p(1)$ is positive requires

$$\frac{(1-a_{11})(1-a_{22})}{a_{12}} > a_{21}, \tag{A1}$$

or equivalently

$$-\frac{1-a_{11}}{a_{12}} < -\frac{a_{21}}{1-a_{22}}.$$

The term on the left of the inequality is the absolute value of the slope of $SS$ whereas the term on the right is the absolute value of the slope of $KK$. Thus, stability requires $KK$ to be steeper than $SS$, as shown in Figure 2.3.

If the condition $p(1) > 0$ holds, the eigenvalues are on the same side of both 1 and $-1$. Moreover, given that $\det \mathbf{A} > 0$, the eigenvalues are of the same sign. With both $a_{21} < 1$ and $a_{22} < 1$, $\mathrm{tr}\mathbf{A}$ cannot exceed 2, that is, $\mathrm{tr}\mathbf{A} \in (-2, 2)$. Consequently, given that $\mathrm{tr}\mathbf{A} > 0$, $\det \mathbf{A} > 0$, the eigenvalues are not only less than unity in absolute terms but actually positive. The steady state is thus a sink (see Azariadis (1993, p. 65)).

To determine the effects of changes in government spending on the steady-state growth rate when $\mu < 1$, note first that from (32) and (33),

$$\mathbf{B}\begin{bmatrix} \ln \tilde{e}^P \\ \ln \tilde{k}^I \end{bmatrix} = \mathbf{C}\begin{bmatrix} \ln \upsilon_E \\ \ln \upsilon_I \end{bmatrix}, \tag{A2}$$

where

$$\underset{2\times 2}{\mathbf{B}} = \begin{bmatrix} (1-a_{11})/a_{12} & -1 \\ \beta(1-\mu)/\Pi & 1 \end{bmatrix}, \quad \underset{2\times 2}{\mathbf{C}} = \begin{bmatrix} -a_{12}^{-1}\nu_1 & 0 \\ 0 & \mu\Pi^{-1} \end{bmatrix}.$$

Solving (A2) using Cramer's rule yields

$$\ln \tilde{e}^P = \frac{1}{\det \mathbf{B}}\begin{vmatrix} -a_{12}^{-1}\nu_1 \ln \upsilon_E & -1 \\ \mu\Pi^{-1}\ln \upsilon_I & 1 \end{vmatrix},$$

$$\ln \tilde{k}^I = \frac{1}{\det \mathbf{B}} \begin{vmatrix} (1-a_{11})/a_{12} & -a_{12}^{-1}\nu_1 \ln \upsilon_E \\ \beta(1-\mu)/\Pi & \mu\Pi^{-1}\ln \upsilon_I \end{vmatrix},$$

so that

$$\ln \tilde{e}^P = \frac{\mu\Pi^{-1}\ln \upsilon_I - a_{12}^{-1}\nu_1 \ln \upsilon_E}{\Delta},$$

$$\ln \tilde{k}^I = \frac{(1-a_{11})\mu \ln \upsilon_I + \beta(1-\mu)\nu_1 \ln \upsilon_E}{a_{12}\Delta\Pi},$$

where, given that $\Pi = 1 - a_{22}$ and the stability condition (A1),

$$\Delta = \det \mathbf{B} = (1-a_{11})a_{12}^{-1} + \beta(1-\mu)\Pi^{-1} > 0.$$

From these expressions, and the fact that $d\ln y/dx = (d\ln y/d\ln x) \times (d\ln x/dx)$, the impact of budget-neutral shocks to $\upsilon_E$ and $\upsilon_I$ on $\ln \tilde{e}^P$ and $\ln \tilde{k}^I$ can be calculated. Note that $d\ln \tilde{k}^I/d\upsilon_E = 0$ if $\mu = 1$ and that because $\Delta < 0$ in that case, $d\ln \tilde{e}^P/d\upsilon_I < 0$, as indicated in the text.

From (34), growth effects can be calculated as

$$\frac{d\ln(1+\gamma)}{d\upsilon_h} = \alpha\left(\frac{d\ln \tilde{k}^I}{d\upsilon_h}\right) + \beta\left(\frac{d\ln \tilde{e}^P}{d\upsilon_h}\right), \quad \upsilon_h = E, I.$$

# 3 | Public Capital and Health

> The annual loss of life from filth and bad ventilation are greater than the loss from death or wounds in which the country has been engaged in modern times...
>
> The primary and most important measures, and at the same time the most practicable, and within the recognized province of public administration, are drainage, the removal of all refuse of habitations, streets, and roads, and the improvements of the supplies of water...
>
> That by the combinations of all these arrangements it is probable that... an increase of 13 years at least, may be extended to the whole of the labouring classes.
>
> —E. Chadwick, *The Sanitary Conditions of the Labouring Population* (1842)

The effect of health on economic growth has been the subject of much recent empirical and analytical research. A key premise of the literature is that good health enhances worker productivity and promotes growth. Accounting for health factors in models of economic growth is thus important for studies focusing on developing countries—particularly the low-income ones, where health indicators are the weakest. An important issue in that regard relates to the fact that the provision of health services, while complementary to other services at the microeconomic level, requires the use of public resources. At the macroeconomic level, there is therefore a potential trade-off between health services and other services that governments can provide—such as education, security, legal protection, and, most important for the present purpose, access to infrastructure. Understanding the nature of these trade-offs is thus critical for public policy.

This chapter begins with a review of the evidence regarding the relationship among health and growth, infrastructure and health, and health persistence. It then presents a two-period framework that extends the model presented in chapter 1 so as to capture the key interactions between infrastructure and health. A novel feature of the analysis is that time allocation is endogenously determined. After solving for, and analyzing the properties of, the balanced growth path, a three-period framework with endogenous fertility is presented. The model accounts for the persistence in health between childhood and adulthood. Alternative approaches to endogenizing life expectancy are then briefly reviewed. The chapter concludes with a discussion of the interactions between health and education, and how these interactions can magnify the impact of public capital on growth.

# 1| Background

## 1.1| Health and Economic Growth

The evidence documenting a significant effect of health on growth is quite substantial. Bloom et al. (2004), in a sample consisting of both developing and industrial countries, found that good health (proxied by life expectancy) has a sizable, positive effect on economic growth. A one-year improvement in the population's life expectancy contributes to an increase in the long-run growth rate of up to 4 percentage points. Sala-i-Martin et al. (2004) also found that initial life expectancy has a positive effect on growth, whereas the prevalence of malaria as well the fraction of a country's territory located within geographical tropics (which may act as a proxy for exposure to tropical diseases) are both negatively correlated with growth.

Jamison et al. (2005), using a sample of 53 countries, found that improvements in health (as measured by the survival rate of males aged between 15 and 60) accounted for about 11 percent of growth during the period 1965–90. In countries like Bolivia, Honduras, and Thailand, health improvements added about half of a percentage point to the annual rate of growth in income per capita. Even more significant, according to the estimation results of Gyimah-Brempong and Wilson (2004), between 22 and 30 percent of the transition growth rate of per capita income in a "typical" country in sub-Saharan Africa can be attributed to health factors. Along the same lines, D. Weil (2007), using microeconomic data (such as height and adult survival rates) to build a measure of average health, found that as much as 22.6 percent of the cross-country variation in income per capita is the result of health factors—roughly the same as the share accounted for by human capital from education, and larger than the share accounted for by physical capital.

Conversely, Lorentzen et al. (2008) found that countries with a high rate of adult mortality also tend to experience low rates of growth—possibly because when people expect to die relatively young, they have fewer incentives to save and invest in the acquisition of skills. They also found that the estimated effect of high adult mortality on growth is large enough to explain Africa's poor economic performance between 1960 and 2000. Indeed, in the 40 countries with the highest adult mortality rates in their sample of 98 countries, all are in sub-Saharan Africa, except 3.

Evidence on the adverse effects of particular diseases is quite significant as well. McCarthy et al. (1999) found that malaria morbidity is negatively correlated with the growth rate of output per capita across countries. In Sub-Saharan Africa, a one-percentage-point in the morbidity rate associated with the disease tends to reduce the annual growth rate per capita by an average of 0.55 percent. In the same vein, estimates by the United Nations (2005) suggest that malaria (which each year claims the lives of 1 million people in poor countries and infects 300 million more) has slowed economic growth in sub-Saharan Africa by 1.3 percentage points a year. According to a report on HIV/AIDS by the same institution, in sub-Saharan Africa—a region where on average 7 out of 100 adults, and up to a quarter of the population in the southern part of the continent, are HIV positive—the epidemic has reduced annual growth rates by anywhere between 0.5 to 1.6 percentage points (see UNAIDS (2004)). McDonald and Roberts (2006) found similar results; HIV prevalence and the proportion of the population at risk of malaria tend to affect negatively health outcomes in Sub-Saharan Africa, and through that channel the rate of economic growth. The World Health Organization (2007) estimated the economic effects of a global influenza pandemic as potentially devastating for many poor countries.

The link among nutrition, health, and growth has also received much emphasis in recent research (see Strauss and Thomas (1998) and Hoddinott et al. (2005)). Inadequate consumption of protein and energy as well as deficiencies in key micronutrients (such as iodine, vitamin A, and iron) are key factors in the morbidity and mortality of children and adults. The United Nations estimated that 55 percent of the nearly 12 million deaths each year among children under five years old in the developing world are associated with malnutrition (Broca and Stamoulis (2003)). Lack of vitamin A causes half a million children to go blind every year, whereas shortage of iron (anemia) weakens the immune system. Iron deficiency is also associated with malaria, intestinal parasitic infestations, and chronic infections. Moreover, the chronically undernourished may be so unproductive that they do not get hired at any wage. If poor people are so badly nourished that they are too weak to perform up to their physical potential, a "nutrition-based" poverty and low-growth trap may emerge. Inadequate nutrition may thus engender poor health, low productivity, and continued low incomes.[1] Malnutrition reduces life expectancy and may therefore have an adverse, indirect effect on growth. Wang and Taniguchi (2003) found indeed that better nutrition—in addition to improving human welfare—enhances growth, directly through the impact of nutrition on labor productivity, as well as indirectly through improvements in life expectancy and possibly by speeding up the adoption of new production techniques.

An important issue with the existing literature is that the direction of causality is not always clearly established. By raising real incomes and tax revenues, in particular, economic growth may enable individuals and the government to spend more on health services. In a study based on panel data for Indian states, Gupta and Mitra (2004) found indeed evidence of bidirectional effects. There may also be nonlinearities in the relationship between health and growth, as documented for instance by Benos (2005) for

[1] See Mayer-Foulkes (2005) and the discussion in chapter 6. As discussed by Galor and Mayer-Foulkes (2004), and later in this chapter, the effect of health on growth may operate through human capital accumulation.

industrial countries. More important for the purpose at hand, much of the literature uses single-equation estimation to assess the impact of health on growth. As argued by Finlay (2007), this may lead to *underestimation* of the impact of health because it does not account for indirect effects—most notably the benefits of health for education. Individuals who are healthier live longer, and this in turn creates incentives to invest more in education. As a result it is possible for the causality between health and growth to go both ways: better health may enhance growth by improving productivity, and higher growth may allow better human capital formation. In the same vein, single-equation estimation may lead to *overestimation* of the impact of health. If access to public capital is critical to improve health outcomes, as discussed next, these regressions may overstate the contribution of health factors to growth.

### 1.2| Infrastructure and Health

It is now well recognized that infrastructure may have a sizable impact on health outcomes in developing countries—and thus possibly account in part for the positive effect of health on economic growth, as discussed earlier. As documented in the various microeconomic studies summarized by Brenneman and Kerf (2002), access to *safe water and sanitation* helps to improve health, as recognized long ago by Edwin Chadwick.[2] This is particularly so for children. Studies suggest that in some African cities, the death rate of children under five is about twice as high in slums (where water and sanitation services are poor, if not nonexistent), compared to other urban communities. According to the World Health Organization, in 2000 diarrhea caused approximately 22 percent of under-five child mortality deaths (about 10 million) worldwide. About 1.5 million child deaths (or 88 percent of those from diarrhea) are caused by ingestion of unsafe water, inadequate availability of water for hygiene, and lack of access to sanitation. Worldwide, 1.8 million people die every year from inadequate sanitation.

Formal studies by Behrman and Wolfe (1987), Lavy et al. (1996), Lee et al. (1997), Shi (2000), Newman et al. (2002), Leipziger et al. (2003), Wagstaff and Claeson (2004, pp. 170–74), and Gamper-Rabindran et al. (2010) found indeed that access to clean water and sanitation infrastructure helps to reduce infant mortality. In their study of Bolivia, for instance, Newman et al. (2002) found that investments in water systems led to declines in under-five mortality that were similar in size to those associated with health interventions. In the same vein, Galiani et al. (2009) examined the effects of the expansion of the water network in urban shantytowns in Argentina.[3] They found large

[2] Chadwick's work led to the passage, in 1848, of the Public Health Act in England, which among other measures gave boroughs responsibility for drainage, water supply, and paving of roads.

[3] See also Galiani et al. (2005).

reductions in the presence, frequency, and severity of diarrhea episodes among children reached by network expansions relative to a control group. Moreover, expanded connections induced savings in water expenditures (and time), as these families were able to substitute piped water for more expensive and distant sources of water provision. These health and savings effects were also important for households that previously had clandestine self-connections to the water network, which were free but of low quality. In a study of Brazil during the period 1980–91, Gamper-Rabindran et al. (2010) found that, when accompanied by a basic level of other public health inputs, greater access to piped water led to a significant decline in the under-one infant mortality rate. Moreover, this effect appears to be nonlinearly related to the level of income or development: at low levels of income, water has a small effect; as income grows, the impact of access to piped water on infant mortality starts to rise rapidly. At sufficiently high levels of income, this impact starts declining and becomes eventually very small.

Greater access to clean water and sanitation also has a significant effect on the incidence of malaria, as documented by McCarthy et al. (1999). Soares (2009) argued that improvements in public infrastructure (namely, the provision of treated water and sewerage services) played a key role in the increase in life expectancy, from 57 to 70 years, recorded in Latin American and Caribbean countries during the period 1960–2000.[4] Even when it does not result in health gains, greater access to clean water through home connections may improve well-being and the quality of life; this is documented for instance by Devoto et al. (2010) in a study of Morocco.

Access to *electricity*, by reducing the cost of boiling water, helps to improve hygiene and health as well, and may help to reduce child mortality.[5] Availability of electricity is also essential for the functioning of hospitals and the delivery of health services. Vaccines, for instance, require continuous and reliable refrigeration to retain their effectiveness. A case in point is the cholera vaccine. Although the Shanchol brand, introduced in 2009, is relatively inexpensive, it must be administered in two doses (with at last one week between) in adults, and three in children. Stockpiling supplies in rural areas may therefore require refrigeration, which is often not available on a sufficient scale. At the time of this writing, one of the key problems that the Global Alliance for Vaccines and Immunization (GAVI) faces in expanding its

[4] Note, however, that these studies do not necessarily account well for the fact that areas with more piped water connections are likely to benefit from other superior, but unobservable, health inputs—such as access to better-equipped medical facilities, more experienced medical personnel, and nutritional supplements.

[5] Wang (2003) found that access to electricity had the greatest impact on decreasing infant mortality in poor countries compared to other significant variables, namely income, access to water and sanitation, vaccination in the first year of life, and the share of health expenditures to GDP. Similarly, access to electricity explained 64 percent of the variation in mortality among children under five.

operations in poor countries is the lack of storage systems, which creates high risks of vaccine wastage and damage.[6]

Getting access to clean energy for cooking in people's homes (as opposed to smoky traditional fuels, such as wood, crop residues, and charcoal) improves health outcomes, by reducing indoor air pollution and the incidence of respiratory illnesses (such as asthma and tuberculosis). According to some estimates, more than half of the population in the developing world still relies on traditional biomass fuels, such as wood and charcoal for cooking and heating (see Saghir (2005) and Rehfuess et al. (2006)). In sub-Saharan Africa alone, the proportion of cooking on biomass is over 90 percent. Traditional sources of energy represent serious health hazards; according to estimates reported by Warwick and Doig (2004), indoor air pollution from the burning of solid fuels kills over 1.6 million people (predominantly women and children) a year.[7] More efficient electric or solar-powered stoves would reduce this death toll, which is almost as great as that caused by unsafe water and sanitation, and greater than that caused by malaria. The environmental benefits (in terms of lower emissions of $CO_2$) would also be substantial, given that in some poor countries a family of five may use up to three tons of wood a year for cooking alone.[8]

Better *transportation networks* also contribute to easier access to health care, particularly in rural areas. Data produced by national Demographic and Health Surveys in sub-Saharan Africa show that a majority of women in rural areas rank distance and inadequate transportation as major obstacles in accessing health care (see African Union (2005)). In Morocco, a program developed in the mid-1990s to expand the network of rural roads led—in addition to reducing production costs and improving access to markets—to a sizable increase in visits to primary health care facilities and clinics (see Levy (2004)). In Malaysia and Sri Lanka, the World Bank (2005*b*, p. 144) found that the dramatic drop in the maternal mortality ratio—from 2,136 in 1930 to 24 in 1996 in Sri Lanka, and from 1,085 in 1933 to 19 in 1997 in Malaysia—was due not only to a sharp increase in medical workers in rural and disadvantaged communities, but also to improved communication and transportation services—which helped to reduce geographic barriers. Transportation (in Malaysia) and transportation subsidies (in Sri Lanka) were provided for emergency visits to health care centers. Moreover, in Malaysia, health programs formed part of integrated rural development efforts that

[6] Lack of transportation may also complicate delivery.

[7] In a study of rural Orissa, India, Duflo et al. (2009) found that over 72 percent of all households in India and 90 percent of households in the country's poorer, rural areas use traditional solid fuels, such as crop residue, cow dung, and firewood to meet their cooking needs. They also found a high correlation between using a traditional stove and having symptoms of respiratory illness, although the direction of causality is not easy to establish.

[8] An example of a company providing cheap and efficient stoves can be found at http://www.envirofit.org/.

included investment in clinics, roads, and schools. A similar approach was followed in Sri Lanka—better roads made it easier to get to rural health facilities, as documented in other countries. At a more formal level, Wagstaff and Claeson (2004, pp. 170–74) found, using cross-section regressions, that road infrastructure (as measured by the length of the paved road network) had a significant effect on a number of health indicators, such as infant and female mortality rates.

### 1.3| Health Persistence

There has been also much research in recent years on the effects of early childhood influences on later life outcomes; studies include Case et al. (2005), Paxson and Schady (2007), Smith (2009), and Grimard et al. (2010).[9] In particular, it has been shown that events before five years old may have a very large long-term impact on adult outcomes: child and family characteristics measured at school entry do as much to explain future outcomes as factors that economists have more traditionally focused on, such as years of education. In a study based on data for Ecuador, Paxson and Schady (2007) for instance found that health measures such as height for age and weight for age are positively related to language development, a measure of cognitive ability. In the same vein, Behrman and Rosenzweig (2004) found that increasing weight at birth raises adult schooling attainment and adult height for babies at most levels of birth weight. In a study of Andhra Pradesh, India, Helmers and Patnam (2011) found that child health at age one influences significantly cognitive abilities at age five. Using data on the malaria-eradication campaigns in the United States (circa 1920) and in Brazil, Colombia, and Mexico (circa 1955), Bleakley (2010*a*) found that, relative to nonmalarious areas, cohorts born after eradication of the disease had higher income as adults than the preceding generation.

The persistent effect of health in childhood on health in adulthood may operate to a significant extent through its impact on educational attainment in early age. Indeed, the available evidence suggests that protein-energy malnutrition during the early stages of a child's life can lead to permanent impairment of central nervous system functions. Folate and iodine deficiency in utero, and iron deficiency during infancy may also cause permanent neurological damage. Adult physical work capacity is thus determined by their entire nutritional history. Consequently, health represents a key inter- and intragenerational mechanism through which poverty is transmitted: people born into poorer families experience poorer childhood health, lower benefits

[9] See Currie (2009) and Almond and Currie (2011) for an overview of the literature on the role of health in the intergenerational transmission of socioeconomic status, with a focus on industrial countries, and Glewwe and Miguel (2008) and Behrman (2009) for a focus on developing countries. The report by the World Health Organization (2005) remains a useful source of data.

from investments in human capital, and poorer health in early adulthood, all of which are associated with lower productivity and earnings in middle age—when children themselves become parents. As discussed in detail in chapter 5, to the extent that health in childhood depends on the time that mothers allocate to child rearing, health dependence gives a crucial role to mothers' time allocation (which itself may depend on access to infrastructure) in shaping the future of their children.

## 2| A Two-Period Framework

Consider, as in chapter 1, an economy populated by three types of agents: households, firms, and the government. Population is constant for now at $N_t = \bar{N}, \forall t$. Households live for two periods and are endowed with one unit of labor services when they are young and zero units when they are old. Capital income accrues to the old only. The government spends now not only on productive investment and unproductive services but also on health; again, it taxes only the young and cannot borrow. Health affects both the utility and the productivity of young individuals. As before, both infrastructure and health services are provided free of charge.

### 2.1| Households

In addition to working, households allocate time, in proportion $\varepsilon_t^H$, to educate themselves about health and taking care of their health needs (going to the hospital, exercising, etc.). When young, all individuals work and care about their health status, $h_t$. Survival from young age to old age is uncertain; the survival rate (that is, one minus the mortality rate) is defined as $p \in (0, 1)$ and is taken as given for the moment. To abstract from unintended bequests, the saving left by agents who do not survive to old age is assumed to be confiscated by the government, which transfers them in lump-sum fashion to surviving members of the same cohort. As shown later, the effective rate of return to saving is thus $(1 + r_{t+1})/p$, where $r_{t+1}$ is the gross rate of return on capital.[10]

Taking care of one's health involves not only time but also a loss of adult consumption equal to a fixed fraction $\theta \in (0, 1)$ of the young's net wage. This loss could be related to the cost of medicines, for instance. Thus, although access to public health services per se is free, maintaining one's health is costly not only in terms of foregone wage income but also in terms of foregone consumption.

[10] See Zhang et al. (2003) for a more general discussion of issues associated with unintended bequests. Alternatively, it could be assumed, as in Zhang and Zhang (2005) for instance, that there is an actuarially fair annuity market through which old-age survivors share the savings plus the interest income left by those who die while young. This gives qualitatively similar results.

Let $\varepsilon_t^W$ denote the amount of time allocated by each agent to market work; the time constraint is thus

$$\varepsilon_t^H + \varepsilon_t^W = 1. \tag{1}$$

The utility function of an agent born at $t$ is specified as

$$U_t = \ln c_t^t + \eta_H \ln h_t + p\frac{\ln c_{t+1}^t}{1+\rho}, \tag{2}$$

where $\rho > 0$, and $\eta_H > 0$ measures the individual's relative preference for health.[11]

Assuming no bequests and no debts to future generations, period-specific budget constraints are now, using (1),

$$c_t^t + s_t = (1-\tau)(1-\theta)(1-\varepsilon_t^H)a_t w_t, \tag{3}$$

$$c_{t+1}^t = (1+r_{t+1})s_t/p, \tag{4}$$

where, as before, $\tau \in (0, 1)$ is the tax rate, $a_t$ is individual labor productivity, and $w_t$ is the *effective* wage rate (again, in terms of efficient units of labor, or productivity-adjusted raw labor). Based on these definitions, the total cost of taking care of one's health, accounting for its opportunity cost, is thus $(\varepsilon_t^H + \theta)a_t w_t$.

Combining (3) and (4), the individual lifetime budget constraint is

$$c_t^t + \frac{pc_{t+1}^t}{1+r_{t+1}} = (1-\tau)(1-\theta)(1-\varepsilon_t^H)a_t w_t. \tag{5}$$

To show that the effective rate of return to saving is $(1+r_{t+1})/p$, let $x_{t+1}$ denote the lump-sum transfer that the government provides to the surviving old agents, $p\bar{N}$. An individual's second-period budget constraint should therefore be

$$c_{t+1}^t = (1+r_{t+1})s_t + x_{t+1}. \tag{6}$$

The total amount of transfers is thus $p\bar{N}x_{t+1}$ and it must be equal to what is "left behind" by those who die, $(1-p)\bar{N}(1+r_{t+1})s_t$. This implies that in equilibrium the transfer per survivor of the same cohort is

$$x_{t+1} = \left(\frac{1-p}{p}\right)(1+r_{t+1})s_t. \tag{7}$$

Combining (6) and (7) gives indeed (4).

[11] With a logarithmic utility function (which is used consistently in this book), utility can be negative. Suppose that utility in the eventuality of death is normalized to zero; then it is possible that today's young could prefer death to surviving to old age. This perverse case, in principle, could be avoided by restricting second-period utility to be strictly positive, for instance by making it also a function of accidental bequests, as in Chakraborty and Das (2005). However, this issue is somewhat tangential to the main point of interest in the present discussion and is ignored for simplicity.

## 2.2| Production of Goods

As in the previous chapters, there is a continuum of identical firms, indexed by $i \in (0, 1)$. They produce a single nonstorable good, which is used either for consumption or investment. Production requires the use of private inputs, effective labor, private capital, $K_t^{P,i}$, and (congested) public infrastructure, $K_t^I$. Effective labor is now defined as $(1-\varepsilon_t^H)A_t N_t^i$, where $A_t$ is average labor productivity.

The production function of individual firm $i$ takes now the form

$$Y_t^i = \left[\frac{K_t^I}{(K_t^P)^\zeta}\right]^\alpha [(1-\varepsilon_t^H)A_t N_t^i]^\beta (K_t^{P,i})^{1-\beta}, \tag{8}$$

where $K_t^P = \int_0^1 K_t^{P,i}$; $\alpha, \zeta > 0$; and $\beta \in (0, 1)$.

Again, each firm's objective is to maximize profits, $\Pi_t^i$, with respect to labor services and private capital, taking $K_t^I$, $K_t^P$, and $A_t$ as given:

$$\max_{N_t^i, K_t^{P,i}} \Pi_t^i = Y_t^i - (r_t + \delta^P)K_t^{P,i} - w_t(1-\varepsilon_t^H)A_t N_t^i.$$

Given that all firms are identical, and that the labor market equilibrium condition requires $\int_0^1 N_t^i di = \bar{N}$, in a symmetric equilibrium the first-order conditions yield

$$w_t = \beta Y_t/(1-\varepsilon_t^H)A_t\bar{N}, \quad r_t = (1-\beta)Y_t/K_t^P - \delta^P, \tag{9}$$

and aggregate output is

$$Y_t = \int_0^1 Y_t^i di = \Xi(k_t^I)^\alpha[(1-\varepsilon_t^H)A_t]^\beta K_t^P, \quad \Xi = \bar{N}^\beta, \tag{10}$$

where again assumption 1.2 in chapter 1, $\beta - \alpha(1-\zeta) = 0$, is imposed to ensure constant returns to private capital and generate long-run growth.[12]

With full depreciation, private capital accumulation is again driven by

$$K_{t+1}^P = I_t. \tag{11}$$

## 2.3| Health Status and Productivity

Health status of each individual depends on the amount of time that he or she invests in own health, $\varepsilon_t^H$ (which includes seeking medical treatment, hygiene, and exercise) and the provision of health services by the government, $H_t^G$:

$$h_t = (\varepsilon_t^H)^\nu \left(\frac{H_t^G}{K_t^P}\right)^{1-\nu}, \tag{12}$$

[12] The condition is the same because *both* the public-private capital ratio and productivity (which depends on health status) are constant in the steady state, as discussed later.

where $\nu \in (0, 1)$. Access to public health services is taken to be congested by the private capital stock. This effect can be justified by assuming for instance that taking children to health facilities is hampered by a more intensive use of roads associated with private sector activity, which is proxied directly by $K_t^P$. Thus, the *delivery* of health services is hampered by excessive private sector use of public infrastructure assets.

Alternatively, it could be assumed that the congestion factor in access to public health services is measured in terms of the number of children in period $t$, $n\bar{N}$, where $n$ is a constant fertility rate, but that the *efficiency* with which these services are delivered depends again on access to congested infrastructure. It is easy to verify that the results would be qualitatively unchanged, as long as an appropriate restriction is imposed on the degree of congestion induced by private capital.[13] To ease the exposition, specification (12) is therefore retained.

In turn, the production of health services by the government exhibits constant returns to scale with respect to the stock of public capital and government spending on health services, $G_t^H$:

$$H_t^G = (K_t^I)^{\varkappa}(G_t^H)^{1-\varkappa}, \tag{13}$$

where $\varkappa \in (0, 1)$. This specification captures, as discussed earlier, the fact that access to infrastructure is critical to produce health services.

Individual productivity, $a_t$, depends solely on health status:

$$a_t = h_t^{\chi}, \tag{14}$$

where $\chi \in (0, 1)$. Thus, healthy individuals are more productive when working, although there are diminishing marginal returns to health. The evidence linking health and productivity is quite compelling. Using a production function approach, Bloom and Canning (2005) for instance found that a one-percentage point increase in adult survival rates raises labor productivity by 2.8 percent.[14] For simplicity, increasing returns in this relationship is abstracted from.[15]

[13] Suppose indeed that the last term in (12) is replaced by $(\varsigma_t H_t^G / n\bar{N})^{1-\nu}$, where $\varsigma_t$ is an efficiency factor defined as $\varsigma_t = [K_t^I / (K_t^P)^{\phi_H}]^{\alpha_H}$, where $\alpha_H, \phi_H > 0$. Rewriting the term $\varsigma_t H_t^G$ as $(\varsigma_t K_t^P)(H_t^G / K_t^P)$, and given that $H_t^G / K_t^P$ is constant in the steady state, ensuring stationarity in health status requires imposing the restriction $\phi_H = 1 + 1/\alpha_H$. Eliminating the scale effect associated with population could be done by assuming for instance that a fraction of adults consists of medical workers.

[14] See also Cole and Neumayer (2006).

[15] As noted earlier, there is strong evidence of a long-term effect of early childhood health on cognitive and physical development that affects productivity as an adult. This effect cannot be captured here, given the two-period nature of model; but it is discussed later on.

### 2.4| Government

In each period, the government invests in infrastructure and spends on health and other (unproductive) items, $G_t^U$. It runs a balanced budget, so that

$$G_t^I + G_t^H + G_t^U = \bar{N}\tau(1 - \varepsilon_t^H)A_t w_t. \tag{15}$$

As in previous chapters, spending shares are all assumed to be constant fractions of government revenues:

$$G_t^h = \upsilon_h \bar{N}\tau(1 - \varepsilon_t^H)A_t w_t, \quad h = I, H, U. \tag{16}$$

Combining (15) and (16) yields therefore

$$\sum \upsilon_h = 1. \tag{17}$$

With full depreciation, and new public capital requiring the combination of both investment and existing infrastructure assets (as discussed in Chapter 1), the stock of public capital evolves as

$$K_{t+1}^I = (\varphi G_t^I)^{\mu}(K_t^I)^{1-\mu}, \tag{18}$$

where again $\mu, \varphi \in (0, 1)$.

### 2.5| Savings-Investment Balance

The asset market clearing condition requires, as before, equality between investment and savings:

$$I_t = \bar{N}s_t. \tag{19}$$

Given the initial capital stocks $K_0^P$ and $K_0^I > 0$, and initial health status $h_0 > 0$, a *competitive equilibrium* is now a sequence of prices $\{w_t, r_{t+1}\}_{t=0}^{\infty}$, allocations $\{c_t^t, c_{t+1}^t, s_t\}_{t=0}^{\infty}$, physical capital stocks $\{K_{t+1}^P, K_{t+1}^I\}_{t=0}^{\infty}$, health status $\{h_{t+1}\}_{t=0}^{\infty}$, a constant tax rate $\tau$, and constant spending shares $\upsilon_I$, $\upsilon_H$, and $\upsilon_U$ such that individuals maximize utility, firms maximize profits, markets clear, and the government budget is balanced. In equilibrium, individual productivity must also be equal to the economy-wide average productivity level, so that $a_t = A_t$. A *balanced growth equilibrium* is a competitive equilibrium in which $c_t^t$, $c_{t+1}^t$, $K_{t+1}^P$, and $K_{t+1}^I$ grow at the constant, endogenous rate $1 + \gamma$, the rate of return on private capital is constant, and health status and productivity are constant.

The requirement that individual health status be constant in equilibrium—as in Osang and Sarkar (2008), for instance—reflects the view that there are limits in the long run as to how much medical science can improve health outcomes.[16]

## 3| Time Allocation and Growth Dynamics

All young individuals maximize (2) subject to (5), (12), and (14) with respect to $c_t^t$, $c_{t+1}^t$, and $\varepsilon_t^H$:

$$\{\varepsilon_t^H, c_t^t, c_{t+1}^t\} = \arg\max \left\{ \ln c_t^t + \eta_H \ln h_t + p\frac{\ln c_{t+1}^t}{1+\rho} \right\},$$

taking $H_t^G$, $K_t^P$, $w_t$, $r_{t+1}$, $\tau$ and $p$ as given; they therefore internalize the impact of their decisions regarding time allocation on their health status and productivity.

The first-order conditions are

$$1/c_t^t = \lambda_t, \tag{20}$$

$$1/(1+\rho)c_{t+1}^t = \lambda_t/(1+r_{t+1}), \tag{21}$$

$$\frac{\eta_H \nu}{\varepsilon_t^H} = \lambda_t(1-\tau)(1-\theta)\left[1 - \nu\chi\left(\frac{1-\varepsilon_t^H}{\varepsilon_t^H}\right)\right] a_t w_t, \tag{22}$$

where $\lambda_t$ denote the Lagrange multiplier associated with (5). Equations (20) and (21) yield the familiar Euler equation,

$$\frac{c_{t+1}^t}{c_t^t} = \frac{1+r_{t+1}}{1+\rho}. \tag{23}$$

Substituting (23) in the intertemporal budget constraint (5) yields

$$c_t^t = \left[\frac{1+\rho}{(1+\rho)+p}\right](1-\tau)(1-\theta)(1-\varepsilon_t^H)a_t w_t, \tag{24}$$

so that

$$s_t = \sigma(1-\tau)(1-\theta)(1-\varepsilon_t^H)a_t w_t, \tag{25}$$

where

$$\sigma = \frac{p}{(1+\rho)+p} \in (0, 1) \tag{26}$$

is the propensity to save, which now depends on the survival probability $p$.

Substituting (20) in equation (22) and using (24) yields

$$\frac{(1-\sigma)\eta_H \nu}{\varepsilon_t^H} = \frac{1}{1-\varepsilon_t^H} - \frac{\nu\chi}{\varepsilon_t^H},$$

[16] See Agénor (2009*a*) for a more detailed discussion. The important implication is that health (unlike knowledge, as discussed in chapter 2) cannot by itself be an engine of permanent growth.

or equivalently

$$\varepsilon_t^H = \frac{\nu[(1-\sigma)\eta_H + \chi]}{1+\nu[(1-\sigma)\eta_H + \chi]} < 1, \tag{27}$$

which is constant at $\tilde{\varepsilon}^H$, $\forall t$. Note that $\varepsilon_t^H$ also depends on the savings rate, in addition to the preference parameter $\eta_H$, and the "technology" parameters $\nu$ and $\chi$.

Equations (25) and (27) yield the following results, which will prove useful later:

**Result 3.1.** *An increase in the survival probability, p, raises the propensity to save, $\sigma$, and reduces time allocated to health care, $\tilde{\varepsilon}^H$.*

By (1), of course, the second result means that time allocated to market work increases in line with the savings rate. A higher survival rate, ceteris paribus, induces the young to save more to finance consumption in old age. This is the Modigliani-Brumberg life-cycle effect identified in a number of studies, including Blackburn and Cipriani (2002) and Zhang and Zhang (2005), and it is consistent with the evidence reported in Kinugasa and Mason (2007), among others. In the present case, there is an additional effect: an increase in the survival rate also raises labor supply, which is matched by a reduction in time allocated to health care.[17]

Now, to study the dynamics in this economy, note first that using (25), and substituting for $w_t$ from (9), the equilibrium condition (19) combined with (11) yields

$$K_{t+1}^P = \bar{N}s_t = (1-\theta)(1-\tau)\sigma\beta Y_t. \tag{28}$$

Substituting for $Y_t$ in this expression using (10), as well as (14), yields

$$\frac{K_{t+1}^P}{K_t^P} = \Xi_2 (k_t^I)^{\alpha} h_t^{\chi\beta}, \tag{29}$$

where $\Xi_2 = (1-\theta)(1-\tau)\sigma\beta\Xi(1-\tilde{\varepsilon}^H)^{\beta} > 0$.

Similarly, from (9), (16), and (18),

$$K_{t+1}^I = (\varphi\upsilon_I\tau\beta Y_t)^{\mu}(K_t^I)^{1-\mu} = (\varphi\upsilon_I\tau\beta)^{\mu}\left(\frac{Y_t}{K_t^P k_t^I}\right)^{\mu} K_t^I. \tag{30}$$

[17] Note that even if $\eta_H = 0$ (health status brings no utility), it is still optimal to allocate time to own health, $\tilde{\varepsilon}^H = \nu\chi/(1+\nu\chi)$, although in that case the savings rate has no impact on the solution. It is also optimal to allocate time to own health if $\chi = 0$ (productivity does not depend on health, which therefore has no effect on wages), as long as health status brings utility. A corner solution ($\tilde{\varepsilon}^H = 0$) obtains only if $\nu = 0$.

Using again (10) to eliminate $Y_t$, together with (14), yields

$$\frac{K_{t+1}^I}{K_t^I} = \Xi_3 (k_t^I)^{-\mu(1-\alpha)} h_t^{\mu\chi\beta}, \tag{31}$$

where $\Xi_3 = [\varphi \upsilon_I \tau \beta \Xi (1 - \tilde{\varepsilon}^H)^\beta]^\mu$.

Combining (29) and (31) yields

$$k_{t+1}^I = \frac{\Xi_3 (k_t^I)^{-\mu(1-\alpha)} h_t^{\mu\chi\beta}}{\Xi_2 (k_t^I)^\alpha h_t^{\chi\beta}} k_t^I = \left(\frac{\Xi_3}{\Xi_2}\right) (k_t^I)^{(1-\alpha)(1-\mu)} h_t^{-\chi\beta(1-\mu)}. \tag{32}$$

The next step is to eliminate $h_t$ from this expression. From (9), (12), (13), and (16),

$$h_t = (\tilde{\varepsilon}^H)^\nu [(k_t^I)^\varkappa \left(\frac{G_t^H}{K_t^P}\right)^{1-\varkappa}]^{1-\nu} = (\tilde{\varepsilon}^H)^\nu [(k_t^I)^\varkappa \left(\frac{\upsilon_H \tau \beta Y_t}{K_t^P}\right)^{1-\varkappa}]^{1-\nu},$$

so that, using (10) and (14),

$$h_t = (\tilde{\varepsilon}^H)^\nu (\upsilon_H \tau \beta)^{(1-\varkappa)(1-\nu)} [(k_t^I)^\varkappa \{\Xi (1 - \tilde{\varepsilon}^H)^\beta (k_t^I)^\alpha h_t^{\chi\beta}\}^{1-\varkappa}]^{1-\nu},$$

which can be solved for $h_t$:

$$h_t = \Xi_4 (k_t^I)^\Omega, \tag{33}$$

where

$$\Theta = \chi\beta(1-\varkappa)(1-\nu) \in (0, 1),$$

$$\Omega = \frac{[\varkappa + \alpha(1-\varkappa)](1-\nu)}{1-\Theta} > 0,$$

$$\Xi_4 = (\tilde{\varepsilon}^H)^{\nu/(1-\Theta)} [(\upsilon_H \tau \beta) \Xi (1 - \tilde{\varepsilon}^H)^\beta]^{(1-\varkappa)(1-\nu)/(1-\Theta)}.$$

Intuitively, public capital affects health status both directly, through its impact on the production of health services, and indirectly, through its impact on output, government revenues, and health spending. Because health itself affects also output (through productivity), its initial impact can be magnified. This translates into the possibility that $\Omega$ may exceed unity, implying in that case a convex relationship between $k_t^I$ and $h_t$.

Substituting (33) in (32) yields

$$k_{t+1}^I = \Phi(k_t^I) = \Xi_5 (k_t^I)^{(1-\mu)[(1-\alpha) - \Omega\chi\beta]}, \tag{34}$$

where

$$\Xi_5 = \left(\frac{\Xi_3}{\Xi_2}\right) \Xi_4^{-\chi\beta(1-\mu)}.$$

Stability of the adjustment process requires

$$|(1-\mu)[(1-\alpha) - \Omega\chi\beta]| < 1. \tag{35}$$

Consider first the case where $\chi = 0$, so that productivity is constant and independent of health. Then the stability condition boils down to $(1-\mu)(1-\alpha) < 1$, which is exactly the condition derived in chapter 1.

With $\chi > 0$, a sufficient (although not necessary) condition for (35) to hold is $(1-\alpha) - \Omega\chi\beta < 1$, or equivalently $-(\alpha + \Omega\chi\beta) < 0$. Given that $\Omega > 0$, this condition is always satisfied.

From (10), (14), (28), and (33),

$$Y_{t+1} = \Xi(1-\tilde{\varepsilon}^H)^\beta (k_{t+1}^I)^\alpha [\Xi_4 (k_{t+1}^I)^\Omega]^{\chi\beta} (1-\theta)(1-\tau)\sigma\beta Y_t,$$

which implies that the steady-state growth rate of output is

$$1+\gamma = \Xi(1-\tilde{\varepsilon}^H)^\beta \Xi_4^{\chi\beta} (\tilde{k}^I)^{\alpha+\Omega\chi\beta} (1-\theta)(1-\tau)\sigma\beta, \tag{36}$$

where, from (34),

$$\tilde{k}^I = \Xi_5^{1/\{1-(1-\mu)[(1-\alpha)-\Omega\chi\beta]\}}. \tag{37}$$

Of particular interest here is the elasticity of output of health services with respect to public capital, $\varkappa$. As can be inferred from (35), because a higher value of $\varkappa$ raises $\Omega$, it enhances the stability of the model. Intuitively, when $\varkappa$ is high, an initial increase in the public capital stock raises significantly the supply of health services, which in turn raises labor productivity and output—thereby magnifying the impact of an increase in access to infrastructure services on total factor productivity. Because higher output raises tax revenues, and thus further stimulates investment in infrastructure and spending on health services, the speed of convergence is faster.

Figure 3.1 illustrates the adjustment process. The panel on the right-hand side is similar to Figure 1.1, whereas the panel on the left-hand side shows curve $HH$, the relationship between the public-private capital ratio and health, as summarized in (33). The figure assumes that $\Omega > 1$, implying that $HH$ is convex. The equilibrium is initially at points $E$ and $B$.

Note also that the model implies that the growth rate depends on the probability of survival (or equivalently, life expectancy). However, an increase in the survival rate has an ambiguous effect on the growth rate, as can be inferred from results 3.1. On the one hand, it raises the steady-state growth rate because it increases savings. This, in turn, lowers time allocated to health. Even though, by implication of the time constraint (1), time devoted to market work increases (thereby raising labor supply), the reduction in time allocated to health reduces productivity and hampers growth. Thus, accounting for the fact that time devoted to health is productive (and depends on the savings rate) yields an ambiguous effect of life expectancy on growth. This result may help to explain conflicting results in the empirical literature on health and economic growth, and possible differences across studies in the magnitude of the effect of life expectancy on growth and standards of living (see Acemoglu and Johnson (2007), Finlay (2007) and Ashraf et al. (2008)).

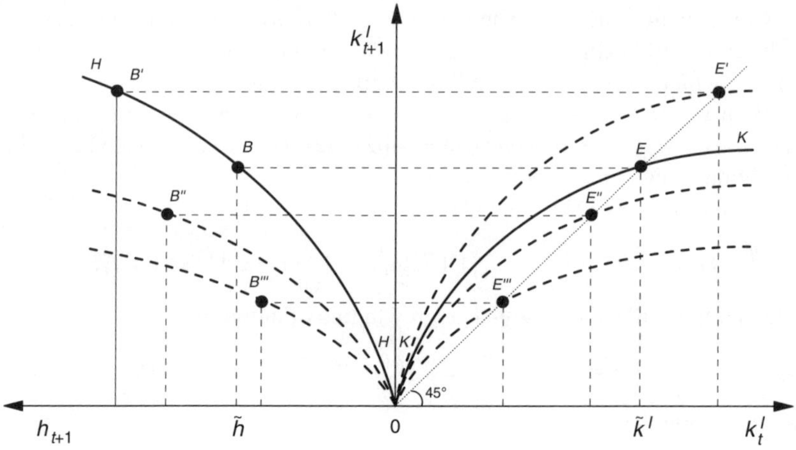


Figure 3.1. Dynamics of the Public-Private Capital Ratio and Health Status.

## 4| Public Spending, Growth, and Human Welfare

A budget-neutral increase in the share of investment on infrastructure ($d\upsilon_I + d\upsilon_U = 0$) leads to an upward shift in $KK$ in Figure 3.1 with no shift in $HH$, given that (as can be inferred from (33)) health status does not depend directly on $\upsilon_I$. The equilibrium shifts therefore from $E$ to $E'$, and from $B$ to $B'$. The public-private capital ratio rises, health status improves, and the steady-state growth rate unambiguously increases. Formally, from (33), (36), and (37),

$$\left.\frac{d\ln\tilde{k}^I}{d\upsilon_I}\right|_{d\upsilon_I+d\upsilon_U=0} = \frac{\upsilon_I^{-1}}{1-(1-\mu)[(1-\alpha)-\Omega\chi\beta]} > 0,$$

$$\left.\frac{d\ln\tilde{h}}{d\upsilon_I}\right|_{d\upsilon_I+d\upsilon_U=0} = \Omega\left.\frac{d\ln\tilde{k}^I}{d\upsilon_I}\right|_{d\upsilon_I+d\upsilon_U=0} > 0,$$

$$\left.\frac{d\ln(1+\gamma)}{d\upsilon_I}\right|_{d\upsilon_I+d\upsilon_U=0} = (\alpha+\Omega\chi\beta)\left.\frac{d\ln\tilde{k}^I}{d\upsilon_I}\right|_{d\upsilon_I+d\upsilon_U=0} > 0.$$

These results are of course consistent with those reported in chapter 1, given that there is no trade-off among components of government spending, and both health and public capital contribute positively to growth by construction.

More interestingly, consider now a budget-neutral increase in the share of spending on health ($d\upsilon_H + d\upsilon_U = 0$). Formally, from (33), (36), and (37) again,

$$\left.\frac{d\ln\tilde{k}^I}{d\upsilon_H}\right|_{d\upsilon_H+d\upsilon_U=0} = \frac{-\chi\beta(1-\mu)(1-\varkappa)(1-\nu)}{\upsilon_H\{1-(1-\mu)[(1-\alpha)-\Omega\chi\beta]\}(1-\Theta)} < 0,$$

$$\left.\frac{d\ln\tilde{h}}{d\upsilon_H}\right|_{d\upsilon_H+d\upsilon_U=0} = \frac{(1-\varkappa)(1-\nu)}{\upsilon_H(1-\Theta)} + \Omega\left.\frac{d\ln\tilde{k}^I}{d\upsilon_H}\right|_{d\upsilon_H+d\upsilon_U=0} \gtrless 0,$$

$$\left.\frac{d\ln(1+\gamma)}{d\upsilon_H}\right|_{d\upsilon_H+d\upsilon_U=0} = \frac{\chi\beta(1-\varkappa)(1-\nu)}{\upsilon_H(1-\Theta)} + (\alpha+\Omega\chi\beta)\left.\frac{d\ln\tilde{k}^I}{d\upsilon_H}\right|_{d\upsilon_H+d\upsilon_U=0} \gtrless 0.$$

Graphically, as also illustrated in Figure 3.1, and as can be inferred from (33) and (34), this policy leads now to an outward shift in $HH$ and a downward shift in $KK$. Thus, the public-private capital ratio always falls. There are now two possible outcomes. If the downward shift in $KK$ is not too large (with a shift in the equilibrium value of the public-private capital ratio from $E$ to $E''$), health status *improves*, with the steady-state value of $h$ moving from $B$ to $B''$. The net effect on growth is ambiguous in that case.

However, if the reduction in the public-private capital ratio is large, and the steady-state public-private capital ratio drops from $E$ to $E'''$, the equilibrium value of health status may actually *fall*, from $B$ to $B'''$, or possibly from $B$ to $B''''$ only, if the shift in $HH$ is more significant. Intuitively, if infrastructure services have a significant effect on the production of health services by the government, a large drop in the public-private capital ratio can eventually prove detrimental to the health status of individuals—even though, at the same time, public spending on health increases. The net effect on growth is unambiguously negative in this case. Of course, this outcome can only occur if $\nu < 1$; with $\nu = 1$, as can be inferred from (33), $\Omega = 0$ and health status is independent of the public-private capital ratio.

By implication, a budget-neutral increase in the share of spending on health that is matched by a reduction in spending on infrastructure ($d\upsilon_H + d\upsilon_I = 0$) makes the possibility of a deterioration in health status and lower growth in the long run more likely, because it implies a further downward shift in $KK$. The implications of this result for optimal spending allocation are discussed next.

## 5| Optimal Spending Allocation

The foregoing discussion suggests that, because there is a trade-off between alternative uses of productive government spending, there is a nontrivial optimal allocation problem—just as occurred with infrastructure investment and education spending in chapter 2.

Suppose again that the government's objective is to maximize growth. Using (36) and (37), it is immediately obvious that the optimal value of

$\upsilon_I$ is unity if financing is through unproductive spending, as discussed in chapter 1.

Consider instead the case where initially $\upsilon_U = 0$, so that from (17), $\upsilon_I + \upsilon_H = 1$. Again, to illustrate the nature of the solution, it is sufficient to consider the case where $\mu = 1$. Using this condition, and using expressions (36) and (37), the condition for determining the optimal (growth-maximizing) share of spending on infrastructure is

$$\frac{\alpha + \Omega\chi\beta}{\upsilon_I} - \frac{\Theta}{(1-\Theta)(1-\upsilon_I)} = 0,$$

which can be solved for $\upsilon_I$:

$$\upsilon_I^* = \frac{(\alpha + \Omega\chi\beta)(1-\Theta)}{(\alpha + \Omega\chi\beta)(1-\Theta) + \Theta} \in (0, 1). \tag{38}$$

Note first that for $\chi = 0$ (in which case $\Theta = 0$ as well) this expression implies that $\upsilon_I^* = 1$, as established in result 1.4 in chapter 1. Thus, if individual productivity (which is the main channel through which public spending on health affects growth) does not depend on health status, then it is optimal to allocate all tax resources to infrastructure investment. The same result holds if health status does not depend on the supply of health services ($\nu = 1$) or if the production of health services is independent of government expenditure on health ($\varkappa = 1$).

Second, for $\varkappa = 0$, the following result can be derived:

**Result 3.2.** *If the production of health services does not depend on access to public capital ($\varkappa = 0$), the optimal share of spending on infrastructure is*

$$\upsilon_I^* = \frac{\alpha}{\alpha + \chi\beta(1-\nu)}.$$

This expression is quite intuitive and can be put in parallel with the optimal allocation rules derived in Chapter 1 (in the case of two productive capital goods, Result 1.5) and Chapter 2 (formula (37)). Essentially, the optimal share of spending on infrastructure should be set equal to the elasticity of output with respect to public capital, relative to the sum of that elasticity and what may be labeled the *effective* elasticity of output with respect to health spending in the production of goods. The latter is a combination of three parameters: the sensitivity of health status with respect to health spending, $1-\nu$ (given that with $\varkappa = 0$, $H_t^G = G_t^H$); the sensitivity of productivity with respect to health status, $\chi$; and the sensitivity of output to effective labor, $\beta$.

From (38) the following result can also be established:

**Result 3.3.** *The larger the impact of public capital on the production of health services (the higher $\varkappa$ is), the higher the optimal share of spending on infrastructure.*

Although tedious to derive, this result is fairly intuitive.

## 6| A Three-Period Framework with Endogenous Fertility

The foregoing analysis is now extended to a three-period setting, with an explicit distinction between the health status of children and adults. The reason for doing so is that the determinants of adult and child mortality are in general different, with mortality reductions in developing countries often translating into rising child survival rates (see Cutler et al. (2006)). The distinction between health in childhood and health in adulthood allows now an explicit analysis of health persistence, a well-documented fact, as discussed earlier. Fertility and thus population growth are now also treated as endogenous. However, to avoid unduly complicating the analysis, it will abstract from survival risk from childhood to adulthood—despite its empirical importance in developing countries.[18]

Individuals now live for three periods: childhood, adulthood, and old age. In the first period of life, children are used only in a nonmarket production activity at home, which brings no direct utility. In the second period of life each individual, by the Virgin Mary hypothesis, gives birth unaided to $n_t$ children, where $n_t$ is the growth rate of the population. They are endowed with one unit of labor, which is allocated to rearing children, $n_t\varepsilon_t^R$ (that is, $\varepsilon_t^R$ units of time on each of them) and market work, $\varepsilon_t^W$. Thus, time allocated to taking care of own health is ignored.[19] They retire in the third period.

The time allocation constraint (1) is now replaced by

$$\varepsilon_t^W + n_t\varepsilon_t^R = 1, \tag{39}$$

whereas the utility function (2) takes now the form

$$U_{t+1} = \ln c_{t+1}^t + \eta_N \ln n_{t+1}h_{t+1}^C + p\frac{\ln c_{t+2}^t}{1+\rho}, \tag{40}$$

where $\eta_N > 0$ measures the preference for healthy children, measured by multiplying the fertility rate (the total number of children per individual), $n_{t+1}$, by the health status of a child, $h_{t+1}^C$.

In the first period of life, children do not consume directly, but parents must spend a fraction $\theta^R \in (0, 1)$ of their after-tax income on rearing each child. The period-specific budget constraints are now

$$c_{t+1}^t + s_{t+1} = (1 - \theta^R n_{t+1})(1-\tau)a_{t+1}\varepsilon_{t+1}^W w_{t+1}, \tag{41}$$

[18] See Agénor (2009*a*) for an explicit analysis of survival between childhood and adulthood, in addition to survival from adulthood to old age, in an extension of the present model. However, an increase in the survival rate between childhood and adulthood has no effect on growth in that model. By contrast, in Ehrlich and Lui (1991) the two survival rates have qualitatively similar effects on growth—with a stronger effect if survival improves in childhood rather than at a later stage. See also Kalemli-Ozcan (2003, 2008) for explicit attempts to incorporate uncertainty about surviving children.

[19] This is for simplicity only, given that the issue of optimal time allocation to own health was considered in the previous section.

$$c_{t+2}^{t} = (1 + r_{t+2})s_{t+1}/p, \tag{42}$$

which imply that the consolidated budget constraint becomes

$$c_{t+1}^{t} + \frac{pc_{t+2}^{t}}{1 + r_{t+2}} = (1 - \theta^{R} n_{t+1})(1 - \tau)a_{t+1}\varepsilon_{t+1}^{W} w_{t+1}. \tag{43}$$

The health status of children, $h_t^C$, depends on the amount of time allocated by their parent to rearing them and access to (congested) public health services:

$$h_t^C = (\varepsilon_t^R)^{\nu_C} \left( \frac{H_t^G}{K_t^P} \right)^{1-\nu_C}, \tag{44}$$

where $\nu_C \in (0, 1)$. Although $h_t^C$ is assumed to exhibit constant returns to scale with respect to its arguments, this is rather inconsequential here, given that time allocated to child rearing turns out to be constant in equilibrium.[20]

Health status in adulthood, $h_t^A$, depends solely on health status in childhood:

$$h_{t+1}^A = (h_t^C)^{\nu_A}, \tag{45}$$

where $\nu_A \in (0, 1)$. There is therefore state dependence in health outcomes, as for instance in De la Croix and Licandro (2007). As discussed earlier, this specification is consistent with the evidence showing that children who experience poor health have on average significantly poorer health (as well as lower educational attainment and lower earnings), as adults.

Adult productivity is again given by (14). Using that equation, with $\chi = 1$ for simplicity, together with (44) and (45), yields

$$a_{t+1} = h_{t+1}^A = (\varepsilon_t^R)^{\nu_A \nu_C} \left( \frac{H_t^G}{K_t^P} \right)^{\nu_A(1-\nu_C)}. \tag{46}$$

Because population is no longer constant, the production side must be modified to eliminate the scale effect associated with population growth (see chapter 1). This is done here in the simplest possible way, by assuming, as in Glomm and Ravikumar (1994), that the public capital stock is congested not only by the aggregate capital stock but also by the size of the adult population, $N_t$:

$$Y_t^i = [\frac{K_t^I}{(K_t^P)^{\zeta} N_t^{\phi}}]^{\alpha} (A_t \varepsilon_t^W N_t^i)^{\beta} (K_t^{P,i})^{1-\beta}, \tag{47}$$

where $\phi > 0$.

Profit maximization now yields

$$w_t = \beta Y_t / A_t \varepsilon_t^W N_t, \quad 1 + r_t = (1 - \beta) Y_t / K_t^P, \tag{48}$$

[20] Note also that health in childhood, as defined in (44), does not depend on the parent's health; thus the model accounts for *intragenerational* health persistence, not *intergenerational* persistence. See Agénor (2009*a*) for an analysis that considers both aspects.

whereas aggregate output is

$$Y_t = \int_0^1 Y_t^i di = N_t^{\beta-\phi\alpha}(A_t\varepsilon_t^W)^\beta (k_t^I)^\alpha (K_t^P)^{1-\beta+\alpha-\zeta\alpha}. \tag{49}$$

To ensure steady-state growth requires now two assumptions:

**Assumption 3.1.** $\beta - \alpha(1-\zeta) = 0$, $\phi = \beta/\alpha$.

The first condition is similar to Assumption 1.2 in Chapter 1, whereas the second ensures that the coefficient of the adult population in (49) is zero. Combining these two conditions yields $\phi + \zeta = 1$, as noted by Glomm and Ravikumar (1994). Intuitively, for small congestion effects, the long-run growth rate is an increasing function of the size of the population, whereas for sufficiently large values of $\phi$ and $\zeta$, the congestion effects dominate and the growth rate decreases with population size (Glomm and Ravikumar (1997, p. 190)).

Under these assumptions, (49) yields aggregate output as

$$Y_t = (k_t^I)^\alpha (A_t\varepsilon_t^W)^\beta K_t^P, \tag{50}$$

which takes, conveniently, a form similar to those used before.[21]

Equations (11) and (15) to (19) remain the same. In addition, the evolution of the population is given by

$$N_t = n_{t-1}N_{t-1}, \tag{51}$$

that is, the number of adults in period $t$ is equal to the total number of children born in $t-1$. For tractability, $n_t$ is assumed to be continuous; integer constraints are thus ignored.

Each individual maximizes (40) with respect to $c_{t+1}^t$, $c_{t+2}^t$, $n_{t+1}$, $\varepsilon_{t+1}^R$, subject to (39), (43), and (44), taking as given the probability of survival $p$, as well as $a_{t+1}$, which depends on $\varepsilon_t^R$. Put differently, time spent by today's old (when they were adults) on child rearing is taken as given by today's adults when choosing how much time they should allocate to caring for their own children; equation (46) is thus ignored in the optimization process.

The first-order conditions are

$$1/c_{t+1}^t = \lambda_t, \tag{52}$$

$$1/(1+\rho)c_{t+2}^t = \lambda_t/(1+r_{t+2}), \tag{53}$$

$$\frac{\eta_N \nu_C}{\varepsilon_{t+1}^R} = \lambda_t(1-\theta^R n_{t+1})(1-\tau)a_{t+1}w_{t+1}n_{t+1}, \tag{54}$$

[21] Of course, there are other ways to eliminate the scale effect; the approach adopted here again has the merit of simplicity.

$$\frac{\eta_N}{n_{t+1}} = \lambda_t[\theta^R \varepsilon_{t+1}^W + (1-\theta^R n_{t+1})\varepsilon_{t+1}^R](1-\tau)a_{t+1}w_{t+1}. \tag{55}$$

Equations (52) and (53) yield the Euler equation (23), so that using (43) consumption and savings are given by

$$c_{t+1}^t = (1-\sigma)(1-\theta^R n_{t+1})(1-\tau)\varepsilon_{t+1}^W a_{t+1}w_{t+1}, \tag{56}$$

$$s_{t+1} = \sigma(1-\theta^R n_{t+1})(1-\tau)\varepsilon_{t+1}^W a_{t+1}w_{t+1}, \tag{57}$$

where $\sigma$ is as defined before.

Substituting (52) and (56) in (54) and (55) yields, using (39) to eliminate $\varepsilon_{t+1}^W$,

$$\frac{\eta_N \nu_C}{\varepsilon_{t+1}^R} = \frac{n_{t+1}}{(1-\sigma)(1-\varepsilon_{t+1}^R n_{t+1})}, \tag{58}$$

$$\frac{\eta_N}{n_{t+1}} = \frac{\theta^R(1-\varepsilon_{t+1}^R n_{t+1}) + (1-\theta^R n_{t+1})\varepsilon_{t+1}^R}{(1-\sigma)(1-\theta^R n_{t+1})(1-\varepsilon_{t+1}^R n_{t+1})}. \tag{59}$$

Equation (58) yields

$$\tilde{n}\tilde{\varepsilon}^R = \frac{\eta_N \nu_C(1-\sigma)}{1+\eta_N \nu_C(1-\sigma)} < 1. \tag{60}$$

Dividing (58) by (59) yields

$$\nu_C[\theta^R(1-\tilde{n}\tilde{\varepsilon}^R) + (1-\theta^R\tilde{n})\tilde{\varepsilon}^R]\tilde{n} = (1-\theta^R\tilde{n})\tilde{n}\tilde{\varepsilon}^R,$$

that is,

$$\theta^R\tilde{n} = \frac{(1-\nu_C)\tilde{n}\tilde{\varepsilon}^R}{\nu_C(1-\tilde{n}\tilde{\varepsilon}^R) + (1-\nu_C)\tilde{n}\tilde{\varepsilon}^R}.$$

Using (60), this expression can be solved for $\tilde{n}$:

$$\tilde{n} = \frac{1-\nu_C}{\theta^R\{1-\nu_C + [\eta_N(1-\sigma)]^{-1}\}}. \tag{61}$$

Thus, in equilibrium, total time allocated to child rearing and the fertility rate are both constant. To avoid convergence of population size toward zero, the condition $\tilde{n} \geq 1$ must be imposed; this requires the following restriction:[22]

**Assumption 3.2.** $\theta^R < (1-\nu_C)/\{1-\nu_C + [\eta_N(1-\sigma)]^{-1}\}$.

Intuitively, the fraction of net income spent on caring for each child cannot be too large.

Equations (60) and (61) yield the following result:

**Result 3.4.** *An increase in unit child rearing costs, $\theta^R$, lowers the fertility rate and raises unit time allocated to child rearing, but it has no effect on*

[22] Note also that $\theta^R\tilde{n} < 1$, $\forall\theta^R$, which ensures that all income is not spent on child rearing.

*total time allocated to child rearing or total rearing costs,* $d(\tilde{n}\tilde{\varepsilon}^R)/d\theta^R = d(\theta^R\tilde{n})/d\theta^R = 0$.

From (39), these results also imply that a change in unit child rearing costs has no effect on time allocated to market work.

Thus, when the unit cost of child rearing increases, the fertility rate falls in the same proportion; consequently, the time allocated to each child by parents increases in the same proportion. There is substitution of quality for quantity ($d\tilde{n}/d\theta^R < 0$, $d\tilde{\varepsilon}^R/d\theta^R > 0$), in the tradition of Barro and Becker (1989). These separate effects matter here because, as shown later, $\tilde{\varepsilon}^R$ and $\tilde{n}$ affect growth independently of each other.

Inspection of equations (57), (60), and (61) shows that, as before, an increase in the survival probability from adulthood to old age increases savings. In addition, the following results can be established:

**Result 3.5.** *An increase in the survival probability from adulthood to old age, p, reduces both the fertility rate and the total time individuals allocate to child rearing.*

The positive effect of the probability to survive from adulthood to old age on savings, which was noted earlier, again reflects the fact that higher longevity dictates a need for higher savings to finance future consumption. The negative effect on the fertility rate is also consistent with the "quantity-quality" trade-off emphasized in Barro and Becker (1989) and for which evidence is provided in a number of studies, including for instance Bleakley (2007) and Bleakley and Lange (2009). Because total rearing time $\tilde{n}\tilde{\varepsilon}^R$ falls, time devoted to market work unambiguously increases. However, the effect on time allocated to each child, $\tilde{\varepsilon}^R$, is ambiguous. This is important because, as shown next, the growth rate depends on $\tilde{\varepsilon}^R$ as well.

Using (11), (48), and (57), the savings-investment equilibrium condition (19) can be rewritten as, instead of (28),

$$K_{t+1}^P = (1-\theta^R\tilde{n})(1-\tau)\sigma\beta Y_t. \tag{62}$$

Using (39), (46), and (50), this expression becomes

$$\frac{K_{t+1}^P}{K_t^P} = \Xi_6(k_t^I)^\alpha(h_t^A)^\beta, \tag{63}$$

where $\Xi_6 = (1-\theta^R\tilde{n})(1-\tau)\sigma\beta(1-\tilde{n}\tilde{\varepsilon}^R)^\beta > 0$.

Equations (16), (18), (46), (48), and (50) yield again (30), which is reproduced here for convenience:

$$K_{t+1}^I = (\varphi\upsilon_I\tau\beta)^\mu\left(\frac{Y_t}{K_t^P k_t^I}\right)^\mu K_t^I.$$

Using (50) to eliminate $Y_t$, together with (46), yields

$$\frac{K_{t+1}^I}{K_t^I} = \Xi_7 (k_t^I)^{-\mu(1-\alpha)} (h_t^A)^{\mu\beta}, \tag{64}$$

where $\Xi_7 = (\varphi \upsilon_I \tau \beta)^{\mu} (1 - \tilde{n}\tilde{\varepsilon}^R)^{\mu\beta}$.

Combining (63) and (64) yields

$$k_{t+1}^I = \left(\frac{\Xi_7}{\Xi_6}\right) (k_t^I)^{(1-\alpha)(1-\mu)} (h_t^A)^{-\beta(1-\mu)}. \tag{65}$$

Substituting (13), (16), and (48) in (46) yields

$$h_{t+1}^A = (\tilde{\varepsilon}^R)^{\nu_A \nu_C} [(k_t^I)^{\varkappa} \left(\frac{\upsilon_H \tau \beta Y_t}{K_t^P}\right)^{1-\varkappa} ]^{\nu_A(1-\nu_C)},$$

that is, using (39) and (50),

$$h_{t+1}^A = \Xi_8 (k_t^I)^{[\varkappa + \alpha(1-\varkappa)]\nu_A(1-\nu_C)} (h_t^A)^{\beta\nu_A(1-\varkappa)(1-\nu_C)}, \tag{66}$$

where

$$\Xi_8 = (\tilde{\varepsilon}^R)^{\nu_A \nu_C} (1 - \tilde{n}\tilde{\varepsilon}^R)^{\beta\nu_A(1-\varkappa)(1-\nu_C)} (\upsilon_H \tau \beta)^{\nu_A(1-\varkappa)(1-\nu_C)}.$$

Equations (65) and (66) represent a simultaneous, nonlinear, first-order difference-equation system in $h_t^A$ and $k_t^I$. Defining $\hat{h}_t^A = \ln h_t^A$ and $\hat{k}_t^I = \ln k_t^I$, this system can be written in linear form as

$$\begin{bmatrix} \hat{h}_{t+1}^A \\ \hat{k}_{t+1}^I \end{bmatrix} = \begin{bmatrix} a_{11} & a_{12} \\ a_{21} & a_{22} \end{bmatrix} \begin{bmatrix} \hat{h}_t^A \\ \hat{k}_t^I \end{bmatrix}, \tag{67}$$

where

$$a_{11} = \beta\nu_A(1-\varkappa)(1-\nu_C) > 0,$$

$$a_{12} = [\varkappa + \alpha(1-\varkappa)]\nu_A(1-\nu_C) > 0,$$

$$a_{21} = -\beta(1-\mu) < 0,$$

$$a_{22} = (1-\alpha)(1-\mu) > 0.$$

These expressions also imply that $a_{11}, a_{22} < 1$, and $|a_{21}| < 1$.

From (65) and (66), the equilibrium values are the solutions of the system

$$\tilde{k}^I = \left(\frac{\Xi_7}{\Xi_6}\right)^{1/\Pi} (\tilde{h}^A)^{-\beta(1-\mu)/\Pi}, \tag{68}$$

$$\tilde{k}^I = \Xi_8^{-1/a_{12}} (\tilde{h}^A)^{(1-a_{11})/a_{12}}, \tag{69}$$

where $\Pi = 1 - (1-\alpha)(1-\mu) > 0$.

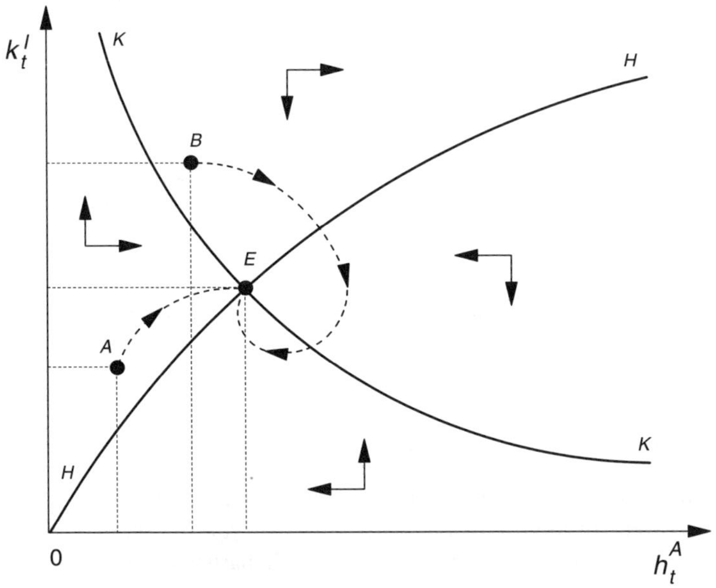


Figure 3.2. Steady-State Equilibrium.

These equations define the steady-state relationships between $h_t^A$ and $k_t^I$. As in chapter 2, equation (68) defines a curve with a negative slope depicted as $KK$ in Figure 3.2. As shown then, $KK$ is convex.

The slope of the curve defined by (69), denoted $HH$ in Figure 3.2, depends on $(1 - a_{11})/a_{12}$, that is

$$\frac{1-a_{11}}{a_{12}} = \frac{1-\beta\nu_A(1-\varkappa)(1-\nu_C)}{[\varkappa+\alpha(1-\varkappa)]\nu_A(1-\nu_C)} > 0,$$

which is positive but may or may not be less than unity. Thus, $HH$ may be either convex or concave; in the figure, it is shown as concave.

As can be inferred from Figure 3.2, the dynamic system has a unique equilibrium, which obtains at point $E$. Health status and productivity are thus both constant in the steady state, together with the public-private capital ratio.[23] If the economy is initially at values $(h_0^A, k_0^I)$ corresponding to, say, point $A$, it will converge monotonically to $E$. However, at initial values corresponding to point $B$, the economy may cycle around the equilibrium point. The appendix to this chapter also shows that the equilibrium is always stable.

[23] The constancy of health status in the steady state is what distinguishes "health" from "human capital" (which can grow without bound) in endogenous growth models of this type. Indeed, a key difference between the analysis of the dynamic system in this chapter and chapter 2 is that here $h_t^A$ itself is a stationary variable, whereas in the previous chapter it is $e_t^P = E_t/K_t^P$, which is stationary (that is, knowledge and the private capital stock grow at the same rate). If health could also grow without bound, there would be nothing that distinguishes it formally from knowledge.

From (39) and (50),

$$Y_{t+1} = (1 - \tilde{n}\tilde{\varepsilon}^R)^\beta (k_{t+1}^I)^\alpha (h_{t+1}^A)^\beta K_{t+1}^P,$$

that is, using (51) for $t+1$ and (62) yields

$$\frac{Y_{t+1}}{N_{t+1}} = (1 - \tilde{n}\tilde{\varepsilon}^R)^\beta (k_{t+1}^I)^\alpha (h_{t+1}^A)^\beta (1 - \theta^R \tilde{n})(1-\tau)\sigma\beta \left(\frac{Y_t}{\tilde{n}N_t}\right),$$

or equivalently,

$$\frac{Y_{t+1}/N_{t+1}}{Y_t/N_t} = (1 - \tilde{n}\tilde{\varepsilon}^R)^\beta \frac{(1 - \theta^R \tilde{n})}{\tilde{n}}(1-\tau)\sigma\beta (k_{t+1}^I)^\alpha (h_{t+1}^A)^\beta.$$

Thus, the steady-state growth rate of output *per worker* is

$$1 + \gamma_{Y/N} = \frac{(1 - \tilde{n}\tilde{\varepsilon}^R)^\beta (1 - \theta^R \tilde{n})}{\tilde{n}}(1-\tau)\sigma\beta (\tilde{k}^I)^\alpha (\tilde{h}^A)^\beta. \tag{70}$$

A full analysis of public policies in this model is discussed in Agénor (2009*a*). Some of the results derived earlier with $\mu = 1$ continue to hold, although there is now more scope for ambiguity. In particular, although spending on infrastructure and health are complementary in terms of their impact on the production of health services, they may be substitutes (depending on how productive spending is financed) in terms of their impact on growth.

As shown in Figure 3.3, an increase in the share of spending on infrastructure financed by a cut in unproductive expenditure ($d\upsilon_I = -d\upsilon_U$) shifts curve $KK$ upward, while leaving $HH$ unchanged. The new equilibrium is at point $E'$, characterized by improved health status and a higher public-private capital ratio. Thus, given that time allocation and the fertility do not change, equation (70) implies that the steady-state growth rate unambiguously increases. However, the same result does not hold for an increase in the share of spending on health financed by a cut in unproductive expenditure ($d\upsilon_H = -d\upsilon_U$). As also shown in Figure 3.3, this policy leads to a downward shift in $HH$, whereas $KK$ does not change. The new equilibrium is now at point $E''$, characterized by improved health status (as can be expected) but by a *lower* public-private capital ratio. Intuitively the reason is that with $\mu < 1$, an improvement in health has a stronger impact on the rate at which private capital is accumulated (through its impact on output and tax revenues). The net effect on the steady-state growth rate is thus ambiguous. These results are qualitatively similar to those obtained in the two-period model—a somewhat intuitive outcome, given that neither policy affects the amount of time allocated to market work or the fertility.

Also just as before, an increase in investment in infrastructure financed by a cut in spending on health ($d\upsilon_I = -d\upsilon_H$) has ambiguous effects. Whether the net effect is positive or negative depends on the technology parameters characterizing the production of both goods and health services. Graphically, as illustrated in Figure 3.4, this policy leads to an upward shift in both $KK$

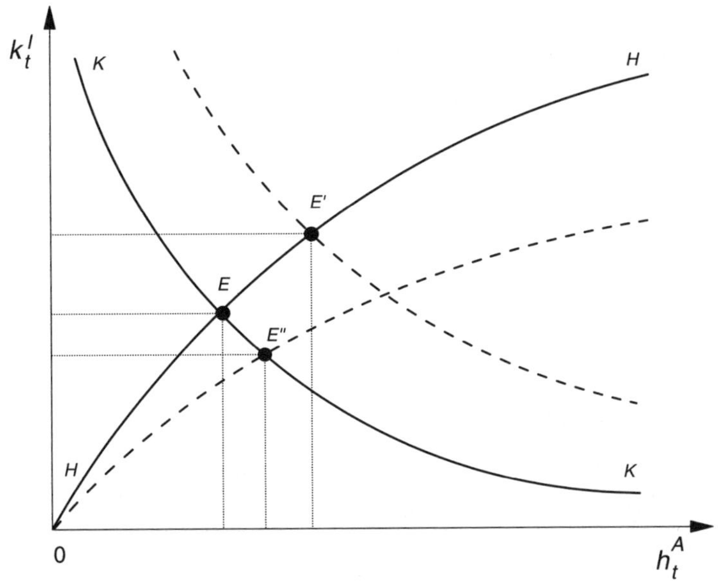


Figure 3.3. Increase in Spending Shares on Infrastructure and Health Financed by a Cut in Unproductive Spending.

and $HH$. If, in particular, public capital is highly productive in the health technology (that is, if $\varkappa$ is sufficiently high), the new equilibrium outcome is likely to be at $E'$, with both improved health status and a higher public-private capital ratio. However, if this is not the case, the outcome is more likely to be at a point such as $E''$, characterized by a higher public-private capital ratio (which always occurs) but lower health status. The net effect on steady-state growth is thus again ambiguous.

Finally, consider, as in chapter 2, the case where the unit cost of child rearing is inversely related to the public-private capital ratio, perhaps because improved access to roads reduces transportation costs (including now the cost of taking children to medical facilities). Thus, $\theta^R = \theta^R(k^I)$, with again $\theta^{R\prime} < 0$. With $\mu = 1$, equation (65) yields

$$J = \frac{\varphi \upsilon_I \tau}{[1 - \theta^R(J)\tilde{n}](1-\tau)\sigma}.$$

However, unlike the result in chapter 2, an increase in $\upsilon_I$ does not have an ambiguous effect on the public-private capital ratio. The reason is that, from results 3.4, the total fraction of income spent on child rearing, $\theta^R \tilde{n}$, does not depend on the unit cost $\theta^R$.

Nevertheless, from (66), $\tilde{\varepsilon}^R$, the share of parental time allocated to rearing each child, has a positive effect on health status; and it can be verified from (60) and (61) that $\tilde{\varepsilon}^R$ is positively related to $\theta^R$. Consequently, an increase in

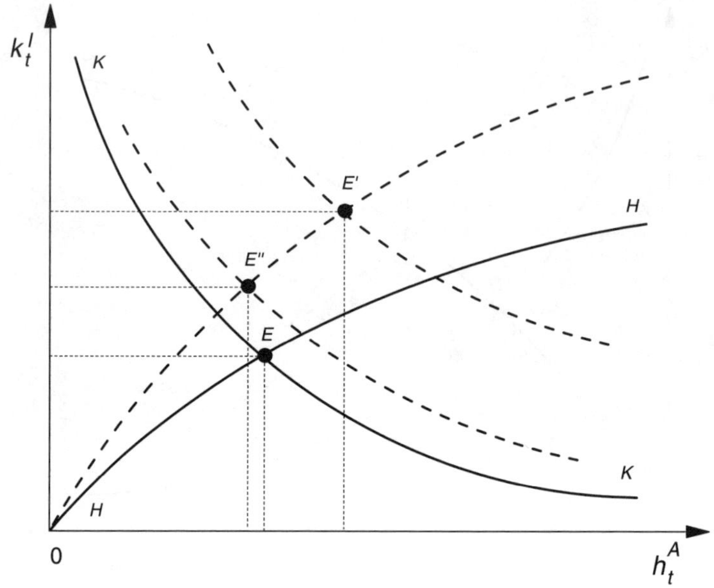


Figure 3.4. Increase in Spending Shares on Infrastructure Financed by a Cut in Spending on Health.

infrastructure investment, by lowering unit child rearing costs and reducing the time parents allocate to each of their children, exerts an indirect, negative effect on health status and growth. However, the elasticity of the unit cost with respect to the public-private capital ratio would have to be relatively large for this effect to dominate the direct, positive impact of that ratio.[24]

## 7| Endogenous Life Expectancy

In the foregoing analysis the survival rate, $p$, was taken as exogenous. There is therefore a one-way effect of life expectancy on income. This unidirectional causal link is a rather restrictive assumption in light of the evidence, which suggests that interactions between these variables go both ways. This section discusses briefly how the survival probability can be endogenized and what this implies for time allocation and growth outcomes.

Conceptually, there are two main approaches to endogenizing the survival rate: the first assumes that households internalize the impact of their decisions on $p$, whereas the second postulates that $p$ depends on an aggregate variable, and is therefore treated as predetermined by households when they optimize;

[24] With $\mu < 1$, a qualitatively similar result would hold, because from results 3.4 $\tilde{n}\tilde{\varepsilon}^R$ is also independent of $\theta^R$.

however, the endogeneity of $p$ is accounted for when solving for the general equilibrium solution of the model.

Regardless of the approach used, some regularity conditions must in general be imposed on the functional relationship between $p_t$ and its main determinant, say $x_t$. Let $p_t = f(x_t)$; the following assumptions are imposed on $f(x_t)$:

**Assumption 3.2.** *(***Concavity***)* $f' > 0$ *and* $f'' < 0$.

These properties imply that increases in $x_t$ lead to higher life expectancy, but that the marginal effect decreases as $x_t$ increases.

**Assumption 3.3.** $\lim_{x_t \to 0} p_t = 0$, *and* $\lim_{x_t \to \infty} p_t \leq 1$; $\lim_{x_t \to 0} f' = \infty$, and $\lim_{x_t \to \infty} f' = 0$.

The first two properties ensure that $p_t \in (0, 1)$. The other properties are often useful to simplify derivations. Together they imply that $x_t$ does *not* need to be bounded from above for $p_t$ to be bounded.

Two examples of functions that satisfy these properties are as follows. The first, suggested by Chakraborty (2004, note 4, p. 122), takes the form

$$p_t = f(x_t) = \frac{\bar{p}x_t}{1 + x_t}, \tag{71}$$

where $\bar{p} \in (0, 1)$. This function satisfies all the properties listed in assumptions 3.2 and 3.3, in particular, $p_0 = 0$ and $\lim_{x_t \to \infty} p_t = \bar{p}$. Thus, the survival probability converges to $\bar{p}$ as $x_t$ goes to infinity. Hashimoto and Tabata (2005, p. 556) generalize specification (71) to

$$p_t = f(x_t) = \frac{\Lambda x_t^{\upsilon}}{1 + \Lambda x_t^{\upsilon}},$$

where $\Lambda > 0$ and $\upsilon \in (0, 1)$.[25]

A second example, resulting from Kalemli-Ozcan (2002), is given by

$$p_t = f(x_t) = \bar{p}[1 - \exp(-\xi x_t)],$$

where $\bar{p}, \xi \in (0, 1)$. The survival rate is again a concave function of $x_t$, reaching a maximum at $\bar{p}$.

A more general example of a concave function, involving a minimum value $p_L \geq 0$ and a maximum value $1 \geq \bar{p} > p_L$, is the piecewise function mentioned in Mariani et al. (2010, p. 803):

$$p_t = f(x_t) = \min(p_L + Ax_t^{\upsilon}, \bar{p}),$$

[25] A related specification, used in Blackburn and Cipriani (2002), is

$$p_t = \frac{p_m + p_M \Phi x_t^{\upsilon}}{1 + p_M \Phi x_t^{\upsilon}},$$

where $p_m$, $p_M \in (0, 1)$, $p_m < p_M$, and $\Phi, \upsilon > 0$. Note that with $\upsilon > 1$, either function could exhibit a convex-concave shape.

where $A > 0$ and $\upsilon \in (0, 1)$. Thus, the survival rate remains constant at $\bar{p}$ once $x_t$ reaches the critical value

$$x^* = \left(\frac{\bar{p} - p_L}{A}\right)^{1/\upsilon}.$$

The next step is to define $x_t$. There are several possibilities to do so.

Consider first the case where the survival probability is a function of first-period consumption, that is, $p_t = f(c_t^t)$.[26]

Agents now internalize the impact of their decisions on $p_t$. The first-order conditions with respect to $c_t^t$ is now, instead of (20),

$$\frac{1}{c_t^t} + f'(c_t^t)\frac{\ln c_{t+1}^t}{1+\rho} = \lambda_t.$$

However, this equation is highly nonlinear, which makes it difficult to obtain closed-form solutions.

Alternatively, $x_t$ can be defined as *individual* health status, $h_t$, so that $p_t = f(h_t)$. Now the first-order conditions with respect to consumption (20) and (21) do not change, but condition (22), given the dependence of $h_t$ on $\varepsilon_t^H$ in the two-period model, becomes

$$\frac{\eta_H \nu}{\varepsilon_t^H} + f'(h_t)\frac{\nu h_t}{\varepsilon_t^H}\frac{\ln c_{t+1}^t}{1+\rho} = \lambda_t(1-\tau)(1-\theta)\left[1 - \nu\chi\left(\frac{1-\varepsilon_t^H}{\varepsilon_t^H}\right)\right]a_t w_t,$$

which again is not tractable in the general case.

Because of the technical difficulties involved in relating the survival rate to individual decisions, for the most part the literature has followed the second approach, which relates life expectancy to an aggregate variable. In the present context, a natural way to proceed is to assume that the survival probability is a function of *average* health status, $H_t$, which is therefore taken as given when households solve their optimization problem.[27] In equilibrium, of course, $h_t = H_t$, so again $p_t = f(h_t)$. In addition to its impact on labor productivity, health status now affects growth through the impact of the survival probability on the savings rate, $\sigma$, which affects not only the pace of private capital accumulation but also time devoted to own health, and thus labor supply (see results 3.1).

[26] This is essentially similar to Sarkar (2007), who relates the discount rate to first-period consumption. This may be viewed as capturing the role of nutrition. Chakrabarty (2004) and Ehrlich and Kim (2005) also relate the survival probability to current consumption. Studies in which the endogeneity of life expectancy with respect to individual health spending choices is internalized include Bhattacharya and Qiao (2007) and Tang and Zhang (2007).

[27] A related specification is to assume that health status itself is related to government spending on health, as in Aísa and Pueyo (2006). Alternatively, as in Blackburn and Cipriani (2002), the survival rate can be directly related to the stock of human capital inherited from parents, which is taken as predetermined by households.

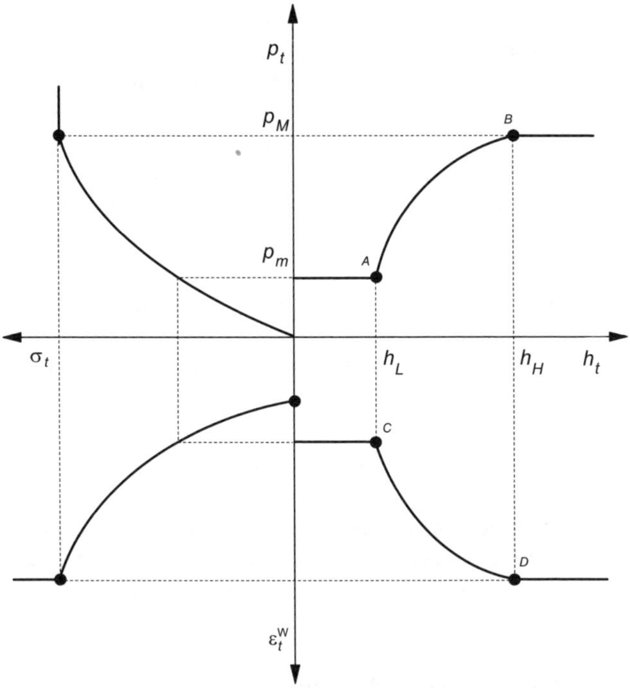


Figure 3.5. Health Status, Life Expectancy, and Labor Supply.

To illustrate further these relationships, consider the two-period model and suppose that the adult survival rate is a piecewise function defined as

$$p_t = \begin{cases} p_m \text{ for } h_t < h_L, \\ f(h_t) \text{ for } h_L \leq h_t < h_H, \\ p_M \text{ for } h_t \geq h_H, \end{cases} \tag{72}$$

where $f' > 0$ and $f'' < 0$. Thus, if health status is below $h_L$, the likelihood of surviving to old age is $p_m$. As health status improves above that threshold, the relationship between $p_t$ and $h_t$ is positive and concave over the interval $(h_L, h_H)$. It becomes constant again at $p_m < p_M < 1$ for values of health status above $h_H$. Put differently, beyond a certain point, further changes in health status have no effect on the probability to survive.

Function (72) is illustrated in the northeast quadrant of Figure 3.5. The northwest quadrant of the figure shows the (concave) relationship between life expectancy and the savings rate, as defined in (26). The southwest quadrant shows the (convex) relationship between the savings rate and time allocated to market work, which can be derived, from (1) and (27), as

$$\varepsilon_t^W = \frac{1}{1 + \nu[(1 - \sigma_t)\eta_H + \chi]}.$$

The southeast quadrant therefore shows the reduced-form relationship between health status and labor supply.[28] More generally, an important implication of the endogeneity of the survival rate is that, to the extent that health status depends indirectly on access to public capital (as discussed in previous sections), there is another channel through which public policy may affect growth: it affects not only changes in the saving rate but also time allocated to market work. Moreover, to the extent that there are nonlinearities in the relationship between health status and the survival rate, as described in (72), multiple equilibria and poverty traps may emerge. A simple example with two equilibria, based on a single threshold, will be discussed in chapter 6.

## 8| Interactions between Health and Education

In Chapters 2 and 3, externalities of public capital on education and health were treated separately, largely for expository purposes. In practice, health and education are largely interlinked in their contribution to growth because they both contribute to human capital accumulation. This section begins by reviewing some of the evidence on interactions between health and education and then examines how the impact of public capital on growth can be enhanced as a consequence of these interactions.

### 8.1| Impact of Health on Education

It is now well recognized that health can have a sizable effect on education and the accumulation of human capital.[29] Indeed, good health and nutrition are essential prerequisites for effective learning. Healthier children tend to do better in school, just like healthier workers perform their tasks better. Conversely, inadequate nutrition, which often takes the form of deficiencies in micronutrients, reduces the ability to learn and study, as noted in chapter 2. Zinc deficiency, in particular, impairs brain and motor functions, causing (according to United Nations estimates) about 400,000 deaths a year. Poor nutritional status can therefore adversely affect children's cognitive development, and this may translate into poor educational attainment, as documented in Behrman (1996, 2009), Miguel (2005), Schultz (2005), and Bundy et al. (2006). Poor health, in the form of respiratory infections for instance, is also an important underlying factor for low school enrollment, absenteeism, and high dropout rates.

Numerous country studies have documented these facts. In Bangladesh, the Food for Education program, which provided a free monthly ration of

[28] The relationship between $h_t$ and $\varepsilon_t^W$ can be concave or convex; in the figure, it is shown as concave.

[29] See Bleakley (2010*b*) for an overview of the evidence on health and human capital, and Hazan and Zoabi (2006) for a simple OLG model where health (in addition to knowledge) is an input in the production of human capital.

food grains to poor families in rural areas if their children attended school, was highly successful in increasing school enrollment (particularly for girls), promoting attendance, and reducing dropout rates (see Ahmed and Arends-Kuenning (2006)). In Tanzania, the use of insecticide-treated bed nets reduced the incidence of malaria and increased attendance rates in schools (Bundy et al. (2006)). In western Kenya, deworming treatment improved primary school participation by 9.3 percent, with an estimated 0.14 additional years of education per pupil treated (see Miguel and Kremer (2004)). McCarthy et al. (1999) found that malaria morbidity, viewed as a proxy for the overall incidence of malaria among children, has a negative effect on secondary enrollment ratios. Bleakley (2007) found that deworming of children in the American South had an effect on their educational achievements while in school, whereas Bloom et al. (2005) found that children vaccinated against a range of diseases (including measles, polio, and tuberculosis) as infants in the Philippines performed better in language and IQ scores at the age of ten, compared to unvaccinated children—even within similar social groups. Thus, early vaccination appears to have a significant effect on subsequent learning outcomes.

Bundy et al. (2006), in their overview of experience on the content and consequences of school health programs (which include for instance treatment for intestinal worm infections), emphasized that these programs can raise productivity in adult life not only through higher levels of cognitive ability but also through their effect on school participation and years of schooling attained. At a more aggregate level, the cross-country regressions of Baldacci et al. (2004) show that health outcomes (as proxied by the under-five child mortality rate) have a statistically significant effect on school enrollment rates.

Another channel through which health can improve education outcomes and spur growth is through higher life expectancy and changes in time allocation within households. Increases in life expectancy tend to raise the incentive to invest in education (in addition to increasing the propensity to save) because the returns to schooling are expected to accrue over longer periods. Thus, at the individual level, to the extent that spending on health increases planning horizons, it may also raise the returns (as measured by the discounted present value of wages) of greater expenditure on education. In a study of Sri Lanka between the period 1946 and 1953, Jayachandran and Lleras-Muney (2009) found that a reduction in maternal mortality risk increases female life expectancy and female literacy. In a study of Brazil, Soares (2006) also found that higher longevity is associated with improved schooling outcomes. These results are both consistent with the view that longer life expectancy encourages human capital accumulation.

The evidence also suggests that intrafamily allocations regarding school and work time of children tend to be adjusted in the face of disease within the family; in turn, these adjustments may influence the aggregate rate of accumulation of physical and human capital and thus the rate of economic growth. As discussed by Corrigan et al. (2005), for instance, when parents become ill, children may be pulled out of school to care for them, take on other responsibilities in the household, or work to support their siblings. Indirect evidence suggesting that reallocation of family time may indeed be important in practice is provided by Kalemli-Ozcan (2006), who found that AIDS lowered school enrollment rates in many countries in sub-Saharan Africa between 1985 and 2000. Hamoudi and Birdsall (2004) also provide evidence that AIDS reduced schooling rates in sub-Saharan Africa. These results are consistent with the view that the risk that children may be infected by AIDS tends to deter parents from investing in their education, as argued by Bell et al. (2006). Put differently, an environment where there is great uncertainty about child survival may create a precautionary demand for children, with less education being provided to each of them. In turn, the lack of human capital accumulation may hamper economic growth, as illustrated by Arndt (2006) in his study of AIDS and growth in Mozambique.

### 8.2| Impact of Education on Health

A significant body of research (at both the micro and macro levels) has also shown that higher education levels can improve health outcomes. The positive effect of education on health works partly through income; but there are other channels as well. Several studies have found that where mothers are better educated (and presumably more aware of health risks to their children), infant mortality rates are lower, and attendance rates in school are higher.[30] Better-educated women tend, on average, to have more knowledge about health risks. For developing countries in general, Smith and Haddad (2000) estimated that improvements in female secondary school enrollment rates are responsible for 43 percent of the 15.5-percentage-point reduction in the child underweight rate recorded during the period 1970–95. For sub-Saharan Africa, it has been estimated that five additional years of education for women could reduce infant mortality rates by up to 40 percent (see Summers (1994)). In the cross-section regressions for developing countries reported by McGuire (2006), average years of female schooling have a statistically significant impact on under-five mortality rates. In Niger alone, researchers have found that infant mortality rates are lower by 30 percent when mothers have a primary education level, and by 50 percent when they have completed secondary education. Paxson and Schady (2007), in a study of Ecuador, found that the cognitive development of children aged 3 to 6 years is positively associated with the level of education of their mother.[31] Of course, third factors could be at play as well; more educated

[30] See Grossman and Kaestner (1997), Glewwe (1999, 2002), and the cross-country regressions of Baldacci et al. (2004) and Wagstaff and Claesson (2004). Tamura (2006) provides a formal analysis of how education affects health outcomes and economic growth.

[31] Evidence that education affects health outcomes is also available for industrial countries; see for instance Cutler and Lleras-Muney (2006) and Altindag et al. (2011) for the United States.

women earn more and are more likely to live in urban areas, where access to health facilities, or nutritional supplements, is easier. But in many instances the positive effect of education on health persists even after controlling for location and other factors.

Conversely, a low level of education may also lead to maternal malnutrition, with dire consequences for children. Inadequate intakes of nutrients during pregnancy have been found to have irreversible effects on children's brain development, as noted earlier. Research at the National institute of Health in the United States, for instance, has shown that the children of mothers who ate food with little omega-3 fatty acids had a lower IQ than children who did. In addition, they also lacked physical coordination and had greater difficulties to engage in normal social relations. Inadequate diets may have adverse effects on mental health as well (and therefore the ability to raise children), as argued in a report by the Mental Health Foundation (2006).

## 8.3| Magnification Effect

The foregoing discussion suggests that the close interactions between health and education can magnify the effects of an increase in public capital on growth. By investing in roads, for instance, governments may not only reduce production costs for the private sector and stimulate investment but also improve education and health outcomes, by making it easier for individuals to attend school and seek health care, as noted earlier. With their health improving, individuals not only become more productive but also may be more inclined to study longer. While this may translate into a lower share of time allocated to market work, the reduction in labor supply may be more than offset through higher productivity. In turn, a higher level of education makes individuals more aware of potential risks to their own health and that of their family members. Moreover, investment in infrastructure, by improving health and life expectancy, may either increase the propensity to save (as discussed earlier) or induce individuals to work longer. As a result of these various effects, the impact of public capital on growth may be enhanced.

Analytically, these interactions among education, health, and public capital can be accounted for by integrating the models of chapters 2 and 3. However, the resulting model would become quite complicated (involving now a three-equation dynamic system in terms of $h_t^A$, $e_t^P$, and $k_t^I$, with $\mu < 1$), and understanding its properties would require numerical simulations. With respect to the optimal allocation of government spending between health, education, and infrastructure, the key intuition can be inferred from the analysis of Agénor and Neanidis (2011): with a binding budget constraint, there are trade-offs between all three components of expenditure, despite the micro complementarities. How acute these trade-offs are depends not only on the magnitude of the externalities associated with public capital (as suggested by the analysis of this chapter and the previous one) but now also on externalities between health and education themselves.

• • •

This chapter has examined interactions among public capital, health, and growth, using both two- and three-period OLG models. The first part began with a review of the large body of evidence that suggests that access to infrastructure may be critical to improving health outcomes. Better transportation networks contribute to easier access to health care, particularly in rural areas. In a number of countries, expanding networks of rural roads led—in addition to reducing production costs and improving access to markets—to a sizable increase in visits to primary health care facilities and clinics. Access to electricity is essential for the functioning of hospitals and the delivery of health services; and by reducing the cost of boiling water, it has a direct effect on health. Direct access to safe water and sanitation has been shown to have a sizable impact on malnutrition and infant mortality.

A review of the evidence on the intergenerational transmission of health, and the persistence of health between childhood and adulthood, was also provided. Children of inadequately nourished mothers are more likely to suffer from low birth weight, stunted growth, susceptibility to disease, and slowed brain development. In addition, health in early childhood has lasting influences on health and other outcomes (productivity, income) in later life. Thus, health represents a key mechanism through which poverty is transmitted: people born into poorer households experience poorer health in childhood and consequently poorer health in early adulthood, which translates into lower earning capacity in middle age.

The first model presented in this chapter focuses on the first issue—externalities associated with public capital in the production of health services. In addition, time allocated to own health was endogenized, health status was related to government-provided on health services and assumed to have a direct effect on productivity, and a nonzero probability of dying before reaching old age was accounted for. Accounting for these links creates several channels through which infrastructure and public policy may affect growth. In particular, it was shown that a budget-neutral increase in the share of spending on health, matched by a reduction in spending on infrastructure, generally leads to a drop in the public-private capital ratio. If that drop is large enough, and if infrastructure services have a significant effect on the production of health services, it may eventually prove detrimental to health outcomes—even though, at the same time, public spending on health may increase. The net effect on growth may thus be ambiguous.

The second model extended further the analysis to capture another feature of the evidence—the persistence in health outcomes between childhood and adulthood. It was shown that health persistence creates an important source of dynamics, although the steady-state effects of some public policies on public capital and growth (especially those that have no effect on fertility and time allocation) may remain qualitatively the same.

The chapter also provided a discussion of growth-maximizing fiscal policy, again in a context where a trade-off may arise in the allocation of government expenditure between two productive uses—infrastructure investment and spending on health. If the production of health services does not depend on access to public capital, the formula for the optimal allocation of tax revenues was shown to bear a close resemblance to the formula derived in Chapter 2 under related circumstances: the optimal share of spending on infrastructure should be set equal to the elasticity of output with respect to public capital, relative to the sum of that elasticity and the *effective* elasticity of output with respect to public spending on health. The latter was shown to be a composite parameter that reflects the fact that the impact of health spending on production operates through its effect on the supply of health services, the link between health and productivity, and the combination of productivity and raw labor. In addition, it was shown that the larger the impact of public capital on the production of health services, the higher the optimal share of spending on infrastructure.

The last part of the chapter examined interactions between health and education, and pointed out that they may serve to magnify the effect of public capital on growth and human welfare. To the extent, for instance, that public capital in water and sanitation helps to promote children's health, and that in turn better health leads to improvements in educational outcomes (as well as, later in life, productivity in adulthood), investing in infrastructure will provide added dividends in the long run.

It is worth noting that in this chapter, the allocation of time, although derived optimally, remained constant over time. However, it is possible to envisage situations where time allocated to own health (as in the two-period model) or time allocated to child rearing (as in the three-period model) is inversely related to access to infrastructure services: better access to roads, for instance, by making it easier for individuals to access health care facilities for themselves and their children, may lead to more time allocated to market work. Accounting for this link would create yet another channel through which public capital may affect growth. If, for instance, greater access to infrastructure services allows parents to devote more time to child rearing, children's health depends positively on parental time, and health is persistence over time, their productivity and earnings in adulthood will also be affected. In such conditions, time allocated to child rearing (which is often considered as unproductive in growth models), may become a critical channel through which public capital affects growth. Chapter 5 will consider more formally the case where access to infrastructure affects directly and endogenously time allocation, through home production.

## APPENDIX: Stability Conditions with Health Persistence

To examine the stability of the dynamic system defined in (67) in the vicinity of the equilibrium, let **A** denote the matrix of coefficients in that system, and let det **A** denote its determinant and tr**A** its trace. Let also $\lambda_j$, $j = 1, 2$ denote the eigenvalues of **A**; the characteristic polynomial is thus $p(\lambda) = \lambda^2 - \lambda \text{tr}\mathbf{A} + \det\mathbf{A}$. Thus, $p(1) = 1 - \text{tr}\mathbf{A} + \det\mathbf{A}$, whereas $p(-1) = 1 + \text{tr}\mathbf{A} + \det\mathbf{A}$.

For convenience, the $a_{ij}$ coefficients are reported here:

$$a_{11} = \beta\nu_A(1-\varkappa)(1-\nu_C) > 0,$$

$$a_{12} = [\varkappa + \alpha(1-\varkappa)]\nu_A(1-\nu_C) > 0,$$

$$a_{21} = -\beta(1-\mu) < 0,$$

$$a_{22} = (1-\alpha)(1-\mu) > 0.$$

From these definitions,

$$\text{tr}\mathbf{A} = \beta\nu_A(1-\varkappa)(1-\nu_C) + (1-\alpha)(1-\mu) > 0,$$

$$\det\mathbf{A} = \beta(1-\mu)\{\nu_A(1-\varkappa)(1-\nu_C)(1-\alpha) + [\varkappa + \alpha(1-\varkappa)]\nu_A(1-\nu_C)\} > 0.$$

Given the signs of $\text{tr}\mathbf{A} = \lambda_1 + \lambda_2$ and $\det\mathbf{A} = \lambda_1\lambda_2$, it is clear that $p(-1) > 0$. In addition,

$$p(1) = 1 - a_{11} - (1-\alpha)(1-\mu) + a_{11}(1-\alpha)(1-\mu)$$

$$+\beta(1-\mu)[\varkappa + \alpha(1-\varkappa)]\nu_A(1-\nu_C),$$

that is

$$p(1) = (1-a_{11})\Pi + \beta(1-\mu)[\varkappa + \alpha(1-\varkappa)]\nu_A(1-\nu_C),$$

where $\Pi = 1 - (1-\alpha)(1-\mu) > 0$, as defined in the text.

Thus, given that $a_{11} < 1$, the condition $p(1) > 0$ always holds. The eigenvalues are therefore on the same side of both 1 and $-1$. Moreover, given that $\det\mathbf{A} > 0$, the eigenvalues are of the same sign. With $a_{11} < 1$ and $a_{22} < 1$, tr**A** cannot exceed 2 (that is, $\text{tr}\mathbf{A} \in (-2, 2)$). Given that $\text{tr}\mathbf{A} > 0$ and $\det\mathbf{A} > 0$, the eigenvalues are not only less than unity in absolute terms but actually positive. The steady state is thus a sink (see Azariadis (1993, p. 65)).

# 4 | Public Capital and Innovation

Increased globalization, through the adoption and adaptation of preexisting technologies imported from more advanced countries, has led to a substantial acceleration in the pace of technological progress in developing countries. Imports of capital and intermediate goods—whose embodied technological knowledge allows domestic firms to employ more efficient production processes and to copy more advanced products—represented in 2002–04 between 6 and 13 percent of their GDP, compared to 5 and 9 percent in 1994–96 (see World Bank (2008*c*)). The easing of restrictions on foreign direct investment has also proved to be a powerful channel for technology diffusion; a significant fraction of these capital flows has helped to finance imported new machinery and equipment purchases in domestic affiliates of foreign firms, and to foster domestic research and development (R&D) activities—eventually leading to greater exports of high-tech goods in a growing number of countries.

However, the capacity of developing countries to absorb foreign technologies has improved at a slower pace. Human capital, a key determinant of a country's capacity to undertake the research necessary to develop new technologies and to understand, implement, and adapt imported technologies (as documented by Coe et al. (2009)), remains a key constraint. Another is access to physical infrastructure. One set of factors, as discussed in chapter 1, is the high production costs that poor access to infrastructure services imposes on sectors producing final goods. Another is the constraints imposed on R&D activities themselves, which may hamper the economy's ability to produce the intermediate goods that are used as inputs in the production of final goods.

This chapter extends the OLG models presented in chapters 1 and 2 to study interactions between infrastructure and human capital with R&D activities and growth.[1] It begins by providing some background evidence on these interactions. The model is then presented and solved, and the impact of public policy, including potential trade-offs associated with the provision of infrastructure and other services by the government, is discussed. Again, this is a critical issue; if governments have access to limited resources to cover their expenditure, different types of government interventions may

[1] The model presented in this chapter is a simplified version of the model in Agénor and Neanidis (2010), which itself dwells on the seminal contribution of P. Romer (1990). In these models, growth is driven by "horizontal" innovations, which involve increases in the quantity of (intermediate) goods available for production. See Aghion and Howitt (1998), Barro and Sala-i-Martin (2003), Gancia and Zilibotti (2005), and Acemoglu (2008) for a discussion of different types of growth models with endogenous technological change.

entail (temporary or permanent) trade-offs at the macroeconomic level—even though at the microeconomic or sectoral level these interventions are largely complementary. In addition, different types of government intervention may generate spillover effects on other sectors, which may have an indirect impact on innovation capacity. If indeed lack of infrastructure and low quality of tertiary education are key constraints on R&D activities (as alluded to earlier), increasing spending on infrastructure or universities may ultimately prove to be more efficient to stimulate innovation than, say, general subsidies to research laboratories. Trade-offs involved in the allocation of public expenditure between infrastructure investment and other components of public spending (namely, education and support for R&D activities) are illustrated both intuitively and numerically. The last part discusses the role of public capital in fostering a shift from imitation activities (copying or adapting foreign products or technologies) to true innovation (invention of new products).

## 1| Background

Poor access to physical infrastructure—especially electrical and road networks, and telecommunications—remains a key constraint on the capacity of developing countries to absorb foreign technologies and engage in R&D activities, bring new goods to markets, and reap the profits that the exploitation of new technologies may generate. In particular, lack of domestic transportation infrastructure and inadequate access to telecommunications may prevent firms from introducing new products and hamper economy-wide dissemination of new and more efficient technologies. Unreliable access to electricity may limit opportunities to use electronic equipment and other advanced devices used in research activities and cross-border knowledge sharing among researchers.[2] In addition, poor access to infrastructure services may constrain the rate of knowledge acquisition (as discussed in chapter 2), thereby indirectly constraining the ability to innovate.

Conversely, the high-speed communication networks available today may support innovation throughout the economy—much as electricity and transport networks spurred innovation in the past. Many governments have promoted information and communication technologies (ICTs) as general-purpose platforms for innovation and knowledge sharing by upholding the open, free, decentralized, and dynamic nature of the Internet.[3] Indeed, broadband networks have been leveraged by other sectors to provide information at no or low cost or to develop other platforms, such as distance education and telemedicine,

[2] Other important constraints may include the regulatory environment and access to finance, especially venture capital.

[3] This has also meant encouraging the adoption of the new standard for Internet Protocol (IPv6), given that the lack of Internet addresses is increasingly a constraint for this key platform, in particular in developing countries.

thereby promoting human capital accumulation and stimulating innovation. In formal econometric studies, Czernich et al. (2011) found that broadband matters for growth, whereas Agénor and Neanidis (2010) found that access to telecommunications has a significant impact on both innovation and growth.[4]

At the same time, lack of human capital continues to limit the capacity of many developing countries (especially the poorest ones) to understand, implement, and adapt imported technologies and to undertake the research necessary to develop new ones. The importance of human capital in an R&D context is well documented (see Coe et al. (2009)). Consequently, when assessing the importance of public capital for innovation and growth, it is essential to capture simultaneously the impact that human capital (or lack thereof) may have on the ability to innovate, and possible interactions between public capital and education outcomes, as discussed in chapter 2.[5]

## 2| The Economy

As in chapter 3, consider an OLG economy where individuals live for three periods, childhood, adulthood, and old age. Each individual is endowed with one unit of time in the first two periods of life, and zero unit in old age. Children allocate all their time to education, as in chapter 2. In adulthood, each individual has one child. Total population is thus constant and the size of each cohort is $\bar{N}$. Adults supply labor inelastically and wages in adulthood are the only source of income.

In addition to individuals, the economy is populated by firms and a government. There are now four sectors in the economy: the first produces as before a final good, the second produces intermediate inputs (which depreciate fully after use), the third produces human capital (which is nonrival), and the fourth conducts R&D activities. Labor is used in the production of the final good and new ideas, and moves freely across sectors.

All other assumptions are the same as in chapter 1. The good can be either consumed in the period it is produced or stored to yield physical capital at the beginning of the following period. Savings can be held only in the form of physical assets. Agents have no other endowments, except for an initial stock of physical capital held by an initial old generation. The government invests in infrastructure and spends on education, subsidies to innovation, and some other unproductive items. It finances its expenditure by taxing wages. It cannot borrow and therefore must run a balanced budget in each period. Finally, all markets clear and there are no debts or bequests between generations.

[4] As discussed in chapter 6, both studies also find evidence of nonlinearities.

[5] An important contribution that also focuses on the interactions between human capital and new technology (in the form of quality improvements of existing intermediate-capital goods) in the growth process is Kosempel (2004). In his analysis, new technologies create new opportunities for learning. However, public capital plays no role.

### 2.1| Households

The household side of the model is the same as in Chapter 2, except for the assumption that $\varepsilon = 0$ (no parental time is allocated to child tutoring) and is presented only briefly. The discounted utility of an individual born at $t$ is

$$U_t = \eta_C \ln c_{t+1}^t + \frac{\ln c_{t+2}^t}{1+\rho}, \quad \rho > 0, \tag{1}$$

whereas the consolidated budget constraint is

$$c_{t+1}^t + \frac{c_{t+2}^t}{1+r_{t+2}} = (1-\tau)e_{t+1}w_{t+1}, \tag{2}$$

with $e_{t+1}$ denoting individual human capital. The parameter $\eta_C > 0$, which measures the household's relative preference for current consumption, is introduced to facilitate the calibration exercise reported later on. In principle, the wage rate appearing in the budget constraint (2) should depend on the sector of occupation of the individual, the production of final goods or R&D. However, as discussed later, with perfect labor mobility the wage rate must be the same across sectors. Thus, to economize on notation, $w_{t+1}$ is defined directly as the economy-wide effective wage.

### 2.2| Production of the Final Good

The final good is produced by identical competitive firms of mass 1, indexed by $i$. Production requires the use of effective labor, given by the product of average human capital of individuals born in $t-1$, $E_t$, and employment, $N_{i,t}^Y$, private capital, $K_t^{P,i}$, and a combination of $M_t$ intermediate inputs (or brands), $x_{s,t}^i$, where $s = 1, ...M_t$. For simplicity, the productivity effect of public capital, considered in chapters 1 to 3, is abstracted from.

The production function of firm $i$ takes therefore the form

$$Y_t^i = (K_t^{P,i})^{\beta_K}(E_t N_{i,t}^Y)^{\beta_N}\left[\sum_1^{M_t}(x_{s,t}^i)^{\eta}\right]^{\varsigma}, \tag{3}$$

where $\beta_K, \beta_N, \varsigma \in (0, 1)$, $\eta \in (0, 1)$, and $1/(1-\eta) > 1$ is the elasticity of demand for each intermediate good. This specific form implies that each new innovation involves the production of a new intermediate good (as in P. Romer (1990)), and that the elasticity of substitution between different intermediate goods is equal to one. In addition, the production function distinguishes between the returns to specialization, as measured by $\varsigma$, and the parameter that determines the demand elasticity, $\eta$. The following restriction is imposed:

**Assumption 4.1.** *Production of the final good exhibits constant returns to scale in private inputs,* $\beta_K + \beta_N + \varsigma = 1$.

With the price of the final good constant and normalized to unity, profits of firm $i$ in the final sector, $\Pi^Y_{i,t}$, are now given by

$$\Pi^Y_{i,t} = Y^i_t - (1+\Lambda_t)\sum_1^{M_t} p^s_t x^i_{s,t} - w_t E_t N^Y_{i,t} - (r_t + \delta^P)K^{P,i}_t,$$

where $p^s_t$ is the price of intermediate good $s$. Transportation costs, $\Lambda_t$, distort the distribution of intermediate goods to producers of the final good.

Each producer maximizes profits subject to (3) with respect to private inputs, labor and capital, and demand for all intermediate goods $x^i_{s,t}$, $\forall s$, taking factor prices, $M_t$, and $\Lambda_t$ as given. This yields

$$r_t = \beta_K \frac{Y^i_t}{K^{P,i}_t} - \delta^P, \quad w_t = \beta_N \frac{Y^i_t}{E_t N^Y_{i,t}}, \tag{4}$$

$$x^i_{s,t} = \left[\frac{\varsigma \eta Z^i_t}{(1+\Lambda_t)p^s_t}\right]^{1/(1-\eta)}, \quad s = 1, \ldots M_t, \tag{5}$$

where

$$Z^i_t = Y^i_t / \sum_1^{M_t} (x^i_{s,t})^\eta. \tag{6}$$

Because each firm demands the same amount of each intermediate good, equation (5) implies that the aggregate demand for intermediate good $s$ is

$$x_{s,t} = \int_0^1 x^i_{s,t} di = \int_0^1 \left[\frac{\varsigma \eta Z^i_t}{(1+\Lambda_t)p^s_t}\right]^{1/(1-\eta)} di. \tag{7}$$

Because all firms producing the final good are identical and their number is normalized to unity, $K^P_t = K^{P,i}_t$, and $Z_t = Z^i_t$, $\forall i$, and the total demand for intermediate goods is the same across firms, $x^i_t = x_t$, $\forall i$. Moreover, in a symmetric equilibrium, $x^i_{s,t} = x^i_t$, $\forall s$. Thus, $\int_0^1 [\sum_1^{M_t} (x^i_{s,t})^\eta]^\varsigma di = M^\varsigma_t x^{\eta\varsigma}_t$. Let also $N^Y_t = \int_0^1 N^Y_{i,t} di$ denote total labor employed in the production of the final good. Given assumption 4.1, aggregate output of the final good is

$$Y_t = \int_0^1 Y^i_t di = \left\{\left(\frac{K^P_t}{M_t}\right)^{\beta_K}\left(\frac{E_t N^Y_t}{M_t}\right)^{\beta_N} x^{\eta\varsigma}_t\right\} M_t. \tag{8}$$

Thus, if the term in brackets is constant in the steady state, the growth rate of output is equal in the long run to the growth rate of innovations.

Transportation costs are assumed to be a decreasing function of the public-private capital ratio:

$$\Lambda_t = \Lambda(k^I_t), \tag{9}$$

where $\Lambda()$ satisfies the following assumptions:

**Assumption 4.2.** $\Lambda(0) = \Lambda_M > 0$, $\Lambda' < 0$, and $\lim_{k^I_t \to \infty} \Lambda(k^I_t) = 0$.

Thus, from (5) and (9), access to infrastructure reduces transportation costs and raises the demand for each intermediate input—thereby promoting growth. This captures one of the "standard" channels through which public capital may affect growth, as discussed in chapter 1.[6]

### 2.3| Production of Intermediate Goods

Firms in the intermediate sector are monopolistically competitive. There is only one producer of each input $s$, and each of them must pay a fee to use the patent (design) of that input to R&D producers. Production of each unit of an intermediate good $s$ requires $\theta$ units of the final good.

Once the fee involved in purchasing a patent has been paid, each intermediate-good producer sets its price to maximize profits, $\Pi^I_{s,t}$, given the perceived total demand function for its good (which determines marginal revenue), $x_{s,t}$:

$$\Pi^I_{s,t} = (p^s_t - \theta)x_{s,t}. \tag{10}$$

Substituting (7) in this expression and imposing $Z^i_t = Z_t, \forall i$, yields

$$\Pi^I_{s,t} = (p^s_t - \theta)\left[\frac{\varsigma\eta Z_t}{(1+\Lambda_t)p^s_t}\right]^{1/(1-\eta)}.$$

Maximizing this expression with respect to $p^s_t$, taking $Z_t$, and $\Lambda_t$ as given, yields the optimal price as

$$p^s_t = p_t = \frac{\theta}{\eta}, \quad \forall s \tag{11}$$

which implies, using (7), that the optimal quantity of each intermediate good demanded by producers of the final good is

$$x_{s,t} = x_t = \left[\frac{\varsigma\eta^2 Z_t}{(1+\Lambda_t)\theta}\right]^{1/(1-\eta)}. \quad \forall s \tag{12}$$

From the definition of $Z^i_t$ in (6), in equilibrium $Z_t = Y_t/M_t x^\eta_t$. Substituting this expression in (12) yields

$$x_t = \frac{\varsigma\eta^2}{(1+\Lambda_t)\theta}\left(\frac{Y_t}{M_t}\right). \tag{13}$$

Because $k^I_t$ is constant in the steady state, so is $\Lambda_t$. As shown in the appendix to this chapter, the ratio $Y_t/M_t$ is also constant in the steady state;

[6] It could be assumed, as in Agénor and Neanidis (2010), that poor access to public capital hampers as well the adoption of new technologies by producers of the final good. By implication, improved access would exert an indirect effect not only by reducing transport costs but also by enabling firms to adopt and exploit at a faster rate the gains from innovation, as measured by a greater variety of intermediate inputs.

thus, the equilibrium quantity of each intermediate good is constant at $\tilde{x}$ as well along the balanced growth path.

Substituting (11) in (10) yields the maximum profit for an intermediate-good producer:

$$\Pi_t^I = \left(\frac{1}{\eta} - 1\right)\theta x_t, \tag{14}$$

which is constant in equilibrium if $x_t$ is constant.

The potential producer of an intermediate input decides to enter the market by comparing the discounted stream of profits generated by producing that input, and the price that must be paid for the patent or new design, $p_t^M$. If the market for new designs is competitive, standard arbitrage implies that the price of a patent must be equal to the present discounted stream of profits that the producer of intermediate inputs could make by producing the intermediate input $s$. For simplicity, each producer of a new intermediate good is accorded a patent only for the period during which it is bought. The (no) arbitrage condition requires therefore that

$$p_t^M = \left(\frac{1}{\eta} - 1\right)\theta x_t. \tag{15}$$

### 2.4| Human Capital Accumulation

As in chapter 2, schooling is mandatory and children allocate all of their time to education. Human capital is produced using a combination of government spending on education per worker, as well as the parent's human capital:

$$e_{t+1} = \left(\frac{G_t^E}{\bar{N}}\right)^{\nu_1} E_t^{1-\nu_1}, \tag{16}$$

where $\nu_1 \in (0, 1)$. Because individuals are identical within a generation, a parent's human capital at $t$ is again taken to be equal to the average human capital of the previous generation, $E_t$. For tractability, the learning technology is assumed to exhibit constant returns to scale in government spending and human capital; and for simplicity, the externality of public capital with respect to knowledge accumulation, discussed in chapter 2, is abstracted from.[7] In a symmetric equilibrium, $e_t = E_t$.

### 2.5| Research and Development Sector

Firms engaged in R&D activities generate designs for new intermediate inputs, using a common technology. Although these activities, at the level of

[7] It could be assumed that, as in McDermott (2002), there is a spillover effect of the stock of ideas on learning, which would make the learning technology depend on $M_t$ as well. A similar idea is developed in Kosempel (2004). However, this would not qualitatively affect the main results.

individual firms, are inherently risky, to simplify matters (and given the book's focus) it will be assumed that there is no uncertainty at the aggregate level.

The production of new designs depends on the existing stock of designs, effective labor, as well as government spending on R&D (measured in units of the final good), $G_t^R$, and access to (congested) public infrastructure:

$$M_{t+1} - M_t = \left(\frac{G_t^R}{E_t}\right)^{\phi_1} \left(\frac{M_t}{E_t}\right)^{\phi_2} (k_t^I)^{\phi_3} E_t N_t^R, \tag{17}$$

where $N_t^R$ is total employment in the R&D sector, $\phi_1, \phi_2 \in (0, 1)$, and $\phi_3 > 0$. As in P. Romer (1990), all R&D firms have free access to the existing stock of ideas, or blueprints, so that each innovation creates a positive externality for future research activities; however, this occurs with diminishing returns. In addition, it is scaled by average human capital, to account for the fact that, as general knowledge increases, the marginal benefit of an increase in the existing stock of ideas (or "specialized" knowledge) becomes less relevant to promote innovation.

Government spending on R&D (in the form of grants for financing lab equipment, improving research facilities, etc.) has a direct impact on the ability to produce new ideas or adapt existing ones. It is scaled again by average human capital, to account for the fact that, as general knowledge increases, government spending—unless it keeps pace with the economy's available human capital stock—becomes less relevant for innovation activities.[8] The following assumption is also imposed:

**Assumption 4.3.** $\phi_1 + \phi_2 < 1$.

This condition ensures that the marginal benefit of an increase in the human capital stock on innovation activity remains positive.

Access to (congested) public capital also has a direct effect on the ability to innovate; this is consistent with the evidence provided in a number of studies (see Agénor and Neanidis (2010)). By fostering innovation today, public infrastructure also has a positive external effect on future research activity.[9]

R&D firms choose labor so as to maximize profits, $\Pi_t^R$, given the dynamics of innovation captured by (17), $N_t^R > 0$, and taking wages, the patent price, $p_t^M$, and the public-private capital ratio as given:

$$\max_{N_t^R} \Pi_t^R = p_t^M (M_{t+1} - M_t) - w_t E_t N_t^R.$$

[8] For instance, with the growth of knowledge, more and more sophisticated computer and lab equipment may be needed to perform research activities.

[9] It could be assumed that public capital is congested by the stock of designs, or equivalently the "size" of the research sector, instead of the private capital stock. This would not affect the results qualitatively.

The first-order condition is

$$w_t = \left\{ \left( \frac{G_t^R}{E_t} \right)^{\phi_1} \left( \frac{M_t}{E_t} \right)^{\phi_2} (k_t^I)^{\phi_3} \right\} p_t^M. \tag{18}$$

Given the linearity of the innovation technology with respect to effective labor, (18) is also the zero-profit condition implied by free entry.

## 2.6| Government

As noted earlier, the government taxes only adult wages. It spends on infrastructure investment, education, subsidies to R&D activities, $G_t^R$, and other items. All its services are provided free of charge. It runs a balanced budget, so that

$$\sum G_t^h = \tau e_t w_t \bar{N}, \quad h = E, I, R, U. \tag{19}$$

In standard fashion, shares of public spending are all assumed to be constant fractions of government revenues:

$$G_t^h = \upsilon_h \tau e_t w_t \bar{N}, \quad h = E, I, R, U. \tag{20}$$

Combining (19) and (20) therefore yields

$$\sum_h \upsilon_h = 1. \tag{21}$$

Assuming full depreciation and full efficiency of spending, and focusing for simplicity on the case where existing capital is not an essential input in the production of new public capital (that is, $\mu = 1$), the stock of infrastructure assets evolves according to

$$K_{t+1}^I = G_t^I. \tag{22}$$

## 2.7| Savings-Investment Balance

With full depreciation, the asset market clearing condition requires as usual equality between tomorrow's private capital stock and today's savings:

$$K_{t+1}^P = \bar{N} s_t. \tag{23}$$

## 2.8| Labor Market

With full employment, labor market equilibrium requires

$$N_t^R + N_t^Y = \bar{N}. \tag{24}$$

Equation (18), given perfect labor mobility, can be used to determine the economy-wide equilibrium wage. If the patent price and the ratios in the curly brackets on the right-hand side of that equation are all constant, then the equilibrium wage will also be constant.

Using equation (4) to substitute out for $N_t^Y$, equation (24) can be used to determine equilibrium employment in the R&D sector:

$$N_t^R = \bar{N} - \beta_N \left(\frac{Y_t}{E_t}\right) w_t^{-1}, \tag{25}$$

which is constant if $Y_t/E_t$ and $w_t$ are constant. In that particular case, the allocation of labor across sectors is also constant.

## 3| Balanced Growth Path

As defined in Agénor and Neanidis (2010), and consistent with the definitions in previous chapters, a *dynamic equilibrium* for the model described above is a sequence of allocations $\{c_t^{t-1}, c_{t+1}^{t-1}, s_t\}_{t=0}^{\infty}$, private and public physical capital stocks $\{K_{t+1}^P, K_{t+1}^I\}_{t=0}^{\infty}$, knowledge $\{E_{t+1}\}_{t=0}^{\infty}$, factor prices $\{w_t, r_{t+1}\}_{t=0}^{\infty}$, prices and quantities of each intermediate input $\{p_t^s, x_{s,t}\}_{s=1,...M_t,t=0}^{\infty}$, available varieties, $\{M_{t+1}\}_{t=0}^{\infty}$, a constant tax rate and public spending shares such that, given initial stocks $K_0^P$, $K_0^I > 0$, $E_0 > 0$, and $M_0 > 0$,

a) Individuals maximize utility subject to their intertemporal budget constraint, taking prices as given;
b) Firms in the final good sector maximize profits, choosing labor, private capital, and intermediate inputs, taking transportation costs and input prices as given;
c) Intermediate goods producers set prices so as to maximize profits, while internalizing the effect of their decisions on the perceived demand curve for their product;
d) Producers of new designs in the R&D sector maximize profits by choosing employment, taking wages, patent prices, the initial stock of designs, the public-private capital ratio, and government spending on R&D, as given;
e) The equilibrium price of each design extracts all profits made by the corresponding intermediate good producer;
f) The government budget is balanced; and
g) All markets clear.

A *balanced growth equilibrium* is a dynamic equilibrium in which

a) $c_t^{t-1}$, $c_{t+1}^{t-1}$, $s_t$, $K_t^P$, $K_t^I$ , $E_t$, $Y_t$, $M_t$, grow at a constant, endogenous rate, implying that the human capital-private capital ratio, as well as the public-private capital ratio, are also constant;
b) The rate of return on private capital $r_t$ and the economy-wide effective wage rate $w_t$ are constant;
c) The price of intermediate goods $p_t$ and the patent price $p_t^M$ are constant; and
d) The fractions of the adult labor force engaged in the production of the final good and ideas, $n_t^h = N_t^h/\bar{N}$, with $h = R, Y$, are constant and $n_t^R + n_t^Y = 1$.

The balanced growth rate of the economy is derived in the appendix to this chapter, in terms of the private capital-human capital ratio, $k_t^P = K_t^P/E_t$, and the ratio of human capital to the stock of innovations, $z_t = E_t/M_t$. As in Chapter 1, with $\mu = 1$ the public-private capital ratio is constant over time:

$$k_t^I = \frac{\upsilon_I \tau}{\sigma(1-\tau)} = J, \quad \forall t \tag{26}$$

where $\sigma = 1/[1+\eta_C(1+\rho)]$ is the marginal propensity to save. The steady-state growth rate of output per worker is now given by[10]

$$1+\gamma = \Xi(\tilde{k}^P)^{\beta_K \nu_1/\Omega(1-\phi_1)}\tilde{z}^{\Gamma}, \tag{27}$$

where $\tilde{k}^P$ and $\tilde{z}$ are steady-state values whose exact expressions are given in the Appendix to this chapter, $\Xi$ is also defined in the Appendix, and

$$\Omega = 1 - \beta_N - \eta\varsigma + \beta_N/(1-\phi_1),$$

$$\Gamma = -\phi\nu_1 + \frac{\nu_1(\beta_K + \beta_N\phi)}{\Omega(1-\phi_1)}.$$

Equation (27) illustrates the fact that now infrastructure affects growth, not through productivity or external effects on the production of human capital or health services (as in previous chapters) but through the capacity to innovate and lower transportation costs of intermediate goods.

## 4| Public Policy

The solution of the model is now too complex to be studied analytically. In particular, the growth-maximizing allocation of public spending between infrastructure, education, and R&D is considerably more involved, even with $\mu = 1$. However, the analysis of the growth effects of spending reallocations remains fairly intuitive. To complement this intuition the model is also calibrated for a "typical" low-income economy and some simple experiments conducted.

### 4.1| Basic Intuition

Consider an increase in the share of government spending on R&D financed by a cut in other spending ($d\upsilon_R = -d\upsilon_U$), or an increase in the share of spending on education financed in the same way ($d\upsilon_E = -d\upsilon_U$). Both policies unambiguously raise the growth rate in the final good sector, although the ratio

[10] Note that the solution displays the typical "scale effect" that is characteristic of Romer-type models of innovation and growth. This scale effect can be eliminated in various ways; see for instance Eicher and Turnovsky (2000), Dinopoulos and Thomson (2000), and Perez-Sebastian (2007). With public capital affecting production of final goods, the approach described in chapter 3 to measure congestion with endogenous population could also be used.

of human capital to the stock of designs falls in the first case and increases in the second. By contrast, an increase in, say, the share of spending on R&D, financed by a cut in spending on either education ($d\upsilon_R = -d\upsilon_E$) or infrastructure ($d\upsilon_R = -d\upsilon_I$), has ambiguous effects on steady-state growth. Intuitively, although spending more on R&D leads to a more rapid pace in the production of new designs, lower spending on education or infrastructure hampers the production of other productive inputs—the stock of human capital and public infrastructure.

The effect of spending shifts on growth may also depend on nonlinearities associated with the effect of infrastructure, be they on production of final goods, education, or innovation. As discussed in more detail in chapter 6, some recent contributions have highlighted the possibility that there may be *critical mass effects* or *network externalities* associated with public capital. These effects imply that the benefits of infrastructure vary with the level of infrastructure itself. Specifically, this could be captured here by assuming that the elasticity $\phi_3$ appearing in equation (17) may change from a relatively low (and possibly empirically insignificant) value to a relatively large (and empirically significant) value, once the public-private capital ratio reaches a certain level. In line with the results in Czernich et al. (2011) for instance, it may be that a telecommunications network must be sufficiently developed to promote interactions between researchers and foster innovation. The evidence on network externalities is further discussed in chapter 6. What they mean here, however, is that the optimal allocation of spending may vary endogenously over time, depending on the magnitude of the policy changes themselves.

## 4.2| Numerical Illustration

To complement the foregoing discussion, the model is now calibrated for a "typical" low-income economy to illustrate the impact of public policy.

On the household side, the annual discount rate is set at 0.04. This implies that the discount factor is equal to 0.96 on a yearly basis—a fairly conventional choice in the literature. Interpreting a period as 20 years in this OLG framework yields the "true" discount factor as $[1/(1+0.04)]^{20} = 0.456$. In line with the evidence on private savings for low-income countries, the savings rate $\sigma = 1/[1+\eta_C(1+\rho)]$ is set at 0.05. The parameter $\eta_C$ is thus calibrated to obtain that value, so that $\eta_C = (\sigma^{-1} - 1)/(1+\rho)$. Given that the discount factor is actually equal to 0.456, this yields $\eta_C = 8.66$.

In the final good sector, the elasticities of production of final goods with respect to public capital, effective labor, and private capital, $\alpha$, $\beta_N$, and $\beta_K$, respectively, are set equal to 0.15, 0.65, 0.2, respectively. Thus, the case considered is that of a low-income country where production of manufacturing goods is highly intensive in labor. These estimates for $\beta_N$ and $\beta_K$

imply an elasticity with respect to intermediate inputs equal to $\varsigma = 1 - \beta_N - \beta_K = 0.15$.[11]

In the intermediate goods sector, the coefficient $\theta$ (which measures marginal cost) is set to 2.5, as in Garcia-Castrillo and Sanso (2002), and the parameter $\eta$ (which measures both the elasticity of substitution between intermediate goods, and the price elasticity of the demand for these goods) is set to 0.85. From (11), this choice implying that the *net* price markup over marginal cost is given by $\eta^{-1} = 17.6$ percent. It also implies that the elasticity of substitution between intermediate goods is $1/(1-\eta) = 6.67$. In the human capital sector, the elasticity with respect to government spending on education services, $\nu_1$, is set equal to 0.3. This implies that the elasticity with respect to the current stock of human capital is equal to 0.7.

In the R&D sector, the elasticity with respect to targeted government spending, $\phi_1$, is set equal to 0.2, whereas the elasticity with respect to the existing stock of ideas, $\phi_2$, is set equal to a higher value, 0.3, to capture the importance of past research for current research. Because of the congestion effects alluded to earlier, these values imply that the net elasticity with respect to human capital alone is $1 - 0.2 - 0.3 = 0.5$. The elasticity with respect to the public-private capital ratio, $\phi_3$, is taken to be 0.2. Thus, access to public infrastructure plays a relatively moderate role in the promotion of R&D activities.

Regarding the government, in line with actual ratios for low-income countries, the tax rate on final output, $\tau$, is set at 0.15 (see Agénor and Neanidis (2010)). The initial shares of government investment in infrastructure, as well as spending on education, and targeted interventions in the R&D sector, $\upsilon_I$, $\upsilon_E$, and $\upsilon_R$, are set at 0.1, 0.15, and 0.05, respectively. These values imply from the budget constraint (21) that the share of spending on unproductive items is $\upsilon_U = 0.7$. Thus, directly productive spending accounts for a relatively small fraction of total expenditure.

Based on these parameter values, equations (A16) and (A20) in the appendix to this chapter can be solved for the steady-state solutions $\tilde{k}^P$ and $\tilde{z}$; these solutions can then inserted in (27), together with a multiplicative constant, in order to yield an annual steady-state growth rate of final output equal to a relatively low value, 1.15 percent.

Consider now a budget-neutral increase in the share of government spending on R&D, $\upsilon_R$, from an initial value of 0.05 to 0.1 of tax revenues. In the first scenario, the increase in $\upsilon_R$ is financed by a cut in unproductive expenditure $(d\upsilon_R + d\upsilon_U = 0)$. The solution of the model yields a growth rate of 1.40 percent, that is, an increase of 0.25 percentage points compared to the baseline value. Thus, consistent with the intuitive discussion, an increase in the share of spending on R&D promotes growth—not only directly, through its effect on

[11] Note that the sum of $\beta_K$ and $\varsigma$ is 0.35, which corresponds to common estimates of the elasticity of final output with respect to private capital; see Agénor (2011*a*) for instance.

R&D activities, but also indirectly, because higher government revenues foster human capital accumulation. In turn, the higher level of human capital further promotes growth by encouraging R&D activities.

In the second scenario, the increase in $\upsilon_R$ is financed by a cut in another productive component of public spending, such as spending on education services ($d\upsilon_R + d\upsilon_E = 0$). The solution of the model gives now a growth rate of 0.45 percent, that is, a drop of 0.7 percentage points compared to the baseline value. Thus, an increase in the share of spending on R&D has now an unambiguously *negative* effect on growth. This is the reflection of the general trade-off that one would expect when considering budget-neutral spending shifts across productive categories, and differences in elasticities with respect to changes in government spending across sectors; the positive effect on growth that higher spending on R&D generates (through the channels identified earlier) is now more than offset because of the reduction in the stock of human capital. Because R&D activities depend *linearly* on human capital, whereas the elasticity of the flow of new ideas with respect to a change in the share of spending on R&D is only $\phi_1 = 0.2$ (see equation (17)), the offsetting cut in the share of spending on education is very costly in terms of growth.

Thus, the key intuition is the same as in chapters 2 and 3: in the presence of alternative uses of public spending, trade-offs inevitably emerge. Moreover, depending on technology parameters and the strength of externalities (in particular, in the R&D technology), the best way to promote innovation may not be necessarily to spend more on research and development, but instead to invest in education or infrastructure.[12]

## 5| From Imitation to True Innovation

In the foregoing analysis the definition of "innovation" or "research and development" was kept relatively vague. In a broad sense, innovation has been defined as the application of new ideas, technologies, or processes to productive activities. Thus, it encompasses not only the creation of new knowledge and technology but also, equally important, the adaptation and diffusion of existing technologies, products, processes, and practices that are "new" to the country or the region—although not necessarily to the world. Innovation is, therefore, also about the transformation of traditional sectors into higher value-added, knowledge-intensive sectors, through the local adoption of already existing technology and processes, as well as increased investments in new technology-intensive sectors. From that perspective,

[12] This point would have come out in an even stronger way had the model and the experiments accounted for the benefits of infrastructure emphasized in the previous chapters.

innovation is of equal relevance to high-technology or research-dependent sectors (such as biotechnology and information technology) and low-technology sectors (such as agriculture, food processing, textiles, and many types of manufacturing).

From the perspective of developing countries, it is useful to distinguish analytically between two types of innovation: *imitation* (or *implementation innovation*), which involves mostly adapting existing products or foreign ideas, often imported from more advanced countries, and *true innovation*, which involves creating or inventing new products, that is, expanding the global technological frontier. The distinction is important because even though both activities can coexist for a while, imitation may be subject to decreasing returns. This implies that, to sustain growth, at some point a switch from imitation to true innovation is essential. Indeed, while imitation may be the main source of productivity growth during early stages of development, as diminishing returns set in and the economy approaches the technology frontier, true innovation needs to become the main engine of growth.[13] However, the transition may prove difficult because by specializing initially in low-skilled intensive activities, poor countries may have diminished incentives to invest in higher education and may therefore be caught in an *imitation trap*—an equilibrium characterized by positive (in both absolute and per capita terms) but moderate growth.[14] In turn, moderate growth lengthens the process of convergence to high-income status.

What then is the role of public capital in facilitating the transition process from imitation to true innovation? To answer this question, it is convenient to think of imitation and true innovation as involving two different production processes, requiring two different types of public capital. The first requires investment in "basic" infrastructure (roads, basic telecommunications services such as fixed and mobile phone lines, connection to electricity grids, and so on) whereas the second requires investment in "advanced" (or R&D-promoting) infrastructure. In particular, access to broadband infrastructure is critical for generating and distributing information and ideas, which in turn are important steps to promote innovation (Czernich et al. (2011)). Thus, advanced infrastructure is important both directly, through its impact on true innovation, and indirectly (as discussed in chapter 2), through its effect on human capital accumulation.

[13] The two activities may also coexist in equilibrium. Growth models with both imitation and innovation sectors include those of Walz (1996), Currie et al. (1999), Perez-Sebastian (2007), and Mondal and Gupta (2009). However, none of these contributions discusses the role of public capital in the transition process.

[14] In that sense, an imitation trap differs from a poverty trap (as discussed in chapter 6), which is characterized by very low (or even negative, in per capita terms) rates of economic growth in equilibrium.

In addition, different types of human capital are needed during the transition process: while imitation can be performed by both low- and higher-skill workers, true innovation normally requires highly educated labor with a broader range of skills.[15] By implication, switching from imitation to true innovation requires improving both access to advanced infrastructure and the quality of the labor force. Moreover, if public capital, private capital, and highly educated labor are close complements in true innovation, the lack of access to advanced infrastructure may also constrain the marginal product of that type of labor in these activities, thereby mitigating the wage signal (relative to wages in other sectors, manufacturing or services) on the basis of which individuals decide to invest or not in higher education. From that perspective, the lack of advanced public capital may be particularly detrimental to true innovation.

This analysis has important implications for the sequencing of growth strategies in developing countries in general, and low-income countries in particular. For many of today's poor countries, imitation is an important initial phase; policy should focus first on strengthening the infrastructure necessary for the successful adoption, diffusion, and implementation of already existing technologies, and on developing basic domestic human capital. At the same time, if there are spillover effects on learning associated with imitation activities, they may also promote knowledge—even though this may occur with decreasing returns. This two-way causality implies that an initial phase of specialization in imitation activities is not necessarily detrimental to sustained growth in these countries. However, the risk for countries specializing in low-skilled intensive activities is that they entail diminishing returns. With inadequate investment in R&D-promoting infrastructure, and with diminished incentives to invest in higher education, their long-term prospects may be constrained and they may be caught in a low-growth imitation trap. It is therefore important, in a second phase, to step up investment in more advanced infrastructure and human capital, to compete at the global technological frontier and ensure sustained growth. Delays in making these investments may be costly, as some slow-growing middle-income countries have now found out.

• • •

This chapter has focused on the links between public capital, innovation, and the diffusion of new products, and growth. The first part provided a brief review of the evidence regarding the impact of infrastructure on innovation. It was noted that access to telecommunications is a particularly important determinant of innovation capacity.

[15] Thus, the closer a country gets to the world technology frontier (which determines opportunities for imitation in poorer countries), the more growth enhancing it becomes to invest in higher education. See Vandenbussche et al. (2006) for a formal discussion and empirical evidence.

The chapter also extended the models presented in chapters 1 and 2 to capture interactions among public capital, human capital, innovation, and growth. This led to introducing two new sectors, one producing intermediate inputs and the other R&D activities. The private production technology was generalized to account for the fact that production requires the use of a large variety of intermediate goods. It was also assumed that access to infrastructure reduces transportation costs and raises the demand for each intermediate input—thereby promoting growth, in line with the review of conventional channels provided in chapter 1. In standard fashion, firms in the intermediate sector were assumed to be monopolistically competitive, with each of them paying a fee (or patent) to use the designs or blueprints created in the R&D sector. An explicit derivation of the equilibrium growth rate showed that infrastructure in this setting affects growth not through external effects on the productivity of private inputs or the production of human capital and health services, as in previous chapters, but through lower transportation costs of intermediate goods and the capacity to innovate.

Potential trade-offs associated with the provision of infrastructure and government support for innovation (as well as education, as in chapter 2) were discussed once again: if governments have access to limited resources to cover their expenditure, different types of government interventions entail trade-offs at the macroeconomic level—even though at the microeconomic or sectoral level these interventions are largely complementary. In addition, different types of government intervention may generate spillover effects on other sectors, which may have an indirect impact on innovation capacity. In particular, if lack of infrastructure or low quality of tertiary education are key constraints on research and development activities, increasing spending on infrastructure or universities may ultimately prove to be more efficient to stimulate innovation than, say, subsidies to research activities in the private sector. These trade-offs were illustrated both intuitively and numerically.

The chapter also discussed the role of public capital in the transition from imitation activities (copying or adapting foreign products or technologies to local markets) to true innovation (which involves the creation of new products, at the global technology frontier). It was argued that this transition may require not only higher quality of labor but also a different *type* of public capital: whereas imitation may necessitate access to basic infrastructure (roads, electricity, basic telecommunications), a more "advanced" type (more complementary with human capital, such as broadband) may be needed beyond a certain stage. Given the externalities in terms of human capital identified in chapter 2, improving access to that type of public capital may create both direct and indirect effects on true innovation and may be an essential step to avoid being caught in an "imitation trap," where growth is positive (in absolute and per capita terms) but moderate.

## APPENDIX: Dynamic System and the Steady State

Each individual maximizes (1) with respect to $c_t^t$ and $c_{t+1}^t$, subject to (2). The first-order conditions give again

$$\frac{c_{t+2}^t}{c_{t+1}^t} = \frac{1+r_{t+2}}{\eta_C(1+\rho)}. \tag{A1}$$

Substituting this result in (2) yields

$$c_{t+1}^t = \left[\frac{\eta_C(1+\rho)}{1+\eta_C(1+\rho)}\right](1-\tau)e_{t+1}w_{t+1}, \tag{A2}$$

so that

$$s_t = \sigma(1-\tau)e_t w_t, \tag{A3}$$

where $\sigma = 1/[1+\eta_C(1+\rho)] < 1$.

Substituting this result in (23) yields

$$K_{t+1}^P = \sigma(1-\tau)e_t w_t \bar{N}. \tag{A4}$$

From (20) with $h = I$ and (22),

$$K_{t+1}^I = \upsilon_I \tau e_t w_t \bar{N}. \tag{A5}$$

Combining (A4) and (A5) yields

$$k_{t+1}^I = \frac{\upsilon_I \tau}{\sigma(1-\tau)} = J. \tag{A6}$$

From (4) and (8),

$$Y_t = \left\{\left(\frac{K_t^P}{M_t}\right)^{\beta_K}\left(\frac{E_t}{M_t}\frac{\beta_N Y_t}{E_t w_t}\right)^{\beta_N} x_t^{\eta\varsigma}\right\} M_t = \beta_N^{\beta_N} x_t^{\eta\varsigma}(k_t^P z_t)^{\beta_K}\left(\frac{Y_t}{M_t}\right)^{\beta_N} w_t^{-\beta_N} M_t,$$

where $k_t^P = K_t^P/E_t$ and $z_t = E_t/M_t$. Equivalently

$$\left(\frac{Y_t}{M_t}\right)^{1-\beta_N} = \beta_N^{\beta_N} x_t^{\eta\varsigma}(k_t^P z_t)^{\beta_K} w_t^{-\beta_N}. \tag{A7}$$

From (13) and (A6),

$$x_t = \frac{\varsigma\eta^2}{[1+\Lambda(J)]\theta}\left(\frac{Y_t}{M_t}\right). \tag{A8}$$

Substituting this result in (A7) and rearranging yields

$$\frac{Y_t}{M_t} = \left[\frac{\beta_N^{\beta_N}}{[1+\Lambda(J)]^{\eta\varsigma}\theta^{\eta\varsigma}}\left(\varsigma\eta^2\right)^{\eta\varsigma}\right]^{1/\omega}(k_t^P z_t)^{\beta_K/\omega} w_t^{-\beta_N/\omega},$$

where

$$\omega = 1-\beta_N-\eta\varsigma > 0.$$

This expression can be rewritten as

$$\frac{Y_t}{M_t} = \Xi_1 (k_t^P z_t)^{\beta_K/\omega} w_t^{-\beta_N/\omega}, \tag{A9}$$

where

$$\Xi_1 = \left[ \frac{\beta_N^{\beta_N}}{[1+\Lambda(J)]^{\eta\varsigma}\theta^{\eta\varsigma}} (\varsigma\eta^2)^{\eta\varsigma} \right]^{1/\omega} > 0.$$

From (15), (A6), and (A8),

$$p_t^M = \left(\frac{1}{\eta} - 1\right) \frac{\varsigma\eta^2}{1+\Lambda(J)} \left(\frac{Y_t}{M_t}\right). \tag{A10}$$

From (20),

$$G_t^h = \upsilon_h \tau e_t w_t \bar{N}, \quad h = E, R. \tag{A11}$$

Substituting (A10) and (A11) for $h = R$ in (18), holding with equality, and using (A6), yields

$$w_t = (\upsilon_R \tau w_t \bar{N})^{\phi_1} z_t^{-\phi_2} J^{\phi_3} \left(\frac{1}{\eta} - 1\right) \frac{\varsigma\eta^2}{1+\Lambda(J)} \left(\frac{Y_t}{M_t}\right),$$

or

$$w_t = \Xi_2 z_t^{-\phi} \left(\frac{Y_t}{M_t}\right)^{1/(1-\phi_1)}, \tag{A12}$$

with

$$\phi = \frac{\phi_2}{1-\phi_1}, \quad \Xi_2 = \left\{ (\upsilon_R \tau \bar{N})^{\phi_1} J^{\phi_3} \left(\frac{1}{\eta} - 1\right) \frac{\varsigma\eta^2}{1+\Lambda(J)} \right\}^{1/(1-\phi_1)} > 0.$$

Substituting (A12) in (A9) yields

$$\frac{Y_t}{M_t} = \Xi_3 (k_t^P)^{\beta_K/\Omega} z_t^{(\beta_K+\beta_N\phi)/\Omega}, \tag{A13}$$

where

$$\Omega = \omega + \beta_N/(1-\phi_1) > 0,$$

$$\Xi_3 = \Xi_1^{\omega/\Omega} \Xi_2^{-\beta_N/\Omega}.$$

Substituting (A13) back in (A12) yields the equilibrium wage as a function of $z_t$ and $k_t^P$:

$$w_t = \Xi_4 (k_t^P)^{\beta_K/\Omega(1-\phi_1)} z_t^{\Gamma_1}, \tag{A14}$$

where

$$\Gamma_1 = -\phi + \frac{\beta_K + \beta_N\phi}{\Omega(1-\phi_1)},$$

$$\Xi_4 = \Xi_2 \Xi_3^{1/(1-\phi_1)} > 0.$$

Next, from (16) and (A11) for $h = E$,

$$\frac{E_{t+1}}{E_t} = \left(\frac{G_t^E}{\bar{N} E_t}\right)^{\nu_1} = (\upsilon_E \tau w_t)^{\nu_1},$$

or equivalently, using (A12) to eliminate $w_t$,

$$\frac{E_{t+1}}{E_t} = \Xi_5 z_t^{-\phi \nu_1} \left(\frac{Y_t}{M_t}\right)^{\nu_1/(1-\phi_1)},$$

where $\Xi_5 = (\upsilon_E \tau)^{\nu_1} \Xi_2^{\nu_1} > 0$.

Substituting (A13) for $Y_t/M_t$ yields

$$\frac{E_{t+1}}{E_t} = \Xi_6 (k_t^P)^{\beta_K \nu_1/\Omega(1-\phi_1)} z_t^{\Gamma_2}, \tag{A15}$$

where

$$\Gamma_2 = -\phi \nu_1 + \frac{\nu_1(\beta_K + \beta_N \phi)}{\Omega(1-\phi_1)} = \nu_1 \Gamma_1,$$

and $\Xi_6 = \Xi_5 \Xi_3^{\nu_1/(1-\phi_1)} > 0$.

Using (A4), (A14), and (A15), the dynamics of $k_t^P$ are determined by

$$k_{t+1}^P = \frac{\sigma(1-\tau)\bar{N}\Xi_4}{\Xi_6} (k_t^P)^{(1-\nu_1)\beta_K/\Omega(1-\phi_1)} z_t^{(1-\nu_1)\Gamma_1}. \tag{A16}$$

To determine the dynamics of $z_t$, divide (17) by $M_t$,

$$\frac{M_{t+1}}{M_t} = 1 + \left(\frac{G_t^R}{E_t}\right)^{\phi_1} z_t^{1-\phi_2} (k_t^I)^{\phi_3} N_t^R,$$

or equivalently, using (A6) and (A11) for $h = R$,

$$\frac{M_{t+1}}{M_t} = 1 + [(\upsilon_R \tau \bar{N})^{\phi_1} J^{\phi_3}] w_t^{\phi_1} z_t^{1-\phi_2} N_t^R. \tag{A17}$$

To eliminate $N_t^R$ from this expression, substitute (A12) for $w_t$ in equation (25) to give

$$N_t^R = \bar{N} - \beta_N \left(\frac{Y_t}{M_t}\right) z_t^{-1} \Xi_2^{-1} z_t^{\phi} \left(\frac{Y_t}{M_t}\right)^{-1/(1-\phi_1)},$$

or equivalently

$$N_t^R = \bar{N} - \frac{\beta_N}{\Xi_2} \left(\frac{Y_t}{M_t}\right)^{-\phi_1/(1-\phi_1)} z_t^{-(1-\phi)}. \tag{A18}$$

Substituting (A13), (A14), and (A18) in (A17) yields

$$\frac{M_{t+1}}{M_t} = 1 + \Xi_7 (k_t^P)^{\omega_2} z_t^{\Gamma_3} [\bar{N} - \Xi_8 (k_t^P)^{-\omega_2} z_t^{-\Gamma_4}], \tag{A19}$$

where

$$\omega_2 = \beta_K \phi_1 / \Omega(1-\phi_1),$$

$$\Gamma_3 = \Gamma_1 \phi_1 + 1 - \phi_2,$$

$$\Gamma_4 = 1 - \phi + \frac{\phi_1(\beta_K + \beta_N \phi)}{\Omega(1-\phi_1)} > 0,$$

$$\Xi_7 = (\upsilon_R \tau \bar{N})^{\phi_1} J^{\phi_3} \Xi_4^{\phi_1} > 0,$$

$$\Xi_8 = \beta_N \Xi_2^{-1} \Xi_3^{-\phi_1/(1-\phi_1)} > 0.$$

Combining (A15) and (A19) yields

$$z_{t+1} = \frac{\Xi_6 (k_t^P)^{\beta_K \nu_1 / \Omega(1-\phi_1)} z_t^{1+\Gamma_2}}{1 + \Xi_7 (k_t^P)^{\omega_2} z_t^{\Gamma_3} [\bar{N} - \Xi_8 (k_t^P)^{-\omega_2} z_t^{-\Gamma_4}]}. \tag{A20}$$

In the steady state, $k_t^P$ and $z_t$ are constant at $\tilde{k}^P$ and $\tilde{z}$, which are obtained by solving (A16) and (A20). By implication, $E_t$, $M_t$, and $K_t^P$ (and thus $K_t^I$ from (A6)) grow at the same constant rate. From (A13), output grows also at the same rate as $M_t$ and other aggregate variables.

From (A15), the growth rate of the economy is given by[16]

$$1 + \gamma = \Xi_6 (\tilde{k}^P)^{\beta_K \nu_1 / \Omega(1-\phi_1)} \tilde{z}^{\Gamma_2}, \tag{A21}$$

Equation (A21) corresponds to (27) in the text, with $\Xi = \Xi_6$ and $\Gamma = \Gamma_2$.

[16] From (A4), (A5), and (A19), three other equivalent expressions can be derived for the growth rate.

# 5 | Public Capital and Women's Time Allocation

> The housewife of the future will be neither a slave to servants nor herself a drudge. She will give less attention to the home, because the home will need less; she will be rather a domestic engineer than a domestic labourer, with the greatest of all hand maidens, electricity, at her service. This and other mechanical forces will so revolutionize the woman's world that a large portion of the aggregate of woman's energy will be conserved for use in broader, more constructive fields.
>
> —Thomas A. Edison, interview in *Good Housekeeping Magazine* (October 1912), cited by Greenwood et al. (2005)

The role of women in promoting growth and development continues to occupy center stage in policy debates. As documented in a number of studies, gender inequality—measured in terms of access to education, health, formal sector employment, or income—remains a significant constraint to growth in many countries. On the one hand, the gender gap in educational attainment has gradually narrowed or moved in favor of women in some regions; and in many individual countries the gender gap in *primary* school enrollment has almost disappeared. According to the United Nations (2010) for instance, in 2007 over 95 girls for every 100 boys of primary school age were in school in developing countries, compared with 91 in 1999. On the other, however, 54 percent of girls in sub-Saharan Africa still do not complete even a primary school education (Herz and Sperling (2004); UNICEF (2005)). In addition, progress toward gender equality in *secondary* schooling has been slower, and in some regions gaps are widening. In sub-Saharan Africa, the percentage of enrolment of girls compared with boys in secondary education fell from 82 percent in 1999 to 79 percent in 2007 (United Nations (2010)). At this rate, achieving the Millennium Development Goal of complete parity by 2015 appears to be out of reach for many countries (see World Bank (2010)). Related in part to gender bias in education, in today's low- and middle-income countries the labor force participation rate for women is only 57 percent, compared to 85 percent for men (International Labour Office (2008)). Wage differentials between men and women exceed 20 percent in many countries. When it comes to taking care of their children's health needs, parents often devote more time and resources to their sons.

This chapter focuses on two aspects of the debate on the role of women in growth and development: the impact of lack of access to infrastructure on women's time allocation and, in line with the discussion in chapter 3, the role of inter- and intragenerational health externalities—namely, how mothers' time allocation decisions affect their children's health, and how health in childhood affects health in adulthood. To do so, a gender dimension is added to the analytical framework presented in the previous chapters. Gender-based OLG models of economic growth are relatively few in the literature; among the notable exceptions are Galor and Weil (1996), Momota (2000), Zhang et al. (1999), Lagerlöf (2003), Andreassen (2004), Greenwood et al. (2005), De la Croix and Vander Donckt (2010), Kimura and Yasui (2010), and Cavalcanti and Tavares (2011).[1] However, none of these contributions analyzes the impact of public capital on women's time allocation, in a context where health status is persistent over time.

This chapter begins with a review of the recent evidence on women's time allocation, with a particular focus on the implications of poor access to infrastructure services, and on intergenerational health externalities. This discussion complements and expands the review of the sources of health persistence provided in chapter 3. The model is then presented and its properties analyzed. The impact of public policy is considered next, and the implications of the analysis for the debate on the relationship between women's labor supply and the level of development are discussed. The concluding section considers various extensions.[2]

# 1| Background

## 1.1| Women's Time Allocation Constraints

Women in developing countries face a number of constraints on the allocation of their time between market and nonmarket activities. There are various factors, including cultural and social norms that may account for these constraints; in many countries, cultural norms are that women are expected to continue to do most of the housework and child rearing—even if they engage in market work full time. This tendency is often exacerbated by a lack of government programs to alleviate constraints associated with child care.

In what follows the discussion will focus on access (or lack thereof) to infrastructure. As documented in previous chapters, there are a number of channels through which infrastructure may promote growth in developing countries; while many of these channels are not gender specific, some of

[1] Galor and Weil (1996) for instance develop a theoretical model that incorporates considerations of fertility and its link to growth. Household fertility and labor supply choices are embedded in a growth model in which wages are endogenously determined. Increases in capital per worker raise women's relative wages, which reduce fertility, and thus raise further capital per worker. This virtuous circle leads to a rapid transition to lower fertility and higher output growth.

[2] The analysis in this chapter draws extensively on Agénor and Agénor (2009) and Agénor et al. (2010).

them do affect disproportionately women and their ability to allocate their time to productive uses. What follows provides a brief review of the empirical evidence on how constraints on access to transport infrastructure, water and sanitation, and electricity affect women's time allocation.

### 1.1.1| *Transportation*

Lack of roads and other transport infrastructure constrains the ability of women to travel to perform activities related to household production and income-generating activities. They often end up traveling on foot, while carrying heavy loads at times. As documented by Riverson et al. (2006), for instance, in Ethiopia, 73 percent of women's trips and 61 percent of their travel time is dedicated to meeting their household's energy, water, and food needs. On average, women in rural Sub-Saharan Africa spend between 0.9 and 2.2 hours per day on transporting water and firewood (see Weiss (1999) and Blackden and Wodon (2006)). They travel on average between 1 and 5 kilometers per day on foot for 2.5 hours, while carrying a load of about 20 kilograms (see Riverson et al. (2006)).

Women also depend on transportation for health care, for themselves and their children. In many countries in sub-Saharan Africa, a majority of women in rural areas rank distance and inadequate transportation as major obstacles in accessing health services (African Union (2005)). Women may have to travel long distances sometimes to reach obstetric care, and may die or lose their babies as a result (see Mills et al. (2007)). Thus, lack of access to transport infrastructure not only constrains time available for market-related activities but may also have direct adverse implications for women's health—and thus their productivity and earning potential.

### 1.1.2| *Water and Sanitation*

Women in low-income countries allocate a significant amount of time to collecting water for household production (see Isha (2007) for an overview). In Pakistan, women devote an average of 27 hours per month—or approximately 15 percent of their monthly work time—to this activity (Ilahi and Grimard (2000)). In Madagascar and Benin, women spend 164 hours per year and 273 hours per year, respectively, collecting water; this corresponds to 14 and 23 hours a month, or 8.8 percent and 14.4 percent, respectively, of monthly working time (Blackden and Wodon (2006)). In Kenya, as documented by d'Adda et al. (2009), women devote 3.8 hours a week collecting water (compared to 1.3 for men), or equivalently 15.2 hours a month (compared to 5.2 hours a month for men). In Guinea, lack of access to water also imposes a very high time cost on women (Bardasi and Wodon (2009)). More generally, the WHO estimates that a staggering 40 billion "woman-hours" are spent carrying water in Africa annually (see Temin and Levine (2009)).

Lack of access to water and sanitation (combined with poor access to transportation services) may also have an adverse, indirect effect on education outcomes for girls—especially in rural areas. As noted in chapter 1, studies have indeed found that when sanitation facilities are lacking, dropout rates for girls tend to be higher.

### 1.1.3| *Electricity*

Various studies have shown that lack of access to electricity acts as a significant constraint on women's time, by forcing them to rely on fossil fuels and to devote less time to income-generating activities, to rearing children and furthering their education, and to accessing health care for themselves and their children. For instance, Ilahi (2001) found that women living in rural Peru who rely on firewood or coal as a source of energy tend to allocate a smaller proportion of their time to self-employment activities and a greater proportion of time to housework, compared to women who use gas or electricity. In Kenya, as documented by d'Adda et al. (2009), women devote 2.7 hours a week collecting firewood (compared to 0.3 for men), in addition to the almost 4 hours a week that they spend collecting water. In many countries, deforestation forces women to go further and further away from their place of residence to collect wood—as documented by Kumar and Hotchkiss (1988) for Nepal—imposing therefore tighter constraints on what else they can do with their time.

Lack of access to electricity may also hamper the ability of women to take care of their own health and the health of their children, as documented in chapter 3. Infants' and children's health may be adversely affected because of greater exposure to indoor air pollution produced by the burning of fossil fuels (as discussed in chapter 2), or greater exposure to bacteria and parasites due to lack of refrigeration of food and boiling of water. Lack of access to electricity may affect child health outcomes indirectly as well, by forcing women to allocate more time to home production activities and consequently reducing the time that they can devote to engaging in market work—thereby inhibiting (as noted earlier) their ability to generate income.[3]

To the extent that it leads to more intensive use of wood charcoal, and thus to environmental degradation, lack of access to electricity may contribute to a larger work burden for children. In turn, children who spend more hours on resource collection work are less likely to go to school; this is particularly so

[3] Conversely, access to electricity, by allowing the use of a wide range of consumer durables, may help to "liberate" women from the home. This is the prediction that Thomas Edison made at the turn of the last century, as quoted earlier. Greenwood et al. (2005) and Greenwood and Seshadri (2005) provide a formal analysis of this effect. However, they focus on technological progress in the market, and technological progress in the home, as determinants of fertility and female labor force participation. By contrast, the focus here is on access to public infrastructure services (whose supply can be directly influenced by policy decisions) on female time allocation decisions, and their interaction with women's health, education outcomes, and economic growth.

for girls. This means that environmental degradation affects children's school performance, but the impact on girls may be much more damaging. It has been argued that this may be one explanation for the increased gender gap in education in Malawi (Nankhuni and Findeis (2003)).

## 1.2| Intergenerational Health Externalities

There is much evidence that a mother's health—which may itself depend on her level of education, as discussed in chapter 3—affects directly the health of her children. In addition, to the extent that health in childhood affects health in adulthood (as also discussed in chapter 3), a mother's health today may determine the health of future mothers and their earning ability.

### 1.2.1| *Mothers' Health Status and Child Development*

It is now well documented that the children of inadequately nourished mothers are likely to suffer systematic negative effects—including low birth weight, stunted growth, susceptibility to disease, and intellectual impairment. This may be the result of either nutritional reasons (insufficient nutrition to the fetus) or physiological factors (the growth potential of a fetus may be hampered in a stunted woman). In turn, the potential damage to low-birth-weight babies from being born undernourished is compounded when they remain undernourished during infancy and early childhood. A malnourished or anemic mother may be unable to produce the quality or the quantity of breast milk needed to help her low-birth-weight baby; and without breast milk, an infant's immune system does not develop properly: it becomes prone to diseases such as malaria, respiratory tract infections, and pneumonia. Early weaning also puts a child at severe risk of infections and disease. In addition, to the extent that a malnourished mother has a low life expectancy, it may induce her to take her daughters out of school because a shorter time horizon lowers the value of educational investments. This may lead to persistence in poor health for women, through the "education channel" discussed later.

Evidence that a mother's poor health actually affects the health of their children in utero, that is, even before they are born, includes Lim et al. (2002) and Field et al. (2008). Lim et al. (2002) found that the nutritional status of Korean women in pre-pregnancy (with respect notably to folate, a B vitamin essential for cell growth and reproduction, as well as iron, and calcium intakes) affects pregnancy outcomes. In a study of Tanzania, Field et al. (2007) found that children who benefited from iodine supplements in utero exhibited higher rates of grade progression at ages 10 to 14. Furthermore, the effects appear to be substantially larger for girls, consistent with the evidence indicating greater cognitive sensitivity of the female fetus to in utero iodine deprivation. Thus, a mother's lack of iodine intake during pregnancy may also help to explain gender differences in schooling, as discussed later.

*A contrario* evidence that low life expectancy for mothers may adversely affect their daughters' health and education prospects is provided by Jayachandran and Lleras-Muney (2009). In a study of Sri Lanka between 1946 and 1953, they found that the increase in life expectancy of girls associated with a large drop in maternal mortality was accompanied (for every extra year of life expectancy) by an increase in female literacy of 0.7 percentage points and years of education by 0.11 years.

Another aspect of the mother-to-child transmission of health that has received much attention in recent years is related to the HIV/AIDS epidemic. As documented by the United Nations (2010), the number of women receiving treatment for prevention of mother-to-child transmission of HIV has increased threefold in recent years, from 15 percent in 2005 to 45 percent in 2008. There have been some notable successes in prevention, most notably in Lesotho (see Agénor et al. (2010)). However, in 2008 only 21 percent of pregnant women worldwide were receiving HIV testing and counseling, while only one-third of those identified as HIV-positive during antenatal care were subsequently assessed for eligibility to receive antiretroviral therapy for their own health. These problems are most pressing in sub-Saharan Africa, where the prevalence of HIV is, by far, the highest.

Finally, there is also evidence that maternal mental health may have a sizable effect on child development, with maternal depression significantly increasing the odds that a child will experience growth faltering (that is, low height for age) and poorer education outcomes (see Das et al. (2009)).[4]

### 1.2.2| *Mothers' Educational Status and Child Development*

A mother's level of education also affects her children's health. A number of studies have found that mothers with higher levels of education have healthier children, even after controlling for variation in household resources, and that the education of mothers has a much stronger impact on children's health than does the education of fathers.[5] Better-educated mothers know more about the benefits of proper diet and hygiene; they are also more likely to seek medical care, ensure that their children are immunized, be better informed about their children's nutritional requirements, and adopt improved sanitation practices. In addition, these women may have better access to information about health care, and to be better able to process and act on the information that they acquire. As a result, infants and children of women with some formal education have higher survival rates and tend to be healthier and better nourished. A mother with a few years of formal education is also more likely to send her children

[4] However, these associations could also reflect genetic links between parents and children.

[5] See Hill and King (1995) and Glewwe (1999) for early surveys. See also Morrison et al. (2007).

to school—which in turn may improve their health, by allowing them to learn better hygiene practices.

The evidence for sub-Saharan Africa for instance shows that children of mothers who received five years of primary education are 40 percent more likely to live beyond age five, and educated mothers are about 50 percent more likely to immunize their children than uneducated mothers (see Morrison et al. (2007)). McGuire (2006) found that the average number of schooling years for women has a statistically significant impact on the mortality rate of children under five. Kiros and Hogan (2001) for Ethiopia, Castro et al. (2006) for Guatemala, and Oloo (2005) for a larger group of developing countries also found that higher levels of female literacy tend to be associated with lower child mortality rates. Similarly, in a study of 47 sub-Saharan African countries over the period 1999–2004, Anyanwu and Erhijakpor (2009) found that female literacy is significantly and negatively related to both infant and under-five mortality rates. A study that followed women for over 35 years in Guatemala showed that the benefits of mothers' schooling for their children's health are even greater than previously estimated from studies conducted at one point in time (Maluccio et al. (2009)).

There are a number of other ways through which maternal education benefits children, boys and girls alike. Better-educated mothers may spend more time and resources on children's health and education (Brown (2006)). Behrman et al. (1999), in a study of rural India, found that literate and better-educated mothers spend more time on children's school work. Educated women tend to have fewer children, which reduces dependency ratios and thus increases (all else equal) per capita consumption within households. In their study of Brazil, Lam and Duryea (1999) found a strong negative effect of women's schooling on fertility. Brazilian women with no schooling at all give birth to 6.5 live children; this number declines to 3 for women with 8 years of schooling. Furthermore, they argue that the effect of schooling on fertility works primarily through increased investment (including time) in child quality. As discussed by Agénor et al. (2010), educated mothers may also have greater bargaining power within the household over intrafamily allocation of monetary resources, be better able to act on their preference for investing in children, and have a greater impact on family decisions regarding the allocation of children's time to household chores (such as meal preparation and cleanup, doing laundry, ironing, dusting, and indoor home cleaning and maintenance).

However, some caution is needed in interpreting the link between mothers' education and children's health. First, it is not simply the completion of a certain number of years of schooling by mothers that may yield the benefits outlined earlier; rather, it is *literacy* that appears to drive the relationship between education and health outcomes. This means that school quality may be what really determines the extent to which children derive health benefits from their parents' education. Moreover, if access to infrastructure is poor, even well-educated mothers may be unable to act upon their health knowledge and take their children to health facilities—an all too common problem in sub-Saharan Africa. Second, there is evidence that better-educated women marry better-educated men; it is thus possible that the observed effect of women's education may also, to some extent, reflect unobserved preferences of their husbands for healthier or better-educated children. A study of rural India, for instance, found that in a setting where educated women do not participate in the labor market, better-educated men are more likely to marry better-educated women (Behrman et al. (1999)).

### 1.3| Analytical Implications

The evidence reviewed in the previous subsections has important analytical implications for understanding and modeling the links among public capital, gender, and growth. First, to the extent that children's health depends on their mother's health and the time that they allocate to child rearing, and that health in childhood is an important determinant of health in adulthood, women's time allocation plays a crucial role in determining health outcomes, productivity and wages in adulthood, and the overall growth process. Second, when women lack access to core infrastructure services, they must allocate a greater proportion of their (and possibly their children's) time to household chores. The opportunity costs of poor infrastructure for women include wage labor, acquiring an education, and investing in their own health and the health of their children. Thus, in a fundamental sense, the gender gap in employment and wages in adulthood may result from women's lack of access to infrastructure.

By implication, improved access to core infrastructure services may enable women to devote more time to market activity and to improve learning monitoring and child care practices. The longer-run benefits in terms of improved health status and learning ability of their children, and eventually economic growth, can be substantial. However, it is possible that the increase in time that women devote to market work come at the expense of time allocated to child care; if so, and given health persistence, the longer-run effects on growth could be mitigated, or possibly reversed—despite the fact that higher earnings may allow mothers to spend more on goods and medical supplies for their children. The key issue to address therefore is how improved access to infrastructure affects, both directly and indirectly, the time women allocate to these various activities and how, in turn, changes in women's time allocation affect economic growth.

## 2| The Economy

Consider an OLG economy where two goods are produced, a marketed commodity and a home good, and individuals live for (at most) three periods: childhood, adulthood (or middle age), and retirement. The marketed commodity can be either consumed in the period it is produced or stored to yield capital at the beginning of the following period. Each individual is either male or female, and is endowed with one unit of time in childhood and adulthood, and zero units when old. As in chapter 2, schooling is mandatory, so children devote all their time to education. They depend on their parents for consumption and any spending associated with schooling and health care. All individuals, males and females, work in middle age; the only source of income is therefore wages in the second period of life.

In adulthood, individuals match randomly into couples with someone of the opposite sex to form a family. Intrafamily distribution of assets and resources is abstracted from by assuming that all income is pooled; couples therefore become joint decision makers. For simplicity, once married, individuals do not divorce; couples retire together (if they survive to old age) and die together.[6] Boys and girls have the same innate abilities and thus the same intrinsic capacity to acquire human capital.

The cost of rearing children involves the cost of schooling and the cost of keeping them healthy. In turn, these costs involve both parental time and spending on marketed commodities (school supplies, medicines, etc.). As a result of biological differences (women are the ones who actually bear children and are capable of breast feeding) or social norms, mothers incur the whole time cost involved in rearing children. Thus, women "specialize" in that activity within the family—even though there are no innate gender differences in home production skills. Male spouses allocate inelastically all their time to market work; by contrast, female spouses must consider four alternatives: market work, raising children, taking care of their own health, and home production.

The health status of children depends on the time mothers allocate to rearing their offspring and access to publicly-provided health services. Health status in adulthood depends on health status in childhood (as in chapter 3) and time spent caring about one's health. Children mature safely into adults, but at the end of the second period (again, as in chapter 3) there is a nonzero probability of dying. At the same time, to simplify the analysis the survival probabilities for men and women are taken to be the same, despite the fact that there are good biological and socioeconomic reasons to suggest that adult mortality rates differ by gender.

In addition to individuals, the economy is populated by firms and an infinitely lived government. Firms produce marketed commodities using public capital as an input, in addition to male and female labor and private capital. Home production combines women's time and infrastructure services. These

[6] Because the focus of the subsequent analysis is on women's health status, the assumption that husbands do not survive their wives and die of sorrow immediately after the passing of their spouse helps to simplify matters. The survival rate for men and women can be kept the same, and the gender composition of the population can be kept constant.

features of the production side of the model capture therefore the productivity effects of infrastructure, as in previous chapters.

Other assumptions remain as before. Savings can be held only in the form of physical capital. Agents have no other endowments, except for an initial stock of physical capital, which is the endowment of an initial old generation. The government invests in infrastructure and spends on education, health, and some unproductive items. It taxes the wage income of adults (males and females), but not the interest income of retirees. It maintains a balanced budget at all times.

## 2.1| Family's Utility and Income

At the beginning of adulthood in $t+1$, all men and women are randomly matched into married couples. Each couple produces $n_{t+1}$ children. [7] A mother raising a child faces two types of costs. First, she must spend $\varepsilon_{t+1}^{f,R} \in (0,1)$ units of time on each of them because she provides tutoring or "home schooling" and takes care of the child's health (taking them to medical facilities for checkups and vaccinations, etc.). Second, raising children involves costs in terms of marketed commodities. Specifically, it entails a cost per child (regardless of gender) equal to a fraction $\theta^R \in (0,1)$ of the family's net income. As in previous chapters, this cost is related to sending children to school and educating them at home (which involves buying school supplies, etc.) and to taking care of their health needs (such as buying medicines). [8] Thus, although access to "out of home" schooling and health services per se is free, families face a cost in terms of foregone wage income and foregone consumption.

In addition to raising children, mothers allocate time to market activity (in proportion $\varepsilon_{t+1}^{f,W}$ ) and to taking care of their own health needs (in proportion $\varepsilon_{t+1}^{f,H}$); this involves seeking medical treatment, personal hygiene, and exercise. For simplicity, these activities involve no pecuniary cost. Let $\varepsilon_{t+1}^{f,P}$ denote the time women allocate to home production (which includes time spent collecting water and firewood, for instance); the time constraint that women face is thus

$$\varepsilon_{t+1}^{f,W} = 1 - \varepsilon_{t+1}^{f,H} - \varepsilon_{t+1}^{f,P} - n_{t+1}\varepsilon_{t+1}^{f,R}. \tag{1}$$

To avoid convergence of population size (and the number of families) toward zero, it is also assumed that $n_{t+1} \geq 2$.

As in chapter 3, the saving left by agents who do not survive to old age is confiscated by the government, which transfers them in lump-sum fashion to surviving members of the same cohort. The gross rate of return to saving is thus $(1+r_{t+2})/p$, where $p \in (0,1)$ is again the probability of survival from

[7] Giving birth is also assumed to involve no time cost—or, equivalently, that the time involved is fixed and normalized to zero.

[8] These two types of costs could be separated by introducing different spending shares for the schooling and health components. This, however, would mainly add notational clutter and produce little value added to the analysis.

adulthood to old age. This probability is independent of gender and assumed constant for the moment.

The good consumed at home is a "composite" good produced by combining marketed commodities and the good produced at home. Assuming that consumption of children is subsumed in their parents' consumption, the family's lifetime utility takes the form

$$U_t = \ln[(c^t_{t+1})^{\omega} q^{1-\omega}_{t+1}] + \eta_N \ln h^C_{t+1} n_{t+1} + \frac{p}{1+\rho} \ln c^t_{t+2}, \tag{2}$$

where $c^t_{t+1}$ ($c^t_{t+2}$), is the family's total consumption in adulthood (old age), $q_{t+1}$ production of home goods, $h^C_{t+1}$ health status of a child, $\rho > 0$ the discount rate, and $\omega \in (0, 1)$. As in the three-period model of chapter 3, the term $h^C_{t+1} n_{t+1}$ can be interpreted as the "effective" number of children. Coefficient $\eta_N > 0$ measures the family's relative preference for healthy children. For simplicity, only the marketed commodity is consumed in old age. It is also assumed that parents have ready access to gender selection techniques, so that half of their children are daughters and half of them sons.[9]

A male (female) adult in period $t + 1$ is endowed with $e^m_{t+1}$ ($e^f_{t+1}$) units of human capital. Each unit of effective labor earns an effective wage, $w^m_{t+1}$ for men and $w^f_{t+1}$ for women, per unit of time worked.

The family's budget constraints for period $t + 1$ and $t + 2$ are given by

$$c^t_{t+1} + s_{t+1} = (1 - \theta^R n_{t+1})(1 - \tau) w^T_{t+1}, \tag{3}$$

$$c^t_{t+2} = (1 + r_{t+2}) s_{t+1} / p, \tag{4}$$

where $\tau \in (0, 1)$ is the tax rate, $s_{t+1}$ is family saving, and gross wage income is defined as

$$w^T_{t+1} = e^m_{t+1} w^m_{t+1} + e^f_{t+1} \varepsilon^{f,W}_{t+1} a^f_{t+1} w^f_{t+1}. \tag{5}$$

In this expression, $a^f_{t+1}$ is female labor productivity. As noted earlier, husbands supply inelastically to paid work the unit of time that they have available. For simplicity, and as discussed further later, it is also assumed that male productivity is constant and normalized to unity.

The family's consolidated budget constraint is thus

$$c^t_{t+1} + \frac{p c^t_{t+2}}{1 + r_{t+2}} = (1 - \theta^R n_{t+1})(1 - \tau) w^T_{t+1}. \tag{6}$$

[9] This assumption can also be justified in terms of equal family preferences for boys and girls. Indeed, the term $\eta_N \ln h^C_{t+1} n_{t+1}$ in (2) can be replaced by the composite term $\eta^B_N \ln h^C_{t+1} n^B_{t+1} + \eta^G_N \ln h^C_{t+1} n^G_{t+1}$, where $n^B_{t+1}$ ($n^G_{t+1}$) is the number of boys (girls). With $\eta^B_N = \eta^G_N$, the solution would then yield $n^B_{t+1} = n^G_{t+1}$.

## 2.2| Home Production

Home production (which includes cooking dinner, washing the kitchen floor, doing laundry, cleaning the house, etc.) involves combining women's time allocated to that activity with (congested) infrastructure services.[10] For simplicity, it is assumed that these factors are perfect substitutes and that production takes place under decreasing returns to scale:[11]

$$q_t = [\varepsilon_t^{f,P} + \zeta^P (k_t^I)]^{\pi^Q}, \tag{7}$$

where $\pi^Q \in (0, 1)$ and $\zeta^P \geq 0$ is an efficiency parameter. Thus, greater access to roads or electricity for instance allows mothers to devote less time to home production.

## 2.3| Market Production

Firms are identical and their number is normalized to unity. They produce a single nonstorable commodity, using male effective labor, $L_t^{m,i}$, and female effective labor, defined as $A_t^f \varepsilon_t^{f,W} L_t^{f,i}$, where $A_t^f$ is economy-wide female labor productivity, and $L_t^{j,i} = E_t^j N_t^{j,i}$ (where $E_t^j$ is average human capital for $j = m, f$), and private capital, $K_t^{P,i}$.[12]

The production function of individual firm $i$ takes the form

$$Y_t^i = (L_t^{m,i})^{\beta} (A_t^f \varepsilon_t^{f,W} L_t^{f,i})^{\beta} (K_t^{P,i})^{1-2\beta}, \tag{8}$$

where $\beta \in (0, 1)$. For simplicity, the elasticity of output with respect to male and female labor is assumed to be the same.

Each firm's objective is to maximize profits, $\Pi_t^i$, with respect to labor services and private capital, given $E_t^m$, $E_t^f$, $A_t^f$, and $\varepsilon_t^{f,W}$:

$$\max_{N_t^{m,i}, N_t^{f,i}, K_t^{P,i}} \Pi_t^i = Y_t^i - (r_t + \delta^P) K_t^{P,i} - w_t^m E_t^m N_t^{m,i} + w_t^f A_t^f \varepsilon_t^{f,W} E_t^f N_t^{f,i}.$$

The results are

$$\frac{\beta Y_t^i}{N_t^{m,i}} - w_t^m E_t^m = 0, \quad \frac{\beta Y_t^i}{N_t^{f,i}} - w_t^f A_t^f \varepsilon_t^{f,W} E_t^f = 0,$$

$$\frac{(1-2\beta) Y_t^i}{K_t^{P,i}} - \delta^P - r_t = 0.$$

[10] It could be assumed that home production requires also the use of marketed commodities. This would not bring additional insight for the purpose at hand. Child labor is also ignored.

[11] An inverse relationship between time allocated to home production and access to infrastructure services (as derived later) could be established with alternative production functions involving either a constant or a variable elasticity of substitution. The specification used here is more tractable.

[12] Again, to clarify matters the productivity effects identified in chapter 1 are abstracted from.

The gender gap in the firm is captured in a very simple way: due to discrimination in the workplace, women only earn a fraction $b \in (0, 1)$ of their marginal product. Thus, the equations above can be rearranged to give [13]

$$w_t^m = \frac{\beta Y_t^i}{L_t^{m,i}}, \quad w_t^f = b\frac{\beta Y_t^i}{A_t^f \varepsilon_t^{f,W} L_t^{f,i}}, \tag{9}$$

$$r_t = (1-2\beta)\frac{Y_t^i}{K_t^{P,i}} - \delta^P. \tag{10}$$

In equilibrium, given that men and women are in equal numbers in the adult population ($N_t^m = N_t^f$),

$$w_t^m = b^{-1}\left(\frac{A_t^f \varepsilon_t^{f,W} E_t^f}{E_t^m}\right) w_t^f. \tag{11}$$

Aggregate output is

$$Y_t = \int_0^1 Y_t^i di = \left(\frac{L_t^m}{K_t^P}\right)^\beta \left(\frac{A_t^f \varepsilon_t^{f,W} L_t^f}{K_t^P}\right)^\beta K_t^P. \tag{12}$$

### 2.4| Human Capital Accumulation

As in chapter 2, schooling is mandatory so children allocate all of their time to education. Boys and girls have identical innate abilities and have access to the same "out of home" learning technology. However, each group's education outcomes depend also on the amount of time that parents devote to tutoring them at home.

Let $e_{t+1}^j$, $j = m, f$ be the human capital of men and women born in period $t$ and used in period $t+1$. The production of either type of human capital requires several inputs. First, it depends on the time allocated to education in childhood, which (as noted earlier) is normalized to unity. Second, it depends on the time that mothers allocate to tutoring their children—an effect that is consistent with various studies (see Moav (2005)). Time allocation is sequential; mothers determine first the total amount of time allocated to child rearing, $\varepsilon_t^{f,R}$, and then subdivide that time into a fraction $\chi \in (0, 1)$ allocated to sons and $1 - \chi$ allocated to daughters. A bias in parental preferences toward boys can therefore be captured by assuming that $\chi > 0.5$.[14]

[13] The loss in income that women suffer as a result of discrimination could be assumed to accrue to capital owners, who use it to finance current consumption. However, to capture the adverse economic effects of gender discrimination, it is assumed instead to be a pure deadweight loss.

[14] See for instance Amin and Chandrasekhar (2009) for some evidence on parental time allocation between sons and daughters for Bangladesh.

Third, knowledge accumulation depends on average government spending on education per child, $G_t^E/n_t N_t$, where $N_t$ is the number of adults alive in period $t$, itself given by

$$N_t = n_{t-1} N_{t-1}, \tag{13}$$

that is, the number of children born in period $t - 1$.

Finally, in line with the empirical evidence (see Blackden et al. (2006)), human capital accumulation depends on a mother's human capital. As in previous chapters, because individuals are identical within a generation, a mother's human capital at $t$ is equal to the average human capital of the previous female generation.[15]

Thus, abstracting from gender-based discrimination in the public education system itself, and assuming no depreciation for simplicity, the human capital that men and women have in the second period of life is

$$e_{t+1}^j = \varepsilon_t^{f,R} \left( \frac{G_t^E}{n_t N_t} \right)^{\nu} (E_t^f)^{1-\nu} \times \begin{cases} \chi & \text{for } j = m \\ 1 - \chi & \text{for } j = f \end{cases}, \tag{14}$$

where $\nu \in (0, 1)$. For tractability, the education technology is taken to be linear in $\varepsilon_t^{f,R}$ and to exhibit constant returns to scale in government spending and the average human capital of mothers.

Combining equations (14) yields

$$\frac{e_{t+1}^m}{e_{t+1}^f} = \frac{\chi}{1 - \chi}, \tag{15}$$

which implies that, if $\chi > 0.5$, a boy's human capital will exceed systematically a girl's human capital—as a result solely of the greater time that mothers allocate to rearing their sons. However, even though the human capital stocks of sons and daughters may differ systematically in the long run, the wage gap in this model does not necessarily perpetuate itself: from (11), as long as the health status of women (and therefore their productivity) improves over time, the wage differential will narrow as well—despite persistent discrimination in the workplace (as measured by $b$ ). The same result would obtain if the time women allocate to market work increases over time, as discussed later.

## 2.5| Health Status and Productivity

Health status in childhood, $h_t^C$, depends on the effective amount of time allocated by the child's mother to rearing her offspring, and the provision of

[15] For simplicity, the impact of infrastructure on human capital (discussed in chapter 2) is abstracted from.

health services by the government, $H_t^G$,

$$h_t^C = (\zeta_t^R \varepsilon_t^{f,R})^{\nu_C} \left( \frac{H_t^G}{K_t^P} \right)^{1-\nu_C}, \tag{16}$$

where $\nu_C \in (0, 1)$ and $\zeta_t^R$ is an efficiency parameter, which is assumed to depend on access to infrastructure:

$$\zeta_t^R = (k_t^I)^{\pi^R}, \tag{17}$$

where $\pi^R \in (0, 1)$. Thus, greater access to (congested) roads or electricity allows mothers to devote less "raw" time to child care, while providing the same effective time. The marginal efficiency gain decreases over time.

As noted earlier, given the focus of this chapter on women's time allocation, the health status of males and their productivity are not modeled explicitly; instead, both are constant and normalized to unity.[16] By contrast, the health status of females in adulthood, $h_{t+1}^f$, is taken to depend on two factors, both of them discussed in chapter 3: their health status in childhood and the time spent taking care of their own health, $\varepsilon_{t+1}^{f,H}$:

$$h_{t+1}^f = h_t^C \left( \varepsilon_{t+1}^{f,H} \right)^{\nu_A}, \tag{18}$$

where $\nu_A \in (0, 1)$. For simplicity, health status is assumed linear in $h_t^C$. This specification is again consistent with the evidence suggesting that early childhood health affects cognitive and physical development, which in turn affects health outcomes later in life.

Female productivity, $a_{t+1}^f$, is simply a linear function of health status:

$$a_{t+1}^f = h_{t+1}^f. \tag{19}$$

Substituting (16) and (18) in (19) yields

$$a_{t+1}^f = (\varepsilon_t^{f,R})^{\nu_C} (\varepsilon_{t+1}^{f,H})^{\nu_A} (k_t^I)^{\pi^R \nu_C} \left( \frac{H_t^G}{K_t^P} \right)^{1-\nu_C}. \tag{20}$$

## 2.6| Government

As noted earlier, the government taxes only the wage income of adults, and spends on infrastructure, education, health, and unproductive items. All its services are provided free of charge. With a balanced budget, spending must

[16] It can be shown that if men's health and productivity depend on the same variables as women's health and productivity, and if in addition women's health generates a positive externality in terms of men's health—perhaps because a healthier wife is more conscious of the benefits of a healthy diet for her husband and prepares home meals accordingly—then what matters fundamentally for the dynamics of the economy is indeed women's health.

equal tax revenues:

$$G_t = \sum G_t^h = \tau(w_t^m L_t^m + w_t^f A_t^f \varepsilon_t^{f,W} L_t^f). \tag{21}$$

Shares of spending are all assumed to be constant fractions of revenues:

$$G_t^h = \upsilon_h \tau(w_t^m L_t^m + w_t^f A_t^f \varepsilon_t^{f,W} L_t^f), \quad h = E, H, I, U \tag{22}$$

so that

$$\sum \upsilon_h = 1. \tag{23}$$

Assuming again full depreciation and that $\mu = 1$, public capital in infrastructure evolves according to

$$K_{t+1}^I = \varphi G_t^I. \tag{24}$$

The production of health services by the government depends solely on government spending on health services, $G_t^H$:

$$H_t^G = G_t^H. \tag{25}$$

Thus, for clarity, the impact of access to infrastructure on the supply of health services, discussed at length in chapter 3, is abstracted from.

## 2.7| Savings-Investment Balance

The asset-market-clearing condition requires private capital stock in $t+1$ to be equal to savings in period $t$ by individuals born in $t-1$. Given that $s_t$ is savings per family, and that the number of families is $(N_t^m + N_t^f)/2$, this yields

$$K_{t+1}^P = 0.5(N_t^m + N_t^f)s_t = N_t^f s_t. \tag{26}$$

A *competitive equilibrium* is now a sequence of prices $\{w_t^m, w_t^f, r_{t+1}\}_{t=0}^{\infty}$, allocations $\{c_t^t, c_{t+1}^t, s_t\}_{t=0}^{\infty}$, physical capital stocks $\{K_{t+1}^P, K_{t+1}^I\}_{t=0}^{\infty}$, human capital stocks $\{E_{t+1}^m, E_{t+1}^f\}_{t=0}^{\infty}$, health status of children and adult females $\{h_t^C, h_{t+1}^f\}_{t=0}^{\infty}$, a constant tax rate, and constant public spending shares such that, given initial stocks $K_0^P, K_0^I > 0$ and $E_0^m, E_0^f > 0$, initial health statuses $h_0^C, h_0^f > 0$, individuals maximize utility, firms maximize profits, markets clear, and the government budget is balanced. In addition, in equilibrium $e_t^j = E_t^j$, for $j = m, f$, and $a_t^f = A_t^f$. A *balanced growth equilibrium* is a competitive equilibrium in which $c_t^t, c_{t+1}^t, K_{t+1}^P, K_{t+1}^I, E_{t+1}^m, E_{t+1}^f$ grow at the constant, endogenous rate $\gamma$, population grows at a constant rate $\tilde{n}$, the rate of return on private capital $r_{t+1}$ and effective wage rates $w_t^m, w_t^f$ are all constant, and health status of both children and adult females, $h_t^C$ and $h_t^f$, are constant.

## 3| Women's Time Allocation and Fertility

As shown in the appendix, solving the family's optimization problem leads to the following solutions for women's time allocation and the fertility rate: [17]

$$\varepsilon_t^{f,P} = \max\left\{\varepsilon_m^{f,P}, \left(1+\frac{\Lambda_1}{\Lambda_2}\right)^{-1}\left(\frac{\Lambda_1}{\Lambda_2} - \zeta^P k_t^I\right)\right\}, \tag{27}$$

$$\varepsilon_t^{f,H} = \nu_A \varepsilon_t^{f,W}, \tag{28}$$

$$\varepsilon_t^{f,W} = \frac{1-\varepsilon_t^{f,P}}{\Lambda_2}, \tag{29}$$

$$\varepsilon_t^{f,R} = \frac{\Lambda_3 \theta^R \eta_N \nu_C (1-\sigma)}{\omega(1-\nu_C)}\left(\frac{1-\varepsilon_t^{f,P}}{\Lambda_2}\right), \tag{30}$$

$$\tilde{n} = \frac{1-\nu_C}{\Lambda_3 \theta^R} > 0, \tag{31}$$

where $\sigma = p/[\omega(1+\rho)+p] < 1$ is the family's marginal propensity to save, $\varepsilon_m^{f,P}$ the minimum amount of time to be allocated to home production, and

$$\Lambda_1 = (1-\omega)\pi^Q(1-\sigma)\omega^{-1} > 0,$$

$$\Lambda_2 = 1 + \nu_A + \eta_N \nu_C (1-\sigma)\omega^{-1} > 1,$$

$$\Lambda_3 = 1 - \nu_C + \frac{\omega}{\eta_N(1-\sigma)} > 0.$$

The properties of these solutions can be summarized as follows:[18]

**Result 5.1.** *Improved access to infrastructure services, up to a critical threshold $k_C^I$, reduces women's time allocated to home production and raises time allocated to market work, own health care, and child rearing. It has no effect on the fertility rate as long as the unit cost $\theta^R$ is constant.*

The decreasing relationship between $k_t^I$ and $\varepsilon_t^{f,P}$ implied by (27), as long as $\varepsilon_t^{f,P} \geq \varepsilon_m^{f,P}$, is the main channel through which access to public infrastructure affects women's time allocation decisions. If $\zeta^P = 0$, $\varepsilon_t^{f,P}$ is constant at $\tilde{\varepsilon}^{f,P} < 1$ and so are the other time allocation parameters. Figure 5.1 illustrates

[17] To ensure that $\tilde{n} \geq 2$ requires imposing an upper bound on $\theta^R$, that is, spending per child on marketed commodities cannot be too high ($\theta^R \leq 0.5(1-\nu_C)/\Lambda_3$). Note also that the solutions do not depend directly on the gender bias parameters, $b$ and $\chi$.

[18] The increase in child rearing time is consistent with the results of Koolwal and van de Walle (2010) on the impact of greater access to water infrastructure on women's time allocation.

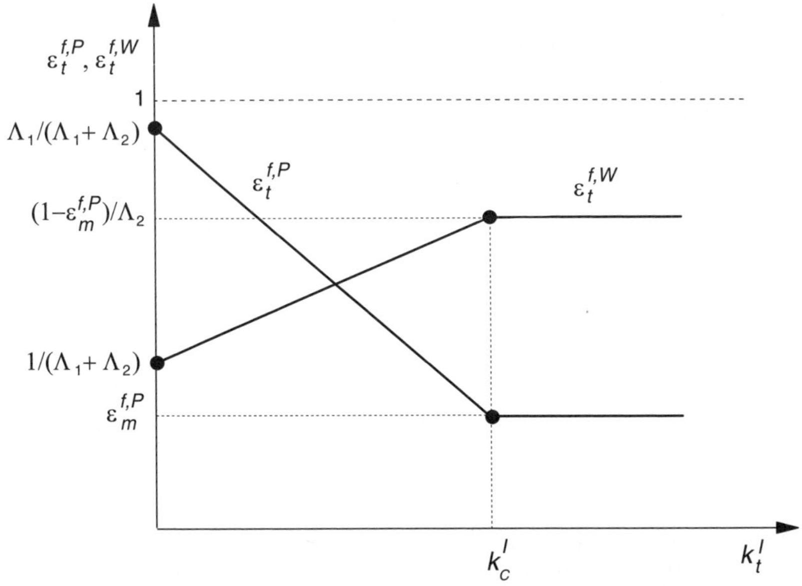


Figure 5.1. Access to Infrastructure and Women's Time Allocation.

the behavior of $\varepsilon_t^{f,P}$ and $\varepsilon_t^{f,W}$ as a function of $k_t^I$. Because $\Lambda_2$ is greater than unity, time allocated to market work grows at a slower rate than the (absolute) rate at which time spent on home production falls. Intuitively, this is because some of the time saving is reallocated not only to market work but also to other activities (own health care and child rearing). The figure assumes that $\Lambda_1 > 1$, to ensure that the initial value $\varepsilon_0^{f,P}$ (for $k_t^I = 0$) is higher than $\varepsilon_0^{f,W}$. In turn, $\Lambda_1 > 1$ requires $1 - \omega > 1/[1 + \pi^Q(1 - \sigma)]$, or equivalently that the home good be sufficiently valued by the family.

From (27) and (29), there is a critical value of the public-private capital ratio, determined by

$$k_C^I = \frac{1}{\zeta^P}\left\{\frac{\Lambda_1}{\Lambda_2} - \left(1 + \frac{\Lambda_1}{\Lambda_2}\right)\varepsilon_m^{f,P}\right\}, \tag{32}$$

above which $\varepsilon_t^{f,P}$ is equal to $\varepsilon_m^{f,P}$ and $\varepsilon_t^{f,W}$ reaches its maximum value, $(1 - \varepsilon_m^{f,P})/\Lambda_2$:

$$\varepsilon_t^{f,P} = \begin{cases} f(k_t^I) \text{ If } k_t^I < \hat{k}^I \\ \varepsilon_m^{f,P} \quad \text{If } k_t^I \geq \hat{k}^I \end{cases}, \quad \varepsilon_t^{f,W} = \begin{cases} \Lambda_2^{-1}[1 - f(k_t^I)] \text{ If } k_t^I < \hat{k}^I \\ (1 - \varepsilon_m^{f,P})\Lambda_2^{-1} \quad \text{If } k_t^I \geq \hat{k}^I \end{cases}. \tag{33}$$

From these solutions, it can be established (as in chapter 3), that an increase in the survival probability from adulthood to old age increases the savings rate and reduces the fertility rate. More important for the purpose at hand, the following results can be established (see the appendix):

**Results 5.2.** *An increase in the survival probability from adulthood to old age, p, for a given public-private capital ratio, raises both the time allocated to market work and the time women allocate to their own health. It also reduces the fertility rate and the amount of time allocated to home production. However, it has an ambiguous effect on women's time allocated to child rearing—both total and on a per child basis.*

The effect of the survival rate on women's time allocation operates essentially through the change in the saving rate. The increase in time allocated to work is also part of the life-cycle effect associated with greater longevity, as noted in chapter 3. At the same time, an increase in the survival rate induces women to allocate more time to their own health (because it affects productivity and income), and to less time being allocated to home production. Thus, the increase in the survival rate leads to intratemporal substitution in mothers' time—between home production, on the one hand, and working time and time allocated to own health, on the other.

However, an increase in the adult survival probability has an ambiguous effect on both total time allocated to child care, $n_t\varepsilon_t^{f,R}$, and time allocated to each child, $\varepsilon_t^{f,R}$.[19] Intuitively, the reason for this is that such time does not have a direct effect on the family's resources, neither today (there is no child labor) nor in the future (there are no intergenerational bequests). The net effect depends, in general, on the structure of preferences (namely, $\eta_N$) and the parameter that measures the response of health status in childhood to mothers' time, $\nu_C$. In particular, as shown in the appendix to this chapter, the less parents value their children (that is, the lower $\eta_N$ is), the more likely it is that total time allocated to child rearing will fall. This ambiguity is quite important. From the perspective of women's time allocation decisions, what matters is total time devoted to children, $n_t\varepsilon_t^{f,R}$, as implied by (1). However, to assess the growth effects of these decisions, time allocated to each child, $\varepsilon_t^{f,R}$, matters as well because it affects directly health outcomes, as implied by (16) and (18).

## 4| The Balanced Growth Path

The balanced growth rate of the economy is derived in the appendix to this chapter. The public-private capital ratio is given by

$$k_{t+1}^I = \frac{\varphi \upsilon_I \tau}{\sigma(1-\tau)(1-\theta^R n_t)} = J, \tag{34}$$

which is constant as long as the savings rate and the fertility rate are constant. This is the same result as obtained in previous chapters with $\mu = 1$. Because

[19] In the three-period model presented in chapter 3, in which individuals can allocate time only to market work or child rearing, an increase in the adult survival probability necessarily raises total time allocated to child care.

the savings rate is positively related to the survival rate (consistent with results 3.1 in chapter 3), the following corollary to results 5.3 can be established:

**Corollary to Results 5.2.** *An increase in the survival probability from adulthood to old age, p, lowers the public-private capital ratio.*

As shown in the appendix, the system boils down to an autonomous, first-order linear difference equation system in $\hat{h}_t^f = \ln h_t^f$ and $\hat{x}_t^f = \ln x_t^f$, where $h_t^f$ is female health status and $x_t^f = K_t^P/e_t^f N_t^f$ is the private capital-female effective labor ratio:

$$\begin{bmatrix} \hat{x}_{t+1}^f \\ \hat{h}_{t+1}^f \end{bmatrix} = \begin{bmatrix} a_{11} & a_{12} \\ a_{21} & a_{22} \end{bmatrix} \begin{bmatrix} \hat{x}_t^f \\ \hat{h}_t^f \end{bmatrix}, \tag{35}$$

where

$$a_{11} = (1-2\beta)(1-\nu) > 0,$$

$$a_{12} = \beta(1-\nu) > 0,$$

$$a_{21} = -2\beta(1-\nu_C) < 0,$$

$$a_{22} = \beta(1-\nu_C) > 0.$$

As also shown in the appendix, the dynamic system (35) is stable under relatively mild conditions.

The steady-state growth rate per worker is given as

$$1+\gamma = \frac{1}{\tilde{n}}\left(\frac{\chi\tilde{\varepsilon}^{f,W}}{1-\chi}\right)^{\beta} b\beta\Phi\sigma(1-\theta^R\tilde{n})(\tilde{h}^f)^{\beta}(\tilde{x}^f)^{-2\beta}, \tag{36}$$

where $\Phi = (1-\tau)(b^{-1}+1)$ and $\tilde{h}^f$ and $\tilde{x}^f$ are steady-state solutions determined by

$$\tilde{h}^f = [\theta^R(\tilde{\varepsilon}^{f,R})^{\nu_C}(\tilde{\varepsilon}^{f,H})^{\nu_A} J^{\Omega_1}]^{1/(1-\Omega_2)} \times \left\{[\upsilon_H\tau(1+b)\beta]^{1-\nu_C}\left(\frac{\chi\tilde{\varepsilon}^{f,W}}{1-\chi}\right)^{\Omega_2}\right\}^{1/(1-\Omega_2)} (\tilde{x}^f)^{-2\Omega_2/(1-\Omega_2)}, \tag{37}$$

$$\tilde{x}^f = \left\{\Gamma\left\{\left[\frac{\chi\tilde{\varepsilon}^{f,W}}{1-\chi}\right]^{\beta}\right\}^{1-\nu}\right\}^{1/\Omega_3} (\tilde{h}^f)^{\beta(1-\nu)/\Omega_3}, \tag{38}$$

with

$$\Omega_1 = \pi^R\nu_C > 0,$$

$$\Omega_2 = \beta(1-\nu_C) \in (0, 1),$$

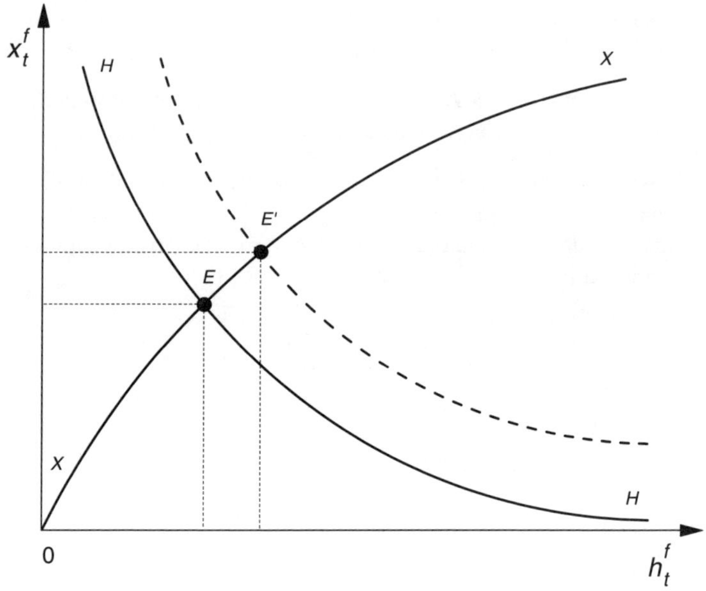


Figure 5.2. Equilibrium and Effect of an Autonomous Increase in Women's Time Allocated to Own Health.

$$\Omega_3 = 1 - (1 - 2\beta)(1 - \nu) > 0,$$

$$\Gamma = \left[ \frac{b\beta\Phi\sigma(1 - \theta^R \tilde{n})}{(1 - \chi)\tilde{\varepsilon}^{f,R}\tilde{n}^{1-\nu}(0.5)^\nu} \right] [\upsilon_E \tau(1 + b)\beta]^{-\nu}.$$

The steady-state relationship (37) is shown as the decreasing convex curve $HH$ in Figure 5.2, whereas the relationship (38) is depicted as the upward-sloping concave curve $XX$. It is immediately clear from the diagram that there is a unique nontrivial equilibrium, located at point $E$. As shown in the appendix, the equilibrium is stable as long as $\nu$ is not too large. Depending on the initial values, however, the economy may converge either monotonically or with cycles.

The following result is immediately clear from those established previously:

**Result 5.3.** *An increase in the survival probability from adulthood to old age has an ambiguous effect on the steady-state growth rate in output per worker.*

As noted earlier, an increase in the survival probability from adulthood to old age tends to increase the saving rate; this tends to promote growth directly, as implied by (36). However, its overall effect can be negative. In the present setting, there are two reasons for this to occur. The first is that higher savings translate into a higher stock of private capital and this tends to worsen, all else equal, congestion effects on public infrastructure. Even in the absence of any effect of public capital on production, education, and health services, a lower public-private capital ratio reduces the efficiency of time allocated to child rearing, thereby affecting negatively female health and productivity in adulthood. The second reason is that higher life expectancy may, as discussed earlier, lower raw time allocated by mothers to child care—which eventually may also affect adversely their health and productivity in adulthood.

The impact of women's time allocation on growth can be summarized as follows: [20]

**Result 5.4.** *An autonomous increase in time allocated to own care improves female health status and raises steady-state growth; an autonomous increase in time allocated to child rearing improves female health status but has an ambiguous effect on long-run growth; and an autonomous increase in time allocated to market work raises the private capital-female effective labor ratio but has an ambiguous impact on female health status and long-run growth.*

These results illustrate the importance of accounting for the productive effects of nonmarket work. In the model, time allocated by women to their own health is productive and always growth promoting. Graphically, an autonomous increase in $\tilde{\varepsilon}^{f,H}$ leads to an upward shift in $HH$ and no change in $XX$, as shown in Figure 5.2. The new equilibrium point $E'$ is located to the northeast of $E$.

By contrast, an autonomous increase in $\tilde{\varepsilon}^{f,R}$ or $\tilde{\varepsilon}^{f,W}$ has an ambiguous effect on growth. In the first case, an increase in child rearing time has a positive impact on growth, as a direct consequence of the serial dependence in female health status, and because it affects positively education outcomes. At the same time, however, it raises family income, savings, and private investment; because both private capital and female human capital increase, the change in $\tilde{x}^f$ (and thus the overall growth effect) is ambiguous. Graphically, an autonomous increase in $\tilde{\varepsilon}^{f,R}$ leads to an upward shift in $HH$ and a downward shift in $XX$; the new equilibrium is now located either to the northeast or the southeast of $E$. Thus, $\tilde{h}^f$ always increases, whereas $\tilde{x}^f$ may go either up or down.

In similar fashion, an autonomous increase in $\tilde{\varepsilon}^{f,W}$ increases savings and private capital; because it has no direct effect on female education, the increase in the private capital stock raises unambiguously the private capital-effective female labor ratio. However, the increase in the private capital stock also compounds congestion problems and lowers the efficiency of rearing time; the net effect on female health status and productivity are thus ambiguous, and so is the overall effect on growth. Graphically, both $HH$ and $XX$ shift upward

[20] An "autonomous" change in time allocation is implicitly assumed here to be offset by a change in time allocated to home production, keeping other components constant.

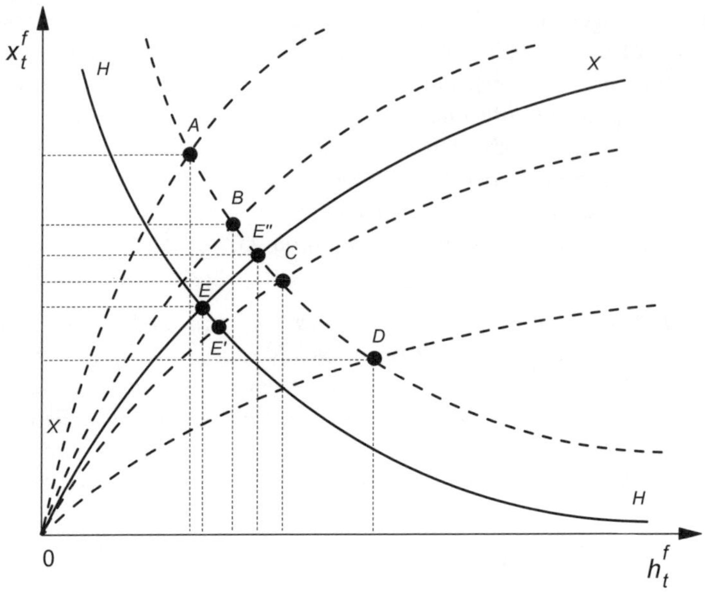


Figure 5.3. Budget-Neutral Increase in Shares of Public Spending on Infrastructure, Health, and Education.

as a result of an increase in $\tilde{\varepsilon}^{f,W}$; the new equilibrium is located either to the northeast or the northwest of $E$. Thus, more time allocated to market work can, in some circumstances, reduce growth.

Equations (36) to (38) can also be used to examine the impact of specific parameters on long-run growth. In particular, the effect of an increase in the parameter characterizing the response of the efficiency parameter $\zeta_t^R$ that affects women's time allocated to child rearing with respect to the public-private capital ratio, $\pi^R$, is illustrated in Figure 5.2 as well. Again, curve $HH$ shifts upward whereas $XX$ does not change; the outcome is both an improvement in health status and a higher private capital-effective female labor ratio in the new long-run equilibrium.

## 5| Public Policy

To begin with, consider a budget-neutral increase in the share of spending on education financed by a cut in unproductive outlays ($d\upsilon_E + d\upsilon_U = 0$).[21] This leads into a downward shift in $XX$ with no change in $HH$; the new equilibrium is at a point like $E'$ in Figure 5.3. Women's health status unambiguously

[21] Budget-neutral increases in one share of productive spending that are offset by changes in another share would, of course, create trade-offs between spending allocations, as discussed in previous chapters.

improves once again, whereas the private capital-effective female labor ratio falls. Both effects combine to promote growth, as formally established in the appendix.

Consider now a budget-neutral increase in the share of spending on health financed by a cut in unproductive spending ($d\upsilon_H + d\upsilon_U = 0$ ). Curve $HH$ in Figure 5.3 shifts upward, whereas curve $XX$ does not change; the equilibrium shifts from $E$ to a point like $E''$ in Figure 5.3. Thus, both women's health status and the private capital-effective female labor ratio increase. Because the latter effect tends to lower growth, the net effect on long-run growth is now ambiguous, as also shown in the appendix. Because the steady-state public-private capital ratio does not depend on the spending shares $\upsilon_E$ and $\upsilon_H$ (as can be inferred from (34), given (31)), women's time allocation is not altered by these policy changes, these results are the same regardless of whether $J \gtrless k_C^I$.

Finally, consider a budget-neutral increase in the share of public spending on infrastructure, such that $d\upsilon_I + d\upsilon_U = 0$. As in previous chapters, the direct effect is an increase in the public-private capital ratio, which promotes growth. The efficiency of women's time allocated child rearing also increases, again with a positive effect on growth. In addition, there are also indirect effects on women's time allocation, as long as initially $J < k_C^I$ and $\tilde{\varepsilon}^{f,P} > \varepsilon_m^{f,P}$. As shown in the appendix, time allocated to home production falls, whereas time allocated to market work, own health, and child rearing increases. However, the net effect on growth is not necessarily positive. As illustrated in Figure 5.3, the increase in $\upsilon_I$ leads to an upward shift in $HH$ but $XX$ can shift either up or down. The reason is that changes in private capital and human capital affect the private capital-female labor ratio in opposite directions: the increase in women's time allocated to market work raises savings and private capital, which tends to increase $x_t$; at the same time, the increase in parental time allocated to child rearing increases human capital, which tends to lower $x_t$.

The new equilibrium can be either at $A$, $B$, $C$, or $D$, depending on which effect dominates. If $XX$ shifts downward (the human capital effect dominates), women's health status unambiguously improves, whereas the capital-effective female labor ratio may either increase (point $C$) or fall (point $D$). If, on the contrary, $XX$ shifts upward (the savings effect dominates), women's health status may either deteriorate (point $A$) or improve (point $B$), depending on the magnitude of the shift.

From (36),

$$\frac{d\ln(1+\gamma)}{d\upsilon_I} = \beta\left[\left(\frac{d\ln\tilde{\varepsilon}^{f,W}}{d\upsilon_I}\right) + \left(\frac{d\ln\tilde{h}^f}{d\upsilon_I}\right)\right] - 2\beta\left(\frac{d\ln\tilde{x}^f}{d\upsilon_I}\right), \qquad (39)$$

implying that, except for the case corresponding to point $D$, the net effect on growth is in general ambiguous. Thus, the thrust of the foregoing analysis is that, even in the absence of trade-offs among productive components of government spending, changes in time allocation may alter in significant ways the growth effect of changes in public investment in infrastructure.[22]

## 6| Women's Labor Supply and Development

The foregoing analysis has useful implications for the long-standing debate on the determinants of women's labor supply in the course of development. Studies based on data pertaining to both developed and developing countries suggest the existence of a U-shaped relationship between women's labor force participation and the level of development, as measured by income per capita, with participation being the highest in the poorest and richest countries (see Mammen and Paxson (2000) and Tam (2011)).

Various explanations have been offered for the existence of this U-shaped relationship. For very poor countries, female labor force participation is high, and women work mainly in labor-intensive farm or nonfarm family enterprises—possibly with less access than men to inputs relevant to farming activities and other productive assets such as labor-saving technologies. Women enter the labor force even at fairly low wages because unearned incomes are also low. Development initially moves women out of the labor force, partly because of the rise in men's wages and earnings (which therefore raise unearned income) and partly because of social barriers against women entering the paid labor force. However, as countries continue to develop, women's education levels rise and women move back into the labor force as paid employees. Thus, at low levels of income, they work more than they would like. As income increases, female labor force participation decreases. Eventually, capital per capita is high enough to induce women to join the labor force again. As income rises, women move from work in family enterprises to work as paid employees. This pattern also has implications for the behavior of fertility over the course of development.

A woman's decision to enter the labor market depends in general on two key components. The first is the opportunity cost of her time; a higher wage induces a *substitution effect* that makes working away from home, and working for a longer period of time, more attractive. As long as this substitution effect dominates the offsetting *income effect*, higher wages (which tend to promote investment in human capital and the acquisition of market-related transferable skills) would tend to increase female labor participation, as suggested by the empirical evidence. The second is income that is not "earned" directly, be it income generated by her husband if she is married or income from other family members. This exerts only *income effects*, therefore depressing female labor participation rates. Thus, the U-shaped pattern alluded to earlier could

[22] Agénor and Agénor (2009) consider the case where changes in government spending are associated with discrete shifts in female productivity, life expectancy, and time allocated to home production.

result from the fact that, at low and high levels of economic development, unearned income is low. Alternatively, the (negative) income effect may dominate the (positive) substitution effect initially, with a reversal at higher levels of development. Indeed, as income increases initially, and with female educational levels relatively low, the demand for children may also increase, causing female participation rates to decrease as the result of a negative income effect. Over time, as income continues to increase, and with opportunities for women to invest in education and engage in paid work improving, there may be a substitution of "quality for quantity" in the desired number of children (as discussed in chapter 3), leading to a stronger substitution effect.

A third possibility is that the U-shaped relationship may be the result of cultural, religious, and social norms, which restrict employment opportunities for women. Indeed, at low levels of income women (who often do not hold any land) may have no choice but to engage in family farm activities or agriculture more generally. If the structure of production changes over time, with a shift first from agriculture to male-labor-intensive manufacturing (associated with the expansion of markets and the creation of new technologies), and subsequently a change in the composition of manufacturing toward female-labor-intensive industries (such as textiles or light electronics), coupled with a shift toward services  and improved opportunities for women to educate themselves), a U-shaped relationship may emerge.

Yet another possibility, in line with the foregoing analysis of women's time allocation, is that the U-shaped curve is a result of a nonlinear relationship between female labor participation and access to infrastructure. In the early stages of economic development, public capital is insufficient, constraining private activities and opportunities for market work for both men and women. For instance, the lack of roads may prevent farmers from investing in transportation equipment. In addition, women must allocate a large fraction of their time to home production. Thus, time devoted to market work is limited and women participate mostly in family farm activities. As access to public capital improves, and (complementary) private capital expands, labor productivity and thus labor demand increase, while time allocated to farm activities and home production (as illustrated in Figure 5.1) falls. But initially women may allocate most of the resulting time savings to their children's health and their own health care (as implied by results 5.1) or possibly also to the acquisition of skills. The former effect would occur if, initially, the preference for children's health is very high. As a result, the *effective* female labor force participation rate may fall. Over time, as access to public capital continues to improve, women may choose to allocate more of their time savings to market work if their preferences toward children diminish and their preference for current and future consumption of market goods increases. Thus, despite the fact that the marginal productivity effect of public capital on labor diminishes over time, female labor force participation rates may increase. As a result, the overall female labor participation rate may again exhibit a U-shaped pattern, with participation in market work alone taking more the form of a J-shaped or simply monotonic curve—the latter possibly concave, rather than convex, in nature.

Testing this relationship may be difficult for a number of other reasons. First, at low levels of income, one constraint on women's time allocation is the lack of availability of child care. If so, even when access to infrastructure improves, it may not lead to increased participation rates due to social norms. Second, time allocated to market work is lumpy, rather than continuous; for instance, a female may not be able to work an extra 30 minutes a week because of improved access to water. Thus, unless there is a very large reduction in time allocated to household chores, women may well allocate the time savings to activities other than market work. In other words, there is a nonlinearity (or discontinuity) associated with time savings. At the same time, however, even though there is a discontinuity at the individual level, it may not emerge at the aggregate level. This is an important issue to address to better understand the relationship among women's labor supply, public capital, and economic development.

## 7| Extensions

### 7.1| Public Capital and Gender Gaps

In the foregoing analysis, the parameters characterizing gender bias in the workplace and mothers' time allocation between sons and daughters, $b$ and $\chi$, were treated as exogenous. Their role, in effect, was to make the model more tractable—a legitimate approach, given the focus on the determinants of women's time allocation. In addition, the analysis showed that gender gaps are not "locked in"; as mothers' health improves, the health status of their daughters also improves, thereby increasing their productivity (and wages) in adulthood. Because access to infrastructure affects the efficiency of time allocated to children, increases in public capital mitigate over time initial gender gaps in income. However, a more general framework would involve endogenizing both parameters—perhaps by relating them to fertility choices, technology in home production, or more generally intertemporal resource allocation. For instance, if boys are perceived as being more likely—or more capable—to support their parents in old age, there may be a bias in choosing the number of boys relative to girls (see Zhang et al. (1999)).

### 7.2| Nonunitary Household Framework

The foregoing analysis was based on a *unitary framework*, that is, a family was treated as a single decision-making unit that pools all the resources of individual members. Thus, issues associated with intrahousehold allocation were not addressed. The early evidence on the unitary framework, as summarized in Behrman (1997) and Hoddinott et al. (1997), is actually mixed for developing countries. In a more recent study of Indonesia, for instance, Park (2007) found that, with respect to children's nutritional status, the resource pooling hypothesis can be rejected and that parental household bargaining has an important impact on outcomes. However, with respect to investment in children's education, results are mixed. The implication is that the process of intrahousehold resource allocation may differ according to the type of decisions being made; thus, it is possible that no single model can explain all these decisions.

Nevertheless, it would be worth exploring issues associated with bargaining power between husbands and wives in the family decision process, the possible influence of the relative level of education and asset distribution among spouses, and the role of public capital in that context. For instance, several observers have argued that with greater control over household resources, women are more likely to invest in their children's health, nutrition, and education. Changes in intrahousehold bargaining between husbands and wives may also have important implications for the gender gap, if they affect how spouses use infrastructure.

To briefly illustrate how such an approach could be implemented in the present context, suppose that the family's (collective) utility takes the composite form

$$U_t = \varkappa_t U_t^f + (1 - \varkappa_t) U_t^m, \tag{40}$$

where $U^j$ is partner $j$'s utility function, with $j = f, m$, and $\varkappa_t \in (0, 1)$ is a weight that measures the wife's bargaining power in the household decision process. Perfect equality corresponds therefore to $\varkappa_t = 0.5$.

Assuming again that consumption of children is subsumed in the family's consumption, the subutility functions are given by, instead of (2),

$$\begin{aligned} U_t^j &= \eta_C^j \ln c_{t+1}^t + \eta_Q \ln q_{t+1} \\ &\quad + \eta_N \ln n_{t+1} + \eta_H^i (\ln h_{t+1}^{C,f} + \ln h_{t+1}^{C,m}) + \frac{p}{1+\rho} \ln c_{t+2}^t, \end{aligned} \tag{41}$$

where $h_{t+1}^{C,j}$ is now health status of a child of gender $j$.

Coefficient $\eta_C^j$ measures relative preference for today's consumption, $\eta_N$ relative preference for surviving children, $\eta_Q$ the family's relative preference for the home-produced good, and $\eta_H^j$ relative preference for children's health (with no distinction between boys or girls). In this specification, both parents benefit equally from consumption of the home good, and care equally about the number of surviving children; neither $\eta_Q$ nor $\eta_N$ depends on $j$. But women are less concerned than men about current consumption ($\eta_C^f < \eta_C^m$) and care more about the health of their children ($\eta_H^f > \eta_H^m$).

In the spirit of De la Croix and Vander Donckt (2010), suppose now that the relative bargaining power of women evolves as a function of the relative levels of human capital of the two spouses:

$$\varkappa_t = (1 - \gamma_B)\bar{\varkappa} + \gamma_B \left( \frac{e_t^f}{e_t^m} \right)^{\mu_B}, \tag{42}$$

where $\gamma_B \in (0, 1)$ measures the importance of relative stocks of human capital on the distribution of bargaining power between spouses. When $\gamma_B = 0$, bargaining power is exogenous and equal to $\bar{\varkappa} \in (0, 1)$, with possibly $\bar{\varkappa} = 0.5$. The parameter $\mu_B \geq 0$ describes the sensitivity of bargaining power to relative stocks of human capital. The larger it is, the stronger the effect of an increase in women's human capital stock on their bargaining power.[23]

From (15), the human capital ratio is given by $e_t^m / e_t^f = \chi/(1 - \chi)$. Substituting this result in (42) yields

$$\varkappa = (1 - \gamma_B)\bar{\varkappa} + \gamma_B \left( \frac{\chi}{1 - \chi} \right)^{-\mu_B}. \tag{43}$$

Thus, in this simple setting women's bargaining power depends fundamentally on a key structural parameter: the allocation of mothers' time to their sons and daughters, as measured by $\chi$. The stronger the bias toward boys in childhood (the higher $\chi$ is), the lower the human capital women eventually accumulate, and the weaker their bargaining position. A key issue to explore therefore is the extent to which $\chi$ depends not only on social norms but also on broader economic forces, including access to infrastructure.

• • •

This chapter focused on the gender dimension of public capital. The first part provided a review of the evidence on women's time allocation constraints, with particular emphasis on the role of access to infrastructure (or lack thereof). Much of the evidence shows that in developing countries, women often bear the brunt of domestic tasks, such as processing food crops, providing water and firewood, and caring for children. As a consequence, their ability to engage in market work or other productive activities is hampered, and this in turn may act as an impediment to growth.

The second part of the chapter presented a gender-based OLG model that generalizes in several respects the models presented in Chapters 1 to 3. The gender dimension was introduced in several ways, most critical of them being the endogenous treatment of women's time allocation among market work, home production, child rearing, and own health care, and by assuming that the production of home goods requires combining women's time and access to public capital. Gender bias in the workplace and in the home was also accounted for. As in chapter 3, health status in childhood was assumed to

[23] De la Croix and Vander Donckt (2010) propose a slightly more general specification. See Agénor (2011*b*) for a more detailed analysis.

depend on the amount of time allocated by mothers to child rearing and access to public health services, whereas health status in adulthood (which affects productivity and wages) was taken to depend on health status in childhood as well as time allocated to own health care. The analysis showed that improved access to infrastructure services (up to a critical threshold level of the public-private capital ratio) reduces women's time allocated to home production and raises time allocated to market work, own health care, and child rearing. An increase in the survival probability from adulthood to old age, for a given public-private capital ratio, increases both the time allocated to market work and the time women allocate to their own health. It also reduces the fertility rate, the amount of time allocated to home production, and the public-private capital ratio. However, it has an ambiguous effect on time allocated to child care. Through all those different channels, an increase in the survival probability from adulthood to old age was shown to have an ambiguous effect on the steady-state growth rate in income per worker. This is in contrast to the conventional view, according to which an increase in life expectancy, by increasing savings (and possibly investment in human capital), has an unambiguously positive effect on growth. This is also consistent with the results reported in chapter 3, with the exception that there is now a gender dimension to the explanation.

The third part of the chapter discussed the possible role of public capital in the long-standing debate on the determinants of women's labor supply in the course of development. Studies based on data pertaining to both developed and developing countries suggest the existence of a U-shaped relationship between women's labor force participation and the level of income per capita. It was argued that changes over time in women's access to infrastructure could possibly explain part of this nonlinear relationship—but perhaps in the form of a J-shaped curve. In the early stages of economic development, public capital is insufficient, constraining private activities and opportunities for market work for both men and women. In addition, women must allocate a large fraction of their time to home production. Thus, time devoted to market work is limited and female labor participation is limited. As access to public capital improves, labor productivity and thus labor demand increase, while time allocated to home production falls. But initially women may allocate most of the resulting time savings to their children's health and their own health care; this would occur if, initially, the preference for children's health is very high. As a result, the *effective* female labor force participation rate may fall. Over time, as access to public capital continues to improve, women may choose to allocate more of their time savings to market work if their preferences toward children diminish and their preference for current and future consumption increases.

In the model presented earlier, just as in previous chapters, the family's utility function was assumed to have a log-linear form. This simplifies significantly the analysis—by permitting an explicit solution to the first-order conditions for household optimization, by leading to a savings function that depends linearly on wages only, and thus by allowing an explicit derivation of the steady-state growth rate. In addition, it implies that neither the wage nor the interest rate matter in fertility and women's labor allocation decisions. Indeed, higher wages normally induce two opposite effects: a positive income effect, which raises both consumption and leisure (and thus reduces women's time allocated to market work), and a substitution effect, which stems from the increase in the opportunity cost of leisure (and therefore raises women's time allocated to market work). These two effects exactly offset each other with logarithmic utility. Because time allocated to market work does not change, the overall constraint on women's time implies that the fertility rate does not change either. Similarly, there are normally two opposite effects when the interest rate goes up: an intertemporal substitution effect, triggered by the fall in the relative price of future consumption (in old age) with respect to present consumption (in adulthood), which induces an increase in women's time allocated to market work, and a positive income effect, which results here from the relaxation of the family's intertemporal budget constraint and leads to lower savings and reduced participation in the labor force for women. Again, both effects exactly offset each other under logarithmic preferences for consumption.

By contrast, with a more general isoelastic utility function (as discussed in chapter 7 for instance), an increase in the wage rate or the interest rate would have ambiguous effects on women's time devoted to market work and the fertility rate. As can be inferred from the results in Boucekkine et al. (2009) in particular, if the intertemporal elasticity of consumption is less than unity, an increase in the market wage would raise women's labor force participation rate and reduce the total fertility rate.

In the context of this book, the fact that a change in the market wage has an ambiguous effect on women's market work with more general utility preferences is potentially important. The reason is that the stock of public capital, through its effect on the marginal productivity of labor, has a positive effect on wages. So when that stock increases, there are now two effects on women's labor supply: a direct effect on time allocated to home production, as identified earlier, and an indirect effect through an increase in wages. If the effect through wages is positive, then the reallocation of time toward market work is magnified; but if it is negative (because the substitution effect dominates the income effect), the net impact on women's time allocated to market work may be negligible or even negative. However, the substitution effect would have to be very large for this case to occur; there is no strong empirical evidence to suggest that this is actually the case for women in poor countries.

Finally, it is worth stressing that although the analysis in this chapter focused on the impact of infrastructure on women's time allocation, the model can be used to study a variety of gender-based policies, such as a reduction in gender bias in the market place (see Agénor et al. (2010) and Agénor (2011*b*)).

The chapter may therefore prove to be of independent interest to those working on gender and growth issues.

## APPENDIX: Solution, Stability Conditions, and Steady-State Effects

Consider first the family's optimization problem. Substituting (7) in (2) yields

$$U_t = \omega \ln c^t_{t+1} + (1-\omega)\pi^Q \ln\left(\varepsilon^{f,P}_{t+1} + \zeta^P k^I_{t+1}\right)$$

$$+\eta_N \ln h^C_{t+1} n_{t+1} + \frac{p}{1+\rho} \ln c^t_{t+2}. \tag{A1}$$

From equation (11),

$$e^m_t w^m_t = b^{-1} a^f_t e^f_t \varepsilon^{f,W}_t w^f_t, \tag{A2}$$

which can be substituted in (5) to give

$$w^T_t = e^m_t w^m_t + a^f_t e^f_t \varepsilon^{f,W}_t w^f_t = (b^{-1}+1) a^f_t e^f_t \varepsilon^{f,W}_t w^f_t. \tag{A3}$$

In turn, this expression can be substituted in the budget constraint (6) to give, using (19) to replace $a^f_t$ and (1) to substitute out for $\varepsilon^{f,W}_{t+1}$,

$$\frac{(1-\theta^R n_{t+1})}{[(1-\tau)(b^{-1}+1)]^{-1}} h^f_{t+1} e^f_{t+1} \left(1 - \varepsilon^{f,H}_{t+1} - \varepsilon^{f,P}_{t+1} - n_{t+1}\varepsilon^{f,R}_{t+1}\right) w^f_{t+1}$$

$$-c^t_{t+1} - \frac{pc^t_{t+2}}{1+r_{t+2}} = 0. \tag{A4}$$

Writing (16) for $t+1$ using (17) and (25), and combining the result with (18), yields

$$h^C_{t+1} = (\varepsilon^{f,R}_{t+1})^{\nu_C} (k^I_{t+1})^{\pi^R \nu_C} \left(\frac{G^H_{t+1}}{K^P_{t+1}}\right)^{1-\nu_C}, \tag{A5}$$

$$h^f_{t+1} = (\varepsilon^{f,R}_t)^{\nu_C} (k^I_t)^{\pi^R \nu_C} \left(\frac{G^H_t}{K^P_t}\right)^{1-\nu_C} \left(\varepsilon^{f,H}_{t+1}\right)^{\nu_A}. \tag{A6}$$

Families maximize (A1) subject to (A4), (A5), and (A6 ), with respect to $c^t_{t+1}, c^t_{t+2}, \varepsilon^{f,H}_{t+1}, \varepsilon^{f,R}_{t+1}, \varepsilon^{f,P}_{t+1}$, and $n_{t+1}$, with $\varepsilon^{f,W}_{t+1}$ solved residually from (1). They take as given all period-$t$ variables (including $\varepsilon^{f,R}_t$), $G^H_{t+1}/K^P_{t+1}$, $e^f_{t+1}$, and the public-private capital ratio, $k^I_{t+1}$. First-order conditions yield the familiar Euler equation

$$\frac{c^t_{t+2}}{c^t_{t+1}} = \frac{1+r_{t+2}}{\omega(1+\rho)}, \tag{A7}$$

together with

$$\frac{\omega(1-\theta^R n_{t+1})}{\Phi^{-1}c_{t+1}^t} e_{t+1}^f w_{t+1}^f \left( \frac{\nu_A \varepsilon_{t+1}^{f,W}}{\varepsilon_{t+1}^{f,H}} - 1 \right) h_{t+1}^f = 0, \tag{A8}$$

$$\frac{\eta_N \nu_C}{\varepsilon_{t+1}^{f,R}} = \frac{\omega(1-\theta^R n_{t+1})}{\Phi^{-1}c_{t+1}^t} h_{t+1}^f e_{t+1}^f w_{t+1}^f n_{t+1}, \tag{A9}$$

$$\frac{(1-\omega)\pi^Q}{\varepsilon_{t+1}^{f,P} + \zeta^P k_{t+1}^I} = \frac{\omega(1-\theta^R n_{t+1})}{\Phi^{-1}c_{t+1}^t} h_{t+1}^f e_{t+1}^f w_{t+1}^f, \tag{A10}$$

$$\frac{\eta_N}{n_{t+1}} = \frac{\omega}{\Phi^{-1}c_{t+1}^t} h_{t+1}^f e_{t+1}^f w_{t+1}^f \left[ \theta^R \varepsilon_{t+1}^{f,W} + (1-\theta^R n_{t+1})\varepsilon_{t+1}^{f,R} \right], \tag{A11}$$

where $\Phi = (1-\tau)(b^{-1}+1)$.

Substituting (A7) in (A4) yields

$$c_{t+1}^t = \left[ \frac{\omega(1+\rho)}{\omega(1+\rho)+p} \right] (1-\theta^R n_{t+1})\Phi h_{t+1}^f e_{t+1}^f \varepsilon_{t+1}^{f,W} w_{t+1}^f. \tag{A12}$$

Thus, family savings, $s_{t+1}$, is equal to

$$s_{t+1} = \sigma(1-\theta^R n_{t+1})\Phi h_{t+1}^f e_{t+1}^f \varepsilon_{t+1}^{f,W} w_{t+1}^f, \tag{A13}$$

where $\sigma = p/[\omega(1+\rho)+p] < 1$.

Equation (A8) implies

$$\varepsilon_{t+1}^{f,H} = \nu_A \varepsilon_{t+1}^{f,W}. \tag{A14}$$

Substituting equation (A12) for $c_{t+1}^t$ in (A9) and (A10) yields

$$\frac{\eta_N \nu_C}{\varepsilon_{t+1}^{f,R}} = \frac{\omega n_{t+1}}{(1-\sigma)\varepsilon_{t+1}^{f,W}},$$

$$\frac{(1-\omega)\pi^Q}{\varepsilon_{t+1}^{f,P} + \zeta^P k_{t+1}^I} = \frac{\omega}{(1-\sigma)\varepsilon_{t+1}^{f,W}},$$

or equivalently

$$n_{t+1}\varepsilon_{t+1}^{f,R} = \frac{\eta_N \nu_C (1-\sigma)\varepsilon_{t+1}^{f,W}}{\omega}, \tag{A15}$$

$$\varepsilon_{t+1}^{f,P} + \zeta^P k_{t+1}^I = \Lambda_1 \varepsilon_{t+1}^{f,W}, \tag{A16}$$

where

$$\Lambda_1 = (1-\omega)\pi^Q(1-\sigma)\omega^{-1} > 0.$$

From the time constraint (1), together with (A14) and (A15) to eliminate $\varepsilon_{t+1}^{f,H}$ and $n_{t+1}\varepsilon_{t+1}^{f,R}$,

$$\varepsilon_{t+1}^{f,W} = 1 - \nu_A \varepsilon_{t+1}^{f,W} - \varepsilon_{t+1}^{f,P} - \eta_N \nu_C (1-\sigma)\omega^{-1}\varepsilon_{t+1}^{f,W},$$

or equivalently

$$\varepsilon_{t+1}^{f,W} = \frac{1-\varepsilon_{t+1}^{f,P}}{\Lambda_2}, \tag{A17}$$

where

$$\Lambda_2 = 1 + \nu_A + \eta_N \nu_C (1-\sigma)\omega^{-1} > 1.$$

This equation can be substituted in (A16) to give

$$\varepsilon_{t+1}^{f,P} = \left\{1 + \frac{\Lambda_1}{\Lambda_2}\right\}^{-1} \left\{\frac{\Lambda_1}{\Lambda_2} - \zeta^P k_{t+1}^I\right\}. \tag{A18}$$

From (A17) and (A18), it can also be shown that, with $\zeta^P = 0$,

$$\varepsilon_{t+1}^{f,P}\Big|_{\zeta^P=0} = \frac{\Lambda_1}{\Lambda_1+\Lambda_2} < 1, \quad \varepsilon_{t+1}^{f,W}\Big|_{\zeta^P=0} = \frac{1}{\Lambda_1+\Lambda_2} < 1, \tag{A19}$$

which also correspond to the values displayed in Figure 5.1 for $k_t^I = 0$. Because

$$\Lambda_1 + \Lambda_2 = 1 + \nu_A + [(1-\omega)\pi^Q + \eta_N \nu_C](1-\sigma)\omega^{-1},$$

it follows that an increase (fall) in $\eta_N$ or $\nu_C$ lowers (raises) $\varepsilon_{t+1}^{f,W}$.

To determine $n_{t+1}$, divide (A9) by (A11) to give

$$\frac{\eta_N \nu_C n_{t+1}}{\eta_N \varepsilon_{t+1}^{f,R}} = \frac{(1-\theta^R n_{t+1})n_{t+1}}{\theta^R \varepsilon_{t+1}^{f,W} + (1-\theta^R n_{t+1})\varepsilon_{t+1}^{f,R}},$$

or equivalently

$$\frac{\nu_C}{\varepsilon_{t+1}^{f,R}} = \frac{1-\theta^R n_{t+1}}{\theta^R \varepsilon_{t+1}^{f,W} + (1-\theta^R n_{t+1})\varepsilon_{t+1}^{f,R}},$$

or again

$$\nu_C \theta^R \left(\frac{\varepsilon_{t+1}^{f,W}}{\varepsilon_{t+1}^{f,R}}\right) = (1-\nu_C)(1-\theta^R n_{t+1}). \tag{A20}$$

From (A15), $\varepsilon_{t+1}^{f,W}/\varepsilon_{t+1}^{f,R} = \omega n_{t+1}/\eta_N \nu_C (1-\sigma)$; substituting this result in (A20 ) yields

$$\left\{\frac{\omega}{\eta_N(1-\sigma)} + (1-\nu_C)\right\}\theta^R n_{t+1} = 1 - \nu_C,$$

or equivalently

$$n_{t+1} = \frac{1 - \nu_C}{\Lambda_3 \theta^R}, \tag{A21}$$

where

$$\Lambda_3 = 1 - \nu_C + \frac{\omega}{\eta_N(1-\sigma)} > 0.$$

Finally, using (A15), (A17), and (A21) yields

$$\varepsilon_{t+1}^{f,R} = \frac{\Lambda_3 \theta^R \eta_N \nu_C (1-\sigma)}{\omega(1-\nu_C)} \left( \frac{1 - \varepsilon_{t+1}^{f,P}}{\Lambda_2} \right). \tag{A22}$$

From (A21), it can be shown that to have $1 - \theta^R n_{t+1} < 1$ (that is, to ensure a positive net before-tax wage) requires $(1-\nu_C)/\Lambda_3 > 0$, which always holds.

From (A13), $d\sigma/dp > 0$. Using this result, it can be established from (A18), with $k_{t+1}^I$ given, that $d\varepsilon_{t+1}^{f,P}/dp < 0$. From (A21), and given that $d\Lambda_3/dp > 0$, $dn_{t+1}/dp < 0$; thus, from (34), $dJ/dp < 0$. From (A14) and ( A17), and given that $d\Lambda_2/dp < 0$,

$$\frac{d\varepsilon_{t+1}^{f,H}}{dp} = \nu_A \frac{d\varepsilon_{t+1}^{f,W}}{dp} > 0,$$

$$\frac{d\varepsilon_{t+1}^{f,W}}{dp} = -\Lambda_2^{-1} \frac{d\varepsilon_{t+1}^{f,P}}{dp} - \left( \frac{1 - \varepsilon_{t+1}^{f,P}}{\Lambda_2^2} \right) \frac{d\Lambda_2}{dp} > 0.$$

From the time constraint (1),

$$n_{t+1}\varepsilon_{t+1}^{f,R} = 1 - \varepsilon_{t+1}^{f,H} - \varepsilon_{t+1}^{f,P} - \varepsilon_{t+1}^{f,W},$$

so that

$$\frac{d(n_{t+1}\varepsilon_{t+1}^{f,R})}{dp} = -\frac{d\varepsilon_{t+1}^{f,H}}{dp} - \frac{d\varepsilon_{t+1}^{f,W}}{dp} - \frac{d\varepsilon_{t+1}^{f,P}}{dp},$$

or equivalently, using the above results,

$$\begin{aligned}\frac{d(n_{t+1}\varepsilon_{t+1}^{f,R})}{dp} &= -(1+\nu_A)\frac{d\varepsilon_{t+1}^{f,W}}{dp} - \frac{d\varepsilon_{t+1}^{f,P}}{dp} \\ &= -\left[1 - \left(\frac{1+\nu_A}{\Lambda_2}\right)\right] \frac{d\varepsilon_{t+1}^{f,P}}{dp} + (1+\nu_A)\left(\frac{1 - \varepsilon_{t+1}^{f,P}}{\Lambda_2^2}\right)\frac{d\Lambda_2}{dp}.\end{aligned}$$

From the definition of $\Lambda_2$ given above,

$$\frac{1+\nu_A}{\Lambda_2} = \frac{1+\nu_A}{1+\nu_A+\eta_N\nu_C(1-\sigma)\omega^{-1}} < 1.$$

Thus, $1-(1+\nu_A)\Lambda_2^{-1}>0$. Given that $d\varepsilon_{t+1}^{f,P}/dp<0$, the first term is positive. However $d\Lambda_2/dp<0$, so the second term is negative. Consequently,

$$\frac{d(n_{t+1}\varepsilon_{t+1}^{f,R})}{dp} \lesseqgtr 0. \tag{A23}$$

More directly, from (A15), and given that $d\varepsilon_{t+1}^{f,W}/dp, d\sigma/dp>0$,

$$\frac{d(n_{t+1}\varepsilon_{t+1}^{f,R})}{dp} = \frac{\eta_N\nu_C}{\omega}\left\{(1-\sigma)\frac{d\varepsilon_{t+1}^{f,W}}{dp} - \varepsilon_{t+1}^{f,W}\frac{d\sigma}{dp}\right\} \lesseqgtr 0. \tag{A24}$$

As shown earlier, the lower $\eta_N$ or $\nu_C$, the higher $\varepsilon_{t+1}^{f,W}$; and the more likely it is that $d(n_{t+1}\varepsilon_{t+1}^{f,R})/dp<0$.

Now,

$$\frac{d(n_{t+1}\varepsilon_{t+1}^{f,R})}{dp} = \varepsilon_{t+1}^{f,R}\left(\frac{dn_{t+1}}{dp}\right) + n_{t+1}\left(\frac{d\varepsilon_{t+1}^{f,R}}{dp}\right). \tag{A25}$$

Thus, rearranging (A25) and given (A23) or (A24),

$$\frac{d\varepsilon_{t+1}^{f,R}}{dp} = (n_{t+1})^{-1}\left\{\frac{d(n_{t+1}\varepsilon_{t+1}^{f,R})}{dp} - \varepsilon_{t+1}^{f,R}\left(\frac{dn_{t+1}}{dp}\right)\right\} \lesseqgtr 0.$$

Because $dn_{t+1}/dp<0$, the second term in brackets on the right-hand side is positive; thus, if $d(n_{t+1}\varepsilon_{t+1}^{f,R})/dp>0$, it must be that $d\varepsilon_{t+1}^{f,R}/dp>0$. In general, however, $d\varepsilon_{t+1}^{f,R}/dp$ is ambiguous.

To study the dynamics in this economy, substitute first (A13) in (26), to give

$$K_{t+1}^P = N_t^f s_t = N_t^f \Phi\sigma(1-\theta^R n_t)h_t^f e_t^f \varepsilon_t^{f,W} w_t^f,$$

that is, substituting for $w_t^f$ from (9) and using (19),

$$K_{t+1}^P = b\beta\Phi\sigma(1-\theta^R n_t)Y_t. \tag{A26}$$

Equation (22) can be rewritten as, given that $L_t^j = e_t^j N_t^j$ and $N_t^m = N_t^f$,

$$G_t^h = \upsilon_h\tau(e_t^m w_t^m + h_t^f e_t^f \varepsilon_t^{f,W} w_t^f)N_t^f,$$

that is, using (A3),

$$G_t^h = \upsilon_h\tau(b^{-1}+1)h_t^f e_t^f \varepsilon_t^{f,W} w_t^f N_t^f. \tag{A27}$$

Substituting for $w_t^f$ from (9) gives, given (19) and $L_t^f = e_t^f N_t^f$,

$$G_t^h = \upsilon_h\tau(1+b)\beta Y_t, \tag{A28}$$

which can be substituted for $h = I$ in (24) to give

$$K_{t+1}^I = \varphi\upsilon_I\tau(1+b)\beta Y_t. \tag{A29}$$

Combining (A26) and (A29), and recalling that $\Phi = (1-\tau)(b^{-1}+1)$, yields

$$k_{t+1}^{I} = \frac{\varphi \upsilon_I \tau}{\sigma(1-\tau)(1-\theta^R n_t)}, \quad \forall t, \tag{A30}$$

which is independent of $b$, as well as $\theta^R$ given (A23). Thus, as noted in the text, $k_t^I = J$ is constant as long as $n_t$ is constant.

The next step is to calculate $G_t^H/K_t^P$ to substitute in (A6) and obtain a dynamic equation for $h_{t+1}^f$. From (A28) with $h = H$,

$$\frac{G_t^H}{K_t^P} = [\upsilon_H \tau(1+b)\beta]\left(\frac{Y_t}{K_t^P}\right). \tag{A31}$$

The next step therefore is to solve for $Y_t/K_t^P$. To do so, note that from (12) and (19), given again that $L_t^j = e_t^j N_t^j$,

$$\frac{Y_t}{K_t^P} = (\varepsilon_t^{f,W})^{\beta}\left(\frac{1}{x_t^m}\right)^{\beta}(h_t^f)^{\beta}\left(\frac{1}{x_t^f}\right)^{\beta},$$

where $x_t^j = K_t^P/e_t^j N_t^j$ is the private capital-$j$ effective labor ratio.

Because $N_t^f = N_t^m$, and given that from (15) $e_t^m = \chi e_t^f/(1-\chi)$, then $x_t^m = (1-\chi)x_t^f/\chi$. Substituting these results in the above expression yields

$$\frac{Y_t}{K_t^P} = \left(\frac{\chi \varepsilon_t^{f,W}}{1-\chi}\right)^{\beta}(h_t^f)^{\beta}(x_t^f)^{-2\beta}. \tag{A32}$$

Substituting (A32) in (A31) gives, given (25),

$$\frac{H_t^G}{K_t^P} = [\upsilon_H \tau(1+b)\beta]\left(\frac{\chi \varepsilon_t^{f,W}}{1-\chi}\right)^{\beta}(h_t^f)^{\beta}(x_t^f)^{-2\beta}.$$

In turn, substituting this expression in (A6) gives, together with ( A30),

$$h_{t+1}^f = (\varepsilon_t^{f,R})^{\nu_C}(\varepsilon_t^{f,H})^{\nu_A} J^{\Omega_1} \times[\upsilon_H \tau(1+b)\beta]^{1-\nu_C}\left(\frac{\chi \varepsilon_t^{f,W}}{1-\chi}\right)^{\Omega_2}(h_t^f)^{\Omega_2}(x_t^f)^{-2\Omega_2}, \tag{A33}$$

where

$$\Omega_1 = \pi^R \nu_C > 0,$$

$$\Omega_2 = \beta(1-\nu_C) \in (0, 1).$$

Equivalently,

$$h_{t+1}^f = g^1(h_t^f, x_t^f; \varepsilon_t^{f,H}, \varepsilon_t^{f,R}, \varepsilon_t^{f,W}), \tag{A34}$$

where $\partial \ln g^1/\partial \ln h_t^f = \Omega_2 > 0$ and $\partial \ln g^1/\partial \ln x_t^f = -2\Omega_2 < 0$.

Next, the dynamic equation for $x^f_{t+1}$ must be derived. From (A28), with $h = E$,

$$\frac{G^E_t}{N_t} = \upsilon_E \tau(1+b)\beta \left(\frac{Y_t}{N_t}\right).$$

Substituting this result in (14) for $j = f$ yields

$$e^f_{t+1} = (1-\chi)\varepsilon^{f,R}_t \frac{[\upsilon_E \tau(1+b)\beta]^\nu}{n^\nu_t} \left(\frac{Y_t}{N_t}\right)^\nu (e^f_t)^{1-\nu}. \qquad \text{(A35)}$$

From (13), (A26), and (A35), given that $N^f_{t+1} = 0.5N_{t+1}$,

$$x^f_{t+1} = \frac{K^P_{t+1}}{e^f_{t+1}N^f_{t+1}} = \Gamma \left(\frac{Y_t}{0.5e^f_t N_t}\right)^{1-\nu}, \qquad \text{(A36)}$$

where

$$\Gamma = \left[\frac{b\beta\Phi\sigma(1-\theta^R n_t)}{(1-\chi)\varepsilon^{f,R}_t n^{1-\nu}_t (0.5)^\nu}\right] [\upsilon_E \tau(1+b)\beta]^{-\nu}.$$

By definition, $Y_t/0.5e^f_t N_t = (Y_t/K^P_t)x^f_t$. Using (A32) to substitute for $Y_t/K^P_t$ yields therefore

$$\frac{Y_t}{0.5e^f_t N_t} = \left(\frac{\chi \varepsilon^{f,W}_t}{1-\chi}\right)^\beta (h^f_t)^\beta (x^f_t)^{1-2\beta}.$$

Substituting this result in (A36) yields

$$x^f_{t+1} = \Gamma \left(\frac{\chi \varepsilon^{f,W}_t}{1-\chi}\right)^{\beta(1-\nu)} (h^f_t)^{\beta(1-\nu)} (x^f_t)^{(1-2\beta)(1-\nu)}, \qquad \text{(A37)}$$

or equivalently

$$x^f_{t+1} = g^2(h^f_t, x^f_t; \varepsilon^{f,R}_t, \varepsilon^{f,W}_t), \qquad \text{(A38)}$$

with $\partial \ln g^2/\partial \ln h^f_t = \beta(1-\nu) > 0$ and $\partial \ln g^2/\partial \ln x^f_t = (1-2\beta)(1-\nu) > 0$.[24]

To determine the growth rate of output per worker, it is convenient to note first that $Y_{t+1}/N_{t+1} = (Y_{t+1}/K^P_{t+1})(K^P_{t+1}/N_{t+1})$. Now, using (13), (A26), and (A32) for $t+1$ yields

$$\frac{Y_{t+1}}{N_{t+1}} = \left(\frac{\chi \varepsilon^{f,W}_{t+1}}{1-\chi}\right)^\beta (h^f_{t+1})^\beta (x^f_{t+1})^{-2\beta} b\beta\Phi\sigma(1-\theta^R n_t)\left(\frac{Y_t}{n_t N_t}\right).$$

[24] Note that although $\varepsilon^{f,P}_t$ does not appear directly in (A34) and (A38), changes in $\varepsilon^{f,P}_t$ as defined in (27) have indirect effects on $\varepsilon^{f,H}_t$, $\varepsilon^{f,R}_t$, and $\varepsilon^{f,W}_t$, as implied by (28), (29), and (30).

The balanced growth rate of output per worker is thus, substituting out for $\Phi$,

$$1+\gamma = \frac{1}{\tilde{n}}\left(\frac{\chi\tilde{\varepsilon}^{f,W}}{1-\chi}\right)^{\beta}\frac{\beta\sigma(1-\theta^R\tilde{n})}{[(1-\tau)(1+b)]^{-1}}(\tilde{h}^f)^{\beta}(\tilde{x}^f)^{-2\beta}, \tag{A39}$$

where $\tilde{h}^f$ and $\tilde{x}^f$ are the steady-state solutions obtained by setting $\Delta h^f_{t+1} = \Delta x^f_{t+1} = 0$ in (A33) and (A37):

$$\tilde{h}^f = [(\tilde{\varepsilon}^{f,R})^{\nu_C}(\tilde{\varepsilon}^{f,H})^{\nu_A}J^{\Omega_1}]^{1/(1-\Omega_2)} \times \left\{[\upsilon_H\tau(1+b)\beta]^{1-\nu_C}\left(\frac{\chi\tilde{\varepsilon}^{f,W}}{1-\chi}\right)^{\Omega_2}\right\}^{1/(1-\Omega_2)}(\tilde{x}^f)^{-2\Omega_2/(1-\Omega_2)}, \tag{A40}$$

$$\tilde{x}^f = \left\{\Gamma\left(\frac{\chi\tilde{\varepsilon}^{f,W}}{1-\chi}\right)^{\beta(1-\nu)}\right\}^{1/\Omega_3}(\tilde{h}^f)^{\beta(1-\nu)/\Omega_3}, \tag{A41}$$

where

$$\Omega_3 = 1-(1-2\beta)(1-\nu) > 0.$$

These equations define the steady-state relationships between $h^f_t$ and $x^f_t$. Equation (A40) defines a curve whose slope in the $\tilde{h}^f$-$\tilde{x}^f$ plane is determined by $-(1-\Omega_2)/2\Omega_2$. Given that $\Omega_2 < 1$, this slope is negative. This curve is defined as curve $HH$ in Figure 5.2, and it is convex, as long as $2\Omega_2/(1-\Omega_2) < 1$.

Equation (A41) defines a curve depicted as $XX$ in Figure 5.2. Its slope is $\beta(1-\nu)/\Omega_3$, which is positive and less than unity:

$$\frac{\beta(1-\nu)}{1-(1-2\beta)(1-\nu)} < 1.$$

Thus, curve $XX$ is concave and there is a unique equilibrium.

To examine stability in the vicinity of that equilibrium, note that equations (A33) and (A37), given time allocation parameters, form a first-order linear difference equation system in $\hat{h}^f_t = \ln h^f_t$ and $\hat{x}^f_t = \ln x^f_t$, which is written in (35), where again

$$a_{11} = (1-2\beta)(1-\nu) > 0, \quad a_{12} = \beta(1-\nu) > 0,$$

$$a_{21} = -2\Omega_2 < 0, \quad a_{22} = \Omega_2 > 0.$$

Let $\mathbf{A}$ denote the matrix of coefficients in (35) and let $\det\mathbf{A}$ denote its determinant and $\operatorname{tr}\mathbf{A}$ its trace. Let $\lambda_j$, $j = 1, 2$ denote the eigenvalues of $\mathbf{A}$; the characteristic polynomial is thus $p(\lambda) = \lambda^2 - \lambda\operatorname{tr}\mathbf{A} + \det\mathbf{A}$. Thus, $p(1) = 1 - \operatorname{tr}\mathbf{A} + \det\mathbf{A}$, whereas $p(-1) = 1 + \operatorname{tr}\mathbf{A} + \det\mathbf{A}$.

From the above definitions,

$$\mathrm{tr}\,\mathbf{A} = (1-2\beta)(1-\nu) + \Omega_2 > 0,$$

$$\det \mathbf{A} = (1-2\beta)(1-\nu)\Omega_2 + 2\Omega_2\beta(1-\nu) > 0.$$

Given the signs of tr $\mathbf{A} = \lambda_1 + \lambda_2$ and det $\mathbf{A} = \lambda_1\lambda_2$, it is clear that $p(-1) > 0$. In addition,

$$p(1) = 1-(1-2\beta)(1-\nu) \\ +\Omega_2[-1+(1-2\beta)(1-\nu)+2\beta(1-\nu)],$$

so that

$$p(1) = 1-(1-2\beta)(1-\nu) - \Omega_2\nu.$$

If $\nu$ is not too large, then $p(1) > 0$ and the steady state is a sink (see Azariadis (1993, p. 65)).

To determine the effects of changes in government spending on the steady-state growth rate, consider first the case where $J \geq k_C^I$, which implies that $\varepsilon_t^{f,P} = \varepsilon_m^{f,P}$, and from (28), (29), and (30),

$$\tilde{\varepsilon}^{f,W} = (1-\varepsilon_m^{f,P})\Lambda_2^{-1},$$

$$\tilde{\varepsilon}^{f,H} = \nu_A \tilde{\varepsilon}^{f,W},$$

$$\tilde{\varepsilon}^{f,R} = \frac{\Lambda_3\theta^R\eta_N\nu_C(1-\sigma)}{\omega(1-\nu_C)}\tilde{\varepsilon}^{f,W}.$$

From (A40) and (A41),

$$\mathbf{B}\begin{bmatrix} \ln \tilde{h}^f \\ \ln \tilde{x}^f \end{bmatrix} = \mathbf{C}\begin{bmatrix} \ln \upsilon_I & \ln \upsilon_E & \ln \upsilon_H \end{bmatrix}^{\mathrm{T}}, \tag{A42}$$

where

$$\underset{2\times 2}{\mathbf{B}} = \begin{bmatrix} 1 & 2\Omega_2/(1-\Omega_2) \\ -\beta(1-\nu)/\Omega_3 & 1 \end{bmatrix},$$

$$\underset{2\times 3}{\mathbf{C}} = \begin{bmatrix} \Omega_1/(1-\Omega_2) & 0 & (1-\nu_C)/(1-\Omega_2) \\ 0 & -\nu/\Omega_3 & 0 \end{bmatrix}.$$

Solving (A42) using Cramer's rule yields

$$\ln \tilde{h}^f = \frac{1}{\det \mathbf{B}}\begin{vmatrix} [\Omega_1 \ln \upsilon_I + (1-\nu_C)\ln \upsilon_H]/(1-\Omega_2) & 2\Omega_2/(1-\Omega_2) \\ -\nu \ln \upsilon_E/\Omega_3 & 1 \end{vmatrix},$$

$$\ln \tilde{x}^f = \frac{1}{\det \mathbf{B}}\begin{vmatrix} 1 & [\Omega_1 \ln \upsilon_I + (1-\nu_C)\ln \upsilon_H]/(1-\Omega_2) \\ -\beta(1-\nu)/\Omega_3 & -\nu \ln \upsilon_E/\Omega_3 \end{vmatrix},$$

so that

$$\ln \tilde{h}^f = \frac{\Omega_1 \ln \upsilon_I + (1-\nu_C)\ln \upsilon_H + (\nu 2\Omega_2/\Omega_3)\ln \upsilon_E}{(1-\Omega_2)\Delta}$$

$$\ln \tilde{x}^f = \frac{-\nu/\Omega_3 \ln \upsilon_E + [\beta(1-\nu)/\Omega_3(1-\Omega_2)][\Omega_1 \ln \upsilon_I + (1-\nu_C)\ln \upsilon_H]}{\Delta},$$

where

$$\Delta = \det \mathbf{B} = 1 + \frac{2\Omega_2\beta(1-\nu)}{(1-\Omega_2)\Omega_3} > 0.$$

From these expressions, it can be shown that

$$\frac{d\ln \tilde{h}^f}{d\upsilon_I} > 0, \quad \frac{d\ln \tilde{h}^f}{d\upsilon_E} > 0, \quad \frac{d\ln \tilde{h}^f}{d\upsilon_H} > 0, \tag{A43}$$

$$\frac{d\ln \tilde{x}^f}{d\upsilon_I} > 0, \quad \frac{d\ln \tilde{x}^f}{d\upsilon_E} < 0, \quad \frac{d\ln \tilde{x}^f}{d\upsilon_H} > 0. \tag{A44}$$

Now, from (A39),

$$\frac{d\ln(1+\gamma)}{d\upsilon_h} = \beta\left(\frac{d\ln \tilde{h}^f}{d\upsilon_h}\right) - 2\beta\left(\frac{d\ln \tilde{x}^f}{d\upsilon_h}\right), \tag{A45}$$

Equations (A43), (A44), and (A45) imply therefore that

$$\frac{d\ln(1+\gamma)}{d\upsilon_I} \gtrless 0, \quad \frac{d\ln(1+\gamma)}{d\upsilon_E} > 0, \quad \frac{d\ln(1+\gamma)}{d\upsilon_H} \gtrless 0.$$

With $J < k_C^I$ (and thus $\varepsilon_t^{f,P} > \varepsilon_m^{f,P}$), given that the steady-state public-private capital does not depend on spending shares on education and health, the above effects remain the same for changes in $\upsilon_E$ and $\upsilon_H$. However, the effect of a change in $\upsilon_I$ is more complicated; from (27) to (30), it can be shown that, using (A30),

$$\frac{d\varepsilon^{f,P}}{d\upsilon_I} = -\zeta^P\left(1+\frac{\Lambda_1}{\Lambda_2}\right)^{-1}\left(\frac{dJ}{d\upsilon_I}\right) < 0,$$

$$\frac{d\varepsilon^{f,W}}{d\upsilon_I} = -\Lambda_2^{-1}\left(\frac{d\varepsilon^{f,P}}{d\upsilon_I}\right) > 0,$$

$$\frac{d\varepsilon^{f,H}}{d\upsilon_I} = \nu_A \frac{d\varepsilon^{f,H}}{d\upsilon_I} > 0,$$

$$\frac{d\varepsilon^{f,R}}{d\upsilon_I} = -\frac{\Lambda_3 \theta^R \eta_N \nu_C (1-\sigma)}{\omega(1-\nu_C)\Lambda_2} \left(\frac{d\varepsilon^{f,P}}{d\upsilon_I}\right) > 0.$$

These results show that the time allocation effects operate in the same direction as the direct effect in the case of $HH$, but now they also affect the position of curve $XX$ in opposite ways, as discussed in the text.

# 6| Public Capital and Poverty Traps

> Means of communication were not constructed in the colonial period... to facilitate internal trade in African commodities. There were no roads connecting different colonies and different parts of the same colony in a manner that made sense with regard to Africa's needs and development. All roads and railways led down to the sea. They were built to extract gold or manganese or coffee or cotton. They were built to make business possible for the timber companies, trading companies and agricultural concession firms, and for white settlers.
>
> —Walter Rodney, *How Europe Underdeveloped Africa* (1973, chap. 6)

The previous chapters have established that improved access to infrastructure in low-income countries serves not only to increase factor productivity and reduce production costs but also to promote private capital formation, to improve education and health outcomes, to foster innovation, and to empower women by alleviating the constraints imposed on their time by household chores.

This chapter focuses on the role that public capital may play in helping a poor country escape from a poverty trap, that is, a low-growth equilibrium. The focus of the discussion is on the nonlinearities that may characterize the benefits associated with public capital: for instance, once an efficient, reliable and uncongested transport network is in place, the direct benefits resulting from building yet another highway may be more limited. These nonlinearities, which may take the form of network externalities, are reviewed in the first part. In the second part the basic model presented in chapter 1 is extended to account for network externalities. The possibility of multiple equilibria, and the role of a Big Push in public investment in infrastructure, is then examined. Several alternative channels through which public capital can produce an escape from a poverty trap are studied next, including effects through time allocated to education, health outcomes, and technology adoption, in a setting where the decision to switch technologies is endogenously determined through a rate-of-return arbitrage condition. The last section discusses how aid volatility, by adversely affecting public investment programs, can also lead to stagnation.

## 1| Background

In general, network externalities exist when the value of a product to any user is greater the larger the number of other users of the same product. They can occur in two ways. *Direct* network externalities exist when an increase in the size of a network raises the number of others with whom one can "communicate" directly. *Indirect* network externalities exist when an increase in the size of a network expands the range of complementary products available to the members of the network.

The network externalities associated with infrastructure have been emphasized in a number of studies on long-run development. Early models in the tradition of Rosenstein-Rodan's (1943) Big Push theory stressed interactions between pecuniary externalities and coordination failures. To the extent that the cost of an infrastructure is fixed, each new firm that uses it helps to defray this cost and in so doing brings the building of the infrastructure closer to profitability. In this way, each user indirectly helps other users and hence makes their development more likely. For instance, in the two-period model analyzed by Murphy et al. (1989), firms with fixed start-up costs have to incur investment expenditure in the first period, prior to the realization of production in the second period. The nonconvexity resulting from the fixed start-up costs produces two equilibria: a nonindustrialization equilibrium and a joint industrialization equilibrium, in which expectations of entrepreneurs are properly coordinated.[1] A Big Push, taking the form of a large increase in investment in a shared infrastructure, can shift the economy from the bad equilibrium to the good equilibrium.

More recent contributions have focused on the productivity dimension of network externalities. Economies of scale due to network externalities are a widely recognized imperfection in infrastructure services (see World Bank (1994)). An important characteristic of modern infrastructure is indeed the fact that services are often supplied through a networked delivery system designed to serve a multitude of users. This interconnectedness means that the benefits from investment at one point in the network will generally depend on capacities at other points. Put differently, inherent to the structure of a network is that many components are required for the provision of a service; these components are thus complementary to each other.

The concept of interconnectedness is important to provide a historical perspective on underdevelopment. Some observers have indeed argued that the inadequacy of transport networks in sub-Saharan Africa today is intimately linked to the history of the continent. Colonization and a focus on resource extraction dramatically affected the use of space in the region, shifting growth and urbanization from inland to coastal areas. Many African capitals today are ports that were built at the end of railways designed to carry flows of raw materials and labor from the inland. Historians like Cooper (1993), as well as geographers and political scientists—particularly those in the Marxist

[1] Matsuyama (1991) provided a dynamic extension of the Murphy et al. model. In his framework, entrepreneurs cannot switch technology at any point in time but only when the "opportunity" comes, and opportunity comes randomly, following a certain process. One can then define a critical minimum effort and evaluate the scope for an economy's takeoff.

tradition, like Rodney (1973), quoted above—have long pointed out that transport networks inherited from that growth were located perpendicularly to the seashores, and were not built to occupy space widely. Massive investment in rail networks is viewed by several prominent observers as a key step in promoting growth and regional trade in Sub-Saharan Africa—especially for land-locked countries.

Interrelations between networks may also generate positive externalities as well. Having electricity to produce goods but no roads to carry them to markets limits the productivity effects of a program designed to increase access to energy. In that sense, electricity and roads are complementary components of the infrastructure network, and only joint availability or operation will generate efficiency gains, that is, positive externalities.

The network character of infrastructure capital typically induces strong nonlinearities in its productivity. Until the network is built, public capital may have a low marginal productivity. Once the basic parts of a network are established, and a critical mass has been reached, strong gains may be associated with small additional increases in infrastructure investment. But beyond a certain point, the marginal productivity gains induced by additional investments may slow down considerably. In Agénor (2010), this is captured by assuming that the degree of efficiency of infrastructure is nonlinearly related to the stock of public capital itself. Depending on how strong nonlinearities are, multiple equilibria may emerge.[2] Provided that governance is adequate enough to ensure a sufficient degree of efficiency of public investment, an increase in the share of spending on infrastructure may shift the economy from a low-growth equilibrium to a high-growth steady state. The model presented in the next section provides an analysis along the same lines.

Evidence of nonlinearities or threshold effects in the relationship between output growth and infrastructure, conditional on the level of infrastructure itself, is provided by Röller and Waverman (2001), Hulten et al. (2006), Égert et al. (2009), Candelon et al. (2009), Kellenberg (2009), Agénor and Neanidis (2010), Czernich et al. (2011), and Roberts and Deichmann (2011). Using data for Indian states, Hulten et al. (2006) found a large externality effect associated with the states' infrastructure on manufacturing industry; over the period 1972-92, the growth of road and electricity-generating capacity accounted for nearly half the growth of the productivity residual of India's (registered) manufacturing firms. Roberts and Deichmann (2011) found that transport and telecommunications infrastructure play a significant role in promoting spillovers when it interacts with regional trade integration. Their results show that the importance of infrastructure may lie not in its direct contribution to economic growth, but rather in making it easier for landlocked countries to absorb beneficial growth spillovers from neighboring countries. Czernich et al.

[2] Futagami and Mino (1995) also showed that multiple equilibria can emerge in the presence of threshold externalities in public capital accumulation.

(2011) found that broadband matters for growth only above a threshold of 10 percent penetration rates (measured as the number of broadband subscribers per 100 inhabitants). In the same vein, and using data for 38 countries covering the period 1981–2008, Agénor and Neanidis (2010) found that access to telecommunications has a strong and significant "critical mass" effect on innovation, and thus indirectly on growth.

## 2| The Economy

To analyze the dynamics of a Big Push, the basic OLG model presented in chapter 1 is extended to account for externalities taking the form of threshold productivity effects. Because the core assumptions are the same, only a brief description is provided here.

### 2.1| Individuals

All individuals solve the problem

$$\max_{c_t^t, c_{t+1}^t} V = \ln c_t^t + \frac{\ln c_{t+1}^t}{1+\rho}, \quad \rho > 0 \tag{1}$$

subject to the intertemporal budget constraint

$$c_t^t + \frac{c_{t+1}^t}{1+r_{t+1}} = (1-\tau)w_t. \tag{2}$$

### 2.2| Firms

The production function of firm $i$ takes the same form as before:

$$Y_t^i = \left[\frac{x_t K_t^I}{(K_t^P)^{\zeta}}\right]^{\alpha} (N_t^i)^{\beta} (K_t^{P,i})^{1-\beta}, \tag{3}$$

except for the variable $x_t$, which is a function measuring network externalities. Specifically, network externalities are assumed to be related directly to the stock of public capital itself, scaled by the aggregate private capital stock:

$$x_t = \left(\frac{K_t^I}{K_t^P}\right)^{\chi}, \tag{4}$$

where $\chi \geq 0$. Thus, the basic model presented in chapter 1 corresponds to $\chi = 0$.

Normalizing the constant population $\bar{N}$ to unity, and with full depreciation, profit maximization and assumption 1.1 in chapter 1 yield again

$$w_t = \beta Y_t, \quad r_t = (1-\beta)\frac{Y_t}{K_t^P} - 1, \tag{5}$$

$$Y_t = (x_t k_t^I)^{\alpha} K_t^P. \tag{6}$$

### 2.3| Government

The government budget constraint and spending shares are defined as before:

$$G_t^I + G_t^U = \tau w_t, \tag{7}$$

$$G_t^h = \upsilon_h \tau w_t. \quad h = I, U \tag{8}$$

Combining these equations gives

$$\upsilon_I + \upsilon_U = 1. \tag{9}$$

The production of public capital requires again combining the flow spending on infrastructure and the existing stock of public capital, in effective terms, that is, assuming full depreciation,

$$K_{t+1}^I = (\varphi G_t^I)^\mu (x_t K_t^I)^{1-\mu}, \tag{10}$$

where $\mu \in (0, 1)$.[3]

### 2.4| Savings-Investment Balance

The savings-investment balance is

$$K_{t+1}^P = s_t. \tag{11}$$

## 3| Balanced Growth Path

The solution of the household optimization problem yields as before

$$s_t = \sigma(1-\tau)w_t, \tag{12}$$

where $\sigma \in (0, 1)$.

With no network externality ($\chi = 0$), and as shown in chapter 1, the dynamics of the public-private capital ratio can be written in terms of a first-order, nonlinear difference equation:

$$k_{t+1}^I = \Phi(k_t^I) = \frac{(\varphi \upsilon_I \tau \beta)^\mu}{\beta\sigma(1-\tau)}(k_t^I)^{(1-\alpha)(1-\mu)}, \tag{13}$$

with a steady-state value given by

$$\tilde{k}^I = \left\{\frac{(\varphi \upsilon_I \tau \beta)^\mu}{\beta\sigma(1-\tau)}\right\}^{1/[1-(1-\alpha)(1-\mu)]},$$

and a steady-state growth rate equal to

$$1+\gamma = \left\{\frac{(\varphi \upsilon_I \tau \beta)^\mu}{\beta\sigma(1-\tau)}\right\}^{\alpha/[1-(1-\alpha)(1-\mu)]} \beta\sigma(1-\tau). \tag{14}$$

[3] In principle, the threshold effect associated with public capital could be different in (6) and (10). However, accounting for these differences would simply complicate the algebra without changing the thrust of the analysis.

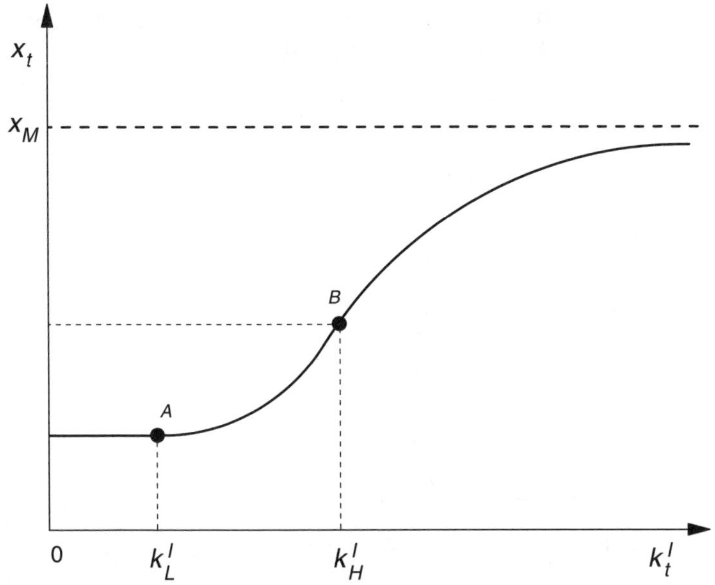


Figure 6.1. Network Externalities and Endogenous Efficiency.

## 4| Network Externalities

Suppose now that the value of the parameter $\chi$ in the externality function (4) depends on the strength of network externalities associated with public capital. Specifically, suppose that

$$\chi \begin{cases} = 0 \text{ for } k_t^I < k_L^I, \\ > \chi_T \text{ for } k_L^I \leq k_t^I < k_H^I, \\ < \chi_T \text{ for } k_t^I \geq k_H^I. \end{cases} \tag{15}$$

Thus, the relationship between $x_t$ and $k_t^I$ is constant over the interval $(0, k_L^I)$ and, in the particular case where $\chi_T = 1$, convex over the interval $(k_L^I, k_H^I)$ and concave over the interval $(k_H^I, \infty[$. This is illustrated in Figure 6.1, where $x_t$ is possibly bounded by a maximum value $x_M$. This specification therefore captures in a simple manner the idea that the marginal benefits of public capital, in terms of its own efficiency, may be highly positive at first, once a "network" is completed (between points $A$ and $B$); but beyond a certain point, these marginal benefits begin to decrease.

For $k_t^I < k_L^I$, the model's dynamics are driven by (13). To determine what happens with $k_t^I > k_L^I$, substitute (5 ), (6), and (12) in (11),

$$\frac{K_{t+1}^P}{K_t^P} = \beta\sigma(1-\tau)(x_t k_t^I)^\alpha, \tag{16}$$

whereas substituting (5) and (8) with $h = I$ in (10),

$$K_{t+1}^I = \left(\varphi \frac{\upsilon_I \tau \beta Y_t}{K_t^I}\right)^\mu x_t^{1-\mu} K_t^I.$$

Using (6), this expression becomes

$$\frac{K_{t+1}^I}{K_t^I} = (\varphi \upsilon_I \tau \beta)^\mu x_t^{1-\mu(1-\alpha)} (k_t^I)^{-\mu(1-\alpha)}. \tag{17}$$

Combining (16) and (17) yields

$$k_{t+1}^I = \frac{(\varphi \upsilon_I \tau \beta)^\mu}{\beta\sigma(1-\tau)} x_t^{(1-\alpha)(1-\mu)} (k_t^I)^{(1-\alpha)(1-\mu)},$$

that is, using (4),

$$k_{t+1}^I = \Phi(k_t^I) = \frac{(\varphi \upsilon_I \tau \beta)^\mu}{\beta\sigma(1-\tau)} (k_t^I)^\Omega, \tag{18}$$

where

$$\Omega = (1-\alpha)(1-\mu)(1+\chi).$$

Because $\Omega > 0$, $dk_{t+1}^I / dk_t^I = \Omega\Phi(k_t^I)/k_t^I > 0$; but given that now $\Omega \lesseqgtr 1$,

$$d^2 k_{t+1}^I / d(k_t^I)^2 = -\Omega(1-\Omega)\Phi(k_t^I)/(k_t^I)^2 \lesseqgtr 0.$$

Thus, if $\chi$ is high enough, so that $\Omega > 1$, then $d^2 k_{t+1}^I / d(k_t^I)^2 > 0$ and the transition function $\phi(k_t^I)$ is convex. Formally, this requires

$$\chi > \chi_T = \frac{\alpha(1-\mu)+\mu}{(1-\alpha)(1-\mu)}.$$

Thus, for $k_L^I \leq k_t^I < k_H^I$, and $\chi > \chi_T$, the transition curve $\Phi(k_t^I)$ is convex; whereas for $k_t^I \geq k_H^I$, and $\chi < \chi_T$, the transition curve is concave. The dynamic equation (18) is unstable over the interval $(k_L^I, k_H^I)$ and stable over the interval $(k_H^I, \infty[$.[4]

There are now a variety of possible outcomes. In particular, the steady-state equilibrium need not be unique. There are up to three possible steady states, two of which at most are stable. Figure 6.2 describes two cases where there

[4] Note that this result may obtain even if $\chi_T < 1$, that is, over a *concave* portion of the curve relating $x_t$ and $k_t^I$. But in practice, $\chi_T$ is likely to be greater than unity. For instance, with $\alpha = 0.15$, $\beta = 0.6$, and $\mu = 0.3$, $\chi_T = 1.21$.

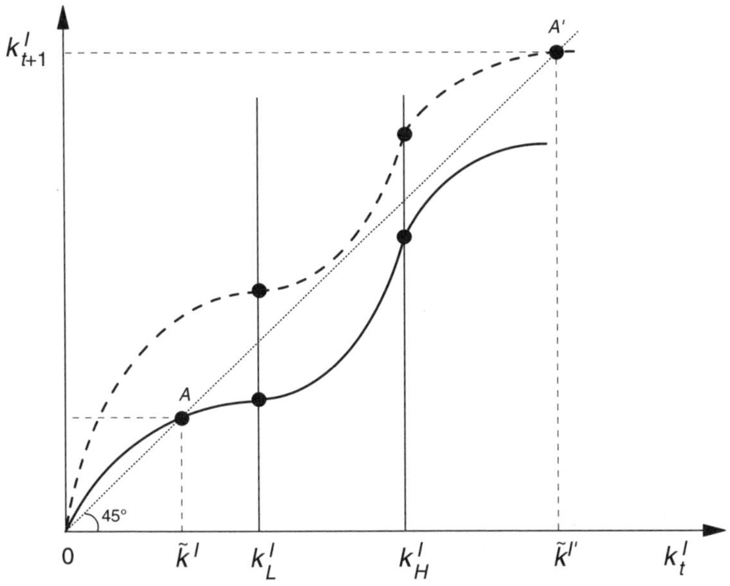


Figure 6.2. Dynamics of the Public-Private Capital Ratio with $\chi > 0$ unique Equilibrium.

exists a unique steady-state equilibrium. For the continuous line, this occurs when $\Phi(k^I_i) < k^I_i$, $i = L, H$, and $\Phi(k^I_t) < k^I_t$, $\forall k^I_t > k^I_H$. If so the condition $\tilde{k}^I < k^I_L$ also holds and the equilibrium is at point $A$. For the dotted line, this occurs when $\Phi(k^I_L) > k^I_L$, in which case $\tilde{k}^{I'} > k^I_H$, and the equilibrium is at point $A'$.[5]

Figure 6.3 describes the case of multiple, locally stable steady-state equilibria; a low public-private capital ratio steady state, $\tilde{k}^I_1$, corresponding to Point $A^1$, and a high public-private capital ratio steady state, $\tilde{k}^I_3$, corresponding to point $A^3$. The intermediate equilibrium, $\tilde{k}^I_2$, corresponding to point $A^2$, is unstable. This occurs if $\Phi(k^I_L) < k^I_L$, $\Phi(k^I_H) > k^I_H$, $\Phi(k^I_t) < k^I_t$, $\forall k^I_t \in (\tilde{k}^I_1, \tilde{k}^I_2)$, and $\Phi(k^I_t) > k^I_t$, $\forall k^I_t \in (\tilde{k}^I_2, \tilde{k}^I_3)$. In this case, initial conditions determine the economy's long-run steady-state equilibrium: economies with a relatively low initial public-private capital ratio may converge to a poverty trap. For instance, if the initial capital ratio is such that $0 < k^I_0 < \tilde{k}^I_2$, the economy will converge to $\tilde{k}^I_1$, whereas if $k^I_0 > \tilde{k}^I_2$, it will converge to $\tilde{k}^I_3$. Put differently, the level of the public-private capital ratio that corresponds to the unstable equilibrium $A^2$ acts as a threshold level that a country must cross if it wants to evolve from being poor to becoming rich.

[5] Note that because $\Phi(k^I_i)$ is increasing, and convex in the interval $(k^I_L, k^I_H)$, the condition $\Phi(k^I_L) > k^I_L$ ensures that $\Phi(k^I_H) > k^I_H$ as well, and that $\Phi(k^I_t) > k^I_t$, $\forall k^I_t \in (k^I_L, \tilde{k}^I_H)$.

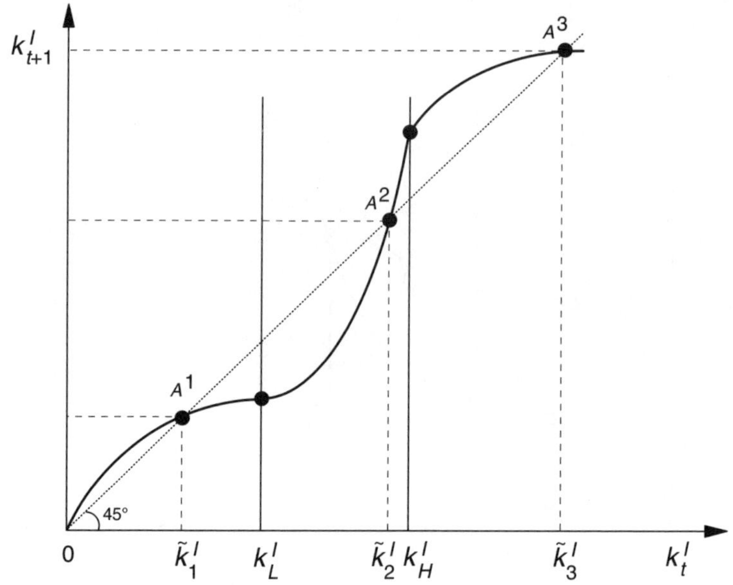


Figure 6.3. Dynamics of the Public-Private Capital Ratio with $\chi > 0$: Multiple Equilibria.

## 5| The Big Push

As noted in the introduction to this book, reports by the United Nations (2005), the Commission for Africa (2005) and the World Bank (2005*a*) and prominent advocates like Jeffrey Sachs (2005, 2008) have supported the idea of a Big Push in public infrastructure investment in poor countries, financed by debt relief and foreign aid. The model developed in the previous sections can be used to address this issue and examine under what conditions such a strategy is likely to be successful.

A Big Push can be captured by considering a budget-neutral increase in $\upsilon_I$ (that is, $d\upsilon_I + d\upsilon_U = 0$) at $t = 0$.[6] The results are illustrated in Figure 6.4. The policy shifts the transition curve $\Phi(k^I_t)$ upward (with no change at the origin). The key issue is whether, starting from a situation where $k^I_0$ is positioned to the *left* of the unstable equilibrium (which implies that the economy would converge to a low-growth trap at $A^1$) to a position where the policy shift is large enough to ensure that $k^I_0$ is now positioned to the *right* of the unstable

[6] In this framework, financing a Big Push through a cut in unproductive spending is equivalent to financing it by an increase in foreign aid, as long as foreign assistance has no distortionary effects—which could occur, for instance, if it reduces incentives to collect taxes. For more general discussions of the role of aid and its composition in growth models with public capital, see Chatterjee et al. (2003), Chatterjee and Turnovsky (2005), Agénor and Yilmaz (2008), and Agénor and Aizenman (2010).

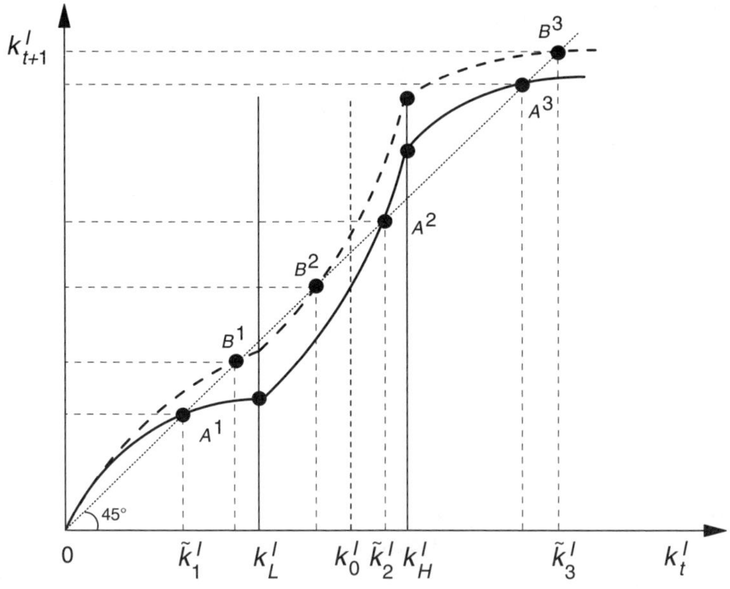


Figure 6.4. The Big Push.

equilibrium, thereby ensuring convergence to the high-growth equilibrium.[7] This is indeed what is shown in the figure; following the policy shift, the new unstable equilibrium is at $B^2$ and the economy converges to the new high-growth state at $B^3$.

Note also that if $k^I_0$ happens to coincide with the poverty trap equilibrium $\tilde{k}^I_1$, or is located anywhere to the left of that point, the increase in government spending in infrastructure must induce an upward shift in $\Phi(k^I_t)$ that is large enough to eliminate the unstable equilibrium and leave only the high-growth equilibrium as a possible outcome, as with the dotted curve in Figure 6.2; otherwise the economy would not be able to escape the low-growth trap.

In the foregoing discussion, the magnitude of the efficiency parameter $\varphi$ was abstracted from. However, in line with the discussion in chapter 1, it is immediately clear that if $\varphi$ is too low, even a large increase in $\upsilon_I$ may not be sufficient to induce an upward shift in $\Phi(k^I_t)$ that puts the economy on a convergent path to the high-growth equilibrium. Thus, to the extent that there is an inverse correlation between the quality of infrastructure investment and the level of corruption, for a Big Push policy to be effective, it must be accompanied by improvements in the selection, implementation, and monitoring of investment projects—or more generally reform of the broad institutional framework underpinning the provision of public capital.

[7] Put differently, the increase in $\upsilon_I$ must be large enough to shift the convex portion of the curve up sufficiently to ensure that it intersects the 45-degree line to the left of $k^I_0$.

# 6| Other Channels

In addition to network effects, there are several other channels through which public capital may affect the ability of a country to escape from a poverty trap. These channels include an effect through time allocation, an effect through health outcomes, and an effect through technology adoption.

## 6.1| Time Allocation

Public capital may help a poor country escape a poverty trap by increasing the efficiency of "raw" time (as discussed in chapters 2 and 5) or by "liberating" time, that is, by allowing individuals to reallocate some of their time from low-productivity activities (such as household chores) to high-productivity, market-related work. This is consistent with the discussion of the previous chapter, where the emphasis was put on changes in women's time allocation, following an increase in government spending on infrastructure. Indeed, time allocated to market work may be lumpy, rather than continuous; this implies that there may be a nonlinearity (or discontinuity) associated with changes in time allocation. A Big Push in public investment, leading to a large reduction in time allocated to household chores and a sharp increase in labor supply to market activities, may shift the economy to a high-growth equilibrium.

## 6.2| Health-Induced Poverty Traps

Interactions among public capital, health, and growth may also lead to poverty traps. Indeed, threshold effects may characterize the impact of infrastructure on human capital and health outcomes, in addition to production externalities or time allocation.[8]

This issue can be analyzed in the context of the three-period model developed in chapter 3.[9] A natural route to follow in the present setting would be to consider the case where the survival rate in adulthood is related (possibly in a nonlinear fashion) to the individual's *own* health status, as discussed in chapter 3. In solving their optimization problem, parents would then internalize the implications of their time allocation decisions. Unfortunately, given the complexity of the resulting framework, doing so precludes an analytical treatment.

Alternatively, as also discussed in chapter 3, suppose that the survival rate of any particular individual depends on *average* health status in the economy—

[8] Threshold effect may also characterize the effect of public capital on research and development activities, as in the analysis presented in chapter 4.

[9] Agénor and Agénor (2009) examine the same issue in the context of the gender-based model developed in chapter 5. For other studies that examine health-related poverty traps, see Chakraborty (2004) and the correction in Bunzel and Qiao (2005), Cervellati and Sunde (2005, 2009), Chakraborty and Das (2005), and Chakraborty et al. (2010). Azariadis and Stachurski (2005) provide a more general discussion of poverty traps.

which, in equilibrium, is of course the same for all individuals. For instance, if one stops smoking, but continues to be surrounded by smokers, one's health prospects will not necessarily improve. If one quits drinking, but nobody else does, one's risk of getting involved in a car accident involving a drunk driver will not necessarily diminish. In an environment where deadly communicable diseases can spread rapidly (as is often the case in urban slums in developing countries), and vaccines do not completely protect from the risk of getting infected, one individual getting immunized will not change the risk to which he or she is exposed (and therefore his or her survival probability), unless all individuals get immunized; and so on. In such conditions, it is natural to retain the assumption that agents do not internalize the effect of their time allocation decisions on their own survival probability.

To illustrate in a simple manner how multiple development regimes may emerge in this context, it is not necessary to assume (as discussed in chapter 3) that life expectancy is related in a continuous fashion to health status; rather, suppose that the adult survival rate is a piecewise function defined as

$$p_t = \begin{cases} p_m \text{ If } h_t^A \leq h_m^A \\ p_M \text{ If } h_t^A > h_m^A \end{cases}, \tag{19}$$

where $p_m$, $p_M \in (0, 1)$. Thus, if health status is below $h_m^A$, the likelihood of surviving into old age is $p_m$, as before. As health status improves above that threshold, the survival probability increases to $p_M > p_m$ and remains insensitive to further changes in health outcomes.

As illustrated in Figure 6.5 (which extends Figure 3.2), the economy may now display multiple development regimes. For $h_0^A \leq h_m^A$, the economy will converge to the low-growth equilibrium point $E$. If the net effect of an increase in the survival rate is positive (as discussed in Chapter 3), once the economy crosses $h_m^A$ it will converge to the high-growth equilibrium point $E'$. Both $KK$ and $HH$ shift upward, and the steady-state growth rate of output per worker increases unambiguously. The stagnation equilibrium (or poverty trap) is thus characterized also by poor health outcomes.

What is the role of policy then? As can be inferred from the results in chapter 3, a shift from unproductive spending toward health outlays may increase health status sufficiently to ensure that over time $h_t^A$ exceeds $h_m^A$, and thereby putting the economy on a new (higher) growth trajectory. At the same time, however, if the degree of efficiency of health outlays is low, or if the increase in health spending is financed by a cut in productive spending, a better strategy may actually be a Big Push in public investment in infrastructure—provided of course that such spending is itself sufficiently efficient. Again, given the complementarity between public capital in infrastructure and other inputs in the production of health services, the best way to improve health outcomes may not be to increase health spending per se—a dimension that is often forgotten in the debate on improving health indicators in poor

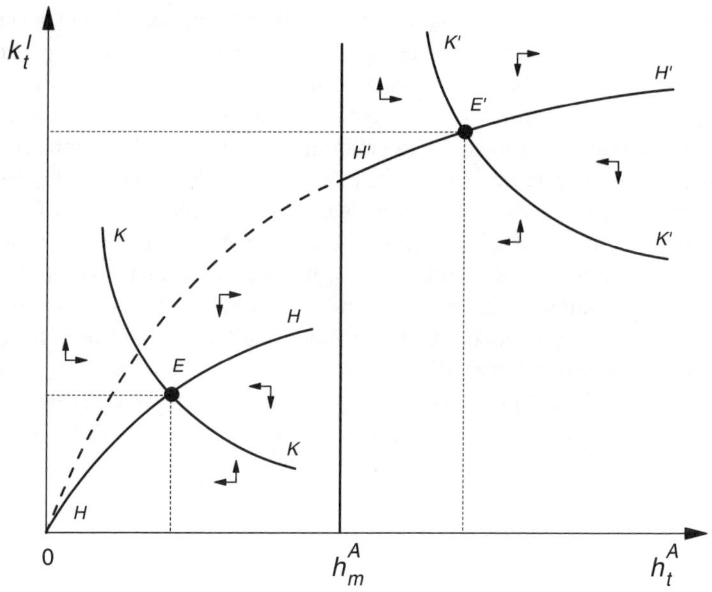


Figure 6.5. Multiple Development Regimes with Threshold Health Effects.

countries. In general, the analysis suggests that a two-pronged strategy, involving spending on both health and infrastructure (given diminishing returns to each production input), accompanied by governance reforms aimed at improving spending efficiency across the board, stands the best chance of helping a country to escape from a poverty trap.

## 6.3| Technology Choice

Access to public capital may affect the choice of production technology itself. At low levels of access, producers may have no choice but to continue to use a subsistence technology—even though it would be profitable to switch to a modern (more productive) technology. In the absence of a reliable power grid, for instance, firms may not be able to switch to more advanced production equipment. With no roads to transport perishable commodities fast enough between rural and urban areas, the adoption of new production techniques in agriculture may not be feasible either.

To illustrate how public capital may affect the choice of technology, suppose that firms have access to two production technologies: a traditional technology (with subscript $T$) and a modern technology (with subscript $M$). Both technologies produce the same good, so the relative price between them is constant; the difference is that the modern technology takes better advantage of public capital. This is captured by assuming that the output elasticity $\alpha^M > \alpha^T$. At the same time, the new technology is taken to be less intensive in labor (or, equivalently, more intensive in private capital), so that $\beta^M < \beta^T$. Access to electricity, for instance, allows firms to use more sophisticated, labor-saving equipment.[10]

From the derivations in chapter 1 with $\mu = 1$, and assuming that the quantity of labor $\bar{N}$ is again normalized to unity, output, the rate of return to capital, and the growth rate of the economy are given by

$$Y_t^j = \left(\frac{K_t^I}{K_t^{j,P}}\right)^{\alpha^j} K_t^{j,P}, \tag{20}$$

$$r_t^j = (1-\beta^j)\left(\frac{Y_t^j}{K_t^{j,P}}\right) - 1, \tag{21}$$

$$1 + \gamma_t^j = (k_t^{j,I})^{\alpha^j} \beta^j \sigma(1-\tau), \tag{22}$$

where $j = M, T$. The assumption that $\mu = 1$ implies that the steady-state public-private capital ratio is the same under the two technologies, so that, as shown in chapter 1, $k_t^{j,I} = \varphi \upsilon_I \tau / \sigma(1-\tau)$, $\forall t$, for $j = M, T$. The wage rate of course differs depending of the technology, with $w_t^j = \beta^j Y_t^j$.

Firms can coordinate their choice of technology, traditional or modern. They adopt the modern technology when $r_t^M \geq r_t^T$, that is, when the differential in the rates of return to private capital turns in favor of that technology. Otherwise, they stick to the traditional technology. Combining (20) and (21), this condition implies the rate-of-return arbitrage condition

$$(1-\beta^M)(k_t^I)^{\alpha^M} = (1-\beta^T)(k_t^I)^{\alpha^T},$$

which can be rewritten as

$$\bar{k}^I = \left(\frac{1-\beta^T}{1-\beta^M}\right)^{1/(\alpha^M - \alpha^T)}. \tag{23}$$

Thus, there is an endogenously determined threshold level of public capital beyond which the technology switch occurs. Because the model displays no transitional dynamics, this threshold is constant. The higher $\alpha^M$ is relative to $\alpha^T$, the lower the threshold needed to induce a switch in technology.

Thus, the determination of the growth rate is quite simple, depending on whether $k^I \lessgtr \bar{k}^I$. Indeed, the growth rate is constant over time at

$$1 + \gamma = \begin{cases} (\varphi \upsilon_I \tau)^{\alpha^T} \beta^T [\sigma(1-\tau)]^{1-\alpha^T} & \text{If } k^I < \bar{k}^I \\ (\varphi \upsilon_I \tau)^{\alpha^M} \beta^M [\sigma(1-\tau)]^{1-\alpha^M} & \text{If } k^I > \bar{k}^I \end{cases},$$

[10] Alternatively, it could be assumed that the traditional technology does not use public capital at all ($\alpha^T = 0$) but that initially growth is generated as a result of an Arrow-Romer learning by doing effect, as discussed in chapter 1.

which implies that

$$\frac{1+\gamma^M}{1+\gamma^T} = (\varphi \upsilon_I \tau)^{\alpha^M - \alpha^T} \left( \frac{\beta^M}{\beta^T} \right) [\sigma(1-\tau)]^{-(\alpha^M - \alpha^T)}. \tag{24}$$

Taking logs on both sides of this equation yields

$$\gamma^M - \gamma^T \simeq (\alpha^M - \alpha^T)\{\ln(\varphi \upsilon_I \tau) - \ln[\sigma(1-\tau)]\} - (\ln \beta^T - \ln \beta^M),$$

Thus, growth is higher with the modern technology if

$$\frac{\ln \beta^T - \ln \beta^M}{\alpha^M - \alpha^T} < \ln(\varphi \upsilon_I \tau) - \ln[\sigma(1-\tau)],$$

a condition that is more likely to hold if, in particular, $\alpha^M$ is large.

Using (23), and the solution of the public-private capital ratio, yields

$$\bar{\upsilon}_I = \left[ \frac{\sigma(1-\tau)}{\varphi \tau} \right] \left( \frac{1-\beta^T}{1-\beta^M} \right)^{1/(\alpha^T - \alpha^M)}. \tag{25}$$

This solution (provided that it is admissible) gives the value of the spending share on investment above which private firms are induced to switch technologies. In particular, the stronger the productivity effect of public capital in the modern production technology (the higher $\alpha^M$ is, relative to $\alpha^T$), the higher the required share of public investment. Note also that the threshold level of investment depends also negatively on the tax rate.

Of course, a more elaborate analysis, involving a more detailed characterization of the transitional dynamics, would be useful.[11] Nevertheless, the intuition would remain fundamentally the same: because of the endogeneity of investors' choice of technology, lack of access to public capital can generate a low-growth equilibrium, because its productivity effects are simply not large enough to make it profitable for private firms to adopt a new, growth-promoting, production process.

## 7| Aid Volatility and Time to Build

Suppose that aid, denoted $A_t$, can serve to finance government expenditure as well and that it is nondistortionary. This can be captured by rewriting the government budget constraint (7) as

$$G_t = \tau w_t + A_t,$$

or equivalently, assuming that aid is a fraction $a \in (0, 1)$ of tax revenues,

$$\upsilon_I + \upsilon_U = 1 + a.$$

[11] Iwaisako (2002) for instance provides a dynamic analysis in a two-period OLG framework where the advanced technology exhibits increasing returns to scale (in labor and private capital) due to specialization of intermediate goods production. His analysis, however, excludes public capital and focuses on taxes and subsidies as ways to escape from poverty traps.

A budget-neutral increase in public investment in infrastructure can now entail an increase in aid, so that $dv_I = da$. Put differently, an increase in aid to finance a Big Push in public investment, as discussed earlier, may allow a country to escape from a poverty trap—to the extent, of course, that aid is efficient, an issue on which there continues to be much debate (see Doucouliagos and Paldam (2009)). The underlying argument is that, given the limited ability of many of these countries to raise domestic resources through taxation, concessional external finance is essential to support a multiyear public investment program.

Rather than the level of aid, some recent thinking has focused on the *volatility* of aid. Pallage and Robe (2001), using data for 63 aid recipients for the period 1969-95, found that aid is approximately twice as volatile as real output. In the same vein, Bulir and Hamann (2003), using data covering 72 countries over the period 1975-97, found that aid flows are significantly more volatile than domestic fiscal revenues; in addition, the information content of aid commitments in predicting actual flows is either very small or statistically insignificant—a result subsequently corroborated by Celasun and Walliser (2008). They also found much larger prediction errors in program assistance than in project aid, and a stronger tendency to overestimation.[12] In a subsequent study, Bulir and Hamann (2007) also found that the volatility of aid is much larger than the volatility of domestic tax revenues, with coefficients of variation in the range of 40 to 60 percent of mean aid flows. The study also found that aid volatility has actually increased since the late 1990s.

By their very nature, some types of aid *should* exhibit a high degree of volatility, because they are designed to deal with local economic and social crises. This is certainly the case for emergency aid. To a lower extent, high volatility may also characterize program assistance, given that it may depend (through conditionality) on short-run macroeconomic performance and disbursement triggers. By contrast, project aid should be relatively stable, given that it is designed to promote (directly or indirectly) investment in physical and human capital. However, in a study of disaggregated aid inflows to 66 low-income recipients over the period 1973-2002, Fielding and Mavrotas (2005) found that project aid (particularly in the more open economies) tends also to be quite volatile. If donor countries provide aid for financing large and lumpy projects, some degree of volatility of that category should naturally be expected; but, more worryingly, it may also result from extrinsic factors, such as the political cycle in donor countries.

[12] Program aid (also referred to as budget or "untied" aid) generally takes the form of a cash disbursement and is perfectly fungible. By contrast, project aid (or "tied" aid) consists of transfers for investment projects agreed between the donor and the recipient country. The extent to which it is fungible depends on whether, prior to the aid commitment, the recipient country intended to finance the project itself.

As emphasized by Agénor and Aizenman (2010), a key implication of lack of predictability in project aid disbursements is that it makes it difficult for recipient governments to formulate medium-term spending plans to spur growth. If aid finances a large fraction of infrastructure investment, as is often the case in low-income countries, and if creating public capital requires time (as a result of a "time to build" assumption, for instance), an aid shortfall could bring the process to a halt if no alternative sources of financing are available.[13] In addition, in response to high volatility, countries may opt to reduce the desired level of investment, which, ceteris paribus, means lower funding requirements; donors, seeing lower requirements, may misinterpret it as a signal of absorption problems, and effectively reduce aid commitments—making the initial concerns about lower assistance self-fulfilling and possibly contributing to the perpetuation of a stagnation equilibrium. Aid volatility may therefore have permanent costs in terms of lost output and exert potentially large adverse effects on growth and human welfare.[14]

• • •

The purpose of this chapter was to study how a Big Push in public capital may help a poor country escape from a poverty or low-growth trap. Dwelling on the basic framework presented in chapter 1, the first part focused on the benchmark case where there are network effects associated with public capital. Network effects typically imply nonlinearities or threshold effects. Specifically, it was assumed that the degree of efficiency of infrastructure is nonlinearly related to the stock of public capital itself; the marginal benefits of public capital, in terms of its own efficiency, are highly positive at first, once a network is completed; but beyond a certain point, these marginal benefits begin to decrease. The analysis showed that, depending on how strong these nonlinearities are, multiple equilibria may emerge. A large increase in the share of spending on infrastructure may shift the economy from a low-growth equilibrium to a high-growth steady state, but only if the quality of governance—including the selection, implementation, and monitoring of investment projects—is adequate enough to ensure a high degree of efficiency of public investment.

The second part of the chapter considered various other channels through which an increase in public investment may help a poor country to escape

[13] More formally, Agénor and Aizenman (2010) consider a two-period model where risk-neutral agents must choose between a traditional and modern technologies. In addition, a "time to build" assumption requires public expenditure in both periods for the modern technology to be adopted. Although aid disbursements are known with certainty in the first period, they are uncertain in the second. In turn, this uncertainty alters the decision to invest—and the incentives for tax reform—in the first period, leading thereby to inertia and stagnation.

[14] Neanidis and Varvarigos (2009) provide evidence that the volatility of project aid has an adverse effect on economic growth.

from a low-growth equilibrium, through a positive impact of public capital on time allocation, health outcomes, and the choice of production technology. In the latter case, the model was extended to consider two technologies (one traditional, one modern, with the latter being more intensive in the use of public capital), under the assumption that the switch among them is endogenously determined through a rate-of-return arbitrage condition. Similar conclusions on the impact of public investment were obtained. These models therefore provide a conceptual underpinning to the Big Push idea, with the important proviso that for this policy to work, governance, or more generally the broad institutional framework underpinning the provision of public capital, may need to be drastically improved. The practical implications of these results for the ongoing debate on "scaling up" public investment in poor countries cannot be overemphasized.

The last part of the chapter focused on the case where foreign aid can serve to finance government expenditure as well. It was argued that the *volatility* (or, rather, lack of predictability) of aid, rather than its *level*, can be a key reason preventing a country from escaping from a poverty trap. If aid finances a large fraction of domestic infrastructure investment, and if building public capital requires time, aid volatility may hamper the ability of recipient governments to formulate medium-term spending plans and may even induce them to reduce the desired level of capital outlays and funding requirements. If donors misinterpret lower aid requirements as a signal of absorption problems, they may reduce their aid commitments—making the initial concerns about the risk of reduced foreign support self-fulfilling and contributing to the perpetuation of a low-growth equilibrium. This point is also particularly important in the current debate on how best to promote growth in low-income countries: it is not simply levels of external financing that matter, but also their predictability over time.

# 7 | Research Perspectives

The previous chapters have documented and formally analyzed a variety of channels, both old and new, through which public capital may affect growth. Various extensions, mostly technical in nature, were outlined at the end of some chapters. This chapter sets out a broader research agenda on the links among public capital, growth, and human welfare. Without being exhaustive, it considers the following areas: heterogeneous infrastructure assets, the political economy of government spending allocation, excludable public goods, interactions between government debt and public capital accumulation in the presence of fiscal rules, spatial and regional dimensions of public capital, infrastructure and trade, public-private partnerships, the impact of public capital on income distribution, negative externalities associated with public capital, and empirical tests of the impact of public capital on growth.

## 1 | Heterogeneous Infrastructure Assets

In previous chapters, public capital was viewed as a homogeneous stock—except in chapter 1, where the case of two public capital stocks was briefly examined. In practice, of course, there are different types of infrastructure—rail, air, sea and road transport, telephone (fixed line and mobile), energy and water, and so on, each possibly affecting private production in a different way. Some components may have a larger multiplier effect due to their impact on human capital, either directly or indirectly—through interactions between health and education in particular, as discussed in Chapter 3. For instance, there is strong evidence to suggest that at low levels of income investments in water and sanitation have very large benefits on health and human welfare. This, in turn, may improve productivity—so much so that the growth benefits may prove to be larger, and accumulate faster, than for other types of investment in infrastructure.

If so, a natural question that arises is whether there is an *optimal sequence* of infrastructure development. Should roads precede railways? Should the development of an electricity network precede the expansion of telecommunications? The discussion in Chapter 4 of the role of different types of infrastructure in the transition from imitation to true innovation provides one perspective on this issue. However, one would expect the optimal sequence to depend on a host of other factors, including geography, initial factor endowments, and political economy considerations. Combining an analytical approach with a historical perspective, based on the experience of currently developed countries, could prove fruitful for further progress.

## 2| Political Economy of Government Spending Allocation

Much of the discussion on optimal spending in previous chapters assumed that spending shares are determined by a benevolent government, intent on maximizing growth. Although this provides a convenient analytical benchmark, in practice political economy considerations are likely to be very important.

Conceptually, it is convenient to distinguish between two issues: (*a* ) the determination of spending levels or shares and (*b*) the quality or efficiency of spending components. Regarding the first issue, two important considerations are demographic factors and the nature of the political process. Surprisingly enough, there has been limited analytical and empirical research on these two possible determinants of government spending behavior. In an OLG context, a key dimension through which political considerations may matter is the conflict between the young and older generations. The former may prefer investment in infrastructure because public capital raises the marginal productivity of labor and thus current and future returns to market work; the latter, by contrast, may prefer immediate transfers. If the old are more likely to vote to reelect the incumbent, it may be rational for the government to bias spending allocation toward transfers to that segment of the population to maximize its immediate chances of reelection. More generally, as discussed by Bohn (2007), both political polarization and political uncertainty may bias a government's intertemporal choices toward redistribution, rather than public investment.[1]

There is evidence suggesting that the composition of public spending depends on the demographic structure of the population. Using data for a large group of industrial and developing countries, Shelton (2007) for instance found that a greater fraction of the population above 65 tends to be accompanied by higher levels of government expenditure on health care, public order, and safety—possibly a reflection of the ability of old agents to exploit the political process to their advantage. Such a bias toward redistribution may result in large adverse effects on infrastructure investment and growth—and eventually the welfare of both old and young generations alike. Supportive evidence is also provided by Vergne (2009), who found in a study based on data for 42 developing countries over the period 1975–2001 that during election years public spending shifts toward more visible current expenditures (in particular wages and subsidies), and away from capital expenditures.

The second issue relates to the determination of the efficiency coefficient $\varphi \in (0, 1)$, which was defined as a parameter that measures the extent to which investment flows translate into actual accumulation of public capital. This

[1] As shown by Kaas (2003), in a model with productive public spending and sequential majority voting, self-fulfilling expectations may also lead to a multiplicity of equilibria, some of which are characterized by an inefficiently low level of government spending.

parameter was introduced exogenously in chapter 1. As indicated then, $\varphi$ may reflect the degree of corruption; there is indeed cross-country evidence to suggest that the quality of investment is inversely related to the quality of governance. Dal Bo and Rossi (2007) found that greater corruption is significantly associated with lower efficiency of electricity distribution. Using panel data for 58 countries, Haque and Kneller (2008) found that corruption reduces the return to public investment and therefore weakens its effect on economic growth, whereas Rajkumar and Swaroop (2008) found that spending on health and education is more effective in developing countries where the quality of governance is high. Alternatively, by the same reasoning as before, it is possible that electoral concerns may induce governments to care less not only about the quantity of infrastructure but also about its quality—with equally adverse effects on growth.

In either case, an important avenue for future research would be to extend the analytical framework presented here in order to account for the endogeneity of government spending choices. Endogenizing $\varphi$ requires a political economy model of the determination of government spending shares by linking it to the degree of corruption or political incentives along the lines of Blackburn et al. (2005), Robinson and Torvik (2005), Cadot et al. (2006), Blackburn and Sarmah (2008), De la Croix and Delavallade (2009, 2011), and Chakraborty and Dabla-Norris (2010). In the model of Blackburn et al. (2005) for instance, corruption is harmful because it implies that public goods are provided at a lower overall quality but greater total expense. In Blackburn and Sarmah (2008), corruption affects growth through demographic outcomes because longevity depends on the public provision of health care. Threshold effects in life expectancy arise from the endogenous change in the incentives of bureaucrats to engage in the embezzlement of public funds. At low levels of development, corruption exists, public goods provision is low, and life expectancy is low; beyond some critical level of development, corruption disappears, public goods provision is higher, and life expectancy improves. A similar analysis could be conducted in terms of public capital, given its effect on health outcomes.

As pointed out by Chakraborty and Dabla-Norris (2010), spending more on fighting corruption, even though it implies less spending for each project, may improve the quality of public capital—so much so that the "quality" effect may more than offset the "quantity" effect. Put differently, any scaling up of public investment needs to be accompanied by improvements in screening, monitoring, and overseeing investment decisions, or more generally the quality of bureaucratic oversight—in line with the analysis of the Big Push developed in chapter 6.

Other considerations may matter as well; policies to achieve greater female political participation (such as quotas in some countries) can lead to the prioritization of investments of particular importance to women, including time-saving infrastructure, which in turn can promote economic growth. There is also evidence to suggest that women's empowerment is associated with improved governance and reduced corruption (see Blackden et al. (2006)).

## 3| Excludable Public Goods

In all of the previous chapters, it was assumed that infrastructure services, although (partially) rival, were provided by the government free of charge. However, in practice, some of these services are *excludable*, that is, potential users can be identified and charged a user fee. This is the case, for instance, for highways, bridges, and electricity grids.

User fees could be introduced in the basic setup of chapter 1 in a relatively simple manner. Suppose that there are two types of infrastructure services provided by the government, one that is not excludable (as before) and another that is excludable. Suppose first that all government resources are pooled, with revenues from selling excludable services generating a unit user fee of $p^X$. Let $G_t^X$ denote the flow supply of excludable public goods; the government budget constraint is now

$$G_t^I + G_t^X + G_t^U = \bar{N}\tau w_t + p^X G_t^{X,d}, \tag{1}$$

where $G_t^{X,d}$ is the demand for excludable goods.

Suppose also that both types of infrastructure services benefit private production and suffer from absolute congestion, measured by the aggregate capital stock:

$$Y_t^i = \left[\frac{K_t^I}{(K_t^P)^{\zeta}}\right]^{\alpha}\left[\frac{G_t^{X,i}}{(K_t^P)^{\zeta^X}}\right]^{\alpha^X}(N_t^i)^{\beta}(K_t^{P,i})^{1-\beta},$$

where $\alpha^X, \zeta^X > 0$ and $G_t^{X,i}$ is firm $i$'s demand for the excludable good.

The profit maximization problem for firm $i$ becomes

$$\max_{N_t^i, K_t^{P,i}, G_t^{X,i}} \Pi_t^i = Y_t^i - (r_t + \delta^P)K_t^{P,i} - w_t N_t^i - p_t^X G_t^{X,i}.$$

The optimality condition with respect to $G_t^{X,i}$ yields, upon aggregation,

$$p_t^X = \alpha^X Y_t / G_t^{X,d}, \tag{2}$$

from which the aggregate demand for excludable public goods can be derived. With the supply of excludable goods given by $G_t^X = \upsilon_X(\bar{N}\tau w_t + p^X G_t^{X,d})$. The equilibrium value of the user fee is obtained by equating supply and demand, that is,

$$\upsilon_X(\bar{N}\tau w_t + p_t^X G_t^{X,d}) = G_t^{X,d},$$

or equivalently, using (2),

$$\upsilon_X \bar{N}\tau w_t = (1 - \upsilon_X p_t^X)\frac{\alpha^X Y_t}{p_t^X}.$$

Using the optimal condition with respect to labor, $w_t = \beta Y_t/\bar{N}$, yields

$$\frac{p_t^X}{1-\upsilon_X p_t^X} = \frac{\alpha^X}{\upsilon_X \tau\beta} \Rightarrow p_t^X = \frac{\alpha^X}{\upsilon_X(\alpha^X+\tau\beta)}.$$

Thus, the optimal user fee is constant; it also increases with the output elasticity with respect to excludable goods and decreases with the tax rate.

Suppose now that provision of the excludable good is financed by tax revenues, whereas provision of the excludable good is financed by user fees; the budget constraint (1) is thus replaced by two separate constraints,

$$G_t^I + G_t^U = \bar{N}\tau w_t, \tag{3}$$

$$G_t^X = p_t^X G_t^{X,d}. \tag{4}$$

Substituting (2) in the second constraint yields $G_t^X = \alpha^X Y_t$, that is, the supply of excludable goods is proportional to output. However, the user fee is indeterminate, given the specification of the production function. This indeterminacy can be eliminated by assuming for instance that the supply of excludable goods, $G_t^X$, depends not only on the expenditure flow associated with the resources generated by the user fee (as in (4)), but also on the existing stock of nonexcludable public capital, $K_t^I$. This would also help to determine the optimal shares of public spending between excludable and nonexcludable goods, $\upsilon_I$ and $\upsilon_X$.

A more thorough analysis, along the lines for instance of Ott and Turnovsky (2006), is warranted to determine the optimal tax and user fee structure. This would imply considering user fees that are paid not only by firms but also by households. A key issue is the extent to which user fees should be used to fully finance the provision of excludable goods or whether cross-subsidization is warranted. Another issue is the extent to which the optimal tax and user fee structure is influenced by administrative capacity constraints, which remain all too common in low-income countries.

## 4| Debt, Public Capital, and Fiscal Rules

Throughout the book, the government was assumed to maintain a balanced budget. This assumption is quite reasonable for many low-income countries, where domestic financial markets remain underdeveloped and the ability of governments to issue bonds is accordingly limited. However, some of these countries have now reached a stage where bond financing has become a viable alternative to tax financing.

In a model with public debt, a first question that must be addressed is whether *Ricardian equivalence* holds. The Ricardian equivalence proposition states that, under certain conditions, deficits and taxes are equivalent in their effect on consumption and saving. Lump-sum changes in taxes have no effect on consumer spending, and a reduction in taxes leads to an equivalent increase in saving. The reason is that a consumer endowed with perfect foresight recognizes that the increase in government debt resulting from a reduction in taxes will ultimately be paid off by increased future taxes, the present value of which is exactly equal to the present value of the reduction in current taxes. Taking the implied increase in future taxes into account, the consumer saves today the amount necessary to pay them tomorrow. However, in OLG economies a change in the timing of taxes that redistributes among generations is in general not neutral in the Ricardian sense—unless there are altruistically motivated transfers.[2]

Suppose then that Ricardian equivalence does not hold. The next question is under what conditions is debt financing sustainable, in the sense of the debt-to-output ratio converging to a stable value, and to what extent it may instead lead to economic instability—by preventing the economy from converging to its long-run equilibrium path. In that context, much attention has been paid, in developed and developing countries alike, to the formulation of fiscal rules. These rules have taken various forms, including maintaining fixed targets for the deficit (variously defined) and/or public debt ratios to GDP. They have been criticized for several reasons; but an important argument, in the context of this book, is that they may discourage public investment and the accumulation of public capital if they are applied too broadly. If indeed the various externalities associated with public capital (as identified in previous chapters) are significant, these rules may impose severe costs in terms of economic growth and human welfare.

Some economists have advocated a "golden rule" approach to budgetary policy, whereby the focus is on maintaining a balance or surplus on the primary fiscal account (that is, current revenues less current expenditures), with net capital expenditure, possibly together with (a fraction of) interest payments, financed by government savings and borrowing. However, this rule has also been criticized on a number of grounds.[3] An important issue in the context of this book is whether a golden rule promotes growth without inducing excessive debt accumulation and a tendency toward instability, that is, as indicated earlier, preventing the economy from converging to its long-run equilibrium position.

The basic analytical framework developed in chapter 1 can be used to illustrate the implications of a golden rule. Suppose that the government can now issue one-period bonds, in quantity $B_{t+1}$, to finance its interest payments

[2] See D. Romer (2011, chap. 12) for a detailed discussion. Even with bequests, Ricardian equivalence would not hold in the model considered later in this section due to the presence of distortionary income taxation.

[3] Critics have pointed out, among other arguments, its vulnerability to creative accounting, and the fact that a preferential treatment of physical investment could bias expenditure decisions against spending on other potentially productive components, such as education and health. Agénor and Yilmaz (2011) provide a summary of some of these arguments.

and investment on infrastructure, $G_t^I$, with tax revenues used to finance other (unproductive) outlays, $G_t^U$.[4] There are therefore two independent budget constraints for the government, given by

$$G_t^U = \tau w_t, \tag{5}$$

$$B_{t+1} = (1 + i_t)B_t + G_t^I, \tag{6}$$

where $i_t$ is the rate of return on government bonds. For simplicity, population is normalized to unity and the government is assumed to tax only wages of adult workers, not interest income on government bonds, which accrues to the old.

The market-clearing condition requires now that private savings be equal not only to tomorrow's stock of physical assets but also to the stock of government bonds:

$$K_{t+1}^P + B_{t+1} = s_t.$$

Given the solution of the individual's optimization problem and the link between wages and marginal productivity derived in chapter 1, $s_t = \sigma(1 - \tau)w_t$ and $w_t = \beta Y_t$, this condition becomes

$$K_{t+1}^P + B_{t+1} = \sigma(1 - \tau)\beta Y_t, \tag{7}$$

with aggregate output given as in that chapter by

$$Y_t = (k_t^I)^\alpha K_t^P. \tag{8}$$

Assuming that physical and financial assets are perfect substitutes from the perspective of households implies the no arbitrage condition $1 + i_t = 1 + r_t$. Thus, using (8), and with full depreciation of private capital,

$$1 + i_t = \frac{(1 - \beta)Y_t}{K_t^P} = (1 - \beta)(k_t^I)^\alpha. \tag{9}$$

With $\mu = \varphi = 1$, and again with full depreciation, public capital evolves as

$$K_{t+1}^I = G_t^I, \tag{10}$$

where $G_t^I$ is now assumed to be a fixed fraction $\theta \in (0, 1)$ of output.

To analyze the dynamics of the economy, begin by substituting (6) in (7) to obtain

$$K_{t+1}^P = [\sigma(1 - \tau)\beta - \theta]Y_t - (1 + i_t)B_t, \tag{11}$$

[4] A more general specification, of course, would involve the government using its tax revenues to finance not only unproductive outlays but also a fraction of investment spending. However, this would not change the key results.

or equivalently, using (8) and (9), and with $b_t = B_t/K_t^P$ defined as the debt-private capital ratio,

$$\frac{K_{t+1}^P}{K_t^P} = [\sigma(1-\tau)\beta - \theta](k_t^I)^\alpha - (1-\beta)(k_t^I)^\alpha b_t. \tag{12}$$

From (10),

$$\frac{K_{t+1}^I}{K_t^I} = \theta\left(\frac{Y_t}{K_t^I}\right) = \theta\left(\frac{Y_t}{K_t^P}\right)\left(\frac{K_t^P}{K_t^I}\right),$$

that is, using (8),

$$\frac{K_{t+1}^I}{K_t^I} = \theta(k_t^I)^{\alpha-1}. \tag{13}$$

Dividing (13) by (12) gives

$$k_{t+1}^I = \frac{\theta}{\nu - (1-\beta)b_t}, \tag{14}$$

where $\nu = \sigma(1-\tau)\beta - \theta$ can be interpreted as the aggregate, after-tax savings rate. Equation (14) determines the dynamics of the public-private capital ratio, as a function of the debt-private capital ratio. In what follows $\nu$ is assumed positive. This condition is necessary, although not sufficient, to ensure that the public-private capital ratio is positive in the steady state.

To determine the dynamics of public debt, note that equation (6) can be written as, with $G_t^I = \theta Y_t$,

$$\frac{B_{t+1}}{B_t} = 1 + i_t + \theta\left(\frac{Y_t}{K_t^P}\right)\left(\frac{K_t^P}{B_t}\right),$$

that is, using (9),

$$\frac{B_{t+1}}{B_t} = [(1-\beta) + \theta b_t^{-1}](k_t^I)^\alpha. \tag{15}$$

Dividing (15) by (12) gives

$$b_{t+1} = \frac{[(1-\beta) + \theta b_t^{-1}]b_t}{\nu - (1-\beta)b_t},$$

or equivalently

$$b_{t+1} = \Phi(b_t) = \frac{\theta + (1-\beta)b_t}{\nu - (1-\beta)b_t}. \tag{16}$$

The model consists therefore of (14) and (16). It is *recursive*: equation (16) can be used to determine the evolution of $b_t$, and by substituting the solution in (14) the evolution of $k_t^I$ can be derived.

To determine the economy's steady-state growth rate, write equation (8) for $t+1$, so that

$$Y_{t+1} = (k_{t+1}^{I})^{\alpha} K_{t+1}^{P},$$

or equivalently, using (11),

$$Y_{t+1} = (k_{t+1}^{I})^{\alpha}[\nu Y_t - (1+i_t)B_t].$$

Substituting (9) in this expression yields

$$Y_{t+1} = (k_{t+1}^{I})^{\alpha}[\nu - (1-\beta)b_t]Y_t,$$

or equivalently, using (14),

$$1+\gamma_{t+1} = \frac{Y_{t+1}}{Y_t} = \theta^{\alpha}[\nu - (1-\beta)b_t]^{1-\alpha}, \tag{17}$$

which implies a negative relationship between the debt-private capital ratio and the growth rate of output. On the one hand, an increase in $b_t$ raises the public-private capital ratio, which tends to promote growth; on the other, it lowers the rate of private capital accumulation, which tends to hamper growth. All else equal (in particular, for $\theta$ constant), the "crowding out" (borrowing) effect dominates the "crowding-in" (productivity) effect—given the linearity of the aggregate production function in the private capital stock and the fact that $\alpha < 1$—and the net impact on growth is negative.

It is easy to verify that the transition curve $\Phi(b_t)$ is convex, with an intercept equal to $\theta/\nu$. Depending on the value of that ratio, the model may exhibit no equilibrium, a single equilibrium, or two equilibria.

The possibility of dual equilibria can be seen by setting $b_{t+1} = b_t$ in equation (16), which yields the following quadratic equation in the steady-state value $\tilde{b}$:

$$(1-\beta)\tilde{b}^2 - [\nu - (1-\beta)]\tilde{b} + \theta = 0,$$

where $\nu - (1-\beta) \lesseqgtr 0$ in general. However, as long as $\nu - (1-\beta) > 0$, this equation can yield at most two admissible (that is, positive) solutions for $\tilde{b}$.[5]

The three cases are illustrated in Figure 7.1, where it can be seen that the transition curve becomes steeper as $\theta/\nu$ rises. If $\theta/\nu$ is too high, there is no equilibrium. Put differently, if the golden rule calls for investing a fraction $\theta$ of output that is too large, the economy cannot reach a steady state because debt grows faster than the stock of public capital, which implies that the debt-private capital ratio explodes. An overambitious, debt-financed program of public investment is not sustainable.

There is a single equilibrium at point $A$, whereas there are two equilibria at points $B$ and $B'$—the latter of which is unstable, given that the transition

[5] This is a direct implication of Descartes's rule of signs, according to which the number of positive real roots of a polynomial is bounded by the number of changes in sign of the sequence of its coefficients.

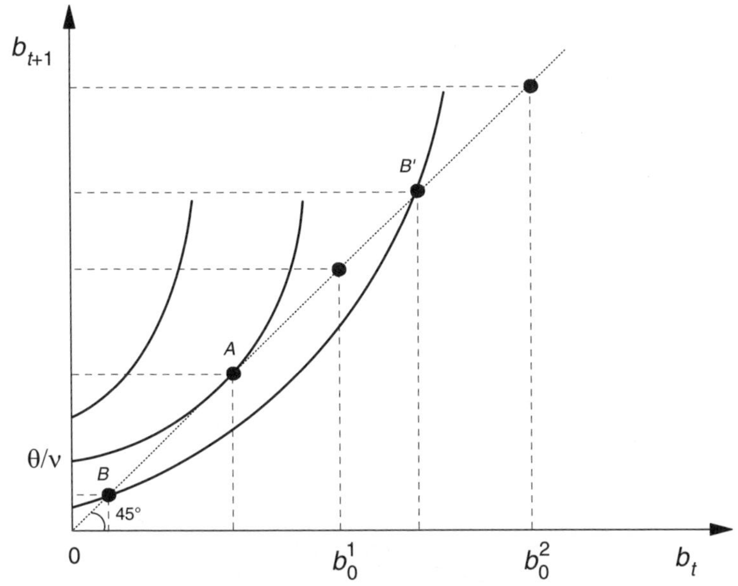


Figure 7.1. Dynamics of the Public Debt–Private Capital Ratio.

curve cuts the 45-degree line from below. At the low debt-private capital ratio, the public-private capital ratio is also low—as implied by (14), which describes a positive and also convex relationship between $\tilde{k}^I$ and $\tilde{b}$. As implied by (17), a low debt-private capital ratio is associated with a high growth rate of output. Conversely, at the high debt-private capital ratio, the public-private capital ratio is also high, whereas the growth rate of output is low.[6] But the economy can attain the high steady state only if it starts there. If the initial debt-private capital ratio is at $b_0^1$, for instance, the economy will converge over time toward the low-debt equilibrium $B$, which is characterized by equality between the growth rates of both capital stocks, output, and public debt. By contrast, if the economy starts at $b_0^2$, it will move over time away from the high-debt growth equilibrium. The growth in public debt always exceeds the growth in the private capital stock, implying that their ratio increases continuously.

Another way to illustrate the possibility of multiple equilibrium values in the public debt-private capital ratio is as follows. In the steady state,

[6] These results are consistent with those obtained in studies that analyze the dynamics of public debt in OLG models of endogenous growth without public capital, such as Brauninger (2005), and those with public capital, such as Yakita (2008). However, if as in chapter 6 public capital displays increasing returns over a certain range (due to network externalities for instance), a low-(high-)debt steady state could be characterized by low (high) growth. See Agénor and Yilmaz (2012) for a formal analysis.

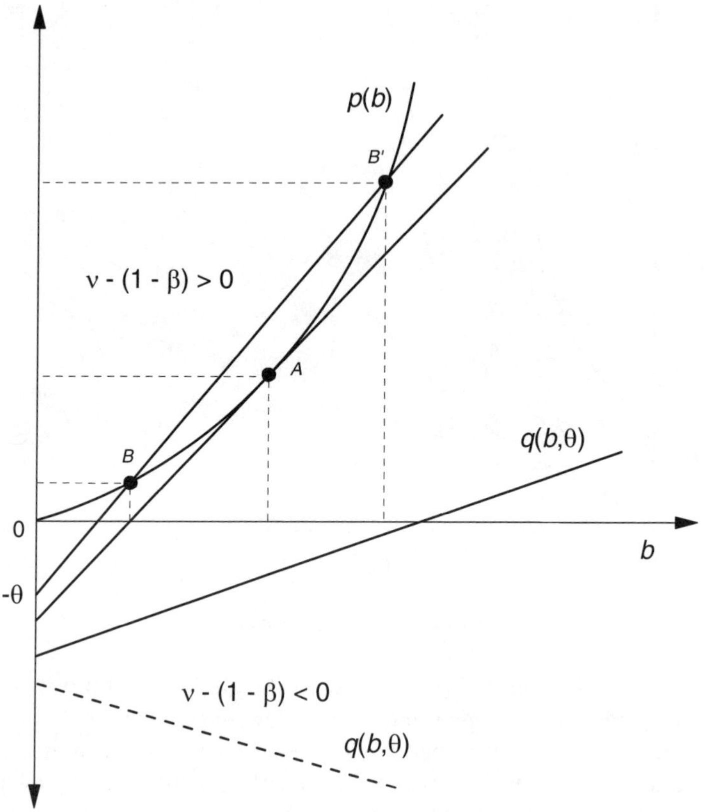


Figure 7.2. Multiple Steady-State Equilbria in the Debt–Private Capital Ratio.

equation (16) can be rewritten as, with $p(b) = (1-\beta)b^2$ and $q(b,\theta) = [\nu - (1-\beta)]b - \theta$,

$$p(b) = q(b,\theta).$$

Function $p(b)$ is a parabola with a minimum at $b = 0$, whereas function $q(b,\theta)$ is linear in $b$ and has an ambiguous slope; it also intersects the horizontal axis at a positive value of $b$, as long as $\theta$ is strictly positive. Under the assumption that only positive values of $b$ are admissible, both curves are shown in Figure 7.2 and alternative outcomes illustrated. It is immediately obvious that if $\nu - (1-\beta) < 0$, a condition that is more likely to occur if $\theta$ is positive and relatively high, there cannot be an equilibrium in which $p(b) = q(b,\theta)$. If $\nu - (1-\beta) > 0$, $q(b,\theta)$ is positively sloped and all three cases illustrated in Figure 7.1 may occur; there may be no equilibrium, a single equilibrium (point $A$), or two equilibria (points $B$ and $B'$). For two (nontrivial) equilibria to emerge, $\theta$ must be *smaller* than the value that it takes at point $A$, to ensure that $\nu = \sigma(1-\tau)\beta - \theta$ is larger and $q(b,\theta)$ steeper. Put differently, there can be neither a single equilibrium nor multiple equilibria if the investment program calls for a value of $\theta$ that is too high, because a higher value of $\theta$ shifts $q(b, \theta)$ downward and makes it flatter, whereas it has no effect on $p(b)$.

The thrust of the analysis is that in a growth context, a simple golden rule of the type specified in (6) may lead to unsustainable public debt and public capital dynamics. Moreover, the sustainable public debt-private capital ratio (which is associated with low in the steady-state growth in output) can be achieved only if the initial value of that variable is not too large. Future research should focus on a more detailed characterization of these dynamics (through calibration and numerical simulations, along the lines of Yakita (2008), for instance), as well as a comparison of alternative rules, such as the "modified golden rule" and the primary surplus rules discussed in Agénor and Yilmaz (2011, 2012).

## 5| Spatial Dimensions of Public Capital

The models developed in the previous chapters had no spatial or regional dimension. However, infrastructure networks are inherently spatial, both reflecting and underpinning the spatial distribution of economic activity. Infrastructure plays a key role in enabling cities to benefit from economies of agglomeration. Transport networks interconnect urban and rural economies, as well as urban centers with each other and with international trading networks. Energy, water, and telecommunications all enhance productivity within urban and rural spaces. Insufficient development of core infrastructure may also lead to *regional poverty traps*, of the type analyzed in Chapter 6.

The spatial (or local vs. global) lens is a useful basis for prioritization of infrastructure investments and provides insight into cross-sectoral links. Looking at infrastructure through a spatial lens allows identification of the key bottlenecks along various trading corridors, which are often high-return interventions. Cross-sectoral links also become more apparent through a spatial perspective, shedding light on the need for coordinating interventions across infrastructure sectors and between infrastructure and other sectors, such as education and health. Because of synergy effects, the returns from bundling multiple infrastructure interventions in a particular spatial area or along a given spatial corridor may be significantly higher than those from making the same investments in a spatially uncoordinated manner. In sub-Saharan Africa, the limited infrastructure available is often thinly spread out, preventing such synergies from being captured (see Simuyemba (2000) and Foster and Briceño-Garmendia (2010)). Network effects, as discussed in chapter 6, are therefore prevented from kicking in. Growth spillovers of strategic, cross-country road networks in particular could be very powerful for resource-poor, landlocked countries in the region.

Indeed, the region's infrastructure networks are highly fragmented. Sub-Saharan Africa comprises 48 countries, many of which are relatively small, and 15 of which are landlocked. The bulk of those countries have populations of fewer than 20 million and fairly small GDPs. International frontiers bear little relation either to natural features (such as river basins) or to artificial features (such as cities and their accessibility to trading channels, such as ports). Intraregional connectivity is therefore very low, whether measured in terms of roads, railways, power interconnectors, or telecommunications. Most continuous transport corridors provide access to seaports (as noted in chapter 6), whereas the intraregional road network is characterized by major discontinuities. Few cross-border interconnectors exist to support regional power exchange, even though many countries are too small to produce electricity economically on their own. Because of their geographic isolation, landlocked countries are at a particular disadvantage in this area. From this perspective, and as argued by Roberts and Deichmann (2011), the benefit of infrastructure may lie not only in its direct contribution to economic growth, but in allowing landlocked countries to absorb beneficial growth spillovers from neighboring countries.

Both the spatial distribution and rapid migration of Africa's population create major challenges for infrastructure development (see Foster and Briceño-Garmendia (2010)). In rural areas, over 20 percent of the population lives in dispersed settlements where typical population densities are less than 15 people per square kilometer; hence, the costs of providing infrastructure are comparatively high. In urban areas, population growth rates averaging 3.6 percent a year have put severe pressure on existing infrastructure. In addition, population densities in African cities remain relatively low by global standards and do not benefit from large economies of agglomeration in the provision of infrastructure services.

The high cost of infrastructure services in sub-Saharan Africa is also partly attributable to fragmentary national boundaries preventing achievement of scale economies. Many of Africa's infrastructure assets and natural resources are regional public goods that cut across national frontiers and can be effectively developed and maintained only through international collaboration (see Foster and Briceño-Garmendia (2010)). Road and rail corridors need to be managed cooperatively to facilitate access to transport and trade services to landlocked countries.

The spatial dimension of infrastructure is also important for other developing regions as well. In Asia, because of trade-related externalities, there remains considerable scope for regional cooperation in infrastructure planning and provision. Island economies, such as those in the Caribbean, are faced with the need to develop regional public goods to cope with small size to foster regional integration and cope with infrastructure vulnerability due to the region's susceptibility to natural disasters such as floods, hurricanes, landslides, and earthquakes.[7] With growing risks of more violent weather in the coming years due to climate change, the scope for large losses in physical assets (including public capital in roads, electricity lines, and power plants) may increase dramatically. Moreover, each time a natural disaster occurs, scarce resources must be redirected to rebuilding damaged infrastructure assets—with consequential pressure on public finances. This in turn may increase macroeconomic instability and real exchange rate volatility, thereby distorting critical signals in relative prices for producers. In fact, the mere possibility that taxes may have to increase in order to help rebuild infrastructure assets may act as a strong deterrent to private investment, both domestic and foreign. This adverse impact may be magnified in the presence of *irreversibility effects*, that is, the fact that a decision taken today may significantly reduce options available in the future. Thus, promoting growth and trade may require an improvement not only in access to infrastructure per se but also in the ability to cope with infrastructure vulnerability. Programs to address infrastructure development at the regional level include the Initiative for the Integration of Regional Infrastructure in South America (IIRSA), which supports the development and integration of an energy, transport, and telecommunications infrastructure program that covers 12 countries, or the more recent Infrastructure Consortium for Africa, which is jointly supported by African countries, the European Commission, G-8 countries, and key multilateral institutions.[8]

In sum, regional coordination can contribute significantly to reducing infrastructure costs, by allowing countries to capture scale economies and economies of agglomeration, facilitate the development of productive activities along key economic corridors, and manage regional public goods effectively. Development of infrastructure networks needs to be strategically informed by the spatial distribution of economic activities and by economies of agglomeration. The regionalization of infrastructure *regulation* may also yield significant benefits—beyond exploiting economies of scale in both infrastructure industries and regulatory institutions (see Kessides et al. (2010)). Regional integration of regulation, combined with regionalization of regulated firms, assists developing countries in overcoming national limits in technical expertise, enhances national capacity to make credible commitments to stable regulatory policy, facilitates the introduction of competition into historically monopolized markets, improves the efficiency of infrastructure industries by allowing them to grow without the constraint of national boundaries, and ultimately increases infrastructure investment. An important issue for

[7] The poorest countries in the Caribbean also have some of the worst infrastructure indicators in the world. See World Bank (2008*b*).

[8] See http://www.iirsa.org/ and http://www.icafrica.org/. See also Corporaci ón Andina de Fomento (2009) for Latin America in general and Fujimura (2004) for a discussion of the experience of Asian countries with cross-border transport infrastructure, particularly the Greater Mekong Subregion.

future research is the design of optimal regulatory rules in a multicountry environment.

## 6| Infrastructure and Trade

As discussed in chapter 1, a key benefit of infrastructure, in particular transport infrastructure, is the reduction of transport costs, which helps to create new markets and realize the returns to agglomeration. However, high production costs continue to be a key constraint on international trade integration, even for the fast-growing economies in Asia, as documented by Brooks (2010). For many low- and middle-income countries, transport costs remain by far the most significant trade friction, accounting in some cases for almost half of total sales costs. Yoshino (2008) for instance found that poor quality of public infrastructure—measured in terms of the average numbers of days per year for which firms experience disruptions in electricity—has an adverse effect on exports in sub-Saharan Africa, whereas Freund and Rocha (2011) found that delays in inland travel time (which are partly attributable to poor road quality) have the most economically and statistically significant effect on exports of the region. In Rwanda, farmers receive only 20 percent of the price of their coffee as it is loaded onto ships in Monbasa; the other 80 percent disappears into the costs of poor roads (as well as red tape) between Rwanda and Kenya. High domestic and international transport costs have also been identified as a key impediment to export growth in South Africa (see Naudé and Matthee (2007)).

Regarding Latin America and the Caribbean, a study by the Inter-American Development Bank suggests that for many countries of the region shipping costs (which depend significantly on port efficiency) may be a greater barrier to U.S. markets than import tariffs (see Micco and Pérez (2002)). Moreover, a comparative study by Dollar et al. (2006) of four countries in Latin America (Brazil, Honduras, Nicaragua, and Peru) and four Asian countries (Bangladesh, China, India, and Pakistan) found that inadequate access to core infrastructure services is one of the key factors that explains the more rapid pace of international trade integration in the latter group of countries.

Conversely, several studies have documented the importance of good infrastructure for trade and export performance, though its impact on trade costs. Brooks and Ferrarini (2010) for instance found that declining trade costs accounted for a large and increasing portion of bilateral trade growth between China and India, explaining approximately 75 percent of trade expansion since the early 1990s.

In addition to reducing transportation costs, there are several channels through which greater access to infrastructure may help to promote exports and foster trade integration. One mechanism is through foreign direct investment (FDI) and the transfer of technology that it is often associated with. There is indeed evidence suggesting that FDI flows are positively related to the availability of infrastructure services, as measured by the number of telephone lines per capita (see Nunes et al. (2006)).

Another way through which infrastructure may enhance trade performance relates to its external effects on human capital. To the extent that, as discussed in previous chapters, core infrastructure exerts positive effects on health and education outcomes, improved access to infrastructure services can generate significant benefits for export activities in terms of a more productive/higher quality labor force. Moreover, if infrastructure capital enhances the degree of complementarity between skilled labor and physical capital, it will also strengthen private incentives to invest in knowledge accumulation. This may in turn create new opportunities for trade (by opening up new areas of specialization) and promote economic growth.

More generally, infrastructure investment may influence a country's absolute and comparative advantage by mitigating the constraints of factor endowments and (as discussed earlier) promoting intra- and interregional integration. This may lead to a complex interdependent process in which infrastructure determines the pattern of trade and in turn the pattern of trade determines the level and type of infrastructure. Indeed, as a country develops, its economy typically moves up the value chain. This process is reinforced by improved access to infrastructure, a crucial factor in attracting overseas investment and thereby contributing to the knowledge transfer. As the economy moves up the value chain, its infrastructure needs to adapt to reflect the changes in production structures. This is related to the sequencing issue discussed in chapter 4 and alluded to earlier in this chapter.

## 7| Public-Private Partnerships

Throughout this book it has been assumed that infrastructure investment and services are provided exclusively by the government. As indicated in the Introduction and Overview, there are three main reasons for government involvement in this context: the large-scale nature and lumpiness of many infrastructure projects, the fact that they are socially desirable but not privately profitable, and the fact that prospects for public-private partnerships (PPPs) in infrastructure, where the government contracts out selected functions to the private sector (such as management, operations, and/or construction), remain limited for poor countries. Part of the problem, as noted by Guasch (2004), is that developing-country legal systems are weaker, making regulation and enforcement more complicated. This makes it more difficult to envisage a greater private sector role in the provision of infrastructure services in these countries.[9] At the same time, inefficient spending allocation and pricing

[9] This also means that scaling up investment programs should be accompanied with regulatory reforms, a point discussed earlier.

policies, and government failures in selecting, managing, and monitoring infrastructure projects, strongly militate in favor of doing so—despite possible short-term political costs.

Yet, despite the proliferation of modalities of regulating infrastructure, little is known about what works and why (see Araral et al. (2011) and Delmon (2011)). Indeed, the experience with PPPs in infrastructure provision and management in developing countries has been mixed. Results in the telecommunications sector, in Africa and elsewhere, were quite positive; as documented by Leigland (2010), over the period 1995–2008, In African IDA countries private participation in infrastructure (PPI) accounted for more infrastructure investment than any other source except government budgets—almost 78 percent more than official development assistance. More than 60 percent of PPI investment in IDA countries during the same period was in telecommunications.

However, in other sectors the benefits were more limited and the experience more problematic. Governments often end up bearing most of the risks associated with PPPs. Studies have found that the fiscal exposure (including implicit liabilities) of governments increase significantly when they offer corporate investors off-budget guarantees and financial support to ensure their profitability. In Latin America, many PPP contracts for infrastructure were renegotiated shortly after they were awarded.

Nevertheless, there are several reasons to believe that PPPs, to the extent that they are feasible, should not be completely discarded in low-income countries. First, given the size of resources required to implement a Big Push in public investment, the limited scope for raising tax revenues (due to the low level of income to begin with), any opportunity to supplement fiscal resources must be explored; the policy implication of the experience of the past two decades with PPPs means that they need to be designed more carefully, not that private financing should be ignored entirely. Private failures are often the result of poor government regulation.

Second, what the experience suggests also is that the benefits of PPPs may vary according to the type of infrastructure; although private financing has made a debatable contribution in areas such as roads, power, and water distribution, it has made a largely positive one in areas such as mobile telephony and ports. What this implies is that the optimal mix of private and public involvement will vary from country to country and may change over time as technology and competitive circumstances evolve.

Third, the experience shows that time and again, when governments come under pressure to reduce fiscal deficits, they are often tempted to cut or postpone investment in new infrastructure and reduce spending on maintaining existing infrastructure because this is seen as being politically easier than raising taxes or cutting social expenditure or public sector wages and salaries. To the extent that long-term arrangements with the private sector are in place, they may mitigate incentives to do so. Understanding the optimality of different types of arrangements, in a context where promoting growth is a key objective, remains an important area of investigation.[10]

## 8| Public Capital and Income Distribution

Some recent evidence has found that improved access to public capital may reduce income inequality. Calderón and Servén (2004) for instance, rely on cross-country regressions to establish this result, using both quantity and quality measures of infrastructure and accounting for possible reverse causality.[11] If inequality is bad for growth—as a result of credit market imperfections and borrowing constraints, as in Galor and Zeira (1993) for instance—then there may be another indirect channel through which public capital may affect growth.[12]

The models developed in this book (except for the gender-based setting of chapter 5) have all excluded within-generation heterogeneity among households, and therefore did not address directly distributional issues. This is a reasonable way to proceed under fairly general assumptions about household preferences (see for instance De la Croix and Michel (2002, pp. 54–56)). In addition, the household utility function used took systematically the form of a log-linear function. As a result, savings were found to be independent of the interest rate (or the rental rate of capital). This allowed the derivation of closed-form solutions and avoided systematic recourse to numerical methods. However, with a more general utility function the savings rate, and thus the pace of private capital accumulation, is positively related to the real interest rate because income and substitution effects do not cancel out.

Suppose for instance that the period utility function takes a constant relative risk aversion (CRRA) form, with the household therefore solving the problem

$$\max_{c_t^t, c_{t+1}^t} U_t = \frac{(c_t^t)^{1-\varsigma^{-1}}}{1-\varsigma^{-1}} + \Omega \frac{(c_{t+1}^t)^{1-\varsigma^{-1}}}{1-\varsigma^{-1}},$$

[10] See Glomm and Ravikumar (1997) for a further discussion and Chatterjee (2007) and Chatterjee and Morshed (2011) for an analysis based on continuous time, representative-agent models. These studies, however, do not account for the fact that some of the externalities that have been highlighted in this book may not be internalized by private agents. This creates, prima facie, a case for (at least joint) government provision of infrastructure services. At the same time, the efficiency of government spending becomes a critical consideration.

[11] Reverse causality is a potential problem in many existing studies, including those based on microeconomic evidence. For instance, data on access to piped water and electricity in Africa show that richer households have higher access rates (Foster and Briceño-Garmendia (2010)). However, this could be because (*a*) households with access to clean water are in better health and more productive, thereby enjoying higher income or (*b*) higher-income households live in urban areas, where connectivity is easier (due to higher population density), or have greater ability to "force" governments to spend on these services.

[12] There is an extensive literature on the effects of inequality on economic growth; see the references in Aghion et al. (1999).

where $\Omega = 1/(1+\rho)$ is the discount factor and $\varsigma$ is the elasticity of intertemporal substitution (that is, the willingness to substitute consumption across periods when the rate of interest changes), subject to

$$c_t^t + \frac{c_{t+1}^t}{1+r_{t+1}} = (1-\tau)w_t.$$

The lower $\varsigma$ is, the greater the incentive to smooth consumption across periods.[13] It can easily be shown that

$$s_t = \frac{(1-\tau)w_t}{1+\Omega^{-\varsigma}(1+r_{t+1})^{1-\varsigma}},$$

from which it can be established that $ds_t/dr_{t+1} < 0$ if $\varsigma < 1$, and $ds_t/dr_{t+1} > 0$ if $\varsigma > 1$. Thus, the effect of the interest rate on savings is generally ambiguous. This ambiguity reflects the familiar fact (already mentioned in chapter 5) that the substitution and income effects on consumption of a change in the interest rate are of opposite signs. Following a rise in the interest rate, for instance, the substitution effect is negative because the higher interest rate makes future consumption cheaper in terms of current consumption, whereas the income effect is positive because a given budget can buy more consumption in both periods. The net effect depends on the value of the intertemporal elasticity of substitution, $\varsigma$.

Based on the evidence reviewed in Agénor and Montiel (2008), the case $\varsigma < 1$ may be the most appropriate for developing countries. The point, however, is that by focusing on a log-linear utility function, redistributional effects of public policy across generations were ignored.[14] The reason is that, as shown in previous chapters, the rental rate of capital is a function of the public-private capital ratio. A policy that leads to a change in that ratio would therefore affect savings both directly through changes in real incomes (as a result of changes in wages) and indirectly through changes in the rate of return on savings, and thus the propensity to save itself. By abstracting from changes in the savings rate, intergenerational distributional effects were not accounted for—despite the fact they may have a significant impact on growth.

More generally, there are several possible factors that may explain a negative correlation between public capital and inequality. One channel through which infrastructure (or lack thereof) may affect inequality is by constraining the ability of poor people to access health care (implying that life expectancy remains low) or by imposing constraints on time allocation (as in the gender-based model of chapter 5); in either case, investment in education may be

[13] By L'Hôpital's rule for $0/0$, the logarithmic function $\ln c_{t+j}^t$ is a limiting form of the function $[(c_{t+j}^t)^{1-1/\varsigma} - 1]/(1-\varsigma^{-1})$ for $\varsigma \to 1$. With this modification, the case considered in the previous chapters corresponds to $\varsigma \to 1$.

[14] This argument essentially follows Rivas (2003).

discouraged.[15] Conversely, an improvement in access to infrastructure increases the efficiency of time allocated to work and own health and, by raising life expectancy (through its impact on the production of health services), lowers the opportunity cost of getting educated; consequently, poor individuals may find it optimal to invest more in human capital accumulation. In turn, greater equality in the distribution of education may increase average life expectancy, and this may affect the human capital of the following generations (see Castelló-Climent and Doménech (2008)). Put differently, an individual who invests in education may improve the life expectancy of all of his or her descendants, thereby allowing the family to escape an intergenerational poverty trap. Thus, improved access to infrastructure (at least, some types of it) may benefit the poor more than proportionally. More generally, to the extent that public capital affects the relative income shares of private inputs, it may have significant indirect effects on income distribution dynamics.

Three studies that have focused specifically on the links among public capital, income distribution, and growth are F. Ferreira (1995), Getachew (2010), and Chatterjee and Turnovsky (2011). Ferreira (1995) developed a general equilibrium model of wealth dynamics with public capital affecting the production function, in a manner similar to that described in the basic OLG model of chapter 1. Public capital is produced by the government and provided at no cost to every firm in the economy, as in the previous chapters. However, private infrastructure capital is available at a cost. There are three sets of agents (subsistence workers, middle-class entrepreneurs, and private infrastructure-owning entrepreneurs), and the main result is that there is a minimum level of public capital below which the middle class disappears, and reductions in the level of public investment led to higher levels of inequality because lower income households do not have the resources to access private infrastructure capital. The analysis also shows that productive public investment has a positive effect in reducing inequality—even if expenditures have no explicit redistributional content. Getachew (2010), in a model in which initial skills (or abilities) among agents are log-normally distributed, emphasized the differential impact of access to particular types of infrastructure on income distribution.[16] However, a key limitation of both models is that they do not account for the impact of infrastructure on time allocation; for the reason mentioned earlier, this may be a critical channel through which infrastructure may affect inequality.

Chatterjee and Turnovsky (2011) accounted for the allocation of time between market work and leisure, while at the same time drawing a distinction between the impact of public capital on the distribution of pre- and after-tax

[15] The link between health and education was discussed in chapter 3. Deaton (2003) provides a broader perspective on the channels through which health may affect inequality.

[16] Getachew's framework is related to the literature on public education, inequality, and growth; see in particular Glomm and Ravikumar (1992, 2003) and Glomm and Kaganovich (2003, 2008).

*income* (as in the previous studies) and the distribution of *wealth* (as measured by the allocation of private capital across individuals). One result of their analysis is that the impact of government investment on infrastructure tends to increase wealth inequality, irrespective of how it is financed. The reason is that such spending (or, rather, the capital stock that it helps to enhance) tends to enhance the productivity of private capital, which tends to stimulate its accumulation. Because private capital is more unequally distributed among agents than is labor (whose productivity tends to increase as well, as a result of gross complementarity with private capital), this tends to increase wealth inequality. By contrast, the effect of public investment on income inequality depends crucially on how government investment is financed; in addition, there may be intertemporal trade-offs, in the sense that the short- and long-run effects of public policy on income distribution may go in opposite directions. The reason is that the short-run response of income inequality is dominated by the initial change in time allocation (between market work and leisure) and its impact on relative factor returns, whereas over time it is more dependent on the evolution of private and public physical capital stocks. While this contribution is important, it does not account for the externalities highlighted in the previous chapters; depending on the strength of these externalities, some of its conclusions can actually be reversed. For instance, if the externality associated with public capital on health is accounted for and is assumed to be sufficiently strong (as could be expected in low-income countries), it is possible that the effect of government accumulation of physical capital may actually *reduce* wealth inequality, through its effect on labor productivity. A fair conclusion from the existing studies is therefore that more research, both theoretical and empirical, is needed to determine the direction and magnitude of the effect of public capital on income and wealth distribution.

## 9| Negative Externalities

Although much of the discussion in this book has emphasized the positive externalities associated with public capital, there are instances where greater access to infrastructure may be either growth or welfare reducing.[17] In Brazil, India, and Nigeria, the expansion of the road network along certain corridors may have contributed to the spread of AIDS, by drawing more sex workers who get involved with truck drivers (see World Bank (2008*d*)). It is also possible that in poor countries more roads may lead to a growing incidence of road traffic injuries if they lead to an increase in motorcycles for the less

[17] As described in chapter 1, crowding-out effects may generate strong negative externalities on private investment. However, there is broad consensus that crowding-out effects tend to be short term in nature if investment in infrastructure is sufficiently productive, and that the positive effect of greater access to public capital on private investment may more than compensate for any adverse effect—even if the latter displays some persistence.

affluent because users (drivers and passengers) of this means of transportation are inherently more at risk than car drivers (see Kjellstrom (2008)).

Another possible negative externality associated with some types of infrastructure is environmental pollution, which could impact growth both directly (through a loss of physical assets important for production) or indirectly (through an adverse effect of pollution on health and productivity).[18] For instance, at the time of this writing, many fear that China's Three Gorges Dam, the world's largest hydroelectric project, may cause massive environmental damage. Similar concerns arise with the Belo Monte Hydroelectric Dam in Brazil. On a smaller scale, the Peligre Dam in Haiti, conceived more than a half century ago, was intended to not only rehabilitate agricultural lands but also provide a reliable supply of hydroelectricity to the country's industries. How much of that happened remains a matter of controversy; in addition, there is some evidence that the construction of the dam actually contributed to deforestation and environmental degradation in its surrounding areas.

Yet another negative externality is related to the fact that by exacerbating urban air pollution, more roads may create new health hazards. A public irrigation program that calls for large-scale deforestation could reduce rainfall and water supply. Water pollution and air pollution create an environment where all types of diseases can thrive, with possible adverse effects on workers' health and productivity. If pollution reduces life expectancy, it may also induce a contraction in savings (through the life-cycle effect discussed in chapter 3) and hamper growth.

The key question is to what extent the negative externalities associated with infrastructure may mitigate the positive effects identified in previous chapters, and therefore affect the allocation of public expenditure. To illustrate this trade-off in a simple manner, suppose that environmental pollution, as measured by $Q_t$, has a direct negative impact on labor productivity. Individual firm $i$'s production function (as defined in chapter 1, section 1.2) becomes

$$Y_t^i = \left[\frac{K_t^I}{(K_t^P)^\zeta}\right]^\alpha \left(\frac{N_t^i}{Q_t^{\epsilon_1}}\right)^\beta (K_t^{P,i})^{1-\beta},$$

where $\epsilon_1 > 0$ measures the strength of the negative externality associated with pollution. Firms take pollution as given when maximizing profits. Suppose also that pollution increases with the scale of economic activity, so that

$$Q_t = q_t Y_t, \tag{18}$$

where $q_t > 0$ measures pollution intensity. Finally, assume that pollution intensity depends negatively on the share of other spending in output, which

[18] See for instance Mariani et al. (2010) for a formal analysis. At the same time, as discussed in chapters 1 and 5, it may be precisely the lack of access to infrastructure that leads to environmental degradation. Deforestation, in particular, has often been the consequence of poor families collecting wood as a source of energy.

consists now of investment in a pollution reduction technology:

$$q_t = \bar{q}(\frac{G_t^U}{Y_t})^{-\epsilon_2}, \tag{19}$$

where $\bar{q}, \epsilon_2 > 0$ and, as before, $G_t^U = \upsilon_U \tau Y_t$ and $\upsilon_I + \upsilon_U = 1$. It is straightforward to show that assumption 1.2 in chapter 1 (which ensures endogenous growth) must now be replaced by $\beta(1+\epsilon_1) - \alpha(1-\zeta) = 0$ and that the growth rate is, with $\mu = 1$,

$$1+\gamma = \Xi \frac{(\varphi \upsilon_I \tau)^{\alpha/(1+\beta\epsilon_1)}}{[\bar{q}(1-\upsilon_I)\tau]^{-\beta\epsilon_1\epsilon_2/(1+\beta\epsilon_1)}} \beta[\sigma(1-\tau)]^{1-\alpha/(1+\beta\epsilon_1)}. \tag{20}$$

Expression (20) provides a good illustration of the trade-off involved in investing in infrastructure: on the one hand, it promotes growth, but on the other, by increasing pollution and lowering labor productivity, it lowers growth. The optimal policy equalizes the marginal benefit and the marginal cost of an increase in investment. More formally, from (20) the growth-maximizing share of investment in infrastructure is determined by the condition

$$\frac{d\ln(1+\gamma)}{d\upsilon_I} = \frac{\alpha}{(1+\beta\epsilon_1)\upsilon_I} - \frac{\beta\epsilon_1\epsilon_2}{(1+\beta\epsilon_1)(1-\upsilon_I)} = 0,$$

so that

$$\upsilon_I^* = \frac{\alpha}{\alpha + \beta\epsilon_1\epsilon_2},$$

which corresponds to result 1.4 in chapter 1 ($\upsilon_I^* = 1$) in the absence of pollution externality ($\epsilon_1 = 0$). Thus, if growth itself creates negative side effects, it is optimal to invest only a fraction of tax revenues in infrastructure and to allocate some of the government's resources to mitigating those effects.[19]

Another illustration of the negative externality associated with public capital involves rewriting the health production function in the two-period model of chapter 3 as

$$h_t = (\varepsilon_t^H)^{\nu} \left(\frac{H_t^G}{K_t^P}\right)^{1-\nu} - \epsilon_Q Q_t,$$

[19] Analytically, this formula is essentially the same as the one derived in chapter 1 in the case of two productive goods. Note also that pollution may reduce the utility derived from consumption, in which case the household utility function may take for instance the form $U_t = \ln(c_t^t Q_t^{-\epsilon_C}) + \ln c_{t+1}^t/(1+\rho)$, with $\epsilon_C > 0$. It can then be shown (following the procedure outlined in the appendix to chapter 1) that the welfare-maximizing share of investment in infrastructure is also lower than unity, even with $\epsilon_1 = 0$.

where $\epsilon_Q > 0$ and environmental pollution $Q_t$ is defined as in (18). Again, if $\epsilon_Q$ is large enough, the growth-promoting effect of investment in infrastructure may be offset by a degradation of health and productivity of the labor force.

There are two issues that deserve further scrutiny. The first is empirical; determining if the net growth benefit of infrastructure is positive or negative is often an empirical question, and few studies have so far attempted to provide rigorous estimates. The second is analytical; even if there are indeed negative externalities, what must be addressed is the extent to which (distortionary) tax policy and expenditure allocation (to finance abatement activities, in the case of environmental pollution) can ensure that agents internalize these negative effects. Gupta and Barman (2010) developed a model of endogenous growth that attempts to address these issues in the presence of public infrastructure expenditure, health capital, and environmental pollution (which, as discussed earlier, affects negatively production). However, the treatment of environmental quality in that model can be improved to account for the *environmental Kuznets curve*, according to which there exists an inverted U-shaped relationship between pollution and income (see, for instance, Hartman and Kwon (2005)).

## 10| Testing for the Impact of Public Capital on Growth

The foregoing analysis also has important methodological implications for the empirical analysis of the determinants of growth, based on either standard growth accounting techniques or cross-country growth regressions. Many existing studies based on this type of regressions tend to focus on flow variables, by considering either investment ratios or capital expenditure. However, as made amply clear in previous chapters, a proper assessment of the supply-side effects of public capital should be based on *stocks*, not spending flows.

Moreover, existing studies (even those based on stocks of infrastructure assets) usually do not capture the externalities associated with public infrastructure, through for instance their impact on the durability of private capital (and thus the rate of return on private investment), their effect on health and education, or innovation activities. Consequently, they are likely to *underestimate* the contribution of public infrastructure to growth. This is a key limitation of the single-equation studies of Bhargava et al. (2001), Esfahani and Ramírez (2003), Baldacci et al. (2004), Calderón and Servén (2004), Loayza et al. (2004), Estache et al. (2005), Bose et al. (2007), Ghosh and Gregoriou (2008), Calderón (2009), Arslanalp et al. (2010), Gupta et al. (2011), and Straub and Terada-Hagiwara (2011).

Indeed, for the reasons discussed in the previous chapters, improvements in human capital (through education or health) may be the consequence of greater access to public infrastructure. Because most cross-country studies do not account for these indirect effects, the true contribution of infrastructure to growth tends to be underestimated. Country-specific studies, such as the analysis of long-run growth in South Africa by Fedderke et al. (2006) or the study on Finnish data using aggregate infrastructure capital series from 1860 to 2003 by Luoto (2011), suffer from the same shortcomings. By implication, simulation exercises in some of these studies aimed at evaluating, say, infrastructure needs and their impact on growth are bound to be seriously misleading because they are based on misspecified models.

Future work based on cross-country growth regressions should provide a more careful attempt to disentangle the various channels through which infrastructure affects growth, through the use of simultaneous equations models. Some existing studies have attempted to do so; for instance, Agé nor and Neanidis (2010) use a sample of 38 industrial and developing countries for the period 1981–2008 and a variety of estimation techniques. These techniques include standard panel regression methods as well as methods that address potential endogeneity (dynamic GMM techniques and 3SLS). The 3SLS system approach is particularly appropriate to capture some of the interactions emphasized in this book. They also estimated the direct and general equilibrium effects of infrastructure on the levels of output per capita. They find that 3SLS yields an estimate of the direct elasticity of output with respect to infrastructure equal to 0.1; however, accounting for the indirect transmission channels raises this figure to a general equilibrium value of 0.25. More studies using system-wide approaches are needed.

As implied by the analysis in chapter 6, there is also a need to account for nonlinearities because estimates from linear models do not account for threshold effects. Existing studies include Röller and Waverman (2001), Candelon et al. (2009), Kellenberg (2009), Agénor and Neanidis (2010), and Roberts and Deichmann (2011), as noted in that chapter, but further tests, involving larger samples, seem warranted.

It is also important to note that although issues associated with the measurement of public capital were not addressed in detail, statistics on the public capital stock are not readily available. Two main approaches have been used in practice for measuring the impact of public capital on growth: an approach based on physical measures of public capital (number of telephone lines, number of kilometers of all-weather roads, production of electricity, and so on), and an approach based on the perpetual inventory method (PIM), which in its standard version corresponds to equation (21) in chapter 1 with $\mu = 0$ and $\varphi = 1$, that is, $K^I_{t+1} = G^I_t + (1 - \delta^I)K^I_t$.[20] Essentially, to arrive at an estimate of the public capital stock, researchers determine an initial value of the capital stock to which they add gross investment flows and subtract depreciation of the existing capital stock (at a fixed rate $\delta^I$), based on the expected life spans of its components. In estimates for developing countries the initial capital stock is often set to zero—an assumption that is not very consequential if

[20] For a detailed description of the perpetual inventory method, see OECD (2009).

the time period covered is sufficiently long. More importantly, in the standard PIM formulation the quality or efficiency of public investment is usually not addressed; given the range of estimates for $\varphi$ discussed in chapter 1 (between 0.4 and 0.6), this may lead to serious overestimation of actual stocks of public capital, and thus underestimation of its marginal productivity effects. This is precisely the conclusion reached by Gupta et al. (2011).

Quality issues arise also with physical measures of public capital; to address them some studies have attempted to calculate separate quality indicators and to test independently their effect on growth. For instance, for transportation infrastructure, the fraction of paved roads is often used as a quality indicator, whereas for telecommunications and the power sector, the number of telephone faults and the percentage of electricity production that is lost due to transmission and distribution problems, respectively, are commonly used. Several of the studies cited earlier indicate that they can make a sizable difference in measuring the impact of public capital on growth (see Hulten (1996), Calderón (2009), and Agénor and Neanidis (2010)). However, all of the existing quality indicators have limitations, and further research is needed to develop more robust measures.

• • •

The purpose of this chapter was to outline a research agenda for understanding further interactions among public capital, economic growth, and human welfare. Issues that were considered important include the sequencing of investment in heterogeneous infrastructure assets, the role of political economy factors in determining government spending allocation, the determination of the level and structure of user fees for excludable public goods, interactions among government debt, public capital accumulation, and growth in the presence of fiscal rules, spatial and regional dimensions of public capital and the role of cooperation and regulation in cross-country infrastructure projects, public-private partnerships, the impact of public capital on income distribution, negative externalities associated with infrastructure (especially in terms of environmental pollution and health), and empirical tests of the impact of public capital on growth. It was noted, in particular, that political economy considerations are likely to play a critical role in both the determination of spending levels and the quality or efficiency of expenditure components. There may be a conflict for instance between young generations (who may value investment in infrastructure because public capital has a positive effect on current and future returns to market activity) and the older generations (who may value immediate transfers more). If older people are more likely to vote to reelect the incumbent, improving chances of reelection may lead to a systematic bias in spending allocation toward transfers—at the cost of lower growth in the longer term and possibly lower welfare for all future generations.

Another issue that was identified is whether infrastructure services, although (partially) rival, should be provided by the government free of charge, as assumed in the previous chapters. In practice, some of these services (bridges, electricity, and so on) are *excludable*, that is, potential users can be identified and charged a user fee, with revenues then allocated to maintenance or another specific activity. Determining the optimal tax and user fee structure, taking into account administrative capacity constraints in low-income countries is an important task.

Yet another issue is the link among public investment, public debt, and economic growth. Once governments have the ability to issue bonds, the issues of fiscal stability and debt sustainability become critical. Various fiscal rules have been proposed to address these issues; however, some of these rules have been criticized on the ground that they tend to discourage public investment and the accumulation of public capital if they are applied too broadly. The golden rule, by contrast, aims at ensuring that a significant fraction of public investment is financed by borrowing. It was shown, however, that this policy may lead to multiple equilibria, and that high debt may be associated with low growth. This occurs because the "crowding-out" effect on private capital accumulation dominates the "crowding-in" effect associated with a higher stock of public capital. Further research on the design of fiscal rules and their implications for growth should aim to clarify conditions under which these results can be reversed.

The design of private-public partnerships in infrastructure development remains an issue where much research is needed. Even though the nature and scale of some infrastructure projects and the lack of access to private capital markets by the poorest countries mean that governments in these countries are likely to continue to carry the bulk of investment in that area, there are some sectors (such as mobile telecommunications) where public-private partnerships have proved possible and viable. In some cases, failure of these partnerships can be found in poorly designed government regulation. It is therefore important to understand what the best long-term arrangements with the private sector are in a context where promoting growth and human development are key objectives. Finally, it was noted that many existing studies, based on linear, single-equation regressions, may seriously underestimate the true impact of public capital on output because they fail to account explicitly for the indirect benefits (studied in previous chapters) that infrastructure may provide in terms of education, health, the capacity to innovate, and the freeing up of women's time allocated to home production. In addition, infrastructure may have strong nonlinear effects on growth, and these need to be accounted for in empirical analysis.

## Lessons for Public Policy |

In recent years there has been a renewed effort by economists to understand how public capital affects economic growth and human welfare. In addition to reviewing the microeconomic and macroeconomic evidence, this book has attempted to provide a unified set of theoretical models that capture some of the key channels identified in recent research and studied how public policy related to infrastructure investment affects growth and human development. By using models based on explicit microeconomic decision rules, the book's objective was to provide rigorous analytical foundations for public policy.

Small analytical models, of course, are not designed to provide detailed policy advice; to do so in a sensible manner requires developing quantified, country-specific models, which account for a host of structural characteristics. In addition, as discussed at length in chapter 7, there are still a number of conceptual and empirical issues that are not fully understood in the relationship among public capital, growth, and welfare: these relate to the sequencing of investment in heterogeneous infrastructure assets, the role of political economy factors in determining government spending allocation, the determination of the level and structure of user fees for excludable public goods, interactions between government debt, public capital accumulation, and growth in the presence of fiscal rules, spatial and regional dimensions of public capital, the design of public-private partnerships, the impact of public capital on income distribution, negative externalities associated with infrastructure, and empirical tests of the impact of public capital on growth. In particular, studies of the public capital-growth nexus based on linear, single-equation regressions face serious limitations and may significantly underestimate the contribution of public capital to economic growth.

At the same time, incorporating the externalities associated with infrastructure in applied macroeconomic models remains a challenging task. Indeed, the optimal spending allocation rules derived in various parts of the book, while useful as simple benchmarks (provided that they are properly calibrated), are not sufficient for practical policymaking. In the real world, the allocation of public expenditure, just like the determination of tax rates, reflects invariably a mix of economic, political, and social considerations. In building growth and development strategies, poor countries must be able to quantify the various channels through which public capital affects the economy. Structural, country-specific structural macroeconomic models are an ideal tool in that regards, because they provide flexibility in accounting explicitly for the various externalities associated with infrastructure. Important classes of models in this area are the SPAHD models developed by Agénor et al. (2008) and the more advanced IMMPA framework described in the contributions contained in Agénor et al. (2006). By their very nature, these models provide an ideal setting for capturing the microeconomic complementarities, and macroeconomic trade-offs, involved in designing growth-promoting, medium-term public investment programs in poor countries. SPAHD models also incorporate a "human development" module that allows one to assess the impact of public capital not only on growth but also on poverty, malnutrition, infant mortality, and life expectancy. Although these models are tractable and have been applied to several poor countries (including Niger; see Pinto Moreira and Bayraktar (2008)), further effort to build capacity in these countries is an essential step to promote their use.

Despite these limitations, there are several broad policy lessons that can be drawn from the results derived in this book and the empirical evidence that served to motivate the theoretical analysis in the first place. First, in low-income countries where stocks of infrastructure assets are low to begin with, the direct productivity and costs effects, and the complementarity effect on private investment, associated with improved access to public capital are likely to be high. On that basis alone, there is a strong case for "scaling up" public investment in infrastructure in these countries. This is particularly important if the role of government is not perceived to be one of "picking winners" (as in the days of old-style industrial policy) but instead to help alleviate constraints to private-sector-led growth. From that perspective, public investment in infrastructure should be thought as one of the means through which governments can create an environment for the private sector to thrive.

Second, there are a number of indirect channels, possibly as important as (if not more important than) direct conventional channels, through which public capital may affect economic growth. These externalities, which by now are all well documented, include positive effects on education and health outcomes, the diffusion rate of new technologies, innovation capacity, and women's time allocation. In particular, improving education outcomes may require not only improving access to basic equipment (such as furniture and adequate textbooks) in rural schools but also alleviating constraints on infrastructure. Greater access to electricity may increase study time at home, improve access to learning programs on television, induce children to stay in school longer, and result in better grades and improved teaching quality. Better roads in rural areas may make it easier for patients to reach medical facilities and for skilled medical personnel to take up positions in rural areas. In addition, interactions between heath and education outcomes are important; higher levels of education increase awareness and the capacity of families to address their health needs. Conversely, better health enhances the effective and sustained use of the knowledge and skills acquired through education, while reducing the rate of depreciation of that knowledge; increased life expectancy may promote investment in skills. Through these interactions, the effect of public investment in infrastructure on growth and human welfare can be magnified. It is thus critical to systematically capture in empirical models, and introduce in policy debates, externalities associated with public capital. In some ways, investing in infrastructure is as much about promoting markets as it is about achieving health or education targets and empowering women. In turn, this has important implications for public expenditure allocation; although spending on infrastructure and spending on other critical areas like education and health are largely complementary at the microeconomic level, in the presence of a binding budget constraint they may be substitutes at the macroeconomic level. Somewhat paradoxically, the best way to improve education or health outcomes in some circumstances could be to spend more on infrastructure and less on education or health.

The presence of these externalities also has substantial implications for the design, selection, and appraisal of infrastructure projects: in addition to internal rates of return, it is essential to account for the benefits that these projects may provide in terms of health and education, that is, in terms of human welfare. This is particularly important for rural infrastructure projects, notably in the transport sector (see Lebo and Schelling (2001)). At the same time, accounting for possible negative externalities associated with the environmental impact of large-scale infrastructure projects, particularly with respect to irrigation and electricity production, may prove critical for assessing the net benefit of public investment.

Third, the nature of public capital goods that need to be supplied varies with the stage of development: whereas *imitation* activities (copying or adapting foreign products or technologies to local markets) may require only access to some "basic" types of infrastructure (roads, basic telecommunications services, electricity connections), a more "advanced" type (more complementary with human capital, such as access to broadband) may be needed to achieve *true innovation* (which involves the creation of new products), along with higher quality of labor. The provision of this type of capital may be an essential step for today's low-income countries to avoid being caught tomorrow in an "imitation trap," where growth is positive, in absolute and per capita terms, but moderate. This transition does not necessarily need to imply only public funds (public-private partnerships may prove to be a viable option), but it is important to prepare early for it.

Fourth, for infrastructure services that are excludable, user fees and congestion charges can play a key role in ensuring that they are used efficiently (an objective that may also require fostering a competitive environment) and that adequate resources are appropriated to ensure maintenance of the underlying assets. They can also provide valuable signals of where additional capacity may be needed. At the same time, however, even when imposing fees or charges are feasible, broader considerations may need to be take into account when setting their level. This is the case for some types of infrastructure services that have a direct effect on poverty, such as rural roads and irrigation. In addition, administrative capacity, which remains all too limited in many low-income countries, may impose constraints on the type of fee structure that can be realistically put in place.

Fifth, throughout the book the focus has been very much on the allocation of public resources. One argument for doing so is the limited tax capacity of low-income countries, and the possibility that foreign aid or foreign borrowing—based on the ability to leverage domestic natural resources, as some countries have started to do in recent years—may alleviate the resource constraint. However, as discussed in chapters 1 and 7, the possibility of crowding out, either directly through taxation or indirectly through the issuance of government debt, should not be discounted. If public capital has a sizable effect on the productivity of private inputs, the growth process that it triggers may generate significant additional resources for the government, allowing it therefore to repay its debt. In that sense, debt may pay for itself. For this to occur, however, much care must be exercised in selecting infrastructure projects with the highest overall impact, that is, those for which externalities are fairly strong. Otherwise, there is a risk that the "crowding-in" effect of public capital may be outweighed by the "crowding-out" effect on private capital accumulation.

Sixth, many of the externalities associated with public capital operate in a nonlinear fashion; improved access to water and sanitation, for instance, may have a large effect on infant mortality rates when, to begin with, access is limited. Network externalities imply that the benefits associated with public capital may depend on the stock of public capital itself—and this suggests that for investment in infrastructure to make a difference in terms of growth, there must be enough of it. Large investments in a road network for instance may magnify economies of agglomeration and facilitate the development of productive activities along key economic corridors. This provides a strong analytical argument in support of a Big Push in public investment in low-income countries, either through a large but temporary increase in foreign aid or by helping these countries to implement adequate mechanisms to leverage their natural resources. However, as made clear in chapter 6, such policies are unlikely to succeed unless there is a concomitant effort to improve governance and ensure that public resources are not wasted, as happened so often in the past. In some countries, this could involve the creation of an *infrastructure bank*, which could depoliticize to some extent the selection of projects, improve monitoring and evaluation, allow the issuance of long-term bonds, and provide greater opportunities to leverage private capital. At the same time, it is important to understand that excessive borrowing could create large contingent liabilities for the government and drive up funding costs across the board. Imposing adequate user fees may be essential to ensure that the flow of revenues is sufficient to service the existing debt and provide resources for future investment.

Seventh, in addition to improving governance, there may be a need for a broader set of *complementary reforms* to promote public infrastructure investment. In particular, clarifying or securing property rights may be an essential step. For instance, at the time of this writing one of the key obstacles to investment in infrastructure in Indonesia (beyond the sheer cost involved, after years of physical neglect following the Asian financial crisis in the late 1990s) is the competing claims on land in areas needed for public infrastructure projects; with this legal uncertainty, compensation levels for land owners cannot be established. In turn, lack of infrastructure (through the complementarity effect discussed in previous chapters) is holding private investment, both domestic and foreign, down.

Eighth, it is important to preserve as much as possible, even during periods when fiscal consolidation cannot be avoided due to severe and long-lasting domestic or external shocks, a core program of spending on infrastructure. If pressure on public finances become particularly acute, governments are often tempted as a first resort to reduce spending on maintaining existing infrastructure and facilities, thereby increasing future rehabilitation costs, and to postpone (and, eventually, cancel) investment in new infrastructure. The reason is that this is often easier, and less costly politically, than raising taxes, cutting social expenditure, or reducing public service wages and salaries. This has happened numerous times during episodes of fiscal retrenchment in developing countries (see Agénor and Montiel (2008)). The consequences, as made clear in the previous chapters, could prove dire in the longer run. In the same vein, donor countries undergoing periods of fiscal adjustment should also strive to preserve aid programs to the poorest countries in some core areas, including infrastructure projects susceptible of generating large externalities.

Ninth, the focus of this book has been mainly on the "why" governments should spend on core infrastructure, rather than the "how." And given the focus on the expenditure side of the budget, most of the analysis was conducted under the assumption of tax financing, with some discussion of the role of foreign financing (chapter 6) and public debt (chapter 7). However, an alternative approach is joint financing with the private sector. As also noted in chapter 7, even though the evidence in favor of public-private partnerships (PPPs) is mixed, poor countries must continue to explore ways through which the private sector can play a greater role in the provision of infrastructure services—at least in some sectors, such as telecommunications (namely, mobile telephony), where the experience has been largely positive. The experience of the past two decades with PPPs suggests that they need to be designed more carefully, not that private financing should be ignored entirely; indeed, in some cases poor government regulation may have been the main culprit for PPP failures. In addition, the existence of PPPs may mitigate the temptation to cut or postpone investment in new infrastructure or spending on maintenance (rather than cutting social expenditure or public sector wages and salaries) during periods of fiscal consolidation, as noted earlier. In effect, what is needed is a less dogmatic, and rather more pragmatic, view of the private sector's role, which acknowledges its potential capacity to contribute in some sectors (mobile telephony, Internet access, power generation, and ports) while recognizing its limitations in others (roads, power and water distribution).

Finally, international development institutions and bilateral donors should strive to incorporate more systematically the broad lessons of the new research on public capital into their day-to-day dialogue with the countries they are supposed to help, given their ability to influence their policy choices—both at the microeconomic (project) level and the macroeconomic level (expenditure allocation, tax effort, etc.). Unfortunately, there are no tangible signs yet that this is happening in a systematic way. Two recent and prominent reports on growth in low- and middle-income countries, one by the Commission on Growth and Development (2008), set up by the World Bank, and the other by UNIDO (2009), do not mention any of the externalities in terms of education, health and gender outcomes discussed in previous chapters; some of the other channels, such as the impact of particular types of public capital on innovation and growth, are barely mentioned—and when they are, their importance is not fully appreciated.[1] My hope is that this book will help, if only in a small way, to put these issues at the forefront of the debate on strategies to promote growth and human development in low-income countries.

[1] In UNIDO (2009, p. 67) for instance, it is stated that "changing public expenditure priorities to increase the share of the budget devoted to infrastructure investments is urgently needed in most low-income countries. However, it will be difficult to implement both domestically, because it involves stark trade-offs between growth and social development objectives." It is hard to disagree of course with the first sentence in this statement but the second suggests that the benefits of infrastructure for social development outcomes, and in turn for growth, are largely underestimated.

# References |


Acemoglu, Daron, *Introduction to Modern Economic Growth*, Princeton University Press (Princeton, N.J.: 2008).

Acemoglu, Daron, and Simon Johnson, "Disease and Development: The Effect of Life Expectancy on Economic Growth," *Journal of Political Economy*, 115 (December 2007), 925–85.

African Union, *Transport and the Millennium Development Goals* (Addis Ababa: February 2005).

Agénor, Pierre-Richard, *The Economics of Adjustment and Growth*, Harvard University Press (Cambridge, Mass.: 2004).

——, "The Analytics of Segmented Labor Markets," in *Adjustment Policies, Poverty and Unemployment: The IMMPA Framework*, ed. by Pierre-Richard Agénor, Alejandro Izquierdo, and Henning Tarp Jensen, Blackwell (Oxford: 2006).

——, "Fiscal Policy and Endogenous Growth with Public Infrastructure," *Oxford Economic Papers*, 60 (January 2008*a*), 57–88.

——, "Health and Infrastructure in a Model of Endogenous Growth," *Journal of Macroeconomics*, 30 (December 2008*b*), 1407–22.

——, "Public Capital, Health Persistence and Poverty Traps," Working Paper No. 115, Centre for Growth and Business Cycle Research, University of Manchester (February 2009*a*).

——, "Infrastructure Investment and Maintenance Expenditure: Optimal Allocation Rules in a Growing Economy," *Journal of Public Economic Theory*, 11 (June 2009*b*), 233–50.

——, "A Theory of Infrastructure-led Development," *Journal of Economic Dynamics and Control*, 34 (May 2010), 932–50.

——, "Schooling and Public Capital in a Model of Endogenous Growth," *Economica*, 78 (January 2011 *a*), 108–32.

——, "A Computable OLG Model for Gender and Growth Policy Analysis," unpublished, University of Manchester and World Bank (November 2011*b*).

——, "Infrastructure, Public Education and Growth with Congestion Costs," forthcoming, *Bulletin of Economic Research* (October 2012).

Agénor, Pierre-Richard, and Madina Agénor, "Infrastructure, Women's Time Allocation, and Economic Development," Working Paper No. 116, Centre for Growth and Business Cycle Research, University of Manchester (March 2009).

Agénor, Pierre-Richard, and Joshua Aizenman, "Aid Volatility and Poverty Traps," *Journal of Development Economics*, 91 (January 2010), 1–7.

Agénor, Pierre-Richard, Nihal Bayraktar, and Karim El Aynaoui, "Roads Out of Poverty? Assessing the Links between Aid, Public Investment, Growth, and Poverty Reduction," *Journal of Development Economics*, 86 (June 2008), 277–95.

Agénor, Pierre-Richard, Otaviano Canuto, and Luiz Pereira da Silva, "On Gender and Growth: The Role of Intergenerational Health Externalities and Women's Occupational Constraints," Policy Research Working Paper No. 5492, World Bank (December 2010).

Agénor, Pierre-Richard, Alejandro Izquierdo, and Henning Tarp Jensen, eds., *Adjustment Policies, Poverty and Unemployment: The IMMPA Framework*, Blackwell Publishing (Oxford: 2006).

Agénor, Pierre-Richard, and Peter J. Montiel, *Development Macroeconomics*, 3rd ed., Princeton University Press (Princeton, N.J.: 2008).

Agénor, Pierre-Richard, and Kyriakos Neanidis, "Optimal Taxation and Growth with Productive Public Goods and Costly Enforcement," unpublished, University of Manchester (March 2009).

——, "Innovation, Public Capital, and Growth," Working Paper No. 135, Centre for Growth and Business Cycle Research, University of Manchester (February 2010).

——, "The Allocation of Public Expenditure and Economic Growth," *Manchester School*, 79 (July 2011), 899–931.

Agénor, Pierre-Richard, and Devrim Yilmaz, "Aid Allocation, Growth and Welfare with Productive Public Goods," Working Paper No. 95, Centre for Growth and Business Cycle Research (January 2008). Forthcoming, *International Journal of Finance and Economics*.

——, "The Tyranny of Rules: Fiscal Discipline, Productive Spending, and Growth," *Journal of Economic Policy Reform*, 14 (March 2011), 69–99.

——, "The Simple Dynamics of Public Debt with Productive Public Goods," unpublished, University of Manchester (January 2012).

Aghion, Philippe, and Peter Howitt, *Endogenous Growth Theory*, MIT Press (Cambridge, Mass.: 1998).

Aghion, Philippe, Eve Caroli, and Cecilia Garcia-Penalosa, "Inequality and Growth: The Perspective of New Growth Theories," *Journal of Economic Literature*, 27 (December 1999), 1615–60.

Ahmed, Akhter, and Mary Arends-Kuenning, "Do Crowded Classrooms Crowd Out Learning? Evidence from the Food for Education Program in Bangladesh," *World Development*, 34 (April 2006), 665–84.

Aísa, Rosa, and Fernando Pueyo, "Government Health Spending and Growth in a Model of Endogenous Longevity," *Economics Letters*, 90 (February 2006), 249–53.

Albala-Bertrand, José M., and Emmanuel C. Mamatzakis, "The Impact of Public Infrastructure on the Productivity of the Chilean Economy," *Review of Development Economics*, 8 (June 2004), 266–78.

Allais, Maurice, *Économie et Intérêt*, Imprimerie Nationale (Paris: 1947).

Allen, Robert C., *The British Industrial Revolution in Global Perspective*, Cambridge University Press (Cambridge: 2009).

Almond, Douglas, and Janet Currie, "Human Capital Development before Age 5," in *Handbook of Labor Economics*, ed. by Orley Ashenfelter and David E. Card, North Holland (Amsterdam: 2011).

Altindag, Duha, Colin Cannonier, and Naci Mocan, "The Impact of Education on Health Knowledge," *Economics of Education Review*, 30 (November 2011), 792–812.

Amin, Sajeda, and S. Chandrasekhar, "Looking Beyond Universal Primary Education: Gender Differences in Time Use among Children in Rural Bangladesh," Working Paper No. 17, United Nations Population Council (May 2009).

Andreassen, Leif, "Mortality, Fertility and Old Age Care in a Two-Sex Growth Model," Discussion Paper No. 378, Statistics Norway, Research Department (May 2004).

Anyanwu, John C., and Andrew E. O. Erhijakpor, "Health Expenditures and Health Outcomes in Africa," *African Development Review*, 21 (September 2009), 400–33.

Araral, Eduardo, Darryl S. Jarvis, M. Ramesh, and Wu Xun, "Regulating Infrastructure: A Review of the Issues, Problems, and Challenges," in *Infrastructure Regulation: What Works, Why, and How Do We Know? Lessons from Asia and Beyond*, ed. by Darryl S. Jarvis, M. Ramesh, Wu Xun, and Eduardo Araral, Imperial College Press (Singapore: 2011).

Arestoff, Florence, and Christophe Hurlin, "The Productivity of Public Capital in Developing Countries," unpublished, University of Orléans (March 2005).

Arndt, Channing, "HIV/AIDS, Human Capital, and Economic Growth Prospects for Mozambique," *Journal of Policy Modeling*, 28 (July 2006), 477–489.

Arrow, Kenneth, "The Economic Implications of Learning by Doing," *Review of Economic Studies*, 29 (June 1962), 155–73.

Arrow, Kenneth J., and Mordecai Kurz, *Public Investment, the Rate of Return, and Optimal Fiscal Policy*, Johns Hopkins University Press (Baltimore, Md.: 1970).

Arslanalp, Serkan, Fabian Bornhorst, Sanjeev Gupta, and Elsa Sze, "Public Capital and Growth," Working Paper No. 10.175, International Monetary Fund (July 2010).

Ashraf, Quamrul, Ashley Lester, and David Weil, "When Does Improving Health Raise GDP?," Working Paper No 2008-7, Brown University (June 2008).

Azariadis, Costas, *Intertemporal Macroeconomics*, Basil Blackwell (Oxford: 1993).

——, "The Theory of Poverty Traps: What Have We Learned?," in *Poverty Traps*, ed. by Samuel Bowles, Steven N. Durlauf, and Karla Hoff, Princeton University Press (Princeton, N.J.: 2006).

Azariadis, Costas, and Allan H. Drazen, "Thresholds in Economic Development," *Quarterly Journal of Economics*, 105 (May 1990), 501–25.

Azariadis, Costas, and John Stachurski, "Poverty Traps," in *Handbook of Economic Growth*, ed. by Philippe Aghion and Steven Durlauf, Vol. 1, North Holland (Amsterdam: 2005).

Baier, Scott L., and Gerhard Glomm, "Long-Run Growth and Welfare Effects of Public Policies with Distortionary Taxation," *Journal of Economic Dynamics and Control* , 25 (December 2001), 1007–42.

Baldacci, Emanuele, Benedict Clements, Sanjeev Gupta, and Qiang Cui, "Social Spending, Human Capital, and Growth in Developing Countries: Implications for Achieving the MDGs," Working Paper No. 04/217, International Monetary Fund (November 2004).

Balducci, Renato, "Public Expenditure and Economic Growth: A Critical Extension of Barro's (1990) Model," *Journal of Analytical and Institutional Economics*, 21 (August 2006), 163–72.

Bardasi, Elena, and Quentin Wodon, "Working Long Hours and Having No Choice: Time Poverty in Guinea," Policy Research Working Paper No. 4961, World Bank (June 2009).

Barro, Robert J., "Government Spending in a Simple Model of Endogenous Growth," *Journal of Political Economy*, 98 (October 1990), s103–25.
Barro, Robert J, and Gary S. Becker, "Fertility Choice in a Model of Economic Growth," *Econometrica*, 57 (March 1989), 481–501.
Barro, Robert J., and Xavier Sala-i-Martin, "Public Finance in Models of Economic Growth," *Review of Economic Studies*, 59 (October 1992), 645-61.
——, *Economic Growth*, 2nd ed., MIT Press (Cambridge, Mass.: 2003).
Bauer, Michal, and Julie Chytilová, "Does Education Matter in Patience Formation? Evidence from Ugandan Villages," IES Working Paper No. 2007/10, Charles University (February 2007).
Becker, Gary, Kevin Murphy, and Robert Tamura, "Human Capital, Fertility, and Economic Growth," *Journal of Political Economy*, 98 (October 1990), 12–37.
Behrman, Jere R., "The Impact of Health and Nutrition on Education," *World Bank Research Observer*, 11 (February 1996), 23–37.
——, "Intrahousehold Distribution and the Family," in *Handbook of Population and Family Economics*, ed. by Mark R. Rosenzweig and Oded Stark, Vol. 1A, Elsevier (Amsterdam: 1997).
——, "Early Life Nutrition and Subsequent Education, Health, Wage, and Intergenerational Effects," in *Health and Growth*, ed. by Michael Spence and Maureen Lewis, World Bank (Washington, D.C.: 2009).
Behrman, Jere R., Andrew D. Foster, Mark R. Rosenzweig, and Prem Vashishtha, "Women's Schooling, Home Teaching, and Economic Growth," *Journal of Political Economy*, 107 (August 1999), 682–714.
Behrman, Jere R., and Mark R. Rosenzweig, "The Returns to Birthweight," *Review of Economics and Statistics*, 86 (May 2004), 586–601.
Behrman, Jere R., and Barbara L. Wolfe, "How Does Mother's Schooling Affect Family Health, Nutrition, Medical Care Usage, and Household Sanitation?," *Journal of Econometrics*, 36 (September 1987), 185–204.
Bell, Clive, Shantayanan Devarajan, and Hans Gersbach, "The Long-Run Economic Costs of AIDS: A Model with an Application to South Africa," *World Bank Economic Review*, 20 (March 2006), 55–89.
Benos, Nikos, "Fiscal Policy and Economic Growth: Empirical Evidence from OECD Countries," Discussion Paper No. 05-01, University of Cyprus (July 2005).
Bhargava, Alok, Dean T. Jamison, Lawrence J. Lau, and Christopher J. Murray, "Modeling the Effects of Health on Economic Growth," *Journal of Health Economics*, 20 (May 2001), 423–40.
Bhattacharya, Joydeep, and Xue Qiao, "Public and Private Expenditures on Health in a Growth Model," *Journal of Economic Dynamics and Control*, 31 (August 2007), 2519–35.
Blackburn, Keith, Niloy Bose, and M. Emranul Haque, "Public Expenditures, Bureaucratic Corruption and Economic Development," unpublished, University of Manchester (September 2005).
Blackburn, Keith, and Giam P. Cipriani, "A Model of Longevity and Growth," *Journal of Economic Dynamics and Control*, 26 (February 2002), 187–204.
Blackburn, Keith, and Rashmi Sarmah, "Corruption, Development and Demography," *Economics of Governance*, 9 (October 2008), 341–62.
Blackden, C. Mark, Sudharshan Canagarajah, Stephan Klasen, and David Lawson, "Gender and Growth in Sub-Saharan Africa: Issues and Evidence," Research Paper No. 2006/37, UNU-Wider (April 2006).

Blackden, C. Mark, and Quentin Wodon, *Gender, Time Use, and Poverty in Sub-Saharan Africa*, World Bank (Washington, D.C.: 2006).

Blankenau, William F., and Nicole B. Simpson, "Public Education Expenditures and Growth," *Journal of Development Economics*, 73 (April 2004), 583–605.

Bleakley, Hoyt, "Disease and Development: Evidence from Hookworm Eradication in the American South," *Quarterly Journal of Economics*, 122 (February 2007), 73–117.

——, "Malaria Eradication in the Americas: A Retrospective Analysis of Childhood Exposure," *American Economic Journal: Applied Economics*, 2 (April 2010*a*), 1–45.

——, "Health, Human Capital, and Development," *Annual Review of Economics*, 2 (September 2010*b*), 283–310.

Bleakley, Hoyt, and Fabian Lange, "Chronic Disease Burden and the Interaction of Education, Fertility, and Growth," *Review of Economics and Statistics*, 91 (March 2009), 52–65.

Bloom, David E., and David Canning, "Schooling, Health, and Economic Growth: Reconciling the Micro and Macro Evidence," unpublished, Harvard School of Public Health (February 2005).

Bloom, David E., David Canning, and Jaypee Sevilla, "The Effect of Health on Economic Growth: A Production Function Approach," *World Development*, 32 (January 2004), 1–13.

Bloom, David E., David Canning, and Mark Weston, "The Value of Vaccination," *World Economics*, 6 (July 2005), 1–13.

Bohn, Frank, "Polarisation, Uncertainty and Public Investment Failure," *European Journal of Political Economy*, 23 (December 2007), 1077–87.

Bom, Pedro R., and Jenny E. Ligthart, "What Have We Learned from Three Decades of Research on the Productivity of Public Capital?," unpublished, Tilburg University (April 2010).

Bose, Niloy, M. Emranul Haque, and Denise R. Osborn, "Public Expenditure and Economic Growth: A Disaggregated Analysis for Developing Countries," *Manchester School*, 75 (September 2007), 533–56.

Boucekkine, Raouf, Rodolphe Desbordes, and Hélène Latzer, "How do Epidemics Induce Behavioral Changes?," *Journal of Economic Growth*, 14 (September 2009), 233–64.

Brauninger, Michael, "The Budget Deficit, Public Debt, and Endogenous Growth," *Journal of Public Economic Theory*, 7 (December 2005), 827–40.

Brenneman, Adam, and Michel Kerf, "Infrastructure and Poverty Linkages: A Literature Review," unpublished, World Bank (December 2002).

Broca, Sumiter, and Kostas Stamoulis, "Micro- and Macroevidence on the Impact of Undernourishment," in *Nutrition Intake and Economic Growth*, ed. by K. Taniguchi and X. Wang, Food and Agriculture Organization (Rome: 2003).

Brooks, Douglas H., "Asia's Infrastructure and Trade," unpublished, Asian Development Bank (March 2010).

Brooks, Douglas H., and Benno Ferrarini, "Changing Trade Costs between People's Republic of China and India," Working Paper No. 203, Asian Development Bank (May 2010).

Brown, Philip H., "Parental Education and Investment in Children's Human Capital in Rural China," *Economic Development and Cultural Change*, 54 (July 2006), 759–89.

Bulir, Ales, and A. Javier Hamann, "Aid Volatility: An Empirical Assessment," *IMF Staff Papers*, 50 (March 2003), 64–89.

——, "Volatility of Development Aid: An Update," *IMF Staff Papers*, 54 (December 2007), 727–39.

Bundy, Donald, et al., "School-Based Health and Nutrition Programs," in *Disease Control Priorities in Developing Countries*, ed. by Dean Jamison et al., 2nd ed., Oxford University Press (New York: 2006).

Bunzel, Helle, and Xue Qiao, "Endogenous Lifetime and Economic Growth Revisited," *Economics Bulletin*, 15 (March 2005), 1–8.

Buys, Piet, Uwe Deichmann, and David Wheeler, "Road Network Upgrading and Overland Trade Expansion in Sub-Saharan Africa," Policy Research Working Paper No. 4097, World Bank (December 2006).

Cadot, Olivier, Lars-Hendrik Roller, and Andreas Stephan, "Contribution to Productivity or Pork Barrel? The Two Faces of Infrastructure Investment," *Journal of Public Economics*, 90 (August 2006), 1133–53.

Calderón, César, "Infrastructure and Growth in Africa," Policy Research Working Paper No. 4914, World Bank (April 2009).

Calderón, César, and Luis Servén, "The Effects of Infrastructure Development on Growth and Income Distribution," Policy Research Working Paper No. 3400, World Bank (September 2004).

Candelon, Bertrand, Gilbert Colletaz, and Christophe Hurlin, "Network Effects and Infrastructure Productivity in Developing Countries," unpublished, University of Orlé ans (September 2009).

Case, Anne, Angela Fertig, and Christina Paxson, "The Lasting Impact of Childhood Health and Circumstance," *Journal of Health Economics*, 24 (March 2005), 365–89.

Castelló-Climent, Amparo, and Rafael Doménech, "Human Capital Inequality, Life Expectancy and Economic Growth," *Economic Journal*, 118 (April 2008), 653–77.

Castro, Juan F., Arlette Beltran, Enrique Vasquez, and Gustavo Yamada, "A Systemic Assessment of MDG Achievement: The Case of Guatemala," unpublished, Universidad del Pacífico (January 2006).

Cavalcanti, Tiago V. de V., and José Tavares, "Women Prefer Larger Governments: Growth, Structural Transformation and Government Size," *Economic Inquiry*, 49 (March 2011), 155–71.

Celasun, Oya, and Jan Walliser, "Predictability of Aid: Do Fickle Donors Undermine Aid Effectiveness?," *Economic Policy*, 23 (July 2008), 545–94.

Cervellati, Matteo, and Uwe Sunde, "Human Capital, Life Expectancy, and the Process of Economic Development," *American Economic Review*, 95 (December 2005), 1653–72.

——, "Life Expectancy and Economic Growth: The Role of the Demographic Transition," Discussion Paper No. 4160, IZA (May 2009).

Chakrabarty, Debajyoti, "Poverty Traps and Growth in a Model of Endogenous Time Preference," unpublished, University of Sydney (June 2004).

Chakraborty, Shankha, "Endogenous Lifetime and Economic Growth," *Journal of Economic Theory*, 116 (May 2004), 119–37.

Chakraborty, Shankha, and Era Dabla-Norris, "The Quality of Public Investment," unpublished, University of Oregon (October 2010).

Chakraborty, Shankha, and Mausumi Das, "Mortality, Human Capital and Persistent Inequality," *Journal of Economic Growth*, 10 (March 2005), 159–92.

Chakraborty, Shankha, Chris Papageorgiou, and Fidel Pérez Sebastián, "Diseases, Infection Dynamics, and Development," *Journal of Monetary Economics*, 57 (October 2010), 859–72.

Chatterjee, Santanu, "Should the Private Sector Provide Public Capital?," *Macroeconomic Dynamics*, 11 (March 2007), 318–46.

Chatterjee, Santanu, and Mahbub Morshed, "Infrastructure Provision and Macroeconomic Performance," *Journal of Economic Dynamics and Control*, 35 (August 2011), 1288–306.

Chatterjee, Santanu, and Stephen J. Turnovsky, "Financing Public Investment through Foreign Aid: Consequences for Economic Growth and Welfare," *Review of International Economics*, 13 (March 2005), 20–44.

——, "Infrastructure and Inequality," unpublished, University of Washington (May 2011).

Chatterjee, Santanu, Georgios Sakoulis, and Stephen J. Turnovsky, "Unilateral Capital Transfers, Public Investment, and Economic Growth," *European Economic Review*, 47 (December 2003), 1077–103.

Chen, Been-Lon, "Public Capital, Endogenous Growth, and Endogenous Fluctuations," *Journal of Macroeconomics* , 28 (December 2006), 768–74.

Coe, David T., Elhanan Helpman, and Alexander W. Hoffmaister, "International R&D Spillovers and Institutions," *European Economic Review*, 53 (October 2009), 723–41.

Cole, Matthew A., and Eric Neumayer, "The Impact of Poor Health on Total Factor Productivity," *Journal of Development Studies*, 42 (August 2006), 918–38.

Commission for Africa, *Our Common Interest: Report of the Commission for Africa*, Department of International Development (London: March 2005).

Commission on Growth and Development, *The Growth Report: Strategies for Sustained Growth and Inclusive Development*, World Bank (Washington, D.C.: 2008).

Cooper, Frederick, "Africa and the World Economy," in *Confronting Historical Paradigms*, ed. by Frederick Cooper, Allen F. Isaacman, Florencia E. Mallon, and Steve J. Stern, University of Wisconsin Press (Madison: 1993).

Corporación Andina de Fomento, *Caminos para el Futuro. Gestió n de la Infraestructura en América Latina*, Reporte de Economía y Desarollo (Caracas: 2009).

Corrigan, Paul, Gerhard Glomm, and Fabio Mendez, "AIDS Crisis and Growth," *Journal of Development Economics*, 77 (June 2005), 107–24.

Corsetti, Giancarlo, and Nouriel Roubini, "Optimal Government Spending and Taxation in Endogenous Growth Models," Working Paper No. 5851, National Bureau of Economic Research (December 1996).

Currie, David, Paul Levine, Joseph Pearlman, and Michael Chui, "Phases of Imitation and Innovation in a North-South Endogenous Growth Model," *Oxford Economic Papers*, 51 (January 1999), 60–88.

Currie, Janet, "Healthy, Wealthy, and Wise: Socioeconomic Status, Poor Health in Childhood, and Human Capital Development," *Journal of Economic Literature*, 47 (March 2009) 87–122.

Cutler, David M., Angus Deaton, and Adriana Lleras-Muney, "The Determinants of Mortality," *Journal of Economic Perspectives*, 20 (June 2006), 97–120.

Cutler, David M., and Adriana Lleras-Muney, "Education and Health: Evaluating Theories and Evidence," Working Paper No. 12352, National Bureau of Economic Research (July 2006).

Czernich, Nina, Oliver Falck, Tobias Kretschmer, and Ludger Woessmann, "Broadband Infrastructure and Economic Growth," *Economic Journal*, 121 (May 2011), 505–32.

Dabla-Norris, Era, Jim Brumby, Annette Kyobe, Zac Mills, and Chris Papageorgiou, "Investing in Public Investment: An Index of Public Investment Efficiency," Working Paper No.11/37, International Monetary Fund (February 2011).

d'Adda, Giovanna, Markus Goldstein, Joshua Graff Zivin, Mabel Nangami, and Harsha Thirumurthy, "ARV Treatment and Time Allocation to Household Tasks: Evidence from Kenya," *African Development Review*, 21 (March 2009), 180–208.

Dal Bo, Ernesto, and Martín A. Rossi, "Corruption and Inefficiency: Theory and Evidence from Electric Utilities," *Journal of Public Economics*, 91 (June 2007), 939–62.

Das, Jishnu, Quy-Toan Do, Jed Friedman, and David McKenzie, "Mental Health Patterns and Consequences: Results from Survey Data in Five Developing Countries," *World Bank Economic Review*, 23 (March 2009), 31–55.

Datta, Saugato, "The Impact of Improved Highways on Indian Firms," unpublished, Ideas42 (June 2011). Forthcoming, *Journal of Development Economics*.

Deaton, Angus, "Health, Inequality, and Economic Development," *Journal of Economic Literature*, 41 (March 2003), 113–58.

De la Croix, David, and Clara Delavallade, "Growth, Public Investment and Corruption with Failing Institutions," *Economics of Governance*, 10 (July 2009), 187–219.

——, "Democracy, Rule of Law, Corruption Incentives and Growth," *Journal of Public Economic Theory*, 13 (April 2011), 155–87.

De la Croix, David, and Omar Licandro, " 'The Child Is Father of the Man': Implications for the Demographic Transition," Working Paper No. 6493, Centre for Economic Policy Research (September 2007).

De la Croix, David, and Marie Vander Donckt, "Would Empowering Women Initiate the Demographic Transition in Least Developed Countries?," *Journal of Human Capital*, 4 (June 2010), 85–129.

De la Croix, David, and Philippe Michel, *A Theory of Economic Growth: Dynamics and Policy in Overlapping Generations*, Cambridge University Press (Cambridge: 2002).

Delmon, Jeffrey, *Public-Private Partnership Projects in Infrastructure: An Essential Guide for Policymakers*, Cambridge University Press (Cambridge: 2011).

Devoto, Florencia, Esther Duflo, Pascaline Dupas, William Parenté, and Vincent Pous, "Happiness on Tap: Piped Water Adoption in Urban Morocco," unpublished, Massachusetts Institute of Technology (September 2010).

Diamond, Peter A., "National Debt in a Neoclassical Growth Model," *American Economic Review*, 55 (December 1965), 1126–50.

Dinopoulos, Elias, and Peter Thompson, "Endogenous Growth in a Cross-Section of Countries," *Journal of International Economics*, 51 (August 2000), 335–62.

Dioikitopoulos, Evangelos V., and Sarantis Kalyvitis, "Public Capital Maintenance and Congestion: Long-Run Growth and Fiscal Policies," *Journal of Economic Dynamics and Control*, 32 (December 2008), 3760–79.

Dollar, David, Mary Hallward-Driemeier, and Taye Mengistae, "Investment Climate and International Integration," *World Development*, 34 (September 2006), 1498–516.

Doucouliagos, Hristos, and Martin Paldam, "The Aid Effectiveness Literature: The Sad Results of 40 Years of Research," *Journal of Economic Surveys*, 23 (July 2009), 433–61.

Duffy, John, and Chris Papageorgiou, "A Cross-Country Empirical Investigation of the Aggregate Production Function Specification," *Journal of Economic Growth*, 5 (March 2000), 87–120.

Duflo, Esther, Michael Greenstone, and Rema Hanna, "Cooking Stoves, Indoor Air Pollution and Respiratory Health in Rural Orissa, India," in *Insights: Closing the Global Gender Gap* , ed. by Women and Public Policy Program, Harvard Kennedy School (March 2009).

Eberhard, Anton, Vivien Foster, Cecilia Briceño-Garmendia, Fatimata Ouedraogo, Daniel Camos, and Maria Shkaratan, "Underpowered: The State of the Power Sector in Sub-Saharan Africa," Background Paper No. 6, Africa Infrastructure Sector Diagnostic, World Bank (April 2008).

Égert, Balázs, Tomasz Koźluk, and Douglas Sutherland, "Infrastructure and Growth: Empirical Evidence," Working Paper No. 685, OECD Economics Department (March 2009).

Ehrlich, Isaac, and Jinyoung Kim, "Endogenous Fertility, Mortality and Economic Growth: Can a Malthusian Framework Account for the Conflicting Historical Trends in Population?," *Journal of Asian Economies*, 16 (October 2005), 789–806.

Ehrlich, Isaac, and Francis Lui, "Intergenerational Trade, Longevity, and Economic Growth," *Journal of Political Economy*, 99 (October 1991), 1029–59.

Eicher, Theo S., and Stephen J. Turnovsky, "Scale, Congestion and Growth," *Economica*, 67 (August 2000), 325–46.

Escribano, Alvaro, J. Luis Guasch, and Jorge Pena, "Impact of Infrastructure Constraints on Firm Productivity in Africa," Working Paper No. 9, Africa Infrastructure Sector Diagnostic, World Bank (June 2008).

——, "Assessing the Impact of Infrastructure Quality on Firm Productivity in Africa: Cross-Country Comparisons Based on Investment Climate Surveys from 1999 to 2005," Policy Research Working Paper No. 5191, World Bank (January 2010).

Esfahani, Hadi Salehi, and María Teresa Ramírez, "Institutions, Infrastructure, and Economic Growth," *Journal of Development Economics*, 70 (April 2003), 443–77.

Estache, Antonio, Biagio Speciale, and David Veredas, "How Much Does Infrastructure Matter to Growth in Sub-Saharan Africa?," unpublished, World Bank (June 2005).

Fedderke, Johanes W., P. Perkins, and John M. Lutz, "Infrastructural Investment in Long-Run Economic Growth: South Africa 1875-2001," *World Development*, 34 (June 2006), 1037–59.

Ferreira, Francisco H. G., "Roads to Equality: Wealth Distribution Dynamics with Public-Private Capital Complementarity," Discussion Paper No. TE/95/286, LSE-STICERD (March 1995).

Ferreira, Pedro C., "Inflationary Financing of Public Investment and Economic Growth," *Journal of Economic Dynamics and Control*, 23 (February 1999), 539–63.

Field, Erica, Omar Robles, and Maximo Torero, "The Cognitive Link between Geography and Development: Iodine Deficiency and Schooling Attainment in Tanzania," Working Paper No. 13838, National Bureau of Economic Research (March 2008).

Fielding, David, and George Mavrotas, "The Volatility of Aid," Discussion Paper No. 0508, University of Otago (June 2005).

Finlay, Jocelyn E., "The Role of Health in Economic Development," PGDA Working Paper No. 21, Harvard School of Public Health (March 2007).

Fisher, Walter H., and Stephen Turnovsky, "Public Investment, Congestion, and Private Capital Accumulation," *Economic Journal*, 108 (March 1998), 399–413.

Food and Agriculture Organization, *Water and the Rural Poor: Interventions for Improving Livelihoods in Sub-Saharan Africa*, FAO (Rome: 2008).

Foster, Vivien, and Cecilia Briceño-Garmendia, eds., *Africa's Infrastructure: A Time for Transformation*, World Bank (Washington, D.C.: 2010).

Freund, Caroline, and Nadia Rocha, "What Constrains Africa's Exports?," *World Bank Economic Review*, 25 (September 2011), 361–86.

Fujimura, Manabu, "Cross-Border Transport Infrastructure, Regional Integration, and Development," Discussion Paper No. 16, ADB Institute (November 2004).

Futagami, Koichi, and Kazuo Mino, "Public Capital and Patterns of Growth in the Presence of Threshold Externalities," *Journal of Economics*, 61 (June 1995), 123–46.

Futagami, Koichi, Yuichi Morita, and Akihisa Shibata, "Dynamic Analysis of an Endogenous Growth Model with Public Capital," in *Endogenous Growth*, ed. by Torben M. Andersen and Karl O. Moene, Basil Blackwell (Oxford: 1993).

Galiani, Sebastian, Paul Gertler, and Ernesto Shargrodsky, "Water for Life: The Impact of Water Supply Privatization on Child Mortality," *Journal of Political Economy*, 113 (February 2005), 83–120.

Galiani, Sebastian, Martin Gonzalez-Rozada, and Ernesto Schargrodsky, "Water Expansions in Shantytowns: Health and Savings," *Economica*, 76 (October 2009), 607–22.

Galor, Oded, *Discrete Dynamical Systems*, Springer Verlag (Berlin: 2006).

Galor, Oded, and David Mayer-Foulkes, "Food for Thought: Basic Needs and Persistent Educational Inequality," unpublished, Brown University (June 2004).

Galor, Oded, and David N. Weil, "The Gender Gap, Fertility, and Growth," *American Economic Review*, 86 (June 1996), 374–87.

——, "Population, Technology, and Growth: From Malthusian Stagnation to the Demographic Transition and Beyond," *American Economic Review*, 90 (September 2000), 806–28.

Galor, Oded, and Joseph Zeira, "Income Distribution and Macroeconomics," *Review of Economic Studies*, 60 (January 1993), 35–52.

Gamper-Rabindran, Shanti, Shakeeb Khanb, and Christopher Timmins, "The Impact of Piped Water Provision on Infant Mortality in Brazil: A Quantile Panel Data Approach," *Journal of Development Economics*, 92 (July 2010), 188–200.

Gancia, Gino, and Fabrizio Zilibotti, "Horizontal Innovation in the Theory of Growth and Development," in *Handbook of Economic Growth*, ed. by Philippe Aghion and Steven Durlauf, Vol. 1A, North Holland (Amsterdam: 2005).

Garcia-Castrillo, Pedro, and Marcos Sanso, "Transitional Dynamics and Thresholds in Romer's Endogenous Technological Change Model," *Macroeconomic Dynamics* (September 2002), 442–56.

García-Peñalosa, Cecilia, and Stephen J. Turnovsky, "Second-Best Optimal Taxation of Capital and Labor in a Developing Economy," *Journal of Public Economics*, 89 (June 2005), 1045–74.

Getachew, Yoseph Y., "Public Capital and Distributional Dynamics in a Two-Sector Growth Model," *Journal of Macroeconomics*, 32 (June 2010), 606–16.

Ghosh, Sugata, and Andros Gregoriou, "The Composition of Government Spending and Growth: Is Current or Capital Spending Better?," *Oxford Economic Papers*, 60 (June 2008), 484–516.

Glewwe, Paul, "Why Does Mother's Schooling Raise Child Health in Developing Countries?," *Journal of Human Resources*, 34 (June 1999), 124–59.

——, "Schools and Skills in Developing Countries: Education Policies and Socioeconomic Outcomes," *Journal of Economic Literature*, 40 (June 2002), 436–82.

Glewwe, Paul, and Michael Kremer, "Schools, Teachers, and Education Outcomes in Developing Countries," in *Handbook of the Economics of Education*, ed. by Eric A. Hanushek and Finis Welch, Vol. 2, Elsevier (Amsterdam: 2006).

Glewwe, Paul, and Edward Miguel, "The Impact of Child Health and Nutrition on Education in Less Developed Countries," in *Handbook of Development Economics*, ed. by T. Paul Schultz and John Strauss, Vol. 4, North Holland (Amsterdam: 2008).

Glomm, Gerhard, and Michael Kaganovich, "Distributional Effects of Public Education in an Economy with Public Pensions," *International Economic Review*, 44 (August 2003), 917–38.

——, "Social Security, Public Education and the Growth-Inequality Relationship," *European Economic Review*, 52 (August 2008), 1009–34.

Glomm, Gerhard, and B. Ravikumar, "Public versus Private Investment in Human Capital: Endogenous Growth and Income Inequality," *Journal of Political Economy*, 100 (August 1992), 813–34.

——, "Public Investment in Infrastructure in a Simple Growth Model," *Journal of Economic Dynamics and Control*, 18 (November 1994), 1173–88.

——, "Productive Government Expenditures and Long-Run Growth," *Journal of Economic Dynamics and Control*, 21 (January 1997), 183–204.

——, "Competitive Equilibrium and Public Investment Plans," *Journal of Economic Dynamics and Control*, 23 (August 1999), 1207–24.

——, "Public Education and Income Inequality," *European Journal of Political Economy*, 19 (June 2003), 289–300.

Gordon, Roger H., and We Li, "Tax Structure in Developing Countries: Many Puzzles and a Possible Explanation," *Journal of Public Economics*, 93 (August 2009), 855–66.

Greenwood, Jeremy, and Ananth Seshadri, "Technological Progress and Economic Transformation," in *Handbook of Economic Growth*, ed. by Philippe Aghion and Steven N. Durlauf, North Holland, Vol. 1B (Amsterdam: 2005).

Greenwood, Jeremy, Ananth Seshadri, and Mehmet Yorukoglu, "Engines of Liberation," *Review of Economic Studies*, 72 (January 2005), 109–33.

Greiner, Alfred, and Willi Semmler, "Fiscal Policy in an Endogenous Growth Model with Productive Government Spending," *Metroeconomica*, 50 (March 1999), 174–93.

Grimard, Franque, Sonia Laszlo, and Wilfredo Lim, "Health, Aging and Childhood Socio-Economic Conditions in Mexico," *Journal of Health Economics*, 29 (September 2010), 630–40.

Grossman, Michael, and R. Kaestner, "Effects of Education on Health," in *The Social Benefits of Education*, ed. by Jere R. Berhman and Nevzer Stacey, University of Michigan Press (Ann Arbor: 1997).

Guasch, J. Luis, *Granting and Renegotiating Infrastructure Concessions: Doing It Right*, World Bank Institute Development Studies (Washington, D.C.: 2004).

Gupta, Indrani, and Arup Mitra, "Economic Growth, Health and Poverty: An Exploratory Study for India," *Development Policy Review*, 22 (March 2004), 193–206.

Gupta, Manash R., and Trishita R. Barman, "Health, Infrastructure, Environment and Endogenous Growth," *Journal of Macroeconomics*, 32 (June 2010), 657–73.

Gupta, Sanjeev, Alvar Kangur, Chris Papageorgiou, and A. Wane, "Efficiency-Adjusted Public Capital and Growth," Working Paper No. 11/217, International Monetary Fund (September 2011).

Gyamfi, Peter, and Guillermo Ruan, "Road Maintenance by Contract: Dissemination of Good Practice in Latin America and the Caribbean Region," Latin America and the Caribbean Regional Studies Program Report 44, World Bank (October 1996).

Gyimah-Brempong, Kwabena, and Mark Wilson, "Health, Human Capital, and Economic Growth in Sub-Saharan African and OECD Countries," *Quarterly Review of Economics and Finance*, 44 (May 2004), 296–320.

Hamoudi, Amar, and Nancy Birdsall, "HIV/AIDS and the Accumulation and Utilization of Human Capital in Africa," in *The Macroeconomics of HIV/AIDS*, ed. by M. Haacker, International Monetary Fund (Washington, D.C.: 2004).

Haque, M. Emranul, and Richard Kneller, "Public Investment and Growth: The Role of Corruption," Working Paper No. 98, Centre for Growth and Business Cycle Research, University of Manchester (February 2008).

Hartman, Richard, and O-Sung Kwon, "Sustainable Growth and the Environmental Kuznets Curve," *Journal of Economic Dynamics and Control*, 29 (October 2005), 1701–36.

Hashimoto, Ken-ichi, and Ken Tabata, "Health Infrastructure, Demographic Transition and Growth," *Review of Development Economics*, 9 (November 2005), 549–62.

Hazan, Moshe, and Hosny Zoabi, "Does Longevity Cause Growth? A Theoretical Critique," *Journal of Economic Growth*, 11 (December 2006), 363–76.

Heijdra, Ben J., and Lex Meijdam, "Public Investment and Intergenerational Distribution," *Journal of Economic Dynamics and Control*, 26 (May 2002), 707–35.

Helmers, Christian, and Manasa Patnam, "The Formation and Evolution of Childhood Skill Acquisition: Evidence from India," *Journal of Development Economics*, 95 (July 2011), 252–66.

Henckel, Timo, and Warwick J. McKibbin, "The Economics of Infrastructure in a Globalized World: Issues, Lessons and Future Challenges," unpublished, Centre for Applied Macroeconomic Analysis, Australian National University (June 2010).

Herz, Barbara, and Gene B. Sperling, *What Works in Girls' Education: Evidence and Policies from the Developing World*, Council on Foreign Relations Press (New York: 2004).

Hoddinott, John, Harold Alderman, and Jere Behrman, "Nutrition, Malnutrition and Economic Growth," in *Health and Economic Growth: Findings and Policy Implications*, ed. by Guillem López-Casasnovas, Berta Rivera, and Luis Currais, MIT Press (Cambridge, Mass.: 2005).

Hoddinott, John, Harold Alderman, and Lawrence Haddad, "Testing Competing Models of Intrahousehold Allocation," in *Intrahousehold Resource Allocation in Developing Countries: Models, Methods, and Policy*, ed. by Lawrence Haddad, John Hoddinott, and Harold Alderman, Johns Hopkins University Press (Baltimore, Md.: 1997).

Hulten, Charles R., "Infrastructure Capital and Economic Growth: How Well You Use It May Be More Important Than How Much You Have," Working Paper No. 5847, National Bureau of Economic Research (December 1996).

Hulten, Charles R., Esra Bennathan, and Sylaja Srinivasan, "Infrastructure, Externalities, and Economic Development: A Study of Indian Manufacturing Industry," *World Bank Economic Review*, 20 (June 2006), 291–308.

Hung, Fu-Sheng, "Optimal Composition of Government Public Capital Financing," *Journal of Macroeconomics*, 27 (December 2005), 704–23.

Hurlin, Christophe, "Network Effects of the Productivity of Infrastructure in Developing Countries," Policy Research Working Paper No. 3808, World Bank (January 2006).

Ilahi, Nadeem, "Gender and the Allocation of Adult Time: Evidence from the Peru LSMS Panel Data," Policy Research Working Paper No. 2744, World Bank (December 2001).

Ilahi, Nadeem, and Franque Grimard, "Public Infrastructure and Private Costs: Water Supply and Time Allocation of Women in Rural Pakistan," *Economic Development and Cultural Change*, 49 (October 2000), 45–75.

International Labour Office, *Global Employment Trends for Women 2008*, ILO Publications (Geneva: 2008).

Isha, Ray, "Women, Water, and Development," *Annual Review of Environment and Resources*, 32 (November 2007), 421–49.

Iwaisako, Tatsuro, "Technology Choice and Patterns of Growth in an Overlapping Generations Model," *Journal of Macroeconomics*, 24 (June 2002), 211–31.

Jamison, Dean T., Lawrence J. Lau, and Jia Wang, "Health's Contribution to Economic Growth in an Environment of Partially Endogenous Technical Progress," in *Health and Economic Growth: Findings and Policy Implications*, ed. by Guillem López-Casasnovas, Berta Rivera, and Luis Currais, MIT Press (Cambridge, Mass.: 2005).

Jayachandran, Seema, and Adriana Lleras-Muney, "Life Expectancy and Human Capital Investments: Evidence from Maternal Mortality Declines," *Quarterly Journal of Economics*, 124 (February 2009), 349–97.

Jones, Charles I., and Paul M. Romer, "The New Kaldor Facts: Ideas, Institutions, Population, and Human Capital," *American Economic Journal: Macroeconomics*, 2 (January 2010), 224–45.

Jones, John T., and Ron W. Zimmer, "Examining the Impact of Capital on Academic Achievement," *Economics of Education Review*, 20 (December 2001), 577–88.

Kaas, Leo, "Productive Government Spending, Growth, and Sequential Voting," *European Journal of Political Economy*, 19 (June 2003), 227–46.

Kalaitzidakis, Pantelis, and Sarantis Kalyvitis, "On the Macroeconomic Implications of Maintenance in Public Capital," *Journal of Public Economics*, 88 (March 2004), 695–712.

Kalemli-Ozcan, Sebnem, "Does Mortality Decline Promote Economic Growth?," *Journal of Economic Growth*, 7 (December 2002), 411–29.

——, "A Stochastic Model of Mortality, Fertility, and Human Capital Investment," *Journal of Development Economics*, 70 (February 2003), 103–18.

——, "AIDS, Reversal of the Demographic Transition and Economic Development: Evidence from Africa," Working Paper No. 12181, National Bureau of Economic Research (May 2006).

——, "The Uncertain Lifetime and the Timing of Human Capital Investment," *Journal of Population Economics*, 21 (July 2008), 557–72.

Kellenberg, Derek K., "US Affiliates, Infrastructure and Growth: A Simultaneous Investigation of Critical Mass," *Journal of International Trade and Economic Development*, 18 (September 2009), 311–45.

Kessides, Ioannis N., Roger G. Noll, and Nancy C. Benjamin, "Regionalising Infrastructure Reform in Developing Countries," *World Economics*, 11 (July 2010), 79–108.

Khandker, Shahidur, Victor Lavy, and Deon Filmer, "Schooling and Cognitive Achievements of Children in Morocco," Discussion Paper No. 264, World Bank (February 1994).

Kimura, Masako, and Daishin Yasui, "The Galor-Weil Gender-Gap Model Revisited: From Home to Market," *Journal of Economic Growth*, 15 (December 2010), 323–51.

Kinugasa, Tomoko, and Andrew Mason, "Why Nations Become Wealthy: The Effects of Adult Longevity on Saving," *World Development*, 35 (January 2007), 1–23.

Kiros, Gebre-Egziabher, and Dennis P. Hogan, "War, Famine, and Excess Child Mortality in Africa: The Role of Parental Education," *International Journal of Epidemiology*, 30 (June 2001), 447–55.

Kjellstrom, Tord, *Our Cities, our Health, our Future: Acting on Social Determinants for Health Equity in Urban Settings*, World Health Organization (Geneva: 2008).

Koolwal, Gayatri, and Dominique van de Walle, "Access to Water, Women's Work and Child Outcomes," Policy Research Working Paper No. 5302, World Bank (June 2010).

Kosempel, Stephen, "A Theory of Development and Long Run Growth," *Journal of Development Economics*, 75 (October 2004), 201–20.

Kumar, Shubh K., and David Hotchkiss, "Consequences of Deforestation for Women's Time Allocation, Agricultural Production, and Nutrition in Hill Areas of Nepal," Research Report No. 69, International Food Policy Research Institute (October 1988).

Lagerlöf, Nils-Petter, "Gender Equality and Long-Run Growth," *Journal of Economic Growth*, 8 (December 2003), 403–26.
Lam, David, and Suzanne Duryea, "Effects of Schooling on Fertility, Labor Supply, and Investments in Children, with Evidence from Brazil," *Journal of Human Resources*, 34 (March 1999), 160–92.
Lavy, Victor, John Strauss, Duncan Thomas, and Philippe de Vreyer, "Quality of Health Care, Survival and Health Outcomes in Ghana," *Journal of Health Economics*, 15 (June 1996), 333–57.
Lebo, Jerry, and Dieter Schelling, "Design and Appraisal of Rural Transport Infrastructure," World Bank Technical Paper No. 496 (Washington, D.C.: 2001).
Lee, Lung-fei, Mark R. Rosenzweig, and Mark M. Pitt, "The Effects of Improved Nutrition, Sanitation, and Water Quality on Child Health in High-Mortality Populations," *Journal of Econometrics*, 77 (March 1997), 209–35.
Leigland, James, "PPI in Poor Countries: How to Increase Private Participation in Infrastructure Management and Investment," PPIAF Note No. 51 (February 2010).
Leipziger, Danny, Marianne Fay, Quentin Wodon, and Tito Yepes, "Achieving the Millennium Development Goals: The Role of Infrastructure," Working Paper No. 3163, World Bank (November 2003).
Levy, Hernan, "Rural Roads and Poverty Alleviation in Morocco," unpublished, World Bank (May 2004).
Li, Zhigang, "Some Evidence on the Performance of Transport Infrastructure Investment in China," unpublished, University of Hong Kong (March 2010).
Lim, Hyeon-Sook, et al., "Low Intakes of Energy, Folate, Iron, and Calcium of Child-Bearing Korean Women," *Ecology of Food and Nutrition*, 41 (September 2002), 401–13.
Lin, Shuanglin, "Labor Income Taxation and Human Capital Accumulation," *Journal of Public Economics*, 68 (May 1998), 291–302.
Lorentzen, Peter, John McMillan, and Romain Wacziarg, "Death and Development," *Journal of Economic Growth* , 13 (March 2008), 81–124.
Luoto, Jani, "Aggregate Infrastructure Capital Stock and Long-Run Growth: Evidence from Finnish Data," *Journal of Development Economics*, 94 (March 2011), 181–91.
Maluccio, John A., John Hoddinott, Jere R. Behrman, Reynaldo Martorell, Agnes R. Quisumbing, and Aryeh D. Stein, "The Impact of Improving Nutrition during Early Childhood on Education among Guatemalan Adults," *Economic Journal*, 119 (April 2009), 734–63.
Mammen, Kristin, and Christina Paxson, "Women's Work and Economic Development," *Journal of Economic Perspectives*, 14 (March 2000), 141–64.
Mariani, Fabio, Agustín Pérez-Barahona, and Natacha Raffin, "Life Expectancy and the Environment," *Journal of Economic Dynamics and Control*, 34 (April 2010), 798–815.
Matsuyama, Kiminori, "Increasing Returns, Industrialization, and Indeterminacy of Equilibrium," *Quarterly Journal of Economics*, 106 (May 1991), 617–50.
Mayer-Foulkes, David, "Human Development Traps and Economic Growth," in *Health and Economic Growth: Findings and Policy Implications*, ed. by Guillem López-Casasnovas, Berta Rivera, and Luis Currais, MIT Press (Cambridge, Mass.: 2005).

McCarthy, Desmond, Holger Wolf, and Yi Wu, "The Growth Costs of Malaria," unpublished, Georgetown University (December 1999).

McDermott, John, "Development Dynamics: Economic Integration and the Demographic Transition," *Journal of Economic Growth*, 7 (December 2002), 371–409.

McDonald, Scott, and Jennifer Roberts, "AIDS and Economic Growth: A Human Capital Approach," *Journal of Development Economics*, 80 (June 2006), 228–50.

McGuire, James W., "Basic Health Care Provision and Under-5 Mortality: A Cross-National Study of Developing Countries," *World Development* (March 2006), 405–25.

Mental Health Foundation, *Feeding Minds—The Impact of Food on Mental Health*, London (January 2006).

Micco, Alejandro, and Natalia Pérez, "Determinants of Maritime Transport Costs," Working Paper No. 441, Inter-American Development Bank (April 2002).

Miguel, Edward, "Health, Education, and Economic Development," in *Health and Economic Growth: Findings and Policy Implications*, ed. by Guillem López-Casasnovas, Berta Rivera, and Luis Currais, MIT Press (Cambridge, Mass.: 2005).

Miguel, Edward, and Michael Kremer, "Worms: Identifying Impacts on Education and Health in the Presence of Treatment Externalities," *Econometrica*, 72 (January 2004), 159–217.

Mills, Samuel, Eduard Bos, Elizabeth Lule, GNV Ramana, Rodolfo Bulatao, "Obstetric Care in Poor Settings in Ghana, India, and Kenya," HNP Discussion Paper, World Bank (November 2007).

Misch, Florian, Norman Gemmell, and Richard Kneller, "Growth and Welfare Maximization in Models of Public Finance and Endogenous Growth," Research Paper No. 08/09 (June 2008).

Mitsui, Hisaaki, "Impact Assessment of Large Scale Transport Infrastructure in Northern Vietnam," unpublished, World Bank (May 2004).

Moav, Omer, "Cheap Children and the Persistence of Poverty," *Economic Journal*, 115 (January 2005), 88–110.

Momota, Michiko, "The Gender Gap, Fertility, Subsidies and Growth," *Economics Letters*, 69 (December 2000), 401–5.

Mondal, Debasis, and Manash R. Gupta, "Endogenous Imitation and Endogenous Growth in a North-South Model: A Theoretical Analysis," *Journal of Macroeconomics*, 31 (December 2009), 668–84.

Monteiro, Goncalo, and Stephen J. Turnovsky, "The Composition of Productive Government Expenditure," *Growth and Development Review*, 1 (March 2008), 57–83.

Morand, Olivier F., "Endogenous Fertility, Income Distribution, and Growth," *Journal of Economic Growth*, 4 (September 1999), 331–49.

Morrison, Andrew R., Dhushyanth Raju, and Nistha Sinha, "Gender Equality, Poverty and Economic Growth," Policy Research Working Paper No. 4349, World Bank (September 2007).

Murphy, Kevin M., Andrei Shleifer, and Robert W. Vishny, "Industrialization and the Big Push," *Journal of Political Economy*, 97 (October 1989), 1003–26.

Nankhuni, Flora, and Jill Findeis, "The Effects of Environmental Degradation on Women's and Children's Time Allocation Decisions in Malawi: Impact on Children's Welfare," unpublished, Pennsylvania State University (July 2003).

Naudé, Wim, and Marianne Matthee, "The Significance of Transport Costs in Africa," Policy Brief No. 5, United Nations University (June 2007).

Neanidis, Kyriakos C., and Dimitrios Varvarigos, "The Allocation of Volatile Aid and Economic Growth: Theory and Evidence," *European Journal of Political Economy*, 25 (December 2009), 447–62.

Newman, John, Menno Pradhan, Laura B. Rawlings, Geert Ridder, Ramiro Coa, and José Luis Evia, "An Impact Evaluation of Education, Health, and Water Supply Investments by the Bolivian Social Investment Fund," *World Bank Economic Review*, 16 (June 2002), 241–74.

Nunes, Luis C., José Oscategui, and Juan Peschiera, "Determinants of FDI in Latin America," Working Paper No. 252, Pontificia Universidad Católica de Perú (October 2006).

OECD, *Measuring Capital: OECD Manual*, 2nd ed. (Paris: 2009).

Oloo, J. O., "Child Mortality in Developing Countries: Challenges and Policy Options," *Eastern Africa Social Science Research Review*, 21 (June 2005), 1–17.

Osang, Thomas, and Jayanta Sarkar, "Endogenous Mortality, Human Capital and Endogenous Growth," *Journal of Macroeconomics*, 30 (December 2008), 1423–45.

Ott, Ingrid, and Stephen J. Turnovsky, "Excludable and Non-excludable Public Inputs: Consequences for Economic Growth," *Economica*, 73 (November 2006), 725–48.

Pallage, Stéphane, and Michel A. Robe, "Foreign Aid and the Business Cycle," *Review of International Economics*, 9 (November 2001), 641–72.

Park, Cheolsung, "Marriage Market, Parents' Bargaining Powers, and Children's Nutrition and Education," *Oxford Bulletin of Economics and Statistics*, 69 (December 2007), 773–93.

Paxson, Christina H., and Norbert Schady, "Cognitive Development among Young Children in Ecuador: The Roles of Wealth, Health and Parenting," *Journal of Human Resources*, 42 (March 2007), 49–84.

Perez-Sebastian, Fidel, "Public Support to Innovation and Imitation in a Non-Scale Growth Model," *Journal of Economic Dynamics and Control*, 31 (December 2007), 3791–821.

Pinto Moreira, Emmanuel, and Nihal Bayraktar, "A Macroeconomic Framework for Quantifying Growth and Poverty Reduction Strategies in Niger," *Journal of Policy Modeling*, 30 (May 2008), 523–39.

Piras, Romano, "Government Spending Composition in an Endogenous Growth Model with Congestion," *Metroeconomica*, 52 (February 2001), 121–36.

——, "Growth, Congestion of Public Goods, and Second-Best Optimal Policy: A Dynamic Analysis," *Rivista Italiana degli Economisti*, 10 (September 2005), 397–416.

Pritchett, Lant, "The Tyranny of Concepts: CUDIE (Cumulated, Depreciated, Investment Effort) Is Not Capital," *Journal of Economic Growth*, 5 (December 2000), 361–84.

Rajkumar, Andrew, and Vinaya Swaroop, "Public Spending and Outcomes: Does Governance Matter?," *Journal of Development Economics*, 86 (April 2008), 96–111.

Raut, Lakshmi K., "Capital Accumulation, Income Distribution and Endogenous Fertility in an Overlapping Generations General Equilibrium Model," *Journal of Development Economics*, 34 (November 1990), 123–50.

Rehfuess, Eva, Sumi Mehta, and Annette Pruss-Ustum, "Assessing Household Solid Fuel Use: Multiple Implications for the Millennium Development Goals," *Environmental Health Perspectives*, 114 (March 2006), 373–78.

Reinikka, Ritva, and Jakob Svensson, "Coping with Poor Public Capital," *Journal of Development Economics*, 69 (October 2002), 51–69.

Rioja, Felix K., "Productiveness and Welfare Implications of Public Infrastructure: A Dynamic Two-Sector General Equilibrium Analysis," *Journal of Development Economics*, 58 (April 1999), 387–404.

——, "The Penalties of Inefficient Infrastructure," *Review of Development Economics*, 7 (March 2003*a*), 127–37.

——, "Filling Potholes: Macroeconomic Effects of Maintenance versus New Investment in Public Infrastructure," *Journal of Public Economics*, 87 (September 2003*b*), 2281–304.

Rivas, Luis A., "Income Taxes, Spending Composition and Long-Run Growth," *European Economic Review*, 47 (June 2003), 477–503.

Riverson, John, Mika Kunieda, Peter Roberts, Negede Lewi, and Wendy M. Walker, "The Challenges in Addressing Gender Dimensions of Transport in Developing Countries: Lessons from World Bank's Projects," unpublished, World Bank (June 2006).

Roberts, Mark, and Uwe Deichmann, "International Growth Spillovers, Geography and Infrastructure," *World Economy*, 34 (September 2011), 1507–33.

Robinson, James A., and Ragnar Torvik, "White Elephants," *Journal of Public Economics*, 89 (February 2005), 197–210.

Rodney, Walter, *How Europe Underdeveloped Africa*, Bogle-L'Ouverture Publications (London: 1973).

Röller, Lars-Hendrik, and Leonard Waverman, "Telecommunications Infrastructure and Economic Development: A Simultaneous Approach," *American Economic Review*, 91 (September 2001), 909–23.

Romer, David, *Advanced Macroeconomics*, 4th ed., McGraw-Hill (New York: 2011).

Romer, Paul, "Increasing Returns and Long-Run Growth," *Journal of Political Economy,* 94 (October 1986), 1002–37.

——, "Endogenous Technological Change," *Journal of Political Economy*, 98 (October 1990), s71-s102.

Romero, Teruel, and Yoshimi Kuroda, "Public Infrastructure and Productivity Growth in Philippine Agriculture, 1974-2000," *Journal of Asian Economics*, 16 (June 2005), 555–76.

Romp, Ward, and Jakob de Haan, "Public Capital and Economic Growth: A Critical Survey," in *Infrastructure, Economic Growth, and the Economics of PPPs*, EIB Papers, Vol. 10, European Investment Bank (Luxemburg: March 2005).

Rosenstein-Rodan, Paul N., "Problems of Industrialisation of Eastern and South-Eastern Europe," *Economic Journal*, 53 (June 1943), 202–11.

Sachs, Jeffrey, *The End of Poverty: Economic Possibilities for Our Time*, Penguin (New York: 2005).

——, *Common Wealth: Economics for a Crowded Planet*, Penguin (New York: 2008).

Saghir, Jamal, "Energy and Poverty: Myths, Links, and Policy Issues," Energy Working Paper No. 4, World Bank (May 2005).

Sala-i-Martin, Xavier, Gernot Doppelhofer, and Ronald I. Miller, "Determinants of Long-Term Growth: A Bayesian Averaging of Classical Estimates (BACE) Approach," *American Economic Review*, 94 (September 2004), 813–35.

Samuelson, Paul A., "An Exact Consumption-Loan Model of Interest With or Without the Social Contrivance of Money," *Journal of Political Economy*, 66 (December 1958), 467–82.

Sarkar, Jayanta, "Growth Dynamics in a Model of Endogenous Time Preference," *International Review of Economics and Finance*, 16 (December 2007), 528–42.

Schultz, T. Paul, "Productive Benefits of Health: Evidence from Low-Income Countries," in *Health and Economic Growth: Findings and Policy Implications*, ed. by Guillem López-Casasnovas, Berta Rivera, and Luis Currais, MIT Press (Cambridge, Mass.: 2005).

Shelton, Cameron A., "The Size and Composition of Government Expenditure," *Journal of Development Economics*, 91 (December 2007), 2230–60.

Shi, A., "How Access to Urban Potable Water and Sewerage Connections Affect Child Mortality," Policy Research Working Paper No. 2274, World Bank (January 2000).

Simuyemba, Shemmy, "Linking Africa through Regional Infrastructure," Economic Research Paper No. 64, African Development Bank (October 2000).

Smith, James, "The Impact of Childhood Health on Adult Labor Market Outcomes," *Review of Economics and Statistics*, 91 (August 2009), 478–89.

Smith, Lisa C., and Lawrence Haddad, "Explaining Child Malnutrition in Developing Countries: A Cross-Country Analysis," Research Report No. 111, International Food Policy Research Institute (May 2000).

Soares, Rodrigo R., "The Effect of Longevity on Schooling and Fertility: Evidence from the Brazilian Demographic and Health Survey," *Journal of Population Economics*, 19 (February 2006), 71–97.

——, "Life Expectancy and Welfare in Latin America and the Caribbean," *Health Economics*, 18 (April 2009), s37-s54.

Straub, Stéphane, and Akiko Terada-Hagiwara, "Infrastructure and Growth in Developing Asia," *Asian Development Review*, 28 (March 2011), 119–56.

Strauss, John, and Duncan Thomas, "Health, Nutrition and Economic Development," *Journal of Economic Literature*, 36 (June 1998), 766–817.

Summers, Lawrence H., *Investing in All the People: Educating Women in Developing Countries*, World Bank (Washington, D.C.: 1994).

Tam, Henry, "U-Shaped Female Labor Participation with Economic Development: Some Panel Data Evidence," *Economics Letters*, 110 (February 2011), 140–42.

Tamura, Robert, "Human Capital and Economic Development," *Journal of Development Economics*, 79 (January 2006), 26–72.

Tang, Kam Ki, and Jie Zhang, "Health, Education, and Life Cycle Savings in the Development Process," *Economic Inquiry*, 45 (July 2007), 615–30.

Temin, Miriam, and Ruth Levine, *Start with a Girl: A New Agenda for Global Health*, Center for Global Development (Washington, D.C.: 2009).

Tsoukis, Chris, and Nigel J. Miller, "Public Services and Endogenous Growth," *Journal of Policy Modeling*, 25 (April 2003), 297–307.

Turnovsky, Stephen J., "Fiscal Policy, Adjustment Costs, and Endogenous Growth," *Oxford Economic Papers*, 48 (July 1996), 361–81.

——, "Fiscal Policy in a Growing Economy with Public Capital," *Macroeconomic Dynamics*, 1 (September 1997), 615–39.

——, "Fiscal Policy, Elastic Labor Supply, and Endogenous Growth," *Journal of Monetary Economics*, 45 (February 2000), 185–210.

Turnovsky, Stephen J., and M. A. Basher, "Fiscal Policy and the Structure of Production in a Two-Sector Developing Economy," *Journal of Development Economics*, 88 (March 2009), 205–16.

Turnovsky, Stephen J., and Walter H. Fisher, "The Composition of Government Expenditure and Its Consequences for Macroeconomic Performance," *Journal of Economic Dynamics and Control*, 19 (May 1995), 747–86.

Turnovsky, Stephen J., and Mihaela Pintea, "Public and Private Production in a Two-Sector Economy," *Journal of Macroeconomics*, 28 (June 2006), 273–302.

UNAIDS, *2004 Report on the Global AIDS Epidemic*, World Health Organization (Geneva: 2004).

UNESCO, *Global Education Digest 2008*, Institute of Statistics (Montreal: 2008).

UNICEF, *Gender Achievements and Prospects in Education: The Gap Report Part I*, UNICEF Headquarters (New York: 2005).

UNIDO, *Breaking In and Moving Up: New Industrial Challenges for the Bottom Billion and the Middle-Income Countries*, Industrial Development Report, United Nations (Vienna: 2009).

United Nations, *The Millennium Development Goals Report 2005*, United Nations (New York: 2005).

——, *Keeping the Promise: A Forward-Looking Review to Promote an Agreed Action Agenda to Achieve the Millennium Development Goals by 2015*, Report No. A/64/665, United Nations (New York: 2010).

Vandenbussche, Jérôme, Philippe Aghion, and Costas Meghir, "Growth, Distance to Frontier and Composition of Human Capital," *Journal of Economic Growth*, 11 (June 2006), 97–127.

Vergne, Clémence, "Democracy, Elections and Allocation of Public Expenditures in Developing Countries," *European Journal of Political Economy*, 25 (March 2009), 63–77.

Vijayakumar, N., and Chandra S. Rao, "Causal Relationship between Foreign Direct Investment and Growth: Evidence from BRICS Countries," *International Business Research*, 2 (October 2009), 198–203.

Wagstaff, Adam, and Mariam Claeson, *The Millennium Development Goals for Heath: Rising to the Challenges*, World Bank (Washington DC: 2004).

Walz, Uwe, "Endogenous Innovation and Imitation in a Model of Equilibrium Growth," *European Journal of Political Economy*, 11 (April 1996), 709–23.

Wang, Limin, "Determinants of Child Mortality in LDCs: Empirical Findings from Demographic and Health Surveys," *Health Policy*, 65 (September 2003), 277–99.

Wang, Xiaojun, and Kiyoshi Taniguchi, "Does Better Nutrition Enhance Economic Growth? Impact of Undernourishment," in *Nutrition Intake and Economic Growth*, ed. by K. Taniguchi and X. Wang, Food and Agriculture Organization (Rome: 2003).

Warwick, Hugh, and Alison Doig, *Smoke—The Killer in the Kitchen*, ITDG Publishing (London: 2004).
Weil, David N., "Accounting for the Effect of Health on Economic Growth," *Quarterly Journal of Economics*, 122 (August 2007), 1265–305.
Weil, Philippe, "Overlapping Generations: The First Jubilee," *Journal of Economic Perspectives*, 22 (December 2008), 115–34.
Weiss, John, "Infrastructure and Economic Development," Economic Research Paper No. 50, African Development Bank (March 1999).
World Bank, *Investing in Infrastructure: World Development Report 1994*, Oxford University Press (New York: 1994).
——, *Vietnam: Moving Forward—Achievements and Challenges in the Transport Sector*, World Bank (Washington, D.C.: April 1999).
——, *Meeting the Challenge of Africa's Development: A World Bank Group Action Plan*, Africa Region, World Bank (Washington, D.C.: 2005*a*).
——, *World Development Report 2006: Equity and Development*, World Bank and Oxford University Press (Washington, D.C.: 2005*b*).
——, *The Welfare Impact of Rural Electrification: A Reassessment of the Costs and Benefits*, Independent Evaluation Group, World Bank (Washington, D.C.: 2008*a*).
——, *Caribbean: Accelerating Trade Integration*, PREM Sector Unit, Latin America and Caribbean Region (Washington, D.C.: 2008*b*).
——, *Technology Diffusion in the Developing World*, Global Economic Prospects Report (Washington, D.C.: 2008*c*).
——, *Lessons Learned from Mainstreaming HIV/AIDS in Transport Sector Projects in Sub-Saharan Africa*, Report No.43075-AFR (Washington, D.C.: 2008*d*).
World Bank, *The MDGs after the Crisis*, Global Monitoring Report 2010, World Bank (Washington DC: 2010).
World Health Organization, *The World Health Report 2005—Make every Mother and Child Count*, WHO Publications (Geneva: 2005).
——, *The World Health Report 2007—A safer future: Global Public Health Security in the 21st Century*, WHO Publications (Geneva: 2007).
Yakita, Akira, "Elasticity of Substitution in Public Capital Formation and Economic Growth," *Journal of Macroeconomics*, 26 (September 2004), 391–408.
——, "Sustainability of Public Debt, Public Capital Formation, and Endogenous Growth in an Overlapping Generations Setting," *Journal of Public Economics*, 92 (April 2008), 879–914.
Yoshino, Yutaka, "Domestic Constraints, Firm Characteristics, and Geographical Diversification of Firm-Level Manufacturing Exports in Africa," Policy Research Working Paper No. 4575, World Bank (March 2008).
Zhang, Jie, Junsen Zhang, and Ronald Lee, "Rising Longevity, Education, Savings, and Growth," *Journal of Development Economics*, 70 (February 2003), 83–101
Zhang, Junsen, and Jie Zhang, "The Effect of Life Expectancy on Fertility, Saving, Schooling and Economic Growth: Theory and Evidence," *Scandinavian Journal of Economics*, 107 (September 2005), 45–66.
Zhang, Junsen, Jie Zhang, and Tianyou Li, "Gender Bias and Economic Development in an Endogenous Growth Model," *Journal of Development Economics*, 59 (August 1999), 497–25.

# Index |


Africa, sub-Saharan. *See* sub-Saharan Africa
Agénor, Madina, 156n, 184n.9
Agénor, Pierre-Richard, 20, 37, 38n.34, 42, 49, 54, 64–65, 67, 91n.18, 98, 107, 111n, 113, 116n, 120, 138, 156n, 176–77, 184n.9, 190, 203, 210, 216, 219–20
AIDS. *See* HIV/AIDS
Aísa, Rosa, 102n.27
Aizenman, Joshua, 190
Albala-Bertrand, José M., 14
Allais-Samuelson Overlapping Generations (OLG) model, 3. *See also* overlapping-generations (OLG) models
Anyanwu, John C., 138
Arestoff, Florence, 24
Arndt, Channing, 106
Arrow, Kenneth J., 4, 22n.15, 39
Azariadis, Costas, 54

Baier, Scott L., 20n
balanced growth path: in the basic model, 26–32; in the Big Push/poverty traps extension, 178; in the education extension, 55–62, 69–71; in the innovation extension, 120–21; in the women's time allocation extension, 150–54, 167–73
Baldacci, Emanuele, 105
Barman, Trishita R., 215
Barro, Robert J., 35–36, 95
Bauer, Michal, 52
Becker, Gary S., 95
Behrman, Jere R., 75, 78, 104, 138, 158
Bell, Clive, 106
Benos, Nikos, 74
Bhattacharya, Joydeep, 102n.26
Birdsall, Nancy, 106
Blackburn, Keith, 85, 101n, 102n.27, 194
Blankenau, William F., 53n.8
Bleakley, Hoyt, 78, 95, 104n.29, 105
Bloom, David E., 73, 82, 105
Bohn, Frank, 193
Boucekkine, Raouf, 162
Brauninger, Michael, 201n
Brazil, 76, 105, 138, 213
Brenneman, Adam, 49, 75
Briceño-Garmendia, Cecilia, 41
broadband networks. *See* communications networks
Brooks, Douglas H., 206
budgetary policy, "golden rule" approach to, 197–203
Bulir, Ales, 189
Bundy, Donald, 104, 105
Buys, Piet, 41

Cadot, Olivier, 194
Calderón, César, 209
Canning, David, 82
Case, Anne, 78
Castro, Juan F., 138
Cavalcanti, Tiago V. De V., 65n.18
Celasun, Oya, 189
Chadwick, Edwin, 72, 75
Chakraborty, Shankha, 80n, 101, 102n.26, 194
Chatterjee, Santanu, 209n.10, 211–12
child-rearing costs, 65–66, 93–95
children: health of, 75–79, 135; health persistence and, 78–79, 82n.15, 91–93; mothers' education or health and development of, 136–39; parental allocation of time for tutoring, 66–67; in three-period framework with endogenous fertility, 91–100, 110. *See also* education
Chytilová, Julie, 52
Cipriani, Giam P., 85, 101n, 102n.27
Claeson, Mariam, 75, 78
communications networks: broadband networks and productivity, 13, 177; innovation and, 112–13
complementarity effect, 14–15, 38–39
congestion effects, 21, 27–28, 67–68
Cooper, Frederick, 175
Corrigan, Paul, 106
Corsetti, Giancarlo, 24n.18
crowding-out effects: economic growth and, 15–16; lessons for public policy and, 222; negative externalities and, 212n; optimal fiscal policy and, 36; tax rate increases and, 33–34
Czernich, Nina, 13, 113, 122, 176–77

Dabla-Norris, Era, 24, 194
d'Adda, Giovanna, 134–35
Dal Bo, Ernesto, 194
Das, Mausumi, 80n
Datta, Saugato, 13
Deaton, Angus, 211n.15
de Haan, Jakob, 12n.2
Deichmann, Uwe, 176, 204
De la Croix, David, 92, 159, 160n, 194
Delavallade, Clara, 194
depreciation, 40–44
Devoto, Florencia, 76
Dioikitopoulos, Evangelos V., 42
Doig, Alison, 77
Dollar, David, 206
Drazen, Allan H., 54
Duffy, John, 20n
Duflo, Esther, 77n.7
Duryea, Suzanne, 138

Edison, Thomas A., 132, 135n
education: balanced growth path in the model extension, 55–62, 69–71; extension of OLG model to, 51–55; gender bias regarding, 132, 135; health and, 104–8, 138, 220–21; infrastructure and, 49–50, 138–39; of mothers, child development and, 137–39; nutrition and, 104–5; optimal allocation of public spending on, 64–65, 67–68; private, 68; public expenditure increase, impact of, 63–64; pupil-to-teacher ratio, 67; schooling quality and investment in, 67–68; technology for, sensitivity of, 62–63; tutoring children, parental allocation of time for, 66–67
Ehrlich, Isaac, 17, 91n.18, 102n.26
environmental degradation, 136, 213–15, 221
environmental Kuznets curve, 215
Erhijakpor, Andrew E. O., 138
externalities: definition of, 13n; negative, research agenda addressing, 212–15; network, 122, 174–77, 179–82

Fedderke, Johanes W., 216
Ferrarini, Benno, 206
Ferreira, Francisco H. G., 211
Ferreira, Pedro C., 13, 24n.18
fertility: child-rearing costs and, 93–95; mothers' education in Brazil and, 138; three-period framework with endogenous, 91–100, 110; women's time allocation and, 148–50

Field, Erica, 136
Fielding, David, 189
Finlay, Jocelyn E., 75
fiscal policy, 34–37, 196–203
foreign aid, 188–90
foreign direct investment, 206–7
Foster, Vivien, 41
Freund, Caroline, 206
Futagami, Koichi, 35n.32, 176n

Galiani, Sebastian, 75
Galor, Oded, 53n.8, 74n, 133n.1, 209
Gamper-Rabindran, Shanti, 75–76
Garcia-Castrillo, Pedro, 123
Garcia-Peñalosa, Cecilia, 18n.7
gender inequality, 132. *See also* women's time allocation
Getachew, Yoseph Y., 211
Glewwe, Paul, 67
globalization, 111
Glomm, Gerhard, 20n, 21n.13, 28n, 92–93, 209n.10
Gordon, Roger H., 38
government: defined in OLG models, 23–25, 54, 82–83, 119, 146–47, 178; political economy of spending allocation, 193–95; public-private partnerships, 207–9, 223–24; reform of, 222–23. *See also* public policy
Greenwood, Jeremy, 135n
Greiner, Alfred, 24n.18
Grimard, Franque, 78
growth effects of public capital: basic channels for, 11; productivity and cost of private inputs, 11–14; reasons for focus on, 34–35; testing for, research agenda addressing, 215–17. *See also* balanced growth path; public capital
Guasch, J. Luis, 207
Gupta, Indrani, 74
Gupta, Manash R., 215
Gyamfi, Peter, 43
Gyimah-Brempong, Kwabena, 73

Haddad, Lawrence, 106
Hamann, A. Javier, 189
Hamoudi, Amar, 106
Haque, M. Emramul, 194
Hashimoto, Ken-ichi, 101
Hazan, Moshe, 104n.29
health: economic growth and, 72–75, 98–100; education and, 104–8, 138, 220–21; endogenous life expectancy and,

100–104; extension of OLG model to, 79–83, 91–100, 110; human capital and, distinction between, 97n; infrastructure and, 75–78, 134–36; of mothers, child development and, 137–39; optimal spending allocation and, 89–90; persistence effect of childhood on adult, 78–79, 82n.15, 91–93; poverty traps and, 184–86; productivity and, 81–82, 84–88; public policy, 98–100; public spending, growth, and human welfare, 88–89
Heijdra, Ben J., 34
Helmers, Christian, 78
heterogeneous infrastructure assets, research agenda addressing, 192
HIV/AIDS, 74, 106, 137
Hoddinott, John, 158
Hogan, Dennis P., 138
Hotchkiss, David, 135
Hulten, Charles R., 41, 176
human capital: accumulation/production of, 53–54, 144–45; foreign technologies and, capacity to absorb, 111, 113; health, 5n, 97n, 104, 106 (*see also* health); imitation to true innovation, transition from, 126; intergenerational externalities, 54; international trade and, 207; knowledge (*see* education); public capital and, 49
Hung, Fu-Sheng, 24n.18
Hurlin, Christophe, 24

Ilahi, Nadeem, 135
IMMPA models, 220
income inequality/distribution, research agenda addressing, 209–12
India, 13, 77n.7, 78, 138–39
infrastructure: child-rearing costs/parental time allocated to tutoring and, 65–67; foreign technologies and, 111–13; growth and, 2, 32, 215–17 (*see also* growth effects of public capital); health and, 75–78; as heterogeneous assets, research agenda addressing, 192; international trade and, 206–7; investment in, 11–12n; maintenance of, 41–44; mothers' education-children's health relationship and, 138–39; network externalities associated with, 175–77. *See also* public capital
innovation: balanced growth path, 120–21; dynamic system and steady state, solution to, 128–31; extension of OLG model, 113–20; human capital and, 111, 113, 126; imitation-true innovation transition, 124–25, 221; public capital and, 111–13, 125–26; public policy and, 121–24; technology choices and poverty traps, 186–88
investment-maintenance trade-off, 41–44
Iwaisako, Tatsuro, 188n

Jamison, Dean T., 73
Jayachandran, Seema, 105, 137
Jones, John T., 49n.2

Kaas, Leo, 193n
Kalaitzidakis, Pantelis, 42
Kalemli-Ozcan, Sebnem, 91n.18, 101, 106
Kalyvitis, Sarantis, 42
Kenya, 105, 134, 135
Kerf, Michel, 49, 75
Kim, Jinyoung, 102n.26
Kinugasa, Tomoko, 85
Kiros, Gebre-Egziabher, 138
Kneller, Richard, 194
knowledge: accumulation of (*see* education); innovation and (*see* innovation); labor productivity and, 22n.15
Koolwal, Gayatri, 148n.18
Kosempel, Stephen, 113n.5, 117n
Kremer, Michael, 67
Kumar, Shubh K., 135
Kuroda, Yoshimi, 12n.2
Kurz, Mordecai, 4, 39

labor: market defined in OLG model, 119–20; public infrastructure and productivity of, 13; supply of women's, development and, 156–58
Lam, David, 138
Lange, Fabian, 95
Lavy, Victor, 75
Lee, Lung-fei, 75
Leigland, James, 208
Leipziger, Danny, 75
lessons for public policy: Big Push and infrastructure bank, potential of and concerns regarding, 222; crowding out, danger of, 222; donor institutions' use of research on public capital, 224; governance reforms, 222; indirect channels for public capital, 220–21; infrastructure spending, preserving core program of, 223; legal structure reforms,

lessons for (*Continued*); 222–23; private sector role in financing infrastructure, 223–24; "scaling up" infrastructure investment in low-income countries, 220; stage of development, imitation *vs.* true innovation and, 221; user fees/congestion charges for excludable infrastructure services, 221–22
Li, We, 38
Li, Zhigang, 13
Licandro, Omar, 92
Lim, Hyeon-Sook, 136
Lin, Shuanglin, 19n.10
Lleras-Muney, Adriana, 105, 137
Lorentzen, Peter, 73
Lui, Francis, 17, 91n.18
Luoto, Jani, 216

magnification effect, 107–8, 220–21
malaria, 1, 73–74, 76, 105
Mamatzakis, Emmanuel C., 14
Mariani, Fabio, 101, 213n
Mason, Andrew, 85
Matsuyama, Kiminori, 175n
Mavrotas, George, 189
Mayer-Foulkes, David, 74n
McCarthy, Desmond, 73, 76, 105
McDermott, John, 117n
McDonald, Scott, 74
McGuire, James W., 106, 138
Meijdam, Lex, 34
Miguel, Edward, 104
Mino, Kazuo, 176n
Misch, Florian, 35
Mitra, Arup, 74
models: IMMPA, 220; overlapping-generations (OLG) models (*see* overlapping-generations (OLG) models); SPAHD, 219–20
Monteiro, Goncalo, 64–65n.17
Montiel, Peter J., 20, 210
Morand, Olivier F., 17
Morocco, 50, 76, 77
Morshed, Mahbub, 209n.10
Murphy, Kevin M., 175

Neanidis, Kyriakos, 38n.34, 54, 107, 111n, 113, 116n, 120, 177, 190n.14, 216
negative externalities, research agenda addressing, 212–15
network effects, 22–23, 190
network externalities, 122, 174–77, 179–82
Newman, John, 75
nutrition: children's well-being and, 78, 104–5; economic growth and, 74

OLG models. *See* overlapping-generations models
Oloo, J. O., 138
optimal spending allocation: education spending and, 64–65, 67–68; health, education and infrastructure, trade-offs between, 107–8; health spending and, 89–90
Osang, Thomas, 83
Ott, Ingrid, 196
overlapping-generations (OLG) models: the Allais-Samuelson Overlapping Generations model, 3; basic version of, 4, 16–26; Big Push and poverty traps, extension to, 177–78; education and growth, extension to (*see* education); extensions of basic version, 37–45; extensions of education version, 65–68; extensions of women's time allocation version, 158–60; golden rule approach to budgetary policy, extension to, 197–203; health and growth, extension to (*see* health); human capital and, 53–54, 117, 144–45; innovation and growth, extension to (*see* innovation); welfare function, difficulty of defining, 34–35; women's time allocation and growth, extension to, 139–47

Pallage, Stéphane, 189
Papageorgiou, Chris, 20n.
Park, Cheolsung, 159
Patnam, Manasa, 78
Paxson, Christina H., 78, 106
persistence effect. *See* health, persistence effect of childhood on adult
Philippines, the, 12n.2, 50, 105
poverty: health and the transmission of, 78–79; number of people living in, 1
poverty traps: aid volatility and time to build, 188–90; balanced growth path, 178; Big Push responses to, 1–2, 175, 182–83, 222; extension of OLG model to Big Push, 177–78; health-induced, 184–86; network externalities and, 174–77, 179–82; public capital and, 174; regional, 203; technology choices and, 186–88; time allocation and, 184

PPPs. *See* public-private partnerships
Pritchett, Lant, 24n.19
public capital: critical mass effects/network externalities associated with, 122; gender dimension of (*see* women's time allocation); growth effect of (*see* growth effects of public capital); household utility and, 39–40; human capital and, 49 (*see also* human capital); law of motion of, 24; model used to illustrate (*see* overlapping-generations (OLG) model); spatial dimensions of, research agenda addressing, 203–6; usage of the phrase, 3–4
public debt: budgetary policy and, research agenda addressing, 196–203; crowding-out effects of public infrastructure investment and, 16; possible assumptions regarding, 24n.18
public goods, excludable, 21n.12, 195–96, 221–22
public policy: country-specific structural macroeconomic models and, 219–20; education and, 63–65, 67–68; growth effects of, 32–34; innovation and, 111–12, 121–24; lessons for (*see* lessons for public policy); limitations of analytical models for making, 219–20; optimal fiscal policy, 34–37; optimal under welfare maximization, 45–48; women's time allocation and, 154–56
public-private partnerships (PPPs), 207–9, 223–24
Pueyo, Fernando, 102n.27

Qiao, Xue, 102n.26

Rajkumar, Andrew, 194
Raut, Lakshmi K., 17
Ravikumar, B., 21n.13, 28n, 92–93, 209n.10
R&D activities. *See* innovation
Reinikka, Ritva, 14
research agenda, 192; debt, public capital, and fiscal rules, 196–203; excludable public goods, 195–96; heterogeneous infrastructure assets, 192; infrastructure and trade, 206–7; negative externalities, 212–15; political economy of government spending allocation, 193–95; public capital and income distribution, 209–12; public-private partnerships, 207–9; spatial dimensions of public capital, 203–6; testing for the impact of public capital on growth, 215–17
Rioja, Felix K., 25n.20, 42
Rivas, Luis A., 210n.14
Riverson, John, 134
Robe, Michael A., 189
Roberts, Jennifer, 74
Roberts, Mark, 176, 204
Robinson, James A., 194
Rocha, Nadia, 206
Rodney, Walter, 174, 176
Romer, Paul, 22, 111n, 114, 118
Romero, Teruel, 12n.2
Romp, Ward, 12n.2
Rosenstein-Rodan, Paul N., 175
Rosenzweig, Mark R., 78
Rossi, Martin A., 194
Roubini, Nouriel, 24n.18
Ruan, Guillermo, 43

Sachs, Jeffrey, 1, 182
Sala-i-Martin, Xavier, 73
Sanso, Marcos, 123
Sarkar, Jayanta, 83, 102n.26
Sarmah, Rashmi, 194
Schady, Norbert, 78, 106
Schultz, T. Paul, 104
Semmler, Willi, 24n.18
Servén, Luis, 209
Seshadri, Ananth, 135n
Shelton, Cameron A., 193
Shi, A., 75
Simpson, Nicole B., 53n.8
Smith, James, 78
Smith, Lisa C., 106
Soares, Rodrigo R., 76, 105
SPAHD models, 219–20
Sri Lanka, 77–78, 105, 137
stagnation equilibriums. *See* poverty traps
sub-Saharan Africa: children's health, mother's education and, 106, 138; cooking on biomass fuels, prevalence of, 77; educational quality, 67; gender gap in educational attainment, 132; health care, inadequate transportation and, 77; health factors, economic growth and, 73–74; HIV/AIDs, 106; infrastructure assets, 2, 11–13; spatial dimensions of infrastructure, 203–4; transportation issues, 41, 134, 175–76
Svensson, Jakob, 14
Swaroop, Vinaya, 194

Tabata, Ken, 101
Tang, Kam Ki, 102n.26
Taniguchi, Kiyoshi, 74
Tavares, José, 65n.18
taxation: assumption regarding, 23n.16; growth effects of, 33–34; indirect, 37–38; optimal rate of, 35–36
technology. *See* innovation
telecommunications. *See* communications networks
Torvik, Ragnar, 194
trade, research agenda addressing, 206–7
Turnovsky, Stephen J., 18n.7, 34n.30, 64–65n.17, 196, 211–12

UNESCO, 67
UNIDO, 224
United Nations, 1, 67, 73–74, 132, 137, 182
United States, 11–12n, 13, 49n.2
user fees, 195–96, 221–22

Vander Donckt, Marie, 159, 160n
van de Walle, Dominique, 148n.18
Varvarigos, Dimitrios, 190n.14
Vergne, Clémence, 193

Wagstaff, Adam, 75, 78
Walliser, Jan, 189
Wang, Limin, 76n.5
Wang, Xiaojun, 74
Warwick, Hugh, 77
Weil, David N., 53n.8, 73, 133n.1
welfare maximization: focus on growth maximization instead of, 34–35; optimal policy under, 45–48
Wilson, Mark, 73
Wolfe, Barbara L., 75
women: education status and children's development, 137–39; gender gaps and public capital, 158; gender inequality and the role of women in economic growth, 132–33; health status and children's development, 136–37; labor market entry by, economic development and, 156–58, 162
women's time allocation: balanced growth path, 150–54, 167–73; constraints on, 133–36; electricity and, 135–36; extension of OLG model to, 139–47; extensions of the model extension, 158–60; the family's optimization problem, 148, 163–67; fertility and, 148–50; infrastructure, implications of access to, 139; in a nonunitary household framework, 158–60; public capital and, 132–33; public policy and, 154–56; survival rate and, 149–50; transportation and, 134; water/sanitation and, 134–35
World Bank, 1–2, 41, 43, 50, 182, 224
World Health Organization (WHO), 74, 75, 134

Yakita, Akira, 201n, 203
Yilmaz, Devrim, 203
Yoshino, Yutaka, 206

Zeira, Joseph, 209
Zhang, Jie, 79n, 85, 102n.26
Zhang, Junsen, 79n, 85
Zimmer, Ron W., 49n.2
Zoabi, Hosny, 104n.29